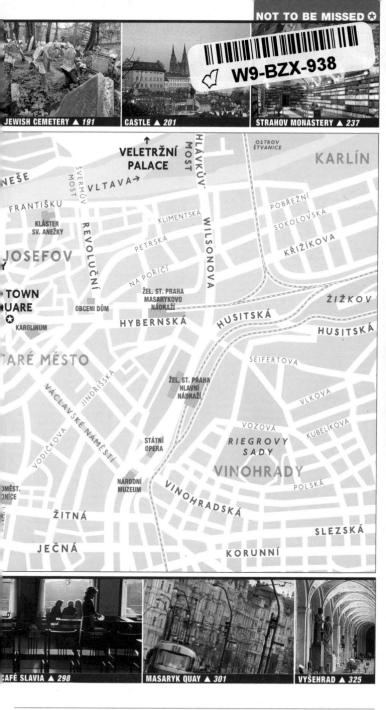

W9-BZX-938

JEWISH CEMETERY ▲ 191 **CASTLE ▲ 201** **STRAHOV MONASTERY ▲ 237**

↑
**VELETRŽNÍ
PALACE**

OSTROV
ŠTVANICE

KARLÍN

NEŠE

ŠVERMŮV
MOST

FRANTIŠKU

HLÁVKŮV MOST

VLTAVA →

REVOLUČNÍ

KLIMENTSKÁ

POBŘEŽNÍ

SOKOLOVSKÁ

KLÁŠTER
SV. ANEŽKY

PETRSKÁ

WILSONOVA

KŘIŽÍKOVA

JOSEFOV

NA POŘÍČÍ

ŽIŽKOV

• TOWN
UARE
✪

OBCENI DŮM

ŽEL. ST. PRAHA
MASARYKOVO
NÁDRAŽÍ

HUSITSKÁ

HUSITSKÁ

KAROLINUM

HYBERNSKÁ

ARÉ MĚSTO

SEIFERTOVA

JINDŘIŠSKÁ

ŽEL. ST. PRAHA
HLAVNÍ
NÁDRAŽÍ

VLKOVA

VÁCLAVSKÉ NÁMĚSTÍ

VOZOVÁ

KUBELÍKOVA

VODIČKOVA

STÁTNÍ
OPERA

RIEGROVY
SADY

OMĚST.
ONICE

NÁRODNÍ
MUZEUM

VINOHRADY

POLSKÁ

ŽITNÁ

VINOHRADSKÁ

SLEZSKÁ

JEČNÁ

KORUNNÍ

AFÉ SLAVIA ▲ 298 **MASARYK QUAY ▲ 301** **VYŠEHRAD ▲ 325**

monastery boasts two magnificent Baroque libraries and a fine picture gallery.
MALÁ STRANA
With its Renaissance and Baroque houses, this district is one of the most atmospheric in Prague.

ST NICHOLAS' CHURCH
This Baroque church in Malá Strana is encrusted with guilding, stucco and trompe l'œil painting.
KAMPA ISLAND
The island's mills, park and lawns make it a haven of peace.

CAFÉ SLAVIA
Favorite haunt of the Czech intelligentsia, this café is imbued with the memories and atmosphere of days gone by.
MASARYK QUAY
The neo-Renaissance, neo-Baroque and Art-

Nouveau façades that line the quay make it a superb architectural ensemble.
VYŠEHRAD
This hill, the legendary birthplace of the princes of Bohemia, commands fine views over Prague.

PRAGUE

KNOPF GUIDES

● Encyclopedia section

NATURE The natural heritage: species and habitats characteristic to the area covered by the guide, annotated and illustrated by naturalist authors and artists.

HISTORY OF PRAGUE The impact of international history on local events, from the arrival of the first inhabitants, with key dates appearing alongside the text.

ARTS AND TRADITIONS Customs and traditions in Prague and their continuing role in contemporary life.

ARCHITECTURE The architectural heritage, focusing on style and topology; a look at urban buildings and major civil, religious and military monuments.

AS SEEN BY PAINTERS A selection of paintings by artists from different periods and countries, arranged thematically.

AS SEEN BY WRITERS An anthology of texts, extracts taken from different periods and countries, arranged thematically.

▲ Itineraries in Prague

Each itinerary begins with a map of the area to be explored.

✪ NOT TO BE MISSED These sites, highlighted in gray boxes, should be seen at all costs.

★ EDITOR'S CHOICE Sites singled out by the editor for special attention.

INSETS On richly illustrated double pages, these insets turn the spotlight on subjects deserving more in-depth treatment.

◆ Practical information

All the travel information you will need before you go and when you get there.

USEFUL ADDRESSES A selection of hotels, restaurants and brasseries.

PLACES TO VISIT A handy table of addresses and opening hours.

APPENDICES Bibliography, list of illustrations and general index.

MAP SECTION Maps of all the areas covered by the guide and a street index; these maps are marked out with letters and figures making it easy for the reader to pinpoint a region or site. A plan of local transport.

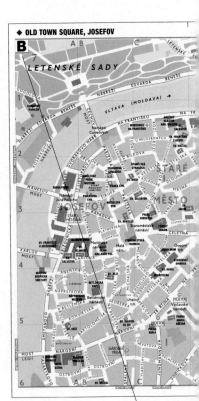

◆ OLD TOWN SQUARE, JOSEFOV

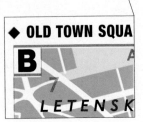

◆ OLD TOWN SQUA

Each map in the section is designated by a letter. In the practical information section, all the sites of interest are given a map reference (for example: ◆ **B** C4).

The mini-map pinpoints the itinerary within the wider area covered by the guide.

★ The star symbol indicates sites singled out by the editor for special attention.

The itinerary map shows the main sites and the places not to be missed.

▲ FROM OLD TOWN SQUARE TO CHARLES BRIDGE

1. QUEEN'S BUILDING 2. SMETANA MUSEUM 3. BELVEDERE ST FRANCIS SVATADÍK 4. CHURCH OF ST SAVIOR 5. ST FRANCIS 6. VLÁŠKA CHURCH 7. ST CLEMENT'S CHURCH 8. CLEMENTINUM 9. KARLOVA STREET 10. NEW TOWN HALL 11. CLAM-GALLAS PALACE 12. MALÉ NÁMĚSTÍ 13. ST NICHOLAS CHURCH 14. TOWN HALL 15. OLD TOWN SQUARE ❂ 16. HOUSE "DE THE WHITE" 17. CHURCH OF OUR LADY OF TÝN

OLD TOWN SQUARE ★   ▲ 138

The histories of Old Town (Staré Město) and its Square (Staroměstské náměstí) are closely inter-related. Much of our knowledge of the city in its earliest days is based

One day
◆ B A4-B4-C4

OLD TOWN SQUARE, THE HEART OF PRAGUE ❂
Old Town Square, an open space in the midst of narrow streets, is dominated by the soaring spires of the Church of Our Lady of Týn, Golz-Kinský Palace and the statue of Jan Hus. It is worth climbing the clocktower of the Old Town Hall for the best view over Prague that it offers. From ground level, the performance of the Apostles in the astronomical clock is an entertaining spectacle. For a drink afterwards, avoid the cosmopolitan café in favor of the quieter ones to be found in Týn Courtyard.

on a document written by an emissary of the Caliph of Cordoba, the diplomat and merchant Ibrahim Ibn Jacob. His stay from 965 to 966 inspired him to write of his journey, during which he came to realize that the city was an important center of commercial exchange. The opening of the city to the west and the development of commerce encouraged Soběslav I (1125–40) to play a more active role in the commercial Týn Courtyard (Ungelt) ▲ 160 behind the Church of Our Lady. This was the start of Prague's role as an important commercial center.
NEWCOMERS. New communities from Piedmont, Burgundy, Germany and Flanders settled in Prague during the 12th century, and their arrival increased the amount of business transactions, already stimulated by the needs of the Royal Court. At this time, the Germans occupied an area that was to become Old Town Square; there, they founded a church dedicated to St Nicholas ▲ 145, the patron saint of merchants, and they also built a hospital, houses and shops. The square began to look a little as it does today: the houses on the north, east and south sides, including Kinský Palace, are aligned on axes already determined in the 12th and 13th centuries.
AIMING FOR MUNICIPAL STATUS. In 1230, Old Town acquired the status of a town, but it was not entitled to have a Town

Hall, the decisive symbol of city freedom in the Middle Ages of another hundred years, in 1338, that John of Luxemburg granted the right to erect a Town Hall in Old Town Square. With political and judiciary power now hand in hand, the bourgeoisie sought to install a prison inside the Town Hall and stocks in the square. As the town's political center, the square established itself as the economic and social epicenter, and it was inhabited by the wealthiest families. Apart from commercial activities, the square also hosted festive occasions, including tourneys.
HISTORIC EVENTS. Down through the centuries, Old Town Square has been the scene of momentous and bloody events: after his victory at White Mountain on November 8, 1620 ● 34, Ferdinand II sent twenty-seven noble and bourgeois rebels to the scaffold (the deed is today marked by a rectangle of black stones); then, twelve heads were hung on the tower on Charles Bridge for ten long years, and were not buried until 1631, by the Lutheran Saxons occupying Prague. On May 8–9, 1945, the partisans fought a ferocious battle here to liberate the city from the Nazis, and then on February 21, 1948, Klement Gottwald proclaimed the victory of Soviet Communism ● 39 from the balcony of Kinský Palace ▲ 139. In a previous age, the Palace had housed the German-language Imperial High School attended by the German-speaking intelligentsia, notably Max Brod and Kafka ▲ 110; and by 1948, the square had come to be known as "Hyde Park" and was soon the favorite venue for student meetings. Today, more people meet up and go for walks here than in Wenceslas Square or any other square in Prague.

Above: an old engraving showing the execution of rebel leaders in 1621. Below: scenes of the liberation of Prague in Old Town Square, May 1945.

136   137

At the beginning of each itinerary, the distance, the suggested mode of travel and the time it will take to cover the area are indicated beneath the maps.
🚶 On foot

❂ This symbol indicates places not to be missed.

● ■ ▲ ◆
The above symbols within the text provide cross-references to a place or a theme discussed elsewhere in the guide.

● Encyclopedia section

▲ Itineraries in Prague

◆ Practical information

FROM OLD TOWN SQUARE TO CHARLES BRIDGE ▲ 135
From this square, the heart of the city and the embodiment of its architectural riches, a maze of cobbled lanes lined with Renaissance palaces and Baroque churches leads to the famous Charles Bridge, blackened by the grime of ages. Of special interest is Malé Náměstí (Little Square), where historic Rott House is to be found.

AROUND WENCESLAS SQUARE ▲ 157
Celetná Street leads from the Old Town to Powder Tower. Further on, around Wenceslas Square, focal point of the Velvet Revolution, stretches the New Town, an administrative and banking district where smart hotels and shopping centers, the result of the introduction of a market economy, are also to be found.

FROM THE NA FRANTIŠKU QUARTER TO JOSEFOV ▲ 179
It was in this quarter of the Old Town that Secessionist and Art Nouveau architecture developed in the late 19th century, exemplified by Paris Avenue, with prestigious shops and restaurants. Vestiges of the former Ghetto, which was razed for health reasons, include several synagogues and one of Europe's oldest Jewish cemeteries.

PRAGUE CASTLE ▲ 199
This extensive complex, ancient seat of Czech spiritual and political power, consists of a harmonious group of buildings, including a palace, churches, a convent, museums and gardens overlooking the city. St Vitus' Cathedral, monumental and richly endowed, and Golden Lane, haunt of alchemists, are unmissable features.

FROM HRADČANY TO MALÁ STRANA ▲ 225
The appeal of the Castle district is due in large measure to the peaceful atmosphere that envelops its many palaces and churches, convents and monasteries. Here is the Church of Our Lady of Loreto and Strahov Monastery, which is surrounded by greenery and boasts an outstanding library.

MALÁ STRANA 1: AT THE FOOT OF THE CASTLE ▲ 245
The appealing and atmospheric "Little Town", is laid out around Malostranské Square, over which towers the dazzling St Nicholas' Church. Baroque palaces, parks and courtyards hidden behind the gateways of ancient houses with magical names invite exploration.

MALÁ STRANA 2: FROM KAMPA TO PETŘÍN HILL ▲ 265
From Kampa Island to the top of Petřín Hill, where a belvedere offers a unique panorama over Prague, this itinerary takes in buildings raised by the Knights of Malta, including Our Lady Under the Chain, the oldest church in Malá Strana, and countless burghers' houses.

FROM THE CAROLINUM TO THE NATIONAL THEATER ▲ 277
Starting at the administrative center of the University of Prague and taking in the Estates Theater, Bethlehem Square and the Rotunda of the Holy Cross, this itinerary leads to Národní Avenue with its Art Nouveau façades and the National Theater, symbol of Czech culture. This district also buzzes with student cafés and trendy restaurants.

AROUND CHARLES SQUARE ▲ 299
The area around Charles Square offers much of interest over a wide area. There are many churches and striking Cubist houses, the splendid neo-Baroque and Secessionist façades of Masaryk Quay and the architectural ensemble of Charles Square. Here also are the devilish Faustus House and Villa Amerika, now the Dvořák Museum.

THE OUTSKIRTS ▲ 315
No visit to Prague would be complete without a visit to the Museum of Modern Art, to Troja Castle, in its bucolic setting, and to Zbraslav Convent and the opulent Villa Bertramka. Finally, climb the hill to Vyšehrad Castle, birthplace of Prague and ancient rival to its castle, to take in a sublime panorama of the city.

**NUMEROUS SPECIALISTS AND ACADEMICS
HAVE CONTRIBUTED TO THIS GUIDE**

● Encyclopedia section

NATURE
Philippe Dubois, Karel Štastný
HISTORY OF PRAGUE
Marie-Elisabeth Ducreux,
Antoine Marès, Zdeněk Hojda
LANGUAGE
Dagmar Hobzova
ARTS AND TRADITIONS
Guy Erismann, Daniela Langer,
Danièle Montmarte, Sylvie Clopet,
Gérard-Georges Lemaire,
Petra Jarošová
ARCHITECTURE
Nathalie Vaillant, Jean-Pierre Lange,
Marie-Élisabeth Ducreux, Aleš Vošahlík,
Bruno Queysanne
PRAGUE AS SEEN BY PAINTERS
Gérard-Georges Lemaire
CZECH ART IN THE EARLY 20TH-CENTURY
Gérard-Georges Lemaire
PRAGUE AS SEEN BY WRITERS
Sylvie Germain
FRANZ KAFKA
Patrizia Runfola

▲ Itineraries in Prague

Patrick Jusseaux, Serge Guilbert,
Guy Erismann, Marie-Élisabeth Ducreux,
Zdeněk Hojda, Gérard-Georges Lemaire,
Françoise de Bonnières,
Catherine Monroy, Dagmar Hobzova,
Milena Braud, Olga Bašeová

◆ Practical information

Grégory Pinson, Iveta Kucerová, and
Robert Anderson of the *Financial Times*
for hotels and restaurants

This is a Borzoi Book
published by Alfred A. Knopf

Completely revised
and updated in 2005

www.aaknopf.com

ISBN 0-375-71111-2

Series editors
Shelley Wanger and Clémence Jacquinet

Translated by
Michael Cunnigham and
Dafydd Rees-Roberts

Originally edited and typeset by
Book Creation Services, London

Practical section updated by
The Content Works
www.thecontentworks.com

Printed and bound in Italy by
Editoriale Lloyd

PRAGUE
ORIGINAL FRENCH-LANGUAGE EDITION
Editors
Julie Wood, Sophie Mastelinck, Anne-J. Magniant,
Claire Burgot (architecture), Alpha Presse (Macha
Séry), Michèle Grinstein, Gonzague de Bouville
(Practical information) Virginia Rigot-Müller
Updating
Anne-Sophie Baumann, Philippe Bénet, Nicolas
Christitch, Fanny Labbé, Florence Picquot,
Grégory Pinson, Odile Simon
Layout
Riccardo Tremori, Nicolas Christitch (Practical
information)
Picture research
William Fischer, Véronique Legrand
Translation
Claudia Ancelot, Marie-Élisabeth Ducreux,
Milena Braud, Radim Brabec, Émilie Djiboghlian
Map section
Édigraphie

ILLUSTRATIONS
Nature:
Jean Chevallier, François Desbordes, Claire Felloni,
Catherine Lachaud
Architecture:
Bruno Lenormand, Maurice Pommier, Amato
Sorro, François Pichon, Jean-Marie Guillou,
Claude Quiec, Jean-Claude Sené, Philippe Candé
Itineraries:
Maurice Pommier, Philippe Candé, Jean-Michel
Kacédan, Laure Massin
Maps:
Éric Gillion, Isabelle-Anne Chatelard, Patrick
Merienne
Computer graphics: Édigraphie, Paul Coulbois,
Antoine Fumet

PHOTOGRAPHY
Serge Guibert, Danièle Rolland, Renata
Holzbachová, Philippe Bénet

SPECIAL THANKS TO
Hélène Bourgois, Jean-Pierre Azvazadourian,
Léopold Chappe (Chambre Française du
Commerce Franco-Tchèque, Paris)
and, especially, Marie-Élisabeth Ducreux

Encylopedia section

"I felt the snow. It was cold, and it warmed the palm of my hand. The most beautiful snow I have ever known – and so dear to my heart . . . Snow gently falling like a hand writing – how many things to cover!"
Jiří Orten

The River Vltava frozen over near Šitek Tower (Šitkovská věž).

"Ah! The good old days
when the whole town resembled a thimble, a fan
and a bird's song or a shellfish on the beach!
– farewell, farewell, you beautiful women
whom we met today
and will never see again."

Jaroslav Seifert

A bus tour of Prague at the beginning of the 20th century.

Nature

THE RIVER VLTAVA

GRASS SNAKE
This snake lives on river banks, and hunts amphibians and small rodents.

The River Vltava (pronounced "Valtava"), which is still called the Moldau in German, rises in the Šumava mountains which run along the German border in the southwest of the Czech Republic. It then crosses Prague along a steep-sided valley before joining the River Labe, or the Elbe as it is known in Germany. The Vltava twists and turns through Prague, making any number of winter refuges for water birds forced off the lakes when they ice over. Every year, the river attracts almost five thousand over-wintering birds. Despite a high degree of pollution (salmon disappeared as many as thirty or forty years ago), people still go fishing from boats in the center of the city.

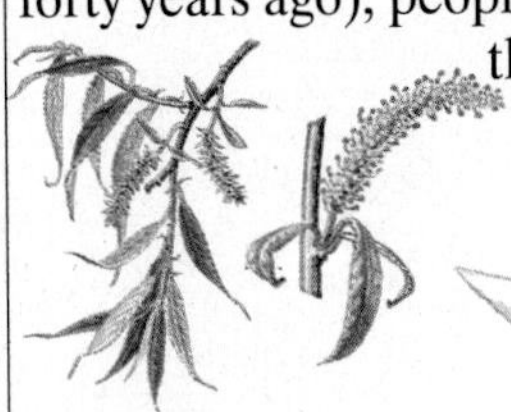

Young

Adult

WHITE WILLOW
The white willow grows abundantly on river banks, and often close to poplars.

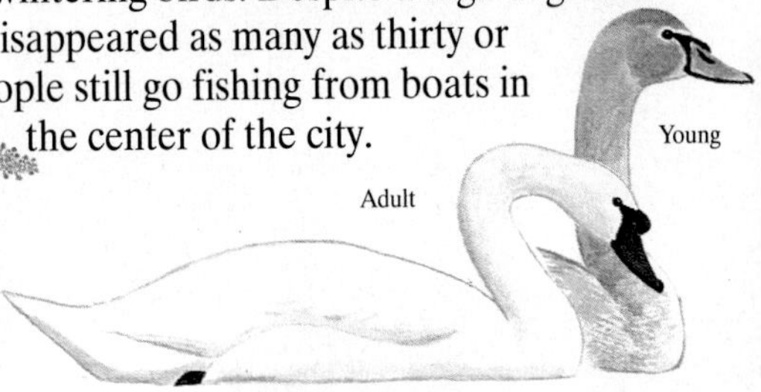

MUTE SWAN
This swan has been known to venture into the very center of Prague, but usually breeds on quiet islands and river banks.

Summer   Winter

LITTLE GREBE
The little grebe gathers in large groups during the winter, but can be difficult to spot when mingling with ducks and larger coots.

16

The construction of dams upstream from Prague has affected the flow of water, and has enabled the population of certain fish to increase in number.

MALLARD
This bird nests in Prague throughout the year. Many have interbred with domestic ducks.

Male   Female

POCHARD
In early autumn, this duck returns to the Vltava where several hundred birds seek refuge, particularly opposite the zoo in Prague.

Male   Female

COOT
The coot feeds on aquatic vegetation, and accounts for the majority of over-wintering birds.

TUFTED DUCK
This kind of duck is extremely common in the Czech Republic. It frequently over-winters with the mallard and the pochard.

Male

Female

CORMORANT
The population of this bird is increasing in Europe. It usually over-winters close to the river, and in the evenings forms large roosting flocks.

BLACK-HEADED GULL
This bird stays in Prague throughout the year. In winter, the black-headed gull is often found scavenging for food thrown by people walking along the quays and over the bridges.

Summer   Winter

Leaf of oak

Leaf of plane

Leaf of horse-chestnut

Petřín Hill has long been wooded, and even now there are signs of the forests of hornbeam, beech, oak, maple and chestnut that once surrounded the city. Almost 250 species of plants and 600 kinds of fungi have been identified on the mountain's slopes; there are also many rare kinds of wild woodland animals. A tower at the summit of Petřín Hill commands a splendid view of Prague.

Where once there were vineyards, beautifully kept orchards now spread out at the foot of Petřín Hill. Plum, pear and apple trees are the dominant varieties. In spring, the beauty of the area is furthered enhanced by white and pink blossom.

TAWNY OWL
A few pairs still nest in the more densely wooded parts of Petřín Hill.

SPARROWHAWK
There are said to be as many a hundred pairs of this magnificent bird of prey in central Prague.

WOODPIGEON
Over the last five to seven years, the woodpigeon has started living in the city.

GREEN WOODPECKER
This large woodpecker feeds mainly on wood-eating insects and ants.

GREAT SPOTTED WOODPECKER
This type of woodpecker is frequently found in wooded areas. It begins its woodpecking activities in early March.

NUTHATCH
The nuthatch searches tree trunks for grubs and insects.

SPOTTED FLYCATCHER
The color of its plumage helps it to merge into the background.

NOCTULE BAT
Has only recently begun hibernating in Prague. It lives in ventilation ducts.

WOOD ANEMONE
This plant flowers in April, covering the slopes of Petřín Hill in white.

WOLF'S-BANE
The flowers are usually violet, or more rarely yellow. They grow in damp, shaded areas.

■ STROMOVKA PARK

This park, laid out on what had once been riverside forest and fields, dates from 1268, when Otakar II turned it into a royal hunting reserve. Stromovka ("Orchard") was turned into a park in 1803 after being almost completely destroyed in the course of the wars that ravaged the region in the 18th century. Today, this 250-acre park contains oak trees over a hundred years old and a remarkable range of original and introduced species. There is also a rose garden, and a number of artificial ponds inhabited by a variety of animals.

RED SQUIRREL
The red squirrel is often found in those parts of the park where there are plenty of large trees.

Small lakes provide a home not only for the semi-wild mallards and moorhens, but also for more inconspicuous species such as frogs, marsh-dwelling warblers and dragonflies.

Oak, ash, elm and maple trees are notable for their height and age.

Pedunculated oak leaf

Ash leaf

Lime leaf

JAY
The jay is particularly common in autumn and winter, but it sometimes stays to breed in the spring.

REDPOLL
This bird has nested in the middle of the city since 1968. Prague is one of the few European cities where this happens.

COLLARED DOVE
This dove sometimes uses wire to makes its nest.

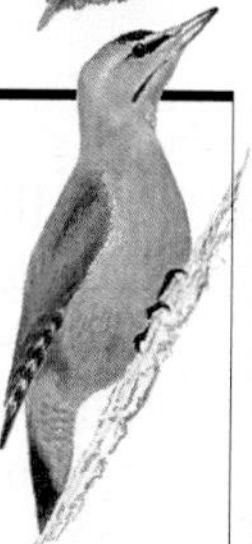

GRAY-HEADED WOODPECKER
Prefers ancient broadleaf forests, but ventures into Stromovka Park ▲ *317*.

ICTERUS
This bird's musical, if sometimes grating, call can be heard in the park from mid-May onward.

BLACKCAP
The melodious song of the blackcap can be heard in all the main parks of Prague.

MARSH WARBLER
The marsh warbler lives in small nests made of reeds. It is found in parks where it is heard practising its imitative song.

TREE CREEPER. This is found in the mountains of southwestern Europe, and in the parks and forests of the plains of the Czech Republic.

BLACKBIRD
The blackbird is one of the most noticeable birds in Stromovka Park.

ROBIN
These birds return from the north in the autumn.

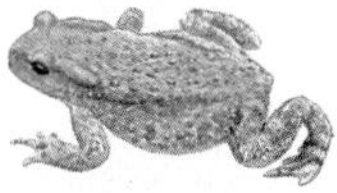

TOAD
In springtime toads gather near ponds to breed.

WILD RABBIT
The wild rabbit sometimes wreaks havoc in flowerbeds.

WILDLIFE IN THE CITY

STONE MARTEN
The stone marten lives in the attics and lofts of Prague, and only emerges at night.

Parks, gardens, old cemeteries and the wooded sections of Petřín Hill are all favorite haunts of the birds of Prague. The countryside is not far away and provides a splendid habitat for the wide variety of local fauna. Prague Castle is home to a small colony of kestrels that spend much of their time hunting pigeons.

Kestrels are increasingly settling in large European cities where they can easily find food.

HOUSE SPARROW
House sparrows can be seen everywhere in Prague, but for some reason their numbers are decreasing.

ROCK PIGEON
About 140,000 rock pigeons inhabit Prague. Wounded individuals are easy prey for kestrels and stone martens.

SWIFT
Large numbers of swifts nest under the gutters and eaves of Prague Castle.

HOUSE MARTIN
The house martin often nests in colonies on the tall buildings of Prague.

KESTREL
About ten pairs nest on various buildings in the castle.

BLACK REDSTART
The black redstart is often heard singing from the tops of chimney stacks and television aerials.

MAGPIE
The magpie population is rapidly increasing in cities; it is able to build its nest almost anywhere.

History of Prague

FROM THE 9TH TO THE 13TH CENTURIES

7TH CENTURY
Legendary birth of the Přemyslid dynasty (prophecies of Libussa and the ploughman, opposite, right) which was to reign until 1306.

880
The Czech Duke Bořivoj is baptized by Bishop Methodius.

929 or 935
Václav (Wenceslas I) is murdered by his brother, Boleslav. Wenceslas later became the country's patron saint.

995
The ruling Přemyslid kings capture Libice Castle, and thereby succeed in unifying Bohemia.

1039
Břetislav I (1034–55) forces his subjects to obey the fundamental laws of Christianity.

Vyšehrad Codex.

1085
Vratislav II ● 30 is crown first king of Bohemia.

1251–78
The Czech State expands into Austria under Přemysl King Otakar II, known as the "the king of iron and gold".

THE CITY'S ORIGINS. Slav tribes built the first villages near modern Prague as early as the second half of the 6th century, but, seeking protection, moved up into the surrounding hills in the 7th century. Around 880, the dukes who commanded the Czech tribe founded Prague Castle on a promontory overlooking the Vltava, and later, in 900, built the Castle of Chrasten-Vyšehrad. For the most part, people inhabited the area that ran between the two fortresses, but the most important of the colonies was established at the foot of the Castle walls where Malá Strana now stands.

THE BEGINNINGS OF A CHRISTIAN CAPITAL. Around 885, Duke Bořivoj (died 895) built a wooden church within the confines of the Castle; it was dedicated to the Virgin Mary and is the oldest church in Prague. St George's Basilica was built later in 915–21, and this was followed by the Rotunda of St Vitus in 925, after an arm allegedly belonging to that saint was acquired by the Emperor Henry I. The foundation of the first monastery in Bohemia around 970, and the establishment of the Archbishopric of Prague in 973, confirmed the Castle as the center of the ecclesiastical activities of the Czech State as it moved slowly toward unity. After 1070, the Czech monarchy took a new interest in Vyšehrad, and a chapter was founded there; it became the residence of Vratislav II (1061–92), and later Soběslav I (1125–40).

ROMANESQUE TOWN AT THE FOOT OF THE CASTLE WALLS. Writing in 1091, Kosmas, the first Czech chronicler, refers to groups of Jewish merchants settling on the hillside below the Castle and along the road to Vyšehrad. After 1100, there was also a market on the right bank of the Vltava where Old Town Square now stands. An early church dedicated to the Virgin Mary was built there before 1135, and the Týn Courtyard (Ungelt) ▲ 160 was attached to it after 1250. The first stone bridge, Judith Bridge, was begun around 1157 and connected the two banks of the Vltava just a short distance upstream from present-day Charles Bridge. The right bank developed rapidly from the middle of the 12th century onward, and by 1230 a group of stone houses and no fewer than twenty-three Romanesque churches had sprung up.

Fresco depicting Charles IV in the chapel of Our Lady of Karlštejn.

13TH TO 14TH CENTURIES: A MEDIEVAL METROPOLIS

A RESIDENCE FIT FOR KINGS AND EMPERORS. In 1231, King Wenceslas I (1230–53) began the fortification of 346 acres of Old Town (Staré Město). Then, after 1257, the Přemyslid King Otakar II (1253–78) brought together the dispersed settlements of inhabitants within a fortified enclosure called the "New Town", a name that derived in part from the "Little City" (Malá Strana). It was not until 1287 that the territory occupied by Old Town, which was already acknowledged as the capital by the other towns of the kingdom, was legally unified; the Jewish town was not, however, included. It was then decided to raise the level of the town by 7–10 feet so as to protect it from flooding. Numerous religious houses were also constructed, including the Convent of St Agnes ▲ 182 and Na Františku founded on the banks of the Vltava around 1294 by Anežka Přemyslovna, the sister of King Wenceslas I, and shared by the Poor Clares and the Franciscans. A form of administration governing the town is documented in texts dated 1258; Old Town had its own Chancellery in 1229 and a Town Hall was built in 1338. The growing power of the nobility was demonstrated when, in 1306, they attempted to seize power after the death of the last of the Přemyslids. Trades were organized into corporations around 1318 and, around 1330, the first hygiene regulation was published and the first roads paved.

PRAGUE, METROPOLIS OF THE EMPIRE. Charles of Luxemburg, son of the last Přemyslid, Eliška, and heir to the throne, settled in Prague in 1333. He had the palace rebuilt within the Castle grounds, and in 1344 obtained from the Pope the right to make the bishopric of Prague an archbishopric. The Gothic cathedral's foundation stone was laid the same year. Even before he was crowned in 1346, Charles IV (whose seal is shown below) announced the establishment of the Universities of Prague and New Town, together with a wide-ranging plan for the town; work began on the two projects in the following year. In 1357, Petr Parléř, who was responsible for so many Gothic buildings in Prague, started work on a new stone bridge (modern Charles Bridge) with two towers, and by 1395, twenty-five new religious houses had been founded in Prague and the surrounding area. The population grew rapidly: with 40,000 inhabitants at the end of Charles IV's reign, it was the largest city in central Europe. Old Town was the bastion of the rich bourgeoisie while New Town attracted artisans and was the scene of the politicization of the corporations. Prague was spared the epidemic that followed the plague of 1348, fell victim to a similar disaster in 1380. In 1389, a huge pogrom against the Jewish inhabitants, who were accused of poisoning the water in the wells, took place.

Vladislav II Jagiello.

1300
Wenceslas II (1278–1305) is elected King of Poland. His monetary reforms included the striking of silver "groš" in Prague.

1306
The last of the Přemyslids, Wenceslas III (1305–6), was murdered at Olomouc at the instigation of his Polish enemies.

1325
The composer Guillaume de Machaut moved to the Court on the invitation of John of Luxemburg.

1348
The Carolinum University is founded in Prague.

1356
Charles IV's Golden Bull proclaimed the Czech State's absolute independence from the Empire, and made the King of Bohemia the first lay Elector of the Empire.

Crown of Bohemia.

THE HUSSITE CRISIS OF THE 15TH CENTURY

1402
John Huss begins preaching at Bethlehem Chapel.

Hussite troops

JULY 6, 1415
John Huss dies at the stake in Constance.

1517
Luther starts to preach reform.

John Huss at the stake.

WENCESLAS IV COMES TO POWER. Under Wenceslas (or Václav) IV, Prague lost the supremacy it had enjoyed as Charles IV's Imperial residence. Trade slackened, the town grew poor, and social and religious disputes flared up. Moreover, preachers such as Waldhauser of St Havel, Milíč of Kroměříž, John Huss, Jakoubek of Stríbro and Nicholas of Dresden denounced the Church's wealth and corruption, and called for a return to poverty and the values set out in the Gospels. Tensions began to mount in 1410. The execution in 1412 of three young men for encouraging people to demonstrate against the sale of indulgences was followed by the executions of both John Huss in Constance and Jeremy of Prague. At that point, the aldermen of Old and New Towns came out against the people; the latter were supported by the Taborites of South Bohemia. On July 30, 1419, the first defenestration at the Town Hall sparked off the revolution, and that same year Prague went to war with Wenceslas IV's successor, his brother King Sigismund. The people's victory, which led to the King's capitulation on June 7, 1421, enabled the town to become a decisive partner in the political life of the Kingdom.

A PARTING OF THE WAYS. The Hussite Wars lasted seventeen years, during which time New Town continued to be more extremist than Old Town; having become more moderate, the latter agreed to the terms proposed by the Four Articles of Prague which had been drawn up in 1419, and had served as the basis for the so-called "Compactata" (Compacts) between the Church, the Christian world, King Sigismund and the Czechs. In Prague, Church property was seized by the Town and no one was able to acquire bourgeois rights without taking Communion in both kinds; the people of Prague vowed that only Czechs should be entitled to this right.

FROM UTRAQUISM TO WHITE MOUNTAIN

1526
Louis Jagiello (above), King of Bohemia and Hungary, is killed by the Turks at Mohács.

Utraquism takes its name from *sub utraque specie* (under both forms, i.e. bread and wine). The Utraquist George of Poděbrady, King of Bohemia from 1458 to 1471, endeavored to make Prague both more beautiful and economically successful, while at the same time respecting the freedom that had been won in the course of the Hussite Wars. In 1463, his councillor, Marini, produced a commercial plan based on the city's merchants more actively seeking business abroad, and in Venice in particular. It was not, however, until the reign of Vladislas Jagiello, also King of Hungary, that foreign merchants began to return to the Czech capital, and an agreement with Nuremberg once more accorded the city a central role in long-distance commerce. The 15th century was a prosperous period for Prague, but it ended with a number of uprisings in the name of the Reformation. In 1502, the

Behem

Rudolph II.

citizens reinforced the Utraquist union and the order of the towns against the power of the King. In 1526, the new King of Bohemia, Ferdinand of Habsburg, sought to bolster royal power by provoking a revolt of the nobility and the towns in 1547, and the repression of this uprising led to a withdrawal of the privileges that Prague had won during the wars. Later, Emperor Rudolph II (1576– 1611) settled in Prague and, for twenty-eight years, the town was again one of the most politically important in Europe. However, the Habsburgs' Catholic absolutism began to weigh on the Czechs, and on May 23, 1618, two Catholic royal lieutenants from Prague were defenestrated at Hradčany. The episode marked the beginning of the Thirty Years' War and foreshadowed the Battle of White Mountain ● *34* in which the Estates of Bohemia were defeated by Catholic forces.

1556
The Jesuits arrive in Bohemia.

1583–1611
The Court of Rudolph II attracts learned men and artists to Prague, including astronomers Tycho Brahe and Johann Kepler, painter Giuseppe Arcimboldo and composer Filippo di Monti.

1686
Buda is wrested from the Turks by the armies of Emperor Leopold I, King of Bohemia and Hungary.

1729
Saint John Nepomuk is canonized.

UNDER THE HABSBURGS

The defeat of the Hussites at White Mountain meant that Protestants were forced to emigrate from Bohemia unless they converted to Catholicism. The victory of the Counter-Reformation was now complete, and the Peace of Westphalia (1648) ensured that Bohemia and Moravia remained under the Habsburgs' Imperial domination. The Kingdom of Bohemia continued to be Catholic until 1781. The Wars of the Austrian Succession (1740–8) against Frederick II of Prussia culminated in the election of Charles of Bavaria by the Diet of Bohemia. Until 1790, the reigns of Maria Theresa of Austria (the wife of Francis of Lorraine, who became Emperor in 1745) and Joseph II (1780–90) marked a period of enlightened absolutism, and the institutions of the Kingdom were fundamentally reformed. From 1749 onward, Bohemia and Moravia were administered in Vienna together with the Habsburgs' "hereditary countries", the future Cisleithenia. Joseph II introduced compulsory education throughout the Habsburg monarchy in 1775, and all schools had to use the vernacular, while in colleges and high schools Latin then German were spoken. He also abolished serfdom in 1780, and established a rule of religious tolerance in 1781 which was also applied to Jews ▲ *185* in 1782.

1784
The four towns of Prague are reunited in a single city.

OCTOBER 29, 1787
Mozart's "Don Giovanni" is premièred at the Nostitz Theater (formerly the Estates Theater).

Joseph II of Habsburg.

The Popular Guard and students standing side by side, 1848.

CZECH NATIONAL AWAKENING

1804
Francis I becomes Emperor of Austria.

DECEMBER 2, 1805
Napoleon I defeats the armies of the Tsar and the Emperor of Austria at the Battle of

Austerlitz (Slavkov, near Brno).

1867
Birth of the Austro-Hungarian Empire.

DECEMBER 8, 1870
Czech Deputies condemn the annexation of Alsace-Lorraine.

Tomáš G. Masaryk arrives in Prague, 1918.

1914
The Archduke Francis Ferdinand is assassinated at Sarajevo. World War One begins.

1938
Under the terms of the Munich Agreement, Czechoslovakia loses a third of its territory to Germany, Hungary and Poland.

THE "AWAKENERS". The beginning of the 19th century was marked by the Czech "national awakening", a movement which received considerable impetus from a group of historians and linguists known as the "Awakeners". As early as 1791, Josef Dobrovský published a manifesto supporting the National Czech Movement, and a history of the Czech language and literature. The Awakeners founded the National Museum ▲ *175* in Prague in 1818; then, Josef Jungmann brought out the first manual of Czech literature (*Slovesnost*) and a history of literature (1825), and František Palacký (left) published a history of Bohemia (*Geschichte von Böhmen*, 1836), which was translated into Czech in 1848. It was during this period that Bohemia, Moravia and Silesia were industrialized.

1848. A pan-Slav congress was held in Prague following the Revolution in France. After forbidding all revolutionary movements, the Diet of the Austrian Empire abolished all feudal rights, putting an end to serfdom. However, following the return of a régime that had reneged on individual freedoms, František Palacký and František Ladislav Rieger sought to gain the support of Napoleon III and the Russians.

LEADING UP TO WORLD WAR ONE. The attempt to link Czechs to the Austro-Hungarian compromise of 1867 foundered, and Czech Deputies joined the opposition. Next, the Czech language acquired the same status as German, and a Czech-language university was re-founded in 1881. As Austrian subjects, the Czechs entered the war in 1914 on the side of their masters, albeit unwillingly, but by 1915 the idea of a Czech and Slovak federation was beginning to gain support in the United States, thanks to the efforts of Masaryk and Beneš.

A REPUBLIC. After the 1918 Armistice, Czechoslovakia became an independent republic, with Tomáš Garrigue Masaryk (1850–1937) as its first president. The country's constitution was influenced by the French model, and an alliance, with an undertaking to provide military assistance, was signed with France in 1925. Edvard Beneš succeeded Masaryk in 1935, and signed a treaty with the USSR.

WORLD WAR TWO. Under the Munich Agreement of 1938, Czechoslovakia was abandoned by the Allies and lost a third of its territory. The Czech Resistance began to form, and in London Beneš took over the Liberal Democratic Movement. Meanwhile, the leaders of the Czech Communist Party, including Gottwald ● *39*, fled to Moscow. Following the National Slovak Revolution, there was an uprising in Prague

Edvard Beneš and Winston Churchill.

on May 5, 1945, and four days later Soviet troops allowed into Prague by the American Army found a city that had already liberated itself. On its return from exile, Beneš' government persuaded the Allies to expel up to two million Germans.

1945
60,000 regular soldiers and 40,000 members of the Resistance fought under the Czechoslovak flag.

FROM STALINIZATION TO NORMALIZATION.
The Communist Klement Gottwald formed a coalition government in 1946 and, in February 1948, the ruling Communists established a Stalinist régime of nationalization and political trials. From 1953 to 1968 Antonín Novotný took over from Gottwald. The historic "Prague Spring" of 1968 ● *40* ended with Czechoslovak resistance being crushed by the USSR; then, the Slovak Gustav Husák, First Secretary of the Communist Party, took control of the country and aligned himself with Moscow. In 1970 and 1971, 500,000 Czechoslovak Communists were expelled from the Party, and society was "normalized". Charter 77, drawn up by Jan Patočka in 1977, was signed by 242 intellectuals, including Václav Havel. In 1986, Jakes replaced Husák, who stayed on as President; the official slogan was "Perestroika" (*přesavba*).

Pro-Soviet demonstration in Prague in 1950.

ENGELS

AUGUST 1968
Troops from Warsaw Pact countries, excluding Ceaucescu's

PRAGUE, CAPITAL OF THE CZECH REPUBLIC

THE VELVET REVOLUTION. The huge demonstrations of November 1989 (below, left) ▲ *173* were sustained by the creation of the Civic Forum: the Velvet Revolution was under way. On December 29, Václav Havel ● *41* was elected President, and from 1990 things began to move quickly with the departure of the Soviet army of occupation, the initiation of parliamentary and local elections, an end to the friendship treaty with the Soviet Union, and the removal of the requirement for visas for most European countries.

TWO REPUBLICS. On June 8, 1992, the party of Václav Klaus and that of Vladimír Mečiar in Slovakia won parliamentary elections, and the process of separating the two countries started. January 1, 1993 marked the end of the Czech and Slovak Federal Republic and of Czechoslovakia, and the birth of two independent States, the Czech and Slovak Republics. Václav Havel (below, right) was elected President of the Czech Republic. He was re-elected in January 1998.

Romania, invade Prague.

JANUARY 16, 1969
Jan Palach makes a political statement by publicly commiting suicide.

OCTOBER 1969
Massive emigration. Frontiers with the West closed.

1991
Dissolution of the USSR.

1991–2
Success of the "small privatization" program.

Crown of the Kings of Bohemia.

The first Czech monarchs were members of the Přemyslid dynasty and were called dukes (Kníže). The title of Duke disappeared under Přemysl Otakar I, and the title of King, which two Přemyslid kings had already had conferred on them personally, became hereditary. If a king had no direct heir, his successor was elected by the Diet. The Jagiellos initiated the practise of having their eldest sons elected and crowned during their own lifetimes. After the Battle of White Mountain, Ferdinand II proclaimed the Kingship of Bohemia to be hereditary in the House of the Habsburgs. In 1804, Francis I became the first Emperor of Austria, a title which his successors retained even after the fall of the Holy Roman Empire (1806).

PŘEMYSLID DYNASTY
The story goes that the founder was a farm-laborer called Přemysl; he became the husband of Princess Libussa, daughter of the patriarch Čech who, legend tells us, led the Czechs to the gates of Prague. The Přemyslid line consists of BOŘIVOJ (9th century),

Barbarossa, PŘEMYSL OTAKAR I (1192–3 and 1197–1230), the first hereditary king after 1198, PŘEMYSL OTAKAR II (1253–78) (right), WENCESLAS I (1230–53), WENCESLAS II (1278–1305), and WENCESLAS III (1305–6), the last member of the Přemyslid Dynasty.

WENCESLAS (or VÁCLAV) (died 929 or 935), VRATISLAV II (1061–92) who was crowned king in 1085 by the Holy Roman Emperor Henry IV, VLADISLAV I (1140–72) who was crowned by the Holy Roman Emperor Frederick

GEORGE OF PODĚBRADY (1458–71), Regent from 1452 to 1458.

JAGIELLO DYNASTY
VLADISLAV JAGIELLO (1471–1516), King of Hungary from 1490. LOUIS JAGIELLO (1516–26) was also King of Hungary, but was killed by the Turks at the Battle of Mohács in 1526.

LUXEMBURG DYNASTY (14TH–15TH CENTURIES)
JOHN OF LUXEMBURG (1310–46) fought on the side of the French during the Hundred Years' War and died at the Battle of Crécy. CHARLES I, known as CHARLES IV (1346–78) (above): during his reign, the Czech State included Bohemia, Moravia, Silesia, the County of Glatz (now Klodsko, Poland), the fief of Cheb, Upper and Lower Lusatia, Brandenburg from 1373 to 1415, and the fief of Upper Palatinate from 1353 to 1373. WENCESLAS, or VÁCLAV IV (1378–1419); and SIGISMUND (1419–20 and 1436–7), who was King of Hungary from 1385.

HABSBURG DYNASTY

16TH–20TH CENTURIES
All the Habsburgs were crowned Kings of Bohemia in Prague, with the exception of Joseph II (who was known in the Estates as the "King wearing a hat") and the last two Habsburgs, Francis Ferdinand I and Charles I. Francis I gave himself the title of Emperor of Austria on the grounds that, although Emperor of the Holy Roman Empire, he was only an Archduke of Austria and King of Bohemia and Hungary.

FERDINAND I
(1526–64) (Opposite)
MAXIMILIAN II
(1564–76)
RUDOLPH II
(1576–1611)
MATTHIAS
(1611–19)
FERDINAND II
(1619–37)
FERDINAND III
(1637–57)
LEOPOLD I
(1657–1705)
JOSEPH I
(1705–11)
CHARLES VI
(1711–40)

RUDOLPH II OF HABSBURG
Rudolph was also King of Hungary until 1608.

HABSBURG-LORRAINE DYNASTY
When Maria Theresa married Francis of Lorraine in 1736, the House of Habsburg became the House of Habsburg-Lorraine.

MARIA THERESA (1740–80) (above)
JOSEPH II (1780–90)
LEOPOLD II (1790–92)
FRANCIS I (1792–1835)
FERDINAND V (1835–48)
FRANZ JOSEF I (1848–1916)
CHARLES I (1916–18)

JOHN HUSS AND THE HUSSITE MOVEMENT

At the end of the 14th century, Prague University was the center of a reform movement favoring a return to fundamental Christianity, and poverty and humility for the clergy and the Church. This movement, influenced by the Oxford theologian, John Wycliffe (1320–84), was driven by a conflict between church and royalty. The leader of the reformers, John Huss, reinforced the movement through his powers of oratory and later as a martyr. In the 19th and early 20th centuries, the role of Hussite Reforms in the development of a national consciousness and Czech policy was as important as that of the Battle of White Mountain.

WENCESLAS IV (reigned 1361–1419, far right) King Wenceslas of Bohemia was one of John Huss' supporters between 1409 and 1412.

SIGISMUND OF LUXEMBURG (1368–1437, right) This king of Hungary, brother of Wenceslas IV, attended the Council of Constance.

JOHN HUSS AND REFORM. John Huss (1371– 1415, left) studied at Prague University and became Rector in 1409. By 1400, he was a preacher and was two years later appointed Curate of the Bethlehem Chapel ▲ 286, where he remained until 1413. Excommunicated at the Council of Constance in 1411, Huss appeared there once more in 1414. Hussite Reform stated that the Bible was the supreme theological and legal authority, superseding human laws The Church was to be divested of material goods and temporal powers, and the State should assume responsibility for them. Huss found an ally in Wenceslas IV, who wanted to re-establish his authority to the detriment of the Church however, growing concerned at the prospect of seeing Bohemia in the grip of heresy, he withdrew his support in 1412.

"Pravda zvítězí"
(Truth shall overcome)

John Huss, at the stake

THE HUSSITE WARS

After Wenceslas IV died, both the Church and King Sigismund, Pretender to the Bohemian throne, were subjected to intense military pressure. The Hussite Wars raged around the country between 1419 and 1435, with the nobility taking arms and the University attesting Huss' integrity.

In 1418, the Synod of Czech Priests approved both the articles of Hussite doctrine and its symbol, the chalice used in Holy Communion.

HUSS AT THE STAKE. John Huss attended the Council of Constance in October 1414 to defend his good faith. He was arrested, thrown into prison and convicted of heresy; on July 6, 1415, Huss was burned at the stake despite a royal safe-conduct and letters of protest from the nobility. As a result of his death, and that of his friend Jeremy of Prague, a year later, the situation intensified. Below: The arrest of John Huss, wearing the cap of a heretic.

33

● THE BATTLE OF WHITE MOUNTAIN

Ferdinand II of
Habsburg

At the end of the 16th century, the political initiative in the kingdom of Bohemia was held by Catholics, who were in a minority, and the most determined section of non-Catholics did not consolidate their position until 1609, when they persuaded Rudolph II of Habsburg to sign a Letter of Majesty which heralded a new era of religious tolerance. These ideological conflicts culminated in the Defenestration of Prague of 1618, and in the Battle of White Mountain of 1620 which brought defeat for the rebelious Estates of Bohemia.

A "COUNTER-KING"
Ferdinand II succeeded Matthias in 1617 but was officially deposed in August 1619; next came the Calvinist elector palatine Frederick V (below), known as the "Winter King".

THE DEFENESTRATION OF PRAGUE
After 1617, inter-religious antagonism sharpened as a result of the pro-Catholic policies introduced by the Emperor Matthias, successor to Rudolph II. On May 23, 1618, in an attempt to gain the support of those still undecided, radical elements threw two of the King's councillors, Jaroslav Bořita of Martinic and William Count Slavata, from the windows of the chancellery. This event sparked off the Thirty Years' War (1618–48).

MILITARY PRELUDE
The election of Frederick V gave the conflict with a dimension, and the formation of new political groupings duly gave rise to a military crisis.

DEFEAT AT THE BATTLE OF WHITE MOUNTAIN

Frederick V left the castle after the defeat on November 8, 1620, and the capital surrendered on November 11. On November 13 the Estates of Bohemia recognized Ferdinand II as king, and Bohemia was integrated into the Habsburg Empire, converting back to Catholicism and losing its political privileges. In the Czech camp, the defeat was followed by executions, including those of twenty-seven insurgent leaders in 1621 (above), confiscation of goods, and forced conversion to Catholicism. The Marian Column (right) in Old Town Square symbolized the triumph of Catholicism.

A KEY HISTORICAL EVENT

The Battle of White Mountain was a major turning point in Czech history. Way beyond the immediate repercussions that helped to create the myth, the battle had long-term consequences. For those promoting the Czech revival, it was a disaster, and it became central to subsequent definitions of national identity during the 19th century. The creation of Czechoslovakia in 1918 was viewed by most Czechs as just reparation.

THE BATTLE OF WHITE MOUNTAIN

This decisive battle was fought on the outskirts of Prague around a knoll known as White Mountain (Bílá Hora) ▲ *321*; it lasted no more than two hours.

The Czechoslovak Republic emerged from the ruins of the Austro-Hungarian Empire, and was born without a single drop of blood being spilled. The new State – it included Czechs, Slovaks, Germans, Hungarians, Rutheno-Ukrainians and Poles – was democratic and secular, and the political spectrum took in everything from the Communist Party to the nationalist right. It was also over-industrialized in the west and under-developed in the east and, although in many ways well balanced, it was a country of great geographical contrasts. Czechoslovakia was a model democracy and was profoundly shaken by the economic crisis of 1929 and, on being abandoned by the western powers, it easily succumbed to pressure from Hitler.

THOMÁŠ GARRIGUE MASARYK
(1850–1937)
This president-philosopher exercised a genuine "respectful dictatorship" because he was able to impress the people with his human and intellectual qualities. As a prominent figure of the expatriate Resistance during the War, he had fought for the emergence of the Czechoslovak State; he then became its President in 1918 and remained in this post until he retired in 1935.

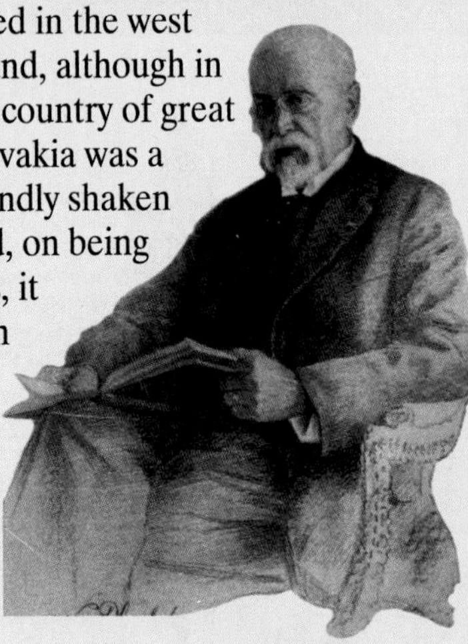

A MAN OF LEARNING
Through his writings and sense of political ethics, Masaryk made a major contribution to the development of the Czech culture.

MASARYK ARRIVES IN WENCESLAS SQUARE IN DECEMBER 1918
Thomáš Garrigue Masaryk returned triumphantly to Prague after four years of exile. He is seen surrounded by Czech and Slovak troops who had fought in Russia on the side of the Allies.

> "The Czech spirit was immediately sensitive to its European mission and . . . took all possible steps to show that it was worthy."
>
> Jan Patočka

EDVARD BENEŠ (1884–1948) Edvard Beneš remains a key figure in Czechoslovakian history.

THE IMPORTANCE OF MINORITIES

Although the State accorded minorities the international rules of protection, it was sometimes difficult for these groups to accept inferior positions. This was particularly true of the Hungarians and Germans. From 1925 onward, democratic Germans adopted Czechoslovakia and from 1927 to 1938 joined the government, although this did not prevent minorities from being used by Hitler as a lever to overturn the State. The German population of the Sudetenland (above) began to adopt radical politics around 1933, and fell heavily under the influence of National Socialism. The independence of which some Slovaks had dreamed back in 1918 would not become reality until October 1938, with Josef Tiso as head of the government.

MASARYK'S SUCCESSOR

After playing a decisive role in securing recognition for his country, Beneš was Minister of Foreign Affairs until 1935, and then President of the Republic. Apostle of collective security, he was appalled by the Munich Agreement of September 1938, but he continued the struggle in exile and returned as leader of his country in April 1945.

● CZECHOSLOVAKIA IN UPHEAVAL 1938–48

Following the Munich Agreement of September 30, 1938, Czechoslovakia was forced to give way to German claims, and the Wehrmacht invaded the Sudetenland. The State was broken up and divided and, on March 14–15, 1939, Hitler invaded, turned Czechoslovakia into a protectorate and lent his support to Slovakian independence. The Slovaks' initial delight soon turned into rejection of their Fascist government, which became increasingly subservient to its protectors. The extermination of the Jews affected both parts of the country but on the whole their experiences were very different. The people therefore remembered things in dissimilar ways, and this meant that they retained different attitudes after the Liberation.

Arrival of Nazi troops in Prague in 1939. The Czech Resistance was harshly put down, and Czech Jews exterminated.

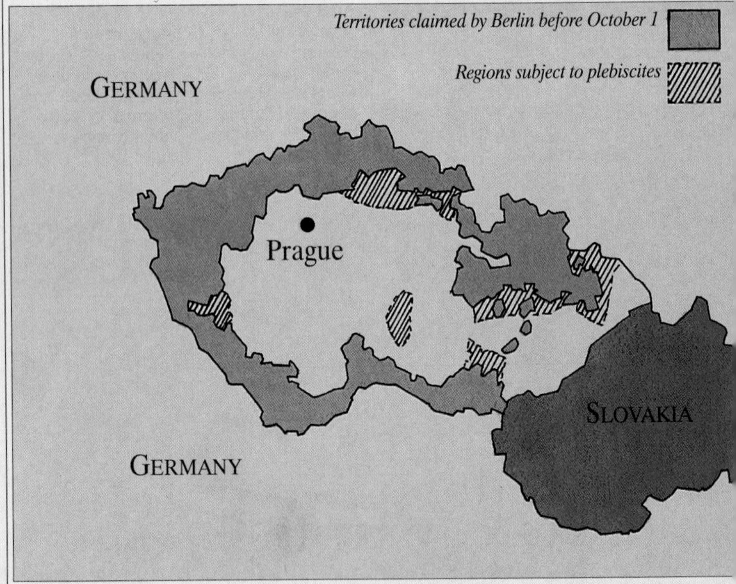

Territories claimed by Berlin before October 1

Regions subject to plebiscites

GERMANY

Prague

GERMANY

SLOVAKIA

A TIME OF ADVERSITY
In September and October 1938, the Czech lands lost their peripheral territories, inhabited by Germans since the 13th century, and Hungary annexed the prosperous areas in the south of Slovakia which had a Hungarian majority. On March 15, 1939, the Wehrmacht invaded the Second Republic and turned it into the Protectorate of Bohemia-Moravia and an independent Slovak State, a satellite of Nazi Germany. Many politicians, under the leadership of Beneš ● 37, fled to London; there, they sought assurance from the Allies that Czechoslovakia would be independent again.

> "Circumstances have made Czechoslovakia into a keystone...
> Everything will collapse if she is unable to resist the attempts
> to crush her."
>
> Paul Valéry (September 1938)

MOVING TOWARD COMMUNISM

Between May 5 and 8, 1945, the people of Prague took control of the city, and Soviet troops entered on May 9. When hostilities ceased, the Communists found themselves in a powerful position, and the Chairman of the Communist Party, Klement Gottwald (above), was quick to pick up the reins of power. The spread of the Cold War and internal struggles soon curtailed the democratic interlude, and the Communist Party eventually took over in February 1948.

Soviet troops arriving in Prague.

POLAND

HUNGARY   ROMANIA

HEYDRICH IS KILLED ▲ *307*
The assassination of Reinhard Heydrich (right), the "hangman" of Czechoslovakia, on May 26, 1942, sparked off a brutal repression which decimated the Resistance. This partly took the form of the destruction of Lidice and Ležáky: these two villages were razed to the ground and the male populations exterminated.

The Communists came to power in February 1948 when the government of the country was in serious crisis. Stalinization was quickly enforced and political repression intensified, affecting even the Communist Party itself. Following Gottwald's death and the waves of anti-authoritarianism that marked the 1960's, the Prague Spring brought real hopes of change, but these were smashed by the Soviet invasion of 1968. That signaled the beginning of normalization, but the Party did not fall until the time of the 1989 demonstrations. Although the new Republic sought European re-integration, it was not able to resist either the national tensions that had been smoldering for so many years, or the dynamic for separation which had been encouraged by politicians – but not noticed by the citizens.

1952: THE GREAT SHOW TRIALS

The trial of Slánský, Secretary General of the Czech Communist Party, was the culmination of a process of repression organized by the Party's upper echelons. Of the fourteen accused, only three escaped execution. This trial was marked by the struggle against "Titoism" in Yugoslavia and by a form of anti-Zionism that came close to anti-Semitism. The rehabilitation of the victims of these trials remained a major political issue until 1968.

1968–9: RESISTANCE

De-Stalinization reached Czechoslovakia late, illustrating the strength of the anti-authoritarian movement of the 1960's. Repression of the opposition did not impede the struggle. As *perestroika* took hold, and the people felt less frightened, the power of the Communists fell away, allowing dissidents to take control.

1968: THE PRAGUE SPRING

In January 1968, the Slovak Alexander Dubček (below) took over from Antonín Novotný as head of the Communist Party. From the spring onward, Dubček opted for reform and the country moved slowly toward liberalization.

NORMALIZATION

Czechoslovakia was invaded by Warsaw Pact troops on August 21, 1968. The country was subjected to a strict régime of normalization and, with the former GDR, became one of the most conservative members of the Soviet bloc. The divorce between power and opinion was now deep-seated.

> "I will take the risk of saying that, despite attractive appearances to the contrary. . . our society is plunging into deeper and deeper crisis."

Václav Havel to Gustav Husák (1975)

1989 THE "VELVET REVOLUTION"

The gap between the official line and personal convictions had never been so great since 1969. Dissidence was born of this unrest, bolstered by a longing for ethical standards. A few hundred people were grouping

round Charter 77 ● *29*, an organization that stood for the defence of human rights; they represented the feelings and aspirations that were now being increasingly shared by the population at large.

1969–89: FROM DISSIDENT TO PRESIDENT

The bourgeois origins of Václav Havel (born 1936) prevented him from having a university education although, as a playwright, he played an important role on behalf of the Writers' Union during the Prague Spring when he was banned from the theater, he became involved in setting up Charter 77, and his activities there earned him several terms of imprisonment. He led the demonstrations of November 17, 1989, and the crowd instinctively called on the man who had always spoken up to take over as President.

Pravda zvítězí: Truth shall overcome. The student struggles of 1989 echoed the last words that John Huss ● *32* uttered at the stake.

PRAVDA ZVÍTĚZÍ

THE KRALICKÁ BIBLE 1579–93

During the 16th century, the Unity of Czech Brethren went to considerable lengths to restore the characteristics of the Czech language and to establish them in written form. As part of this work, they published grammars and made important contributions to a consolidation of the rules of spelling. However, their finest work was a remarkable translation of the Bible; this was to remain a touchstone of the Czech language's purity and style.

JOHN HUSS, CAMPAIGNER FOR A NEW LANGUAGE

"I have written here as I normally speak," John Huss states in one of his books. Elsewhere he recommends, "I ask that anyone who writes should not write in any way differently from me."

INTRODUCTION

Czech is a Western Slavic language like Polish, Slovak and Serb. It is the official language of the Czech Republic. The Czech alphabet has thirty-four letters, which are pronounced as follows:

a (ah)	f (eff)	l (ell)	r (err)	v (vay)
b (bay)	g (gay)	m (emm)	ř (rzh)	w (dvoyitay
c (tsay)	h (hah)	n (enn)	s (ess)	vay)
č (chay)	ch (chah)	ň (enye)	š (esh)	x (iks)
d (day)	i (ee)	o (oh)	t (tay)	y (ypsilon)
ď (diay)	j (yay)	p (pay)	ť (tiay)	z (zett)
e (ay)	k (kah)	q (kvay)	u (oo)	ž (zhet)

Czech makes distinctions between long and short vowels, the main stress of a word being fixed and usually occurring on the first syllable of each word. There are no articles in Czech. As in Latin and German, nouns and adjectives are declined; there are seven cases.

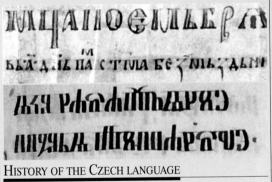

HISTORY OF THE CZECH LANGUAGE

Until the 14th century, Czech was essentially no more than a spoken language, although during the 10th and 11th centuries it sometimes combined with written languages, such as Latin and Old Slav, to form occasional words (*Bohemica*) and glosses. Following the political, economic and cultural expansion that took place toward the end of the 13th century (in the final years of the Přemyslid dynasty) and during the 14th century (particularly under the reign of Charles IV), Czech rapidly became the kingdom's language of literature, administration and law. From the 13th century onward, Czech underwent major vocalic, consonantal and morphological changes, and these extended into the 16th, and even the 18th, centuries. Ultimately, they formed the basis of modern Czech. Syntax developed under the influence of Latin. Czech literature grew in stature in the course of the 14th century. Many literary works of the period are notable for their concentration on form and their search for elaborate syntax in the style of medieval Latin prose; the theological works of Tomáš de Štítný are fine examples of this. Other works drew their inspiration from the spoken language and the flavor of popular expressions. Under the influence of religious reformers and the Hussite movement ● *32*, during a period extending from the end of the 14th century to the 15th century, the influence of the spoken language over literary language became even more marked. As a result many preachers and theologians, such as John Huss and Petr Chelčický, used the spoken tongue as part of a deliberate policy to popularize the Church's teachings. In an attempt to unite the Czech language, John Huss gave pride of place to the dialect spoken both in Prague, a university city and economic and cultural center, and in the surrounding area. The standard features of Czech are based on this dialect.

JOHN HUSS AND SPELLING REFORM. Until the time of John Huss, Czech sounds that did not exist in Latin were transcribed by means of two letters. For example, č was written cz (pronounced "ts") and the long a vowel was written aa; this made writing as complicated as it did reading. Huss suggested that spelling could be simplified by the use of diacritics placed over the relevant letter. He also introduced an acute accent to indicate a long vowel, and a dot to indicate a palatalized consonant. Huss's spelling reforms were revised by the Czech Brethren in the 16th century, and later on in the 19th century it was once again simplified by religious reformers.

THE SPREAD OF THE CZECH LANGUAGE. Interest in the Czech language grew toward the end of the 15th century, and even more so during the 16th century. Czech Humanists devoted many of their works to a defence of their mother tongue, which continued to develop throughout this period; for the most part, Latin served as a model for syntax. Lexicological works played a key role, and contained virtually every word in existence together with its Latin, Greek or German equivalent. The activities of the Unity of Czech Brethren also showed the reviving interest in the national language. Of no less importance were the didactic and pedagogical works of Jan Ámos Komenský ▲ 262 (Comenius), the last bishop of the Unity of Czech Brethren.

J.A.Comen:s
DIDACTICA OPERA
OMNIA.
Ab Anno 1627 ad 1657.
continuata.

THE VYŠEHRAD CODEX
The manuscript of this Codex, which dates from 1085, is kept in the library of Clementinum University ▲ 150. The illustration above is of Saint Wenceslas. The Vyšehrad Codex, the Veleslav Bible, an extract from the Gutenberg Bible and John Huss' manuscripts are the oldest items held in the library. At the time of the Treaty of Versailles in 1919, the Codex was valued at 50 million gold francs.

J. Á. KOMENSKÝ (1592–1670)
Komenský's dictionary, the *Thesaurus linguae bohemicae,* was intended to provide an overall survey of language study during the 16th century. Unfortunately it was almost entirely destroyed in a fire at Lešno, where Komenský was living.

43

AN INTERMINGLING OF LANGUAGES

In the early part of the 20th century, about 415,000

inhabitants of Prague were Czech, 100,000 were Germans, and 25,000 were Jews, of whom some spoke Czech and the rest German. The German minority enjoyed supremacy, but the various languages continued to influence one another: Czech abounded in German words, while German was full of Bohemian expressions. This was the origin of a new language which was far removed from pure German, although it shared the latter's constructions and pronunciation. Writers such as Rilke and Werfel fulminated against this underdeveloped language; by contrast, Kafka found something authentic in its poverty of expression, and this contributed to the purity of his written style.

The poster (right) was designed by Viktor Oliva in 1898 for the Prague review *Zlatá Praha*.

THE PRE-EMINENCE OF GERMAN. The development of literary Czech slowed down in the 17th century, and even more so during the 18th century. Defeat at the Battle of White Mountain (1620) ● *34* forced the non-Catholic intellectual élite to emigrate. Czech was gradually supplanted by German, particularly as the language used in government and in secondary and university teaching; however, it survived orally in religious chants, songs, poetry and popular stories.

REVIVAL. The Czech language began to be revived during the so-called period of "national awakening" which lasted from the late 18th century through the first half of the 19th century. This advance was both demanded and conditioned by various social developments, including the abolition of serfdom in 1781. It also led to an increase in the number of publications in Czech and to developments in literature and the theater. At the end of the 18th century, scholars, linguists, journalists and writers like F. M. Pelcl, J. Nejedlý, Josef Dobrovský, Josef Jungmann and A. J. Puchmajer allotted themselves the task of restoring self-respect to Czech; they aimed to do this by recalling its glorious past. They also produced works of considerable importance including grammars and dictionaries. It was not until the late 19th century that the language was decisively codified through the works of Jan Gebauer, Professor at the Czech University of Prague. These developments survive to the present day. After the Republic was founded in 1918 ● *36*, Czech flourished without impediment and continued its process of modernization. Literary works from the inter-war period show both the language's richness and the enthusiasm that it stimulated in writers such as Karel Čapek, Vítězslav Nezval and V. Vančura. It was around this time that the word robot first appeared; this was a neologism created by Čapek for his play *RUR* (*Rossum's Universal Robots*) ● *55* and deriving from the Slavonic stem *rab* (to work, drudge). In 1926 the Prague Circle was founded; it numbered among its members many linguists, including V. Mathesius, B. Havránek, M. Weingart and Roman Jakobson.

Arts and traditions

Latin Gregorian chant began to evolve in the 9th century. The existence of a canticle in Slavonian, *Hospodine pomiluj ný*, attributed to Saint Adalbert and dating from the same period, establishes that there co-existed in Prague two liturgies that were celebrated in two different languages and which derived from two quite distinct schools of music. Over the centuries, the advances made by Czech music were closely linked to the political, religious and cultural histories of Bohemia and Moravia; this also applied to the history of the whole of western and eastern Europe, of which Prague remained one of the major centers.

The training of cantors ensured the survival of Czech singing. Above: A music lesson.

ANTONÍN DVOŘÁK (1841–1904) Thanks to a cantor from Zlonice, this child of a peasant family, destined to be a butcher, came to Prague and enrolled at the Organ School. He later played viola with the Orchestra of the Provisional Theater under Bedřich Smetana. While Smetana was the musical standard-bearer, Dvořák was more successful at expressing the links that bound the original characteristics of a form of music that was both national and universal. He shone as a symphonist and composer of chamber pieces, and also in the field of oratorios. Only opera, despite his determination to succeed in this field, failed to bring him renown.

"Czech life is in the music."

Bedřich Smetana

The Hussite Movement ● 32 generated a style of canticles in the vernacular which was to have an undisputed impact nationwide. Above: John Huss at the stake; 15th-century gradual.

MUSIC AND HISTORY

Secular music of the Middle Ages reached its apogee during the reigns of Přemysl Otakar II ● 30 and of Charles IV, a man who had been brought up at the French Court. Later, despite defeat at the Battle of White Mountain, music prospered with the assistance of the Unions of Czech and Moravian Brethren, and thanks to the brilliance of the King's Court. During the time of the Thirty Years' War, Czechs made a major impact on the Baroque era. The period of the Enlightenment and the "national awakening" saw the rejection of Italian ideas and oppressive German influences.

BEDŘICH SMETANA

(1824–84). Smetana, who became famous through his *Má vlast*, was the most combative musician in the Czech National Movement. He fought for a National Theater in Prague ▲ 294, his objective being to provide the theater with a Czech repertoire that was worthy of the patriotic ideas of the period.

CZECH SCHOOL

Many composers who followed Smetana contributed to the Czech school's reputation. They included Zdeněk Fibich (1850–1900), Karel Bendl (1830–97) and J. B. Foerster (1859–1951); the most celebrated,

however, was Antonín Dvořák. Later came Josef Suk (1874–1935) and Vítězslav Novák (1870–1949), but none of them challenged the uniqueness and power of Leoš Janáček (1854–1928, left). He was followed by Bohuslav Martinů (1890–1959, above). After Independence in 1918, new talents including Alois Hába (1893–1973) and Jaroslav Ježek (1882–1969) gave Prague an avant-garde reputation. Since World War Two, and in the face of fierce political pressures, a number of composers have made a deep impression through their daring and copious output.

Prague's international image as a musical capital has more to do with respect for certain places, monuments and institutions than with the reputation of its great composers. An example of this is the "Prague Spring" Festival which was founded in 1946 and attracts the world's great performing artists. This event is associated with the city's supposed image as the "conservatoire of Europe". The Museum of Musical Instruments which opened, in the Palace of the Order of Malta in 1954, contains three thousand instruments. It is currently closed, and will soon be moved to new premises.

VIOLIN
Made by Gasparo da Salo, Brescia (c. 1584). This violin, richly decorated, is carved from a single block of maple wood.

GREAT INTERPRETERS
The reputations of many great soloists, and the long line of Czech violinists, provide a rich counterpoint to the fame of Prague's musical institutions. The vitality of the School of String Quartets was demonstrated by the celebrated Czech Quartet founded by Josef Suk at the end of the 19th century. The tradition has been sustained to this day through the emergence of immensely talented groups.

IMPORTANT ORCHESTRAS
The Czech Philharmonic Orchestra ▲ *166* was founded in 1894 and gave its first concert in 1896 under Antonín Dvořák. It shares the Rudolfinum ▲ *194* and the Town Hall with the Prague Symphony Orchestra.

> "Master Poverty taught Dalibor to play the violin."
>
> Czech proverb

MUSICAL EDUCATION

The Academy of Music, the city's senior music school, grew out of the prestigious Prague Conservatoire (1811). When the Association for Musical Development in Bohemia took the initiative to establish the Academy, it was the first musical event linked to the period of "national awakening" ● 28.

"SEDIFONY" HORNS

J. Sediva, Odessa (1901–13). These instruments dating from the early 20th century were made by a Czech manufacturer who lived in Russia. They had two tubes and produced a shriller sound than modern horns.

GIRAFFE PIANO

The name of this early 18th-century instrument derives from the fact that it is shaped like the neck of a giraffe. It is one of the curiosities on display in the Museum of Musical Instruments.

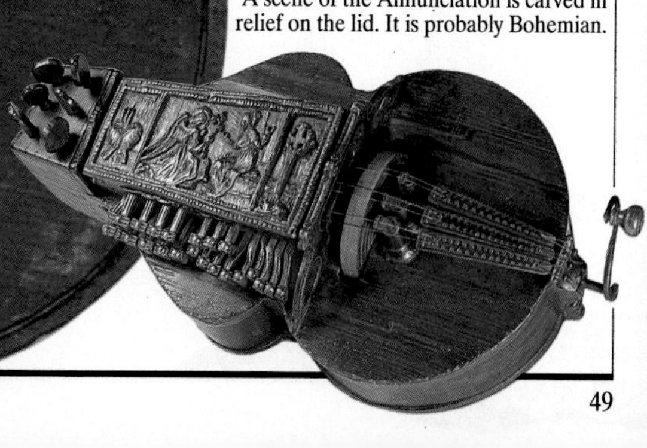

AN 18TH-CENTURY HURDY-GURDY

A scene of the Annunciation is carved in relief on the lid. It is probably Bohemian.

● THE POLKA

The polka is often described as a dance of Polish origin, but in fact it is Czech; it was strongly influenced by the *écossaise* and the Polish *krakowiak*. The name was probably inspired by the presence of Poles in Prague following the 1831 uprising and the enormous feelings of sympathy that they engendered; some people believe, however, that the word derives from the Czech *pole* (field) or *pulka* (half). There were a number of regional variations of the polka that appeared after 1840, including the polka waltz and polka mazurka.

SMETANA'S "THE KISS" AT THE PROVISIONAL THEATER, PRAGUE (1876)
The patriotic composer Bedřich Smetana (1824–84) wrote many well-known polkas; he used this popular form in his large-scale symphonic works as well as in several of his operas, including *The Kiss*.

"BARREL BEER POLKA"
Cover of the score of the most famous polka in the world. It was composed in the 1920's by Jaromir Vejdova, and is known internationally by its American title, *Barrel Beer Polka*.

PIANO SCORE FOR THE "POLKA ESMERALDA"

After 1830, the polka replaced the waltz in the hearts of Czech people, particularly those who frequented the city's more popular meeting places. The first scores of this dance appeared in Prague in the form of loose sheets. F. M. Hilmar's *Esmeralda* was inspired by a character in Victor Hugo's novel *Notre-Dame de Paris*.

SCORE OF "THE BARTERED BRIDE"

Smetana started composing and playing polkas at the age of fifteen. He was an excellent dancer and, at a time when the polka was already sweeping the country, he used to entertain the bourgeois drawing-rooms of Prague and Plzen with demonstrations of the dance. *The Bartered Bride*, the first great Czech opera, made use of stylized polka tunes; the finale to the last act is a celebration of this popular dance.

The basic step, which is alternated and repeated in an unceasing swirl, had been used in several Czech dances since the beginning of the 19th century.

● FESTIVALS AND SOCIETY BALLS

There is no question that music continues to play a major role in Prague life, but society balls are a thing of the past.

Lively festivals and balls were once an integral part of the city's life: in the 19th century, the German and Austrian bourgeoisies would mingle at big society balls, while the city's parks played host to numerous, more popular festivals. However, festivals and balls did not simply provide sources of entertainment; for many years, they had a political objective, bringing together Czechs who yearned to affirm their nationalism. As early as 1848, Czechs were devising their own *besedas*; many years later, in the 1970's, soirées were being organized by Prague dissidents at the National House in Vinohrady and at other gatherings sponsored by Charter 77.

SOCIETY BALL IN PRAGUE (1830)
During the 18th century, the Austrian nobility and the German bourgeoisie held *Societäts-Bälle* and *Privat-Bälle* in their opulent residences. The most popular dances were the polonaise, the gavotte, the *ländler* and, later on, the waltz. At the beginning of the 19th century, they owned as many as sixteen dancing salons.

FUNFAIR IN HVEZDA PARK
In the early 19th century, the parks around Prague were thronged with Czechs enthusiastically indulging in the simple, catchy rhythms of popular dances like the *rejdovák*, *trasák*, *dupák* and *britva*. There had hardly been a Czech nobility of any description for two hundred years.

"POMNĚNKA", (MEMORIES), DANCE CARD
The first Czech *beseda* took place in April 1848. It was organized by the city's artists and intellectuals, who used the proceeds to build the National Theater.

FAN FROM THE PRAGUE STUDENTS' BALL, 1849
From 1840 onward, all sectors of Prague society, including cultural associations and professional bodies, had their own balls. Student *merendas* and masked *redutas* were the most popular.

PATRIOTIC BALLS
From 1830 onward, the Czech intelligentsia, led by the playwright Josef Kajetán Tyl ▲ *280*, organized private balls in aid of patriots, mainly in the Malá Strana district. The first "Czech ball" took place around 1840 in the Jesuit College ▲ *288* in the city center and in the Žofín Palace ▲ *302* on Bavířka Island, nowadays known as Slav Island.

BALLROOM AT THE TOWN HALL
The tradition of Prague society balls may not have survived the test of time, but dancing lessons remain very popular. Today, the Town Hall (*Obecní dům* ▲ *164*) is one of the many places where large numbers of young people come to learn all about the polka, waltz, tango and samba – and even the paso doble.

53

The theater has always played an extremely important role in Prague, and this goes some way toward explaining how Czechs were able to protect their language and maintain their national identity while under Austrian rule. The theater was traditionally a place where people came together during important events, and dramatists always played decisive roles at these times. Both Karel Čapek and Václav Havel have been central figures in their country's destiny.

ABC THEATER
This was the home of the "Liberated Theater", Prague's most popular company during the years 1927–38 and 1946–8. The show had two singing clowns who put on a musical, usually anti-Fascist, revue. The duo was disbanded largely as a result of events in Munich in 1938 and the Prague Coup of 1948, but Voskovec and Werich nonetheless became legends in their own lifetime. Václav Havel first wrote for the theater in 1958.

NÁRODNÍ DIVADLO

Collections that formed part of the *Národ sobě* (Nation for the Nation) appeal paid for the construction in 1883 of what Czechs called "the Golden Chapel on the Vltava". The National Theater's curtain, painted by Vojtěch Hynais ▲ *295* and designed like a Gobelin tapestry, recounts this episode in allegorical style.

"DIVADLO NA ZÁBRADLÍ" ▲ *156*

For the most part, the Theater "on the Balustrade" (the costume above is from a 1972 production of *The Marriage of Figaro*) concentrated on the theater of the absurd when Václav Havel worked there as a playwright in the 1960's.

STAVOVSKÉ DIVADLO

The "Theater of the Estates", built by Count Nostic, was one of the most important theaters in central Europe at the end of the 18th century; the foundation stone was laid by Emperor Joseph II. Mozart wrote *Don Giovanni* for it in 1787, and Milos Forman filmed *Amadeus* here in 1984 with sets by Josef Svoboda. The theater was restored to its original appearance in building works in 1992.

"The theater must not simply be the mechanical sum of text, actors, directors, audience and usherettes. It has got to be something more than that – the spiritual home of its time."

Václav Havel

Left: A set by V. Novák for a 1921 production of *RUR* at the National Theater.

55

The Czech puppet theater tradition was born in the 17th century and rapidly became the favorite diversion of the country's middle classes. In the 19th century, Prague was the third most important puppetry center, after Bohemia in the south and the region of Mount Krkonoše (Mountain of Giants). Since the 1960's, a whole generation of professional puppet theater producers has emerged from the Faculty of Theater at Prague's Academy of Arts. They include Zdeněk Bauer, Pavel Kalfus, Petr Matasek and Jaroslava Žatková, who are particularly noted for bringing new ideas to the use of scenery.

THE REPERTOIRE
Puppets were hugely popular in Bohemia thanks to shows mounted by itinerant troupes from Britain, Germany, the Netherlands and Italy. Many early puppetry plays were influenced by Shakespeare, Molière and other famous playwrights. The fairy stories that are so typical of the present-day repertoire, including Božena Memcová's celebrated "The Grandmother", were neglected for many years.

The traveling puppet-master normally owned about a dozen puppets: six male, three female, Kaspárek (Punch), the Devil and Death. At one time in Bohemia, families of puppeteers passed their art on from father to son. One of the most popular and most skilled puppeteers of the second half of the 19th century was Jan Nepomucký Laštovka.

Poster for the Puppet Theater in Prague.

Group of musicians at the Špejbl and Hurvínek Theater.

OLD PUPPETS

Puppets have varied in size over the centuries. There have been times when heads and extremities were lengthened; sometimes, the bodies became no more than accessories. In the 17th century, puppets were approximately 20–32 inches tall, and the bodies were hollowed out to make them lighter. The 19th century saw numerous technical advances which facilitated more precise designs and a higher degree of realism.

THE ŠPEJBL AND HURVÍNEK THEATER

This theater, which was opened in 1945, is devoted to the adventures of two characters created by Josef Skupa. Špejbl and Hurvínek, father and son, use a technique and style of humor that are both grotesque and satirical, and portray immediately identifiable characters who are seeking remedies to the ills of the world. The production includes visual images, scenes from pantomime and musical numbers which accompany the dialogue.

● LITERARY CAFÉS

It was a Levantine who introduced the idea of café life to both Prague and Paris. In Prague, this was just after the Siege of Vienna and the victory over the Turks at Kalhenberg in 1683. Then, in the early 18th century, one Theodat (or Deodatus) opened a café "At the sign of the Three Ostriches" near Charles Bridge, and shortly afterward another establishment called "Of the Golden Snake" in Karlova Street. By the 19th century, cafés in Prague were the equal of the "temples of the intelligentsia" patronized by Vienna's high society. For civil servants and obscure artists alike, a visit to a café was an essential element of daily life.

THE CAFÉ ARCO
This café was the rallying point for intellectuals with a German-language culture. They included Franz Kafka, Max Brod, Franz Werfel and Egon Erwin Kisch, cosmopolitan writers hostile to pan-Germanism. Members of the Devětsil Group took over the Café Arco in later years.

KAFKA'S CAFÉS
Franz Kafka used to sit in the Louvre Café, alongside the likes of Hugo Bergmann, Emil Ulitz and Ernst Pollak; he also enjoyed going to the less salubrious Ú Brejšků, a haunt of the "Young People's Circle", a group of Czech writers who sought to defend their culture and promulgate socialist ideas. On other evenings, he preferred the Savoy Café where Yitshak Löwy's Yiddish theater company sometimes gave performances. There was also the Stefan Café where Else Kornis attended a reading of the first version of *The Metamorphosis* given by Ernst Pollak.

PRAVÁ ZÁT

DEVĚTSIL

THE DEVĚTSIL GROUP
Poets and painters in the circle of Karel Čapek, Jaroslav Seifert, Vítězslav Nezval and Teige founded this innovatory movement in the *Café Union* ▲ 291 on November 5, 1920. In their search for a form of "new beauty", they chose cafés as their favorite observation points.

THE CAFÉ SLAVIA
Poets in the Devětsil Group often met at the Café Slavia ▲ 298. According to Seifert, "Our table was crowded with the foreign poets and painters whom we talked about in our discussions and arguments. Apollinaire was often there, of course, with his head bandaged as in Picasso's painting. And Jakobson lured many others to our gatherings. That was how Mayakovsky would sometimes be seated amongst us, chatting away . . ."

Below, a caricature of the writer Rainer Maria Rilke.

THE NATIONAL CAFÉ
Rainer Maria Rilke was taken aback by the informality of these hospitable places, where people spent much of the night in an intimate club-like atmosphere, consoling each other for everything, or nearly everything. He preferred to patronize the National Café and "silently listen to older and more serious men who he could see were the local élite". A few years later, Jaroslav Seifert welcomed a newcomer, Roman Jakobson, as if he were "a celebrated guest".

The first brewery in Prague was probably established in 1082, but it was the town of Plzeň in Bohemia which became the undisputed capital of hop fermentation toward the end of the 13th century. The breweries of Plzeň were enormously successful, and in the 19th century they began exporting to the rest of Europe, and Paris and Vienna in particular. At that time, there were no fewer than 1,057 breweries in Bohemia-Moravia. Modern Prague boasts hundreds of taverns; they are the second homes for the city's inhabitants, who go there to make generous sacrifices to their household gods.

"VINO CORRUPTUS"
Tacitus' scornful remark about German beer does not go down well with the Czech people, who have an inordinate passion for this beverage. The Italian Jesuit, Giovanni Botero, has described how enraged he was by the Bohemians who "never stopped drinking" – no doubt because of that "pestilential heresy", the Hussite reforms ● *32*.

Just as much beer was being drunk at the beginning of the 20th century. Jaroslav Hašek, the author of *The Good Soldier Schweik*, urged his compatriots to drink at least thirty-five glasses of beer a day.

TOP-QUALITY BEERS

Prague still produces a large number of beers, most of them made by craftsmen brewers. The best include "Flekovský ležák" made at the U Fleků tavern, "Staropramen" which dates from 1869, "Pražán" which has been produced at Holešovice since 1895, and "Special Braník", first brewed in 1898.

U FLEKŮ ▲ *306*

The U Fleků is still typical of the old-style Prague tavern with its wood-paneling, long tables and huge courtyard. One of the oldest beers in Prague, "Flekovský ležák", has been brewed there since 1499; this dark beer made with roasted malt is 13° Balling, and is only produced in small quantities (3,650 barrels a year).

"In certain well-known bars in the Old Town (*U zlatého Tygra*), amidst the smoke and babble of voices, people stand elbow to elbow next to high, narrow shelves as if in the storage vaults of some arch spanning a sea of nothingness."

Petr Král

V 6 VEČER
U KALICHA

U KALICHA

This is the tavern where Jaroslav Hašek● *126* begins the tale of the Good Soldier Schweik's tribulations. On the day that the Archduke Ferdinand is assassinated in Sarajevo, Schweik goes to the U Kalicha for a chat with Palivec, the proprietor and an old friend of his. Sadly, this leads to them being arrested by a spy working for the political police. On his release, Schweik hurries straight round to his favorite bar: "I'm back!" he cries cheerfully, "Mine's a half!"

Loin of pork with cabbage and dumplings (*Vepřová s knedlíkem a se zelím*) is one of Czech cuisine's most typical dishes. Of course, pork, cabbage and dumplings are to be found in many central European cuisines – in Bohemia, Austria and Germany, for instance – but the cooking always varies slightly from one place to the next.

However, it is delicious wherever it is cooked and if, as is customary, it is preceded by soup, it is a complete meal in itself.

KNEDLÍKY. Ingredients:
3 cups of finely sieved flour, ¾ pint of milk, 2 egg yolks, ½ teaspoonful of baker's yeast, half a baguette cut into ½ inch dice, and a little salt.

1. Pour the milk into a shallow dish. Add the salt, the egg yolks and the flour mixed in with the yeast. Mold the mixture to cover the side of the dish with a wooden spoon for 3 mins.

SAUERKRAUT. Ingredients: 1½ lbs of sauerkraut, 1 tablespoonful of flour, 1 onion, ½ teaspoon of lard or margarine, 1 teaspoonful of vinegar, and 1 or 2 teaspoonfuls of sugar.

4. Sauté the onion in the lard until golden brown. Add the flour and mix, and then pour in one glass of water. Let the roux thicken, and allow to simmer until it sticks to the dish.

LOIN OF PORK

Ingredients for four people: 1½ lbs of fatty pork, 2 ozs of lard or margarine, 1 teaspoonful of caraway seeds, cooking salt, pepper.

6. Place the meat in a shallow dish with the lard. Add the salt and sprinkle caraway seeds. Cook at medium oven heat. After 15 mins, add some water regularly to prevent the joint from getting dry. The meat must be well cooked and golden brown on the outside.

2. Add the cubes of bread. Mix in well and leave. Put the water on to boil, and meanwhile cut the paste in half under running water to prevent it from sticking to your hands.

3. Roll each half into large sausage shapes approximately 6 inches long and 2½ inches wide. Leave the dumplings to cook in boiling water for 25–30 mins. Then cut them into equal, thick slices.

On each plate, place a helping of meat, 3 or 4 slices of dumpling and some cabbage. Add gravy. The best drink to go with this dish is a good light beer such as Pilsner.

5. Remove from the heat and leave for 5 mins for the crust to separate. Mix well. Lastly, add the salt, the sugar and the vinegar. Reheat before serving.

● SPECIALTIES

PUPPETS

The craze for puppet theaters that has gripped Prague since the 17th century lives on. Wooden and string puppets are on sale in street stalls and in specialist shops.

COMPACT DISCS

Recordings of music by the great Czech composers performed by the world's top musicians are available on CD. These recordings are of excellent quality, and are on sale throughout Prague at competitive prices.

Toys made by craftsmen with untreated wood can be bought from street vendors and in specialist shops.

BOHEMIAN CRYSTAL

Crystal made Bohemia famous, and many shops in Prague have superb collections of glassware on sale.

NEWSPAPERS

In addition to Czech newspapers, there is a weekly English-language newspaper called *The Prag Post*. It is an English version of the weeklies *Přehled*, *Pro* and *Programm*, and provides a run-down of the city's cultural events.

BEER AND BECHEROVKA

These two national drinks are on sale in all food shops. Bohemian beer was first exported to other European countries in the 19th century, but brewing dates from the Middle Ages. "Pilsner" beer is one of the best known. Becherovka liqueur (38°) is best drunk cool as an aperitif or a digestive.

Architecture

● THE CONSTRUCTION OF PRAGUE

Libussa, legendary founder of Prague.

During the 9th and 10th centuries, the Slav peopl abandoned the hills overlooking the Vltava and built settlements down in the valley, now defended by two fortresses. The 13th-century ramparts around Staré Město were the beginning of a real medieval city. Space was limited, however, and this led to the construction of Nové Město in 1348 and an extension of the ramparts. Later, after coming under attack during the 17th centur new ramparts reinforced by thirty-nine bastions were built around Prague. Industrialization in the 19th century also gave rise to a modern infrastructure with the first railroad station, numerous bridges and the first trams.

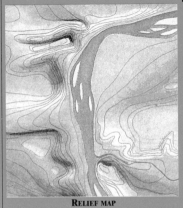

RELIEF MAP

Prague, like Rome, is encircled by seven hills and has often been compared with the Eternal City. The first Slav settlements in the 7th and 8th centuries were located in the fortified highlands. During the 8th century, the Slavs moved down toward the Vltava and, when Prague and Vyšehrad Castles were constructed in the 9th and 10th centuries respectively, they resolved to stay. The Malá Strana area was chosen because it afforded protection from flooding, and was also a healthier environment than the marshy district where Staré Město was eventually built.

PRAGUE CASTLE
The Přemyslids had this fortress residence built in about 880–90.

VYŠEHRAD
Legend has it that Libussa ▲ *324* lived in this 10th–century fortress.

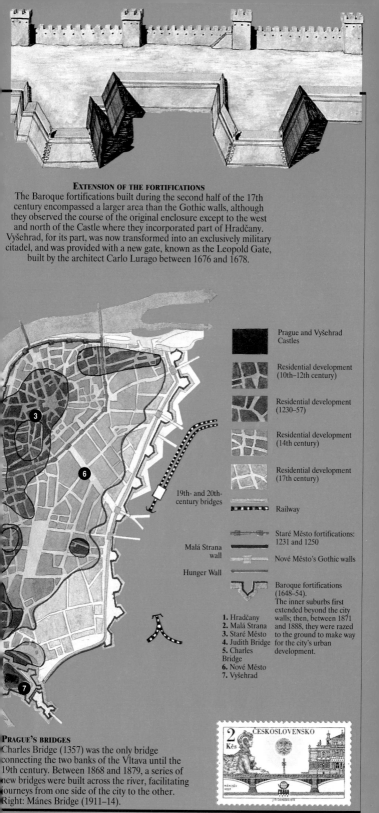

EXTENSION OF THE FORTIFICATIONS

The Baroque fortifications built during the second half of the 17th century encompassed a larger area than the Gothic walls, although they observed the course of the original enclosure except to the west and north of the Castle where they incorporated part of Hradčany. Vyšehrad, for its part, was now transformed into an exclusively military citadel, and was provided with a new gate, known as the Leopold Gate, built by the architect Carlo Lurago between 1676 and 1678.

Prague and Vyšehrad Castles

Residential development (10th–12th century)

Residential development (1230–57)

Residential development (14th century)

Residential development (17th century)

19th- and 20th-century bridges

Railway

Staré Město fortifications: 1231 and 1250

Nové Město's Gothic walls

Malá Strana wall

Hunger Wall

Baroque fortifications (1648–54).
The inner suburbs first extended beyond the city walls; then, between 1871 and 1888, they were razed to the ground to make way for the city's urban development.

1. Hradčany
2. Malá Strana
3. Staré Město
4. Judith Bridge
5. Charles Bridge
6. Nové Město
7. Vyšehrad

PRAGUE'S BRIDGES

Charles Bridge (1357) was the only bridge connecting the two banks of the Vltava until the 19th century. Between 1868 and 1879, a series of new bridges were built across the river, facilitating journeys from one side of the city to the other. Right: Mánes Bridge (1911–14).

Romanesque art first appeared in Bohemia in the 11th century during the reign of the Přemyslid Dynasty; three stone rotundas and one basilica, St George's, remain. Later, as the Gothic style, which was popular in Prague during the reign of Charles IV (1346–78), developed, architecture became lighter. An example of this is St Vitus' Cathedral where the Swabian architect Petr Parléř married French influences and Bohemian Gothic. Buildings constructed thereafter were characterized by a search for greater luminosity.

Paving stones at St Laurence's Basilica in Vyšehrad.

ROMAN ROTUNDA

The 11th-century rotunda of the Holy Cross in Karoliny světlé Street perpetuated the Byzantine tradition of centrally planned buildings. It was a novelty for Prague in that it was circular, approximately 16 feet in diameter, and also had a choir. On the exterior, the stone cupola was covered with tiles and surmounted by a lantern ▲ 289.

INTERIOR DESIGN

Frescos, like this 14th-century example, were a common form of decoration in medieval churches.

ROMANESQUE BASILICA

St George's Basilica ▲ 220 in Prague Castle was rebuilt after a fire in 1142. It is made of beautiful white stone and accords with the principles of a basilica groundplan: a nave bordered by two narrow aisles and a central apse with vaulting in the form of a semi-cupola.

ROMANESQUE STRUCTURE

(section)
The vault is supported by huge semicircular arches and massive square pillars. In line with traditional basilica design, the choir is raised above the level of the nave.

MODELED ON THE RHENISH SCHOOL

The influence of the Rhenish School is evident from the two square clock towers which frame the two lateral bays at the entrance to the choir.

Carved coats of arms of the architects Matthew of Arras and Petr Parléř, who were in charge of work on St Vitus' Cathedral.

MONUMENTAL GOTHIC WINDOW

The frame of this 16th-century window in the south transept of St Vitus' Cathedral ▲ *214* is the work of Matthew of Arras. The fine stairwell beside it is by Petr Parléř. The stone armature with polylobed motifs dates from the 20th century.

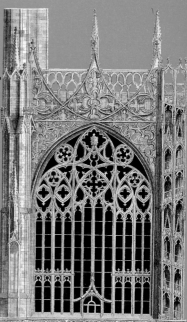

BOHEMIAN VAULTING

Petr Parléř introduced Europe to reticulated vaulting; it is characterized by an entanglement of ribbing.

FROM FRENCH GOTHIC TO BOHEMIAN GOTHIC

Matthew of Arras introduced the canons of the French Gothic to Bohemia and Cathedral with in 1344 built the choir of St Vitus' two rows of an ambulatory and radiating chapels. The of the vaults flying buttresses neutralize the pressure on intersecting ribs, and return it to ornate buttresses and blind arcades. The Bohemian Gothic style is well illustrated by Petr Parléř's triforium with reticulated vaults.

PRIMACY OF CHURCH LIGHTING

The oriel window in the Carolinum ▲ *278* in Železná Street dates from 1383. It is an example of fully

blown Gothic design, characterized by the elegance of the walls and the importance of the bays; this was made possible by the vaulting with intersecting ribs.

After the defeat of the Bohemian reformers in 1620, Catholicism became the State religion and the Baroque movement took on political and religious significance. In the hands of Caratti and Mathey, the so-called "Jesuit" Baroque sought balance within classical sobriety; then with the Dientzenhofers, the countries bordering the Danube breathed a new dynamism into spaces and volumes, and a tension and sensuality into lines. Under Maria Theresa, the Baroque began to evolve toward an affected delicacy known as the "Rococo".

WREATHED COLUMNS in U Svatého Jiří Square. The Baroque enthused over wreathed columns, like those (right) framing the door to a chapel adjoining St George's Basilica. The spiral design of the columns emphasizes their architectural function, and skilfully brings them to life.

INTERRUPTING THE FLOW
The door (1740) to Břevnov Abbey ▲ *320* is a good example of Baroque art at the height of its maturity. This work by Kilián I. Dientzenhofer (1689–1751) is notable for the fact that the architectural flow is broken without altering the balance: a curvilinear pediment overlaps with a broken pediment with scrolls, columns set at an angle, a broken cornice, and a contrast between the curves of the consoles and straight lines. Standing in isolation like a triumphal arch, it was the final touch to the reconstruction of the Abbey.

JESUIT STYLE. Between 1638 and 1640, Carlo Lurago carried out alterations to the Church of St Savior ▲ *153* in Křížovnické Street, taking as his model Church of Il Gesù in Rome. Its austere, triumphant façade is decorated with a porch and gallery (1653–9) by Francesco Caratti; the statues glorifying mystical life observe the façade's vertical organization.

DRAMATIC STYLES
The tormented treatment of the folds on this statue of Saint John Nepomuk are a good illustration of the Baroque movement's taste for theatricality.

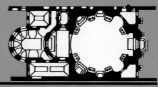

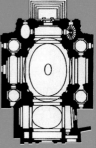

OVERLAPPING SPACE
In the Church of St-John-Nepomuk-on-the-Rock (1729–39) (left) interactive space generates unusual tensions (see groundplan below) ▲ 313. It was built by Kilián I. Dientzenhofer.

CENTRALIZED PLAN
The Baroque greatly preferred centralized plans to cruciform plans. Examples include the Churches of St Joseph (top) and St Francis Seraphim (above).

A THEATRICAL FAÇADE
It is claimed by some that the crooked corner towers curve the façade in such a way as to encourage the faithful to come into the church. This presentation is accentuated by a four-flight staircase which partly compensates for the difference in level in relation to the street.

ONION DOMES
Onion-shaped clock towers like that of St Giles' (above) are typical of the Baroque.

THE ROCOCO
[Th]e narrow façade of the Loreto Church is [ex]travagantly carved with biblical scenes, [in]cluding the theme of the Annunciation. [Th]e church was built by the Dientzenhofers in 1721.

● St Nicholas' Church, Malá Strana

St Nicholas' Church in Malá Strana Square is one of the most dazzling examples of Baroque style in Prague. The surface, the elegance and balance of the exterior, and the opulence of the trompe l'oeil Rococo decoration, all reflect the supreme technical skills of the Czech artists who worked on it. The façade and nave were built between 1703 and 1711 by Kryštof Dientzenhofer; his son, Kilián Ignác, added the choir in 1713 and the cupola in 1752. Anselmo Lurago added the clocktower in 1755. Artists involved in the decoration included the sculptors Jan Kohl, Ignác Platzer and members of the Prachner family.

IMITATION MARBLE
The general decoration and the pulpit (1765) are in polished stucco in imitation of marble.

TROMPE L'OEIL
Baroque art, a spearhead of the Counter-Reformation, sought to rouse souls by favoring luxuriant decoration enriched by illusions. The osmosis between architecture and décor is here sublimated by the use of trompe l'oeil, a device widely used in the decoration of St Nicholas' Church. In fact, the marble is false, and the pictorial perspective alters the cornice by making it undulate, and even creates an illusion of space in the vaults covered with figurative frescos.

A STATELY ART
A fascination with form and color characterizes Baroque style.

ROCAILLE
The conch on which the Rococo pulpit stands is a common motif in rocaille style.

DIDACTIC ART
Through its taste for ostentatious opulence, the Baroque reminded humanity of its mortal condition and the "Vanity" of worldly goods. This death's head is on the carved corbels of St Nicholas' Church.

CLASSICAL HERITAGE
The cupola, which reaches a height of 230 feet, is built according to a circular centralized plan inherited from the classical Renaissance.

CURVES AND COUNTER-CURVES
Baroque style frequently used curved lines to express movement both in architecture and in ornamentation. This 130-foot-long façade comprises a continuous display of curves and counter-curves. Inside the church, there are curved lines painted in trompe l'oeil.

EMPHATIC BODY MOVEMENT
This statue in the choir, of a saint fighting heresy, twists and turns in a manner characteristic of the Baroque.

"JESUIT ARCHITECTURE" AND ROCOCO DÉCOR
The façade is organized in three parts, and the unity of the axial and centralized plans testify to the Jesuits' austere, classical tastes. The plastic elements of the décor, by contrast, anticipate Rococo style.

A PROFUSION OF LITTLE ANGELS
The organ is adorned by as many groups of little angels as there are families of instruments in an orchestra.

73

The lower part of Staré Město was banked up during the 13th century to protect it from flooding when the Vltava overflowed. In this way, what had been a ground floor in Romanesque times became a cellar in the Gothic period; what is more, since 1230, the design of dwellings had changed substantially with houses becoming taller, narrower and deeper. After the fire of 1316, they were rebuilt on a larger scale and in stone. Many buildings retained their Gothic infrastructure over the centuries, as in later periods architects simply remodeled the façade in Renaissance or Baroque style.

THE GOTHIC FAÇADE
The house "At the sign of the Stone Bell" (U kamenného zvonu) ▲ *143* in Starometské Square is a somewhat controversial re-construction of a patrician Gothic residence. It has three stories, and the alternating niches and windows are surmounted with a décor consisting of gables. The Gothic façade, which is covered with a Baroque facing, was discovered in 1965.

MEDIEVAL DWELLINGS
Arched passages and gabled walls are characteristic of the façades of medieval houses. Ground plans show that the first floors had barrel or groined vaults; they were often used as workshops.

GABLES SURVIVE
The Nové Město Town Hall dates from the Renaissance, but the medieval tradition of gables was artificially preserved.

THE TRADITION OF ORNAMENTAL TILING
Streets have been paved since the Middle Ages. In the 19th century, pavements were covered with white, blue and pink marble, and some have survived despite heavy wear.

Barrel vault   Ribbed vault

ROOFS
During the Gothic period, flat and curved Roman tiles were fixed to the lattice with lugs.

MEDIEVAL TO BAROQUE
A series of façades attached to medieval buildings: here, the façade was remodeled in the Renaissance by the addition of a decorative gable with scrolls and sgraffito. In the Baroque era, the façade was altered to suit tastes of the time by adding stucco moldings which covered the Renaissance sgraffito.

ROMANESQUE TO GOTHIC
In the Gothic period the outward appearance of houses changed though their infrastructure, consisting of an arcaded ground floor and two upper stories, was not altered.

75

Arched pediment in the Venetian style.

With the accession of the Catholic Habsburg Dynasty to the throne of Bohemia in 1526, the Kingdom acquired a powerful political personality in the person of Ferdinand I. He soon established his influence by giving commissions to Italian artists, and one result was the Royal Summer Palace which introduced the estheticism of the Italian Renaissance to Prague. In the reign of Rudolph II (1576–1611), Prague became the capital of the Empire and attracted the greatest minds in Europe. Bohemian art then established its own style with brick and elaborated gables and sgraffito decoration.

A UNIQUE CURVED LINE
The façade of Martinic Palace sweeps round in a continuous curve.

RENAISSANCE DOOR
Two carved wolves are just one unique feature of this townhouse in Kožná Street (1580). The elegant doorway is framed by an arch resting on pilasters, but the clumsily made foliage is more reminiscent of northern than of Italian workmanship.

RENAISSANCE FAÇADE OF FORMER MARTINIC PALACE, HRADČANSKÉ SQUARE
During the Renaissance period, three Gothic houses were converted into a palace (1618–24). The gables continue the medieval tradition while the décor, particularly the sgraffito ▲ *232*, is in the Renaissance style.

ROYAL BELVEDERE "IN THE ITALIAN MANNER"
Paolo della Stella built this summer pavilion (1538–64) at the request of King Ferdinand I for his wife, Anne. This rectangular two-story building encircled by a gallery of Ionic capitals recalls the Foundling Hospital in Florence. The alternating niches and windows on the first floor are the work of Bonifác Wohlmut, who completed the building between 1554 and 1564. Its copper roof in the shape of an inverted ship's hull seems to have been inspired by the Palladian Basilica in Vicenza. The garden, which is laid out in the Italian manner, has geometrically shaped flowerbeds that contain exotic plants.

The Czech Renaissance

Schwarzenberg Palace (1545–63) in Hradčanské Square, a fine example of the Czech Renaissance, imitated not only the massive structure of Florentine palaces but also the false bosses decorated with diamond-point sgraffito. Northern influence is concentrated on the gables: three levels of pilasters are super-imposed on them, their entablature set with urns.

Gables in the Venetian style

Gables in Týn Courtyard ▲ 160 and Husova Street are topped by semicircular gables in the Venetian style.

House "At the sign of the Golden Lion" (U zlatého Iva)

The façade (1608) of this house ▲ 248 in Malá Strana Square is an example of the purity of the late Czech Renaissance. It consists of an arch, on two stories pierced by windows, and lastly a gable adorned with scrolls surmounted by a broken pediment.

Trompe l'oeil décor

This mullioned window in the old Martinic Palace has sgraffito decoration in the form of trompe l'oeil garlands and foliage.

● SGRAFFITO

The technique of sgraffito decoration was imported from Italy, and it spread rapidly throughout Prague and Bohemia round the middle of the 16th century. Palaces and residences belonging to the bourgeoisie were swathed in sgraffito decoration, particularly their exteriors. Sgraffito was especially well adapted to trompe l'oeil imitations of stone designs such as diamond-point bosses, but was also used to depict figurative scenes based on mythological, biblical or historical themes. Neo-Renaissance style in the 19th century revived the use of sgraffito to illustrate the Czech National Awakening with the representation of historical scenes and allegorical figures.

against a black background.
7. Bad weather and atmospheric humidity can lead to deterioration.
8. The design peels and then falls off.

HISTORIC PORTRAIT
Right, unidentified portrait of a monarch, applied in 1610 to the cornice of the House "Of the Minute" (Dum U minuty), 3 Old Town Square.

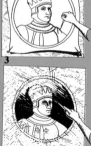

APPLICATION AND DECOMPOSITION
1. First, either black mortar (ground charcoal) or blackish-brown mortar (pigments of ferric minerals) is applied.
2. A second, white, lime-based coating (the *intonaco*) is then smoothed on with a trowel.
3. and **4.** The design is transferred onto the coating by means

of perforations.
5. and **6.** The white coating is scratched with small mattocks and scrapers to obtain a design in two colors, in this case, white

BIBLICAL THEME
The House "Of the Minute" ▲ 146 is covered in early 17th-century sgraffito decoration. A frieze (below), so finely etched it might be a copper engraving, relates the story of Joseph being taken out of a pit to be sold to the Ishmaelites. The sgraffito on this house was discovered at the beginning of the 20th century and has been frequently restored.

THE CZECH NEO-RENAISSANCE

The Renaissance bossage on the Schwarzenberg Palace (above, right) was restored by Josef Schulz at the height of the Czech National Awakening in the 19th century ● 28.

FRIEZES IN THE ANTIQUE STYLE

These sgraffito friezes on the cornice of Schwarzenberg Palace ▲ 230 could be mistaken for reliefs. The motifs used derive from designs popular in antiquity.

A MYTHOLOGICAL THEME

This 16th-century representation of Hercules at 4 Old Town Square was preserved after the house was rebuilt by Pavel Janák in 1938.

FLORAL AND ANIMAL DECORATION ▲ 232
This decoration on the main façade of Martinic Palace dates from the late 15th century.

ALLEGORICAL THEMES

The neo-Renaissance Hlávka houses (Hlávkovy domy) ▲ 291 date from 1889. The façades are adorned with allegorical sgraffito figures, including Vanity (below).

INFLUENCE OF PAINTING

In the Martinic Palace ▲ 232, a technique of linear perspective on a convex surface ● 76 is used to represent the episode of Joseph and Potiphar's wife.

● BAROQUE HOUSES AND PALACES

Urns provide the finishing touch to gardens of Prague.

The ravages caused by the Thirty Years' War provided the new aristocracy with an opportunity to fill Malá Strana with huge palaces and gardens. During the 17th century, these palaces, many of them built by Italian architects, were characterized by simple, geometrical spaces marked by rich decoration. As early as the beginning of the 18th century Prague had become one of the leading Baroque capitals in Europe. Dientzenhofers, Santini-Aichl, and other great masters who had trained in Vienna including Alliprandi and Fischer von Erlach, conceived of space in terms of curves and countercurves that stimulated the play of light and shade. The Baroque also gave prominence to colossal orders of columns of the type favored in Prague by the architect Kaňka. The decorative exuberance of the Rococo appeared after 1740.

BAROQUE PEDIMENT
A stucco molding of curves and countercurves on the pediment of 2 Celetná Street ▲ 158.

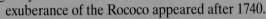

ČERNÍN PALACE
This palace (1669–79) in Loretánské Square ▲ 234 was built by Francesco Caratti on an earlier plan by Bernini (1598–1680).

FROM THE GOTHIC TO THE BAROQUE
The House "At the sign of the Two Suns" (U dvou slunců) (1673) at 47 Nerudova Street has a Baroque façade with two attics topped by pediments; they replaced the gables that had adorned the earlier Gothic façade ▲ 254, 256.

AMBIVALENCE OF BAROQUE SCULPTURE

It is difficult to draw the line between sculpture and architecture on this Baroque door (1714) to Clam-Gallas Palace ▲ *149*. The sculptor, Matthias Bernhard Braun, constructed two pairs of atlantes that act as columns and which contort beneath the weight of the upper balcony. This kind of presentation, and the expressiveness of the figures, owe much to the influence of Bernini. The remainder of the façade overlooking Husova Street is classical.

MONUMENTAL ARCHITECTURE

The impressive façade of Černin Palace is notable for an order of thirty huge columns that rest on a high crepidoma adorned with diamond-point bosses, a direct reference to the work of Palladio (1508–80).

TRANSITION BETWEEN CLASSICISM AND THE BAROQUE

Černín Palace's high, embossed crepidoma and huge orders derive from the classical Renaissance, while its porches with their concave and convex lines foreshadow the Baroque.

LIGHT AND SHADOW

The façade of Alliprandi's Lobkowicz Palace (1703–13) that overlooks the street is flat. By contrast, on the garden side, the Baroque has imbued the façade with great movement and, together with the central oval pavilion flanked by the two concave wings, it provides opportunities for plays of light and shadow. The curb roof and the urns which crown the building are typically Baroque devices.

PASSAGEWAYS AND GALLERIES

COVERED IN GLASS
The tradition of vaults has been maintained in modern times by the use of reinforced concrete and glass.

Houses have incorporated passageways since the Middle Ages, but there were huge changes in Prague between the late 19th century and World War Two when galleries and many new passageways were built. This more modern style of town planning was appended to older methods in such a surprising manner that, for Surrealists poets, Prague represented the urban archetype of wandering and melancholy. A specifically Czech hallmark of the galleries came from their architectural boldness and the avant-garde ideas propounded by the theater and the cinema.

STARÉ MĚSTO
This map reveals the dense network of passageways and galleries criss-crossing Staré Město.

SECRET PASSAGEWAY
The typically Prague passageway, *pruchod* in Czech, is supposed to "shorten" one's journey by enabling the walker to pass through a number of buildings instead of having to walk round them. According to a medieval tradition,

the passageway took its name from the owner of the house the walker was passing through, or from the coat of arms that sometimes surmounted the entrance. The entrance to a passageway was only marked by an anonymous door which was no different from an ordinary house door; in this way, these doors were ambiguous in that they both announced and concealed the presence of these pedestrian ways.

GALLERIES, AN IDEAL OF MODERN DESIGN
The Prague gallery was first known as *bazar* and then as *pasáž*. It constitutes an ideal of modern design in that it forms part of large urban dwellings referred to locally as "palaces", a modern concept with commerical, social and cultural uses. Important characteristics are pomp, functionalism and versatility. The gallery's luxurious interior contrasts sharply with the sobriety of the entrance (below Novak Gallery).

J. NOVAK

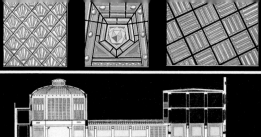

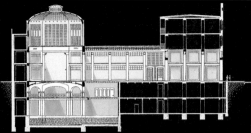

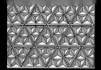

KORUNA GALLERY, WING AND CUPOLA

The gallery was built between 1911 and 1914 to plans by Antonín Pfeiffer (1879–1938) to a commission by the Koruna company, the first Czech limited company specializing in life insurance ▲ 174. It stands on the corner of Wenceslas Square

and Na Příkopě Street. This perfect illustration of Secession ● 86 style is joined to an enormous town palace, one of the earliest buildings in Prague to be built of reinforced concrete. There were once offices, businesses and apartments upstairs, but a café downstairs was

replaced between 1931 and 1978 by a self-service restaurant by the architect and stage designer. Ladislav Machoň (1888–1973). The basement contained a swimming pool and a movie theater. The gallery's overall décor includes tall stained-glass windows and bronze reliefs on the walls.

GLASS CUPOLA

The original cupola, which was restored in 1980, comprised 3,800 pieces of glass cut diamond-style, and was held in position by ribs of reinforced concrete. The prismatic range of the glass generated enough light to illuminate the underground swimming pool through the translucent concrete floor.

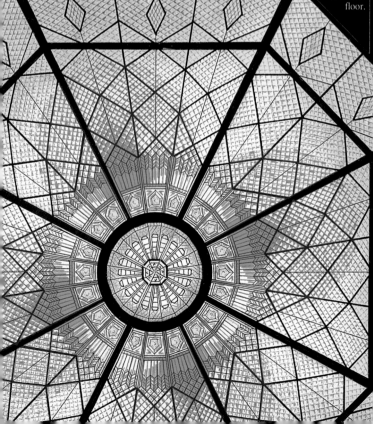

HISTORICISM

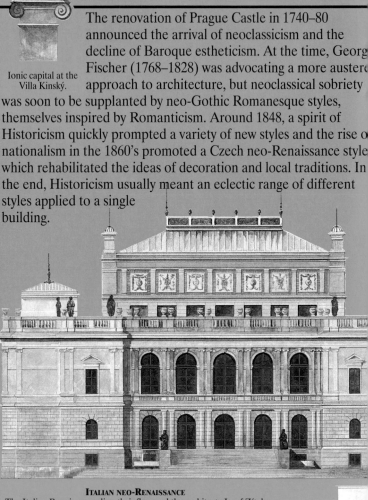

Ionic capital at the Villa Kinský.

The renovation of Prague Castle in 1740–80 announced the arrival of neoclassicism and the decline of Baroque estheticism. At the time, Georg Fischer (1768–1828) was advocating a more austere approach to architecture, but neoclassical sobriety was soon to be supplanted by neo-Gothic Romanesque styles, themselves inspired by Romanticism. Around 1848, a spirit of Historicism quickly prompted a variety of new styles and the rise of nationalism in the 1860's promoted a Czech neo-Renaissance style which rehabilitated the ideas of decoration and local traditions. In the end, Historicism usually meant an eclectic range of different styles applied to a single building.

ITALIAN NEO-RENAISSANCE
The Italian Renaissance directly influenced the architects Josef Zítek and Josef Schulz in the construction of the Rudolfinum (1872). This building houses a concert hall and exhibition facilities.

CZECH NEO-RENAISSANCE
Novotného lávka
Some of the inspiration for the façade of the Smetana Museum (1883)
▲ 156 in Novotného Passage is to be found in Bohemia's Renaissance architecture. The elaborate gable is typically North European, and the relief decoration is also adorned with sgraffito in the Italian manner.

HISTORICISM IS BORN
The birth of Historicism was here marked by the resurgence of a decorative technique, sgraffito ● 78, and by the representation of a historic subject, the story of the battle against the Swedish Army on Charles Bridge in 1648.

NEO-BAROQUE

This building in
Old Town Square
designed by Karel
Osvald Polívka in
1900 is decorated in
the Baroque style.
There is a protruding
porch, medallions, a
rocaille frieze, scrolls,
and some urns and
genuine Baroque
statues on the roof.

CHRONOLOGY OF NEO-STYLES

Late 18th-century
neoclassicism was
fired by the need for
archeological
authenticity.
However, around
1850, Romanticism
emphasized a more
Romanesque vision,
and was challenged
by fin de siècle
Historicism,
which in turn
led to neo-
Renaissance.

NEO-GOTHIC STYLE

This building at
8 Masaryk Quay
illustrates how a
wall containing
decorative, rather
than architectural,
neo-Gothic elements,
like the lancet
windows, can evoke
an image of real
Gothic style.

NEOCLASSICAL STYLE

Georg Fischer's
Customs House
(1808–11) in
Republiky Square is
decorated with
Antique motifs
including Doric
columns framing the
entrance, metopes
and triglyphs on the
entablature, and a
classical pediment.
The tympanum,
carved by Lederer,
takes the form of a
two-headed eagle, the
symbol of the Holy
Roman Empire.

FALSE KEYSTONE
This Art Nouveau device does not fulfil its role as a keystone.

Art Nouveau in Prague was influenced by Symbolism and looked to Paris for inspiration, bu it also derived in part from German Jugendstil (1894–1914), the Viennese Secession (1897–1907) and the School of Otto Wagner where many Czec architects were trained. In Prague, these artistic trends were initially to be found in the applied arts; later, they found expression in architecture where they were combined, concordantly or conflictingly, on façades of buildings, many of them Historicist in design.

URN WITH GARLANDS OF PLANT MOTIFS.
Na příkopě 7

GILDED STUCCO
In its pursuit of Symbolism, Art Nouveau returned to the ornamental themes of the classical and Baroque periods, imposing on them curvilinear forms of plant motifs.

THE PEACOCK
Pelikán Building (1904–6), Na příkopě 7

UNDULATIONS AND BROKEN LINES
Extravagantly undulating spaces give way to the sobriety of geometrical lines and simply defined spaces. The combination of curves and broken lines prefigure Art Deco.

THE SECESSION
Tower of the Koruna Gallery (1912–14) Wenceslas Square Outlines remained classical (square towers, octagonal drums and circular coronas), and the o concessions to Secession styles were symbolic subjects ▲ *171* and plastic applications (plays of materials a of colors and light).

PLANT MOTIFS
Like the peacock, the Ginkgo biloba was a recurrent motif in Art Nouveau decoration.

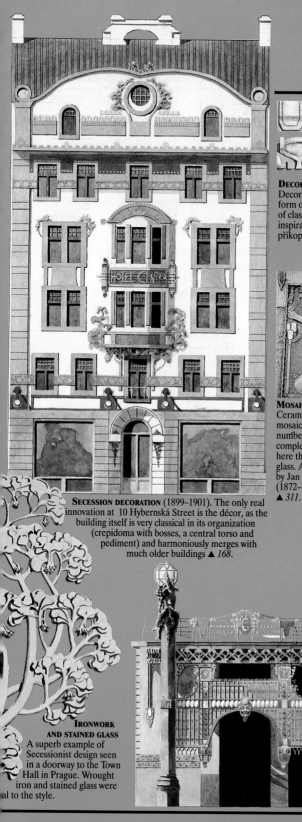

SECESSION DECORATION (1899–1901). The only real innovation at 10 Hybernská Street is the décor, as the building itself is very classical in its organization (crepidoma with bosses, a central torso and pediment) and harmoniously merges with much older buildings ▲ *168*.

DECORATIVE MOLDING
Decoration in the form of molding also of classical inspiration, at Na příkopě 7.

MOSAICS
Ceramic or glass mosaics adorn a number of façades completely or in part; here they recall a pier glass. Above: Mosaic by Jan Preisler (1872–1918) ● *104*, ▲ *311*.

IRONWORK AND STAINED GLASS
A superb example of Secessionist design seen in a doorway to the Town Hall in Prague. Wrought iron and stained glass were al to the style.

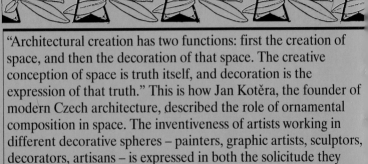

"Architectural creation has two functions: first the creation of space, and then the decoration of that space. The creative conception of space is truth itself, and decoration is the expression of that truth." This is how Jan Kotěra, the founder of modern Czech architecture, described the role of ornamental composition in space. The inventiveness of artists working in different decorative spheres – painters, graphic artists, sculptors, decorators, artisans – is expressed in both the solicitude they bring to the play of form and color and their choice and treatment of materials. This "global art", which was to culminate in Cubism, developed with astonishing stylistic diversity.

PAINTING (1910) Alfons Mucha (1860–1939) A painting decorating the Mayor's Room in the Town Hall (Obecní dům) ▲ 164.

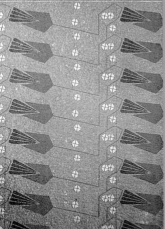

WALLPAPER (1900) Vojtěch Preissieg (1873–1944) An example of the search for novel symmetries by which to produce stylized motifs, and of the dynamic relationship between pattern and background (Museum of Decorative Arts ▲ 195).

CERAMIC TILES

PAINTED STUCCO
Glass and gilting used to enhance stucco scrolls on the Town Hall ▲ 164.

STAINED GLASS
Stained glass in the main entrance to the Praha Insurance Company building (1905–7) by Osvald Polívka (1859–1931) ▲ 176, ▲ 293.

CUBIST
ARCHITECTURE
1910–20

Prague was the only city in which an architectural style inspired by Cubism developed. Evolving in the wake of Secession in decline and invigorated by Prague's late Gothic and Baroque heritage, Cubist architecture influenced the design of both furniture and everyday objects. Although shortlived, it foreshadowed Art Deco, and carried the seeds of modern, post-war architecture.

BENCH AND STREET LAMP (1912–13) 310 Jungmann Square by Matěj Blecha. ▲ *310*.

CUBIST BUILDING (1913) 30 Neklanova Street by Josef Chochol (1880–1956) ▲ *326*.

Though medieval vaulting spread throughout
Europe, in Prague it became an art form in the hands
of such innovative architects as Petr Parléř (1333–99)
and Benedikt Ried (c. 1454–1534). Central to Czech
tradition, vaults remain in the forefront of 20th-
century design, whether made of reinforced
concrete, or decorated with glass or multifaceted.

A TRADITION OF VAULTS IN PRAGUE
Vaulted arcades are a prominent feature of
Prague. Above: Malé náměstí ▲ *148*.

FAN VAULTS. Church of
the Ascension,
Bechyně (1490–1513).

90

Gilt and polychrome
boss with a carving of
a heraldic lion.
Vladislas II Jagiello's
room in Prague
Castle.

LIERNE VAULT
The Riders' Staircase in Prague
Castle (left) ▲ 205 leads to
Vladislav Hall (right). It is the
work of Benedikt Ried.

Banisters round the stairwell in the Evropa Hotel, 25–7 Wenceslas Square ● 86, ▲ 174.

Balcony of a residential building at Na příkopě 7, Secession style ● 86.

Balcony of the Jewish Town Hall, Maislova Street, Rococo style ▲ 193.

Décor beneath the eaves of the Belvedere ▲ 224.

Balcony of the Church of Our-Lady-of-Perpetual-Succor-of-the-Gaetani, Nerudova Street, Baroque style ▲ 255.

Railing in the garden of Strahov Monastery ▲ 237.

Railing of the Royal Mausoleum at St Vitus' Cathedral ● 68, ▲ 216.

Panel of a lift shaft in Malé náměstí ▲ 148, (detail, above).

Prague
as seen by painters

> "I love to go for walks in Prague at night time:
> it is like gathering in each gasp of its soul."
>
> Jiří Karásek

Jakub Schikaneder (1855–1924) first studied in Munich (1886–7) and then at Prague Academy. At first he was attracted to the post-Impressionists, but later he moved toward Symbolism. In letters, he explained how he wanted to turn the landscape into an expression of states of mind: "Man watches and forgets everything... He only sees kinds of phantom colors leaning further and further out as they get nearer. At that moment, the tree has neither branches nor leaves; it has only spots of fire describing ornaments which we had never even suspected."

No one has been more successful than Schikaneder at enhancing the myth of Prague's obscure, ghostly beauty, a beauty that has survived until today. He recalls the Belgian Symbolist painter, William Degouve de Nuncques (1867–1935). He produces a powerful effect with his rarefied, unreal atmospheres, his detached, meticulous style, and the profound sense of mystery in which he wraps compositions such as *Carriages in the Night* (1911)

ANTONÍN SLAVÍČEK

Schikaneder gave expression to Old Prague, but it was left to Antonín Slavíček (1870–1910) to reinvent it; this he did within the radiant perspective of pure colors based on post-Impressionism and a very personal technique. He spent much of his time roaming the streets of Prague, and strove to reproduce its paradoxical beauty – luminous yet changing, and enamored with shadow. *Square in the Old Town, St Mary's Square* (1906) (**2**, detail **4**), and *Tower of St Vitus' Cathedral at Hradčany* are evocations of the more charming corners. Slavíček hoped to eulogize Prague in a cycle of paintings with one panorama for each season that was sadly never completed. Encouraged by the success of his "blue Prague", he painted *View of Prague from Letná* in 1908 (**1**, detail **3**), and then started work on a third panorama using the mixed, nostalgic tones of autumn rain.

1		
2	3	
	4	

97

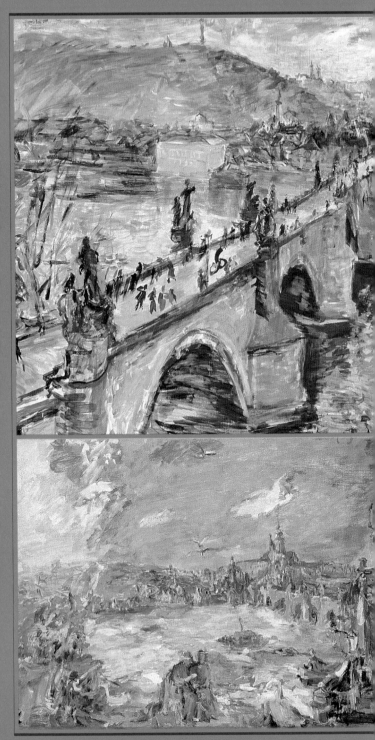

On wearying of the political and social instability that pervaded Vienna in the early 1930's, Oskar Kokoschka (1886–1980) decided to settle in Prague. He stayed there for four years until political events moved him on yet again. It was in Prague that he did his portrait of Tomáš G. Masaryk. He recalls his days there in his memoirs: "Compared with modern metropolises with their uniform skyscrapers and concrete shacks, Prague had remained, or had once again become, the creation of a cultured society." He undertook to do a "portrait" of this small city in the form of a series of panoramic views that concentrated on its mysterious, tormented, almost magic, character. "In four years," he wrote, "I have completed sixteen paintings, mostly of Prague and from quite different places where I had a view of the Vltava. The river cast a spell over me, like the Thames." He painted *Prague, view of Charles Bridge from the Monastery of the Cross* (**1**) and *Charles Bridge at Prague* (**3**) in 1934. While in exile in London, he finished his last painting of Prague, *Nostalgia* (**2**).

> "The importance of color lies in the fact that it has a real harmonic property, and a true mystical symbolism that is appropriate to modern life."
>
> Bohumil Kubišta

During 1910, Kubišta (1884–1918) spent several months in Paris where, using a new technique, he completed a number of works which revealed the profound influence of French Cubism, particularly that of André Derain. He then returned to Prague, a changed man. He did not reject his passion for Expressionist and Fauvist painting, and enthusiastically applied the constructive principles that he had

been taught by the French school. His artistry found expression in works which heralded the birth of a characteristically Czech form of Cubism. One of these, *Motif of Old Prague* (1911) (left), was unquestionably his manifesto. The buildings display a complex geometry while the clouds consist of no more than sinuous, energetic lines. The whole painting is done in blue and grey tones with white and black counterpoint. It was Kubišta's only painting of Prague. His friends thought little of Prague, but Cubist designers went to great lengths to transform it.

Using photographs, Jiří Kolář painted a series of froissages of Prague's main buildings, including *The Powder Tower* (below). These strange deformations are accompanied by quotations from Kafka, and present the great novelist's confused and disquieting view of the city.

"Was the world turned upside down?
Where was I?
What had happened?"

Franz Kafka

Czech art in the
early 20th century

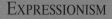

If a date needs to be put on the birth of modern art in Bohemia, it will have to be 1894, the year in which the first issue of *Moderni revue* appeared. It was brought out by the painter Arnost Procházka and the writer Jiří Karásek, and constituted an embodiment of decadent and Symbolist art. The various movements that came after it opened up increasingly toward European culture: cultural exchanges were stepped up, and these culminated in new artistic conceptions which, inspired by Viennese Secession and Parisian Cubism and Surrealism, articulated a need to imbue Czech art with its own identity.

František Bílek (1872–1941) *Ploughing and punishment for our sorrows* (1892).

> "The Munch Exhibition dropped
> like a bomb
> in the middle of our dreams and our desires."
>
> Václav Špála

The Edward Munch Retrospective of 1905 in Prague stimulated keen interest in Expressionism, and in 1908, a number of Czech and German artists founded the OSMA group. It included Emil Filla who, in *Man reading Dostoevsky* (1907, opposite), sought to heighten the pathos and intensity of his feelings through the conjunction of violent colors. Arnost Kubišta Procházka (1882–1945), with *The Circus* (1907, opposite), and Bohumil Kubišta with *The triple portrait*, also attempted to develop their own personal adaptations of Expressionist themes. They shared an ambition to break with Symbolism and Post-Impressionism. Instead, they aimed to promote a representation of the dramatic world delivered within, and by, the free play of a plastic relationship of forces that eschewed all references to reality. Jan Preisler ● 87, ▲ 311 quickly moved away from neo-Impressionism and, as early as 1902, embarked on innovatory work with *Picture from a larger cycle* (3). His sparse style, which was based on a highly synthetic concept and a considerable simplification of form, had already become known in 1894 through *The black lake.* The setting up of OSMA was a signal that modern art had arrived in Prague.

BOHUMIL KUBIŠTA (1884–1918)
Still life with skull, 1912

BOHUMIL KUBIŠTA
St Sebastian, 1912

EMIL FILLA (1882–1953)
Dish with a bunch of grapes, 1915

> "A work of art is the immediate expression
> of the artist's intimate being."
>
> Emil Filla

BOHUMIL KUBIŠTA
The Fakir, 1914

JOSEF ČAPEK (1887–1945)
The Accordionist, 1913

Czech Cubism was in no way an off-shoot of the French model. It was a genuinely Czech product. It consisted of a very original synthesis of a number of esthetic biases and, as Bohumil Kubišta's *St Sebastian* demonstrates, it provided a unique re-interpretation of the Baroque. In fact, these artists only derived any formal training in Cubist concepts during the war or shortly before. *Still life with bottle* (1913–14, below) by Arnost Procházka (1882–1945), *Filla's Dish with a Bunch of Grapes* and the plaster *Woman's Head* (1913) by Otto Gutfreund (1889–1927) express this wish to forego meticulous construction of space. However, none of these painters allowed himself to be hamstrung by restrictive formulas. Indeed, their searches moved simultaneously in completely divergent directions; an instance of this is Špála's *Song of Spring* which consists of a geometrization of the figures and a chromatic range that uses only blue, white and red.

VÁCLAV ŠPÁLA *Song of Spring*, 1915

From the Devětsil Group to Surrealism

The artistic climate changed radically toward the end of the war, with Čapek and Špála rejoining the "Obstinates" who had by this time picked up the torch of modern art. The Devětsil Group ● 59, founded in 1920, continued this trend, its members taking their viewpoint as much from German Dadaism as from the Italian Futurists. Profoundly anti-bourgeois and champions of a form of proletarian art suggested by the heros of popular fiction and folk art, they brought fresh inspiration and adopted a naive style. The Devětsil Group folded in 1924 in order to embrace the "poetists" including Štyrskí, Toyen and Teige, their theoretician and founder. In 1927, they published the Manifesto of Artificialism, which opposed André Breton's Surrealism on the grounds that it was no more than an "infra-red splendor on the threshold of consciousness", whereas Artificialism "lived in the ultra-violet world of full consciousness". It was not until 1934 that the Prague Surrealist Group was founded under Breton; it included most of the "poetists" among its members. In Paris, Josef Šima (1891–1971) worked closely on *Le Grand Jeu*, and mingling the dream-related qualities of Surrealism with a metaphysical conception of the world. In 1927, he painted *Europa* (above) and *At four o'clock in the Afternoon* (right).

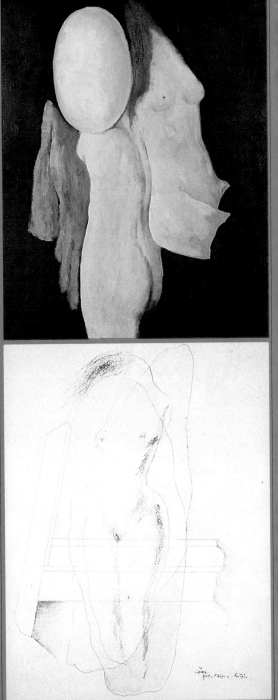

Prague
as seen by writers

● Franz Kafka

Kafka aged five.

"Kafka was Prague and Prague was Kafka," wrote Jan Urzidil. "Nothing had been so completely and typically Prague as what happened during Kafka's lifetime – and nothing ever will be. We, his friends, the 'happy few', knew that Prague was everywhere in Kafka's work, in tiny bits. . . . It is to Kafka's credit if the Prague that disappeared with him was not buried at the same time as he was." Kafka's very existence unfolded in the maze of narrow streets of the Old Town. However, his was a "provincial" life; for all his childhood dreams that took him to far-off countries he never managed to visit them in real life.

AN "IMPENETRABLE, POISONOUS AND DESTRUCTIVE" FAMILY LIFE

Franz Kafka was born in Prague on July 3, 1883, into a Jewish family that was typical of the social and linguistic intermingling typifying Old Bohemia. His Czech father, Hermann, came from provincial, proletarian stock and hailed from Prague's old ghetto, while his mother, Julie Löwy, had been born into a well-off, cultured family that belonged to the Judeo-German bourgeoisie.

THE FAMILY STORE

The success of their ironmongery store (its emblem was a crow, or *kavka* in Czech) brought the family immediate prosperity, and the parents entrusted their children to the care of nurses, governesses and other servants. One of these, a cook, made repeated invocations and regularly reprehended the young Kafka. This source of anxiety and torment became a recurrent theme in Kafka's books.

THE INSURANCE INSTITUTE

A brief period of articles in a lawyer's chambers followed by a year's legal practise coincided with various improbable plans to get as far away from Prague as possible. In the end, Kafka resigned himself to accepting a job at the Insurance Institute where he remained until 1922, fourteen years later.

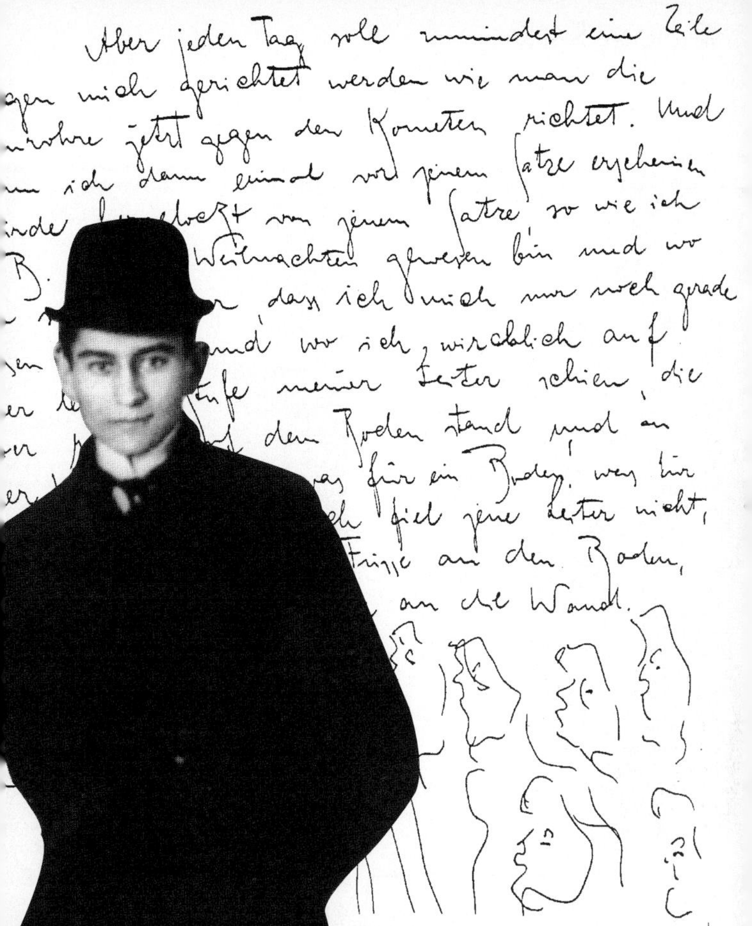

Aber jeden Tag soll zumindest eine Zeile
gegen mich gerichtet werden wie man die
Rohre jetzt gegen den Kometen richtet. Und
daß ich dann einmal vor jenem Satze erscheine
[...] von jenem Satze so wie ich
B. [...] Weihnachten gewesen bin und wo
[...] daß ich mich nur noch gerade
[...] und wo ich, wirklich auf
[...] meiner Leiter schien, die
[...] dem Boden stand und an
[...] was für ein Boden, was für
[...] fiel jene Leiter nicht,
[...] Finger an den Boden,
[...] an die Wand.

CREATIVITY
The acid, droll style
that made such a
deep impression on
writers such as André
Breton and Jean-Paul
Sartre was developed
during long nights of
waking solitude.

The Kafka family
tomb is in the Jewish
Olšany Cemetery,
not far from the
grave of Max Brod.

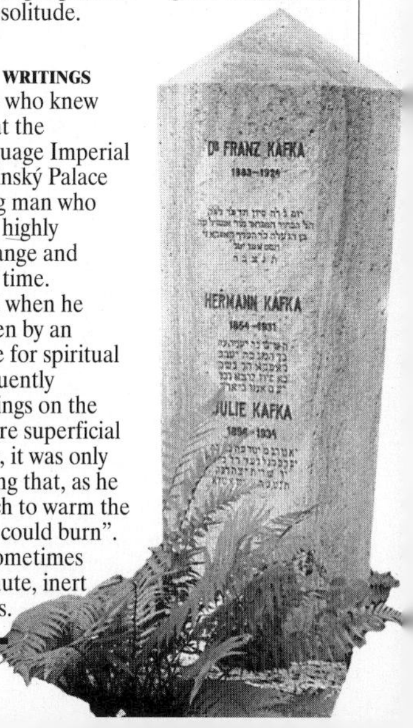

EARLY WRITINGS
Those who knew
Kafka at the
German-language Imperial
High School at Kinský Palace
remember a young man who
was well liked and highly
thought of, but strange and
distant at the same time.
This was the period when he
began writing. Driven by an
overwhelming desire for spiritual
salvation, he subsequently
destroyed these writings on the
grounds that they were superficial
and pompous. In fact, it was only
in, and through, writing that, as he
said, " a fire with which to warm the
icy space of our world could burn".
It was a world which sometimes
seemed to him like a mute, inert
accumulation of objects.

MILENA
For Kafka, writing quickly took on a life of its own. Even his various attempts at establishing long-term emotional attachments, as evidenced by his correspondence with Felice Bauer and Julie Wohrysek, tragically came to nothing. His friendship with Milena Jesenská might have brought him better fortune, but he was too late; the beautiful letters he wrote to her are tinged with undisguised sadness.

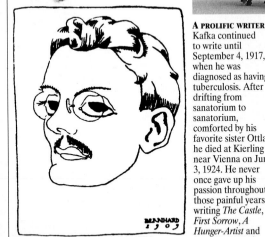

A PROLIFIC WRITER
Kafka continued to write until September 4, 1917, when he was diagnosed as having tuberculosis. After drifting from sanatorium to sanatorium, comforted by his favorite sister Ottla, he died at Kierling near Vienna on June 3, 1924. He never once gave up his passion throughout those painful years, writing *The Castle, First Sorrow, A Hunger-Artist* and *Investigations of a Dog* (1922). In 1923, he had a brief period of independence and happiness when he lived with Dora Dymant in Berlin. It was there that he wrote his last prose works: *A Little Woman, The Burrow* (1923) and *Josephine the Songstress* (1924).

BERNHARD
1909

MAX BROD,
A LIFE-LONG FRIEND
Kafka's enrolment in the Law Faculty of the German University of Prague, insisted on by his father, was supposed to bring him weighty responsibilities within the Austrian bureaucracy. In fact, he found it torture.

His friendship with Ernst Pollak gave him some peace of mind, and a subsequent friendship with Max Brod, who devoted his life to publicizing Kafka's works, proved invaluable. Kafka received his degree in jurisprudence on June 28, 1906.

> "Prague doesn't let go. Either of us. This Little Mother has claws. You have to submit or else."

Franz Kafka, letter to Ernst Pollak, December 20, 1902

A MAN OF HIS TIME Kafka's sensitivity to social and political issues increased as he grew older. He attended public meetings addressed by the more important Czech politicians and followed these debates in the *Cas* review edited by Tomáš G. Masaryk. He also took part in demonstrations organized by the "Vilém Körber" workers' association and by a Social Democratic group, the "Klub mladých". In June 1912, he chanced to attend lectures given by the Social Democratic Soukup on the American political system; they were to have a profound influence on his descriptions of elections in his last novel, *Amerika*.

"THE METAMORPHOSIS"
This novel came out in 1915. The above illustration is by Hans Fromus (1948).

KAFKA DISAPPEARS After Kafka's death, events forced his work into a period of total obscurity. A start was made on the complete edition in 1935, but publication was delayed and subsequently banned. Belongings found in Dora Dymant's flat in Berlin were impounded and many manuscripts were destroyed. Meanwhile, in Prague, the occupying Nazi forces ransacked his archives, removing documents and letters, and his three sisters, together with innumerable friends and relations, disappeared into concentration camps. It was not until the 1950s that his books were again made available.

Left, a scene from Steven Soderbergh's film *Kafka*, made in Prague in 1992.

FIRST IMPRESSIONS

A RENAISSANCE TOWN

The memoirs of Chateaubriand (1768–1848), published posthumously, give a shrewd and fascinating account of the author's life against the background of Europe in turmoil. He traveled widely and lived in exile in London between 1793 and 1800.

❝On Monday the 28th May . . . I found myself free to go through, or rather to revisit the town which I had already seen and seen again in coming and going. I do not know why I had imagined that Prague was nestled in a gap of mountains that threw their black shadow over a huddled kettleful of houses. Prague is a bright city, in which twenty-five or thirty graceful towers and steeples rise up to the sky; its architecture reminds one of a town of the Renascence. The long sway of the Emperors over the Cisalpine countries filled Germany with artists from those countries; the Austrian villages are villages of Lombardy, Tuscany or the Venetian main-land: one would think one's self under the roof of an Italian peasant, if, in the farm-houses, with their great bare rooms, a stove did not take the place of the sun. . . . In the constructions of which Hradschin is composed one sees historic halls, museums hung with the restored portraits and the furbished arms of the Dukes and Kings of Bohemia. Not far from the shapeless masses, there stands detached against the sky a pretty building decked with one of the graceful porticoes of the Cinquecento: this architecture has the drawback of being out of harmony with the climate. If at least one could, during the Bohemian winter, put those Italian palaces in the hot-house, with the palm-trees? I was always preoccupied with the thought of the cold which they must feel at night.❞

MEMOIRS OF FRANÇOIS RENÉ VICOMTE DE CHATEAUBRIAND, VOL. V, TRANS. ALEXANDER TEIXERA DE MATTOS, PUB. FREEMANTLE & CO., LONDON 1902

THE WANDERING JEW

Guillaume Apollinaire (1880–1918), the French poet, prose writer and art critic, describes a Jewish character visiting and commenting on the sights of Prague.

❝We visited the majestic, desolate halls of the Royal Castle of Hradschin, then the cathedral, containing the Royal tombs and the silver funerary casket of St. John Nepomuk. In the chapel, where the Kings of Bohemia were once crowned, and where King Wenceslas succumbed to his martyrdom. Laquedem pointed out to me that the walls were of semiprecious stones – agates and amethysts. He showed me one piece of amethyst in particular:

'See, the one in the middle; the veins trace a portrait with wild, crazed eyes. They say the features are Napoleon's.'

'But it is my own face!' I cried. 'My own face, with its sombre jealous eyes!'

And it is true. My portrait, painfully outlined, is there, by the bronze door on which hangs the ring that supported St. Wenceslas when he was martyred. I had to leave the chapel. I was pale and distressed to have seen myself as a madman, I, who am so afraid of becoming one. **"**

GUILLAUME APOLLINAIRE, *THE WANDERING JEW*,
PUB. RUPERT HART-DAVIS, LONDON 1967

A FINE WELCOME

Washington Irving (1783–1859) wrote sketchy notes and lively descriptions of places he visited. The following piece was written on November 22, 1822.

"A little after Six we arrive at Prague.

Approach to the town – Moonlight on the walls – dry moat and gateway – towers of churches dark – Streets spacious – (post) (I like to enter old walled towns in the evening, fine effect of passing under the old gateways – with sentinels (passi) loitering about – lanterns &c – to hear the reëchoing of the postilions horn)

put up at the Stadt Wien – very civil people. Go to theatre – beautiful moonlight night – fine effect of the light on the white spacious buildings of the (new) Streets – & the walls & columns of the theatre – Much pleased with the theatre – Spacious and cheerful – good Scenery, good dresses, good music. The piece a German translation of the Barber of Seville, the part of Rosina charmingly played by a beautiful actress of the name of Madmoiselle Sontag. – (the part of [*unrecovered*]) blue eyes, auburn hair, fine teeth small mouth – The part of Figaro very well played – The whole got up very well – price, for admission to the pit 1 paper florin, I E one franc – or if you take a locked seat a florin and half – Madmoiselle Sontag is about to leave this for Vienna where she is engaged at a very high price. Fine contrast after travelling thro sombre monotonous country of boors & rude villages, to arrive in the evening at a fine town and in half an hour be ushered into a splendid theatre –**"**

WASHINGTON IRVING, *JOURNALS AND NOTEBOOKS, VOL III, 1819–27*,
EDITED BY WALTER A. REICHART, PUB. UNIVERSITY OF WISCONSIN PRESS

THE REAL PRAGUE

Vernon Lee, otherwise known as Violet Paget (1856–1935), was a prolific British essayist and novelist, who spent most of her life in Italy. Here she describes how the city of Prague revealed itself to her.

"Ever since my childhood the mere name of Prague had awakened emotions of mystery and wonder, only the more potent for being, so to speak, a mere disembodied essence; a shapeless perfume of romance.

One has to pay, occasionally, for such imaginary raptures; and heaven knows we have paid for them during these three dreary, chilly autumn days in the Prague which exists outside the fancy. . . .

This afternoon, having disconsolately dragged our bicycles along muddy tramlines crowded with drays, and gaunt, unfinished streets and mangy playgrounds garnished with dustheaps, we subsided to coffee and sponge-cake on a promenade terrace overlooking the town and the river. The gravel was strewn with singed lime leaves, the coffee was grounds, and the sponge-cake was sand. But from that height, and in the reddened afternoon mists, the city took an odd look, with its snaking quays and its many domed churches, of Rome seen from the Janiculum; the Prague of our fancy, the *real* Prague began to take body for our eyes. And when we were refreshed and a little comforted, we bicycled along the low, half-built-over hills in the direction of the citadel. The weather, as I have said, had been intolerably gloomy, though not actually raining; but the sky opened at sunset, and the dust and powdered brickbat of the unfinished roads gathered in ambrosial halos round the trees, round the towers and cupolas, the triumphal eighteenth century gables of the palace, and the cathedral spires and gargoyles and flying buttresses.❞

VERNON LEE, *THE SENTIMENTAL TRAVELLER: NOTES ON PLACES*,
PUB. JOHN LANE, THE BODLEY HEAD, LONDON 1908

GHOSTS

THE PRINCIPAL CHARACTERS

Many visitors report sightings of long-dead figures in the city, as if their memories are retained by the walls and streets.

❝Ascending the broad flight of steps to the Hradschin, I paused a moment to gaze upon the scene below. A slight blue haze hung over the clustering towers, and the city glimmered through it, like a city seen in a dream. It was well that it should so appear, for not less dim and misty are the memoires that haunt its walls. There was no need of a magician's wand to bid that light cloud shadow forth the forms of other times. They came uncalled for, even by fancy. Far, far back in the past, I saw the warrior-princess who founded the kingly city – the renowned Libussa, whose prowess and talent inspired the women of Bohemia to rise at her death and storm the land, that their sex might rule where it obeyed before. On the mountain opposite, once stood the palace of the bloody Wlaska, who reigned with her Amazon band for seven years over half Bohemia. Those streets below had echoed with the fiery words of Huss, the castle of whose follower – the blind Ziska, who met and defeated the armies of the German Empire – moulders on the mountain above. Many a year of war and tempest has passed over the scene. The hills around have borne the armies of Wallenstein and Frederick the Great; the war-cries of Bavaria, Sweden, and Poland have echoed in the valley, and the glare of the midnight cannon or the flames of burning palaces have often reddened the blood-dyed waters of the Moldau. 99

BAYARD TAYLOR, *VIEW AFOOT; OR, EUROPE SEEN WITH KNAPSACK AND STAFF*, PUB. SAMPSON LOW, MARSTON, LOW & SEARLE, LONDON 1871

PAST LIVES

Rainer Maria Rilke (1875–1926), the German lyric poet, wrote in November 1927 of the memories awakened by a visit to Prague.

66When will one come here and be able to see this city, see it and say it, from visit to visit? When will one have to bear its heaviness no longer, the immense meaning it took on when one was small and *it* was already big and spread out far beyond one; in those days it needed you in order to feel itself . . . It makes me sad to see these houses at the corners, these windows and porticos, squares and church-roofs, to see them all humbled, smaller than they were, abased and completely in the wrong. And it is just as impossible for me to get the upper hand of them in their new guise as it was when they were overweening. Their heaviness as a whole has been transformed into its opposite, yet, taken piecemeal, how much it has remained heaviness! More than ever I have felt since this morning the presence of this city as something incomprehensible and confusing. Either it must have vanished with my childhood, or else my childhood must have flowed away from it, later, leaving it behind, real beside all other realities, something that could be seen and expressed objectively like a

Cézanne thing, inconceivable as far as I am concerned, yet still tangible. In this way it is somehow ghostly, like the people who were part of it and of me long ago and who bring us together and speak of us among themselves. – I have never felt it with such astonishment, my aversion has never been so great as this time (probably because my tendency to see everything with reference to my work has grown so much more marked).

Well then, I have been in Prague since this morning and am just writing you this as the first greeting from the first halt on my journey. Naturally everybody is asking after you and Ruth. But you are just as far from them as I am, and somehow this brings us together and away from this immitigable old town. 99

SELECTED LETTERS OF RAINER MARIA RILKE, 1902–1926, TRANS. BY R. F. C. HULL, PUB. MACMILLAN & CO. LTD. LONDON 1946

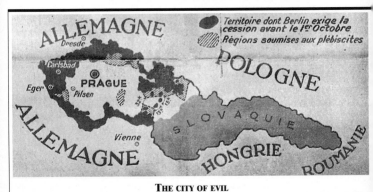

ALLEMAGNE — Dresde, Carlsbad, Eger, **PRAGUE**, Pilsen — **POLOGNE** — **ALLEMAGNE** — Vienne — **SLOVAQUIE** — **HONGRIE** — **ROUMANIE**

Territoire dont Berlin exige la cession avant le 1er Octobre
Régions soumises aux plébiscites

THE CITY OF EVIL

Czech novelist Milan Kundera (b. 1929) wrote in the semi-autobiographical novel "The Book of Laughter and Forgetting" of the hardships of life under the Communist regime.

❝Prague, as Max Brod used to say, is the city of evil. After the defeat of the Czech Reformation in 1621 the Jesuits tried to re-educate the nation in the true Catholic faith by overwhelming the city with the splendor of Baroque cathedrals. The thousands of stone saints looking out from all sides – threatening you, following you, hypnotizing you – are the raging hordes of occupiers who invaded Bohemia three hundred and fifty years ago to tear the people's faith and language from their hearts. The street Tamina was born on was called Schwerin. That was during the war, and Prague was occupied by the Germans. Her father was born on Cernokostelecka Avenue – the Avenue of the Black Church. That was during the Austro-Hungarian Monarchy. When her mother married her father and moved there, it bore the name of Marshal Foch. That was after World War I. Tamina spent her childhood on Stalin Avenue, and when her husband came to take her away, he went to Vinohrady – that is, Vineyards – Avenue. And all the time it was the same street; they just kept changing its name, trying to lobotomize it.

There are all kinds of ghosts prowling these confused streets. They are the ghosts of monuments demolished – demolished by the Czech Reformation, demolished by the Austrian Counterreformation, demolished by the Czechoslovak Republic, demolished by the Communists. Even statues of Stalin have been torn down. All over the country, wherever statues were thus destroyed, Lenin statues have sprouted up by the thousands. They grow like weeds on the ruins, like melancholy flowers of forgetting.❞

MILAN KUNDERA, *THE BOOK OF LAUGHTER AND FORGETTING*,
TRANS. MICHAEL HENRY HEIM, PUB. FABER AND FABER, LONDON 1982

A LONG HISTORY

ACCIDENT OR MIRACLE?

British historian Dame Cicely Veronica Wedgwood (b. 1910) describes the defenestration of Prague during the Thirty Years War.

❝The city was already alive with excitement and when on the following morning the Protestant deputies were seen making their way towards the royal castle of the Hradschin an immense crowd followed in their wake. Through the portals surmounted by the outspread eagle of the Hapsburg they surged into the courtyard, up the staircase the deputies led the way, through the audience hall and into the small room where the governors sat. Trapped between the council table and the wall, the crowd before and the blank stones behind, Slavata and Martinitz stood at bay. Neither doubted that his last hour had come.

A hundred hands dragged them towards the high window, flung back the casement and hoisted them upwards. Martinitz went first. 'Jesu Maria! Help!' he screamed and crashed over the sill. Slavata fought longer, caling on the Blessed Virgin and

> "It is the town that conceived the Reformation and
> hatched the Thirty Years' War."
>
> Jerome K. Jerome

clawing at the window frame under a rain of blows until someone knocked him senseless and the bleeding hands relaxed. Their shivering secretary clung to Schlick for protection; out of sheer intoxication the crowd hoisted him up and sent him to join his masters. One of the rebels leant over the ledge, jeering: 'We will see if your Mary can help you!' A second later, between exasperation and amazement, 'By God, his Mary has helped,' he exclaimed, for Martinitz was already stirring. Suddenly a ladder protruded from a neighbouring window; Martinitz and the secretary made for it under a hail of misdirected missiles. Some of Slavata's servants, braving the mob, went down to his help and carried him after the others, unconscious but alive.The extraordinary chance which had saved three lives was a holy miracle or a comic accident according to the religion of the beholder, but it had no political significance.**99**

C. V. WEDGWOOD, *THE THIRTY YEARS WAR*,
PUB. JONATHAN CAPE, 1938

THE OLD JEWISH CEMETERY
The following piece appeared in "Action Praha" in 1960:

66In the centre of the Old Town of Prague and right on the boundary of what was formerly the ghetto, there sprawls the uneven ground of a cemetery, one of the most fascinating and most frequently visited places in the capital of Czechoslovakia. The mass of ancient, weather-worn gravestones of such varied shapes and sizes, packed so close together and overhung by the gnarled and rugged branches of century-old trees and shrubs, gives the impression of a forgotten corner of the Orient in the very heart of Europe. It is, in fact, the least ancient of the medieval Jewish cemeteries in Prague, and only survived through the ages thanks to its position in the centre of the former Jewish Town . . . Some reports say 11,000 stones, and others up to 20,000, make up this picturesque corner, so full of melancholy and mysticism. The oldest gravestone dates back to the first half of the fifteenth century. By the buying up of additional surrounding land, the Garden of the Dead was enlarged many times between then and 1768, but its area was always far from being adequate. As religious precepts forbade the Jews to dig up old graves, more earth was brought in and added to the level of the cemetery, so that new layers of graves could be dug. This process was repeated several times, until in some places there, as indeed there are to this day, up to twelve layers, one above the other. The gravestones of the lower layers, however, were raised to the new level each time, thus creating that chaotic jumble which has charmed and attracted so many generations of artists and writers.**99**

J. LION AND J. LUKAS, *THE OLD PRAGUE JEWISH CEMETERY*,
ACTION PRAHA, 1960

THE JEWISH MUSEUM

Egon Erwin Kisch (1855–1948), Czech journalist, poet and novelist, writes here of the creation of a Jewish museum. Brainchild of the Nazis, it was completed by the Jews of Prague.

66This was the plan: to exterminate a nation of many millions and then to demonstrate by means of a museum which was to be established by the murderers, what fanatical and dangerous enemies of the millennial Third Reich the victims, i.e. the Jews, had been. The richer and bigger we make this museum – such was the argument of the Nazis – the more convincingly it will show the coming generations how fundamentally we have changed the world, how greatly we influenced the course of history. "But I," – the executor of the plan, the Obersturmbannführer added in his thoughts – "I will get a lecturership out of it."

It didn't come off as planned. And it may yet come to pass that the fugitive Obersturmbannführer and former future lecturer will turn up one day to claim a reward from the Jews for his creation of the mausoleum-museum. Of course it wasn't so completely his creation: the foundation for it was the historical collection of the Israelitic community of Prague. But the Nazis provided plenty of additions.**99**

EGON ERWIN KISCH, *TALES FROM SEVEN GHETTOS*,
TRANS. EDITH BONE, PUB. ROBERT ANSCOMBE & CO. LTD., LONDON 1948

SECRET AGENTS

In "Prague Orgy" Philip Roth (b. 1933) speculates about the waiters in a café.

66On the chance that he has decided to wait inside rather than under the scrutiny of the plainclothes security agents patrolling the halls, I enter the café and look around: a big dingy room, a dirty, airless, oppressive place. Patched, fraying tablecloths set with mugs of beer, and clinging to the mugs, men with close-cropped hair wearing gray-black work clothes, swathed in cigarette smoke and saying little. Off the night shift somewhere, or maybe tanking up on their way *to* work. Their faces indicate that not everybody heard the president when he went on television for three hours to ask the people not to drink so much.

Two waiters in soiled white jackets attend the fifty or so tables, both of them elderly and in no hurry. Since half of the country, by Olga's count, is employed in spying on the other half, chances are that one at least works for the police. (Am I getting drastically paranoid or am I getting the idea?) In German I order a cup of coffee.

The workmen at their beer remind me of Bolotka, a janitor in a museum now that he now longer runs his theater. "This," Bolotka explains, "is the way we arrange things now. The menial work is done by the writers and the teachers and the construction engineers, and the construction is run by the drunks and the crooks. Half a million people have been fired from their jobs. *Everything* is run by the drunks and the crooks. They get along better with the Russians." I imagine Styron washing glasses in a Penn Station barroom, Susan Sontag wrapping buns in a Broadway bakery, Gore Vidal bicycling salamis to school lunchrooms in Queens – I look at the filthy floor and see myself sweeping it.**99**

PHILIP ROTH, *THE PRAGUE ORGY*,
PUB. JONATHAN CAPE, LONDON 1985

DUBČEK AND HAVEL

Timothy Garton Ash's book "We The People" celebrates the revolutions of 1989, as witnessed in Warsaw, Budapest, Berlin and Prague.

❝In the early afternoon comes Dubček. He looks as it he has stepped straight out of a black-and-white photograph from 1968. The face is older, more lined, of course, but he has the same grey coat and paisley scarf, the same tentative, touching smile, the same functionary's hat. Protected by Havel's bodyguards – lead on, John Bok – we emerge from the belly of the Lantern, Dubček and Havel side by side, and scuttle through covered shopping arcades and tortuous back passages to reach the balcony of the Socialist Party publishing house and the offices of *Svobodné Slovo:* the balcony of the free word. Along the arcades people simply gape. They can't believe it. Dubček! It is as if the ghost of Winston Churchill were to be seen striding down the Burlington Arcade. But when he steps out on to the balcony in the frosty evening air, illuminated by television spotlights, the crowds give such a roar as I have never heard. 'DUBČEK! DUBČEK!' echoes off the tall houses up and down the long, narrow square. Many people mourn his ambiguous role after the Soviet invasion, and his failure to use the magic of his name to support the democratic opposition. He has changed little with the times. His speech still contains those wooden newspeak phrases, the *langue de bois.* (At one point he refers to 'confrontationist extremist tendencies'.) He still believes in socialism – that is, reformed communism – with a human face. The true leader of this movement, in Prague at least, is Havel not Dubček. But for the moment none of this matters. For the moment all that matters is that the legendary hero is really standing here, addressing a huge crowd on Wenceslas Square, while the emergency session of the Central Committee has, we are told, been removed to a distant suburb. 'Dubček to the castle!' roars the crowd – that is Dubček for president. The old man must believe he will wake up in a moment and find he is dreaming. For the man who supplanted him and now sits in the castle, Gustav Husák, it is the nightmare come true. After Dubček comes Havel. 'Dubček-Havel,' they chant, the name of '68 and the name of '89.❞

TIMOTHY GARTON ASH,
WE THE PEOPLE, PUB. GRANTA BOOKS
IN ASSOC. WITH PENGUIN BOOKS, CAMBRIDGE 1990

ARCHITECTURE

Dr Charles Burney (1726–1814), a musical historian, visited the city shortly after the battle of Prague in 1757 gave Frederick the Great his first success against the Austrians in the Seven Years' War.

❝This city is extremely beautiful, when seen at a distance. It is situated on two or three hills, and has the river Mulda running through the middle of it. It is divided into three different quarters, or districts, which are distinguished by the names of Ult Stadt, Neue Stadt, and Kleine Stadt, or Old Town, New Town, and Little Town; the Kleine Stadt is the most modern, and the best built of the three. The houses are all of white stone, or stucco, in imitation of it, and all uniform in size and colour. The hill of St. Laurence, the highest about the town, commands a prospect, not only of the whole city, but of all the adjacent country: the declivity of this hill is covered with wood, consisting chiefly of fruit-trees, and vineyards. A great part of the town is new, as scarce a single building escaped the Prussian batteries, and bombardment during the blockade, in the last war. A few churches and palaces only, that were strongly built, and of less combustible materials than the rest, were proof against their fury; and in the walls of these, are still sticking innumerable cannon balls, and bombs, particularly, in the superb palace of count Czernin, and in the Capuchin's church. This palace, which is of the Ionic order, and built of whitestone, has thirty windows in front, the chapel, at the Capuchins, is an exact copy, in stone, of that at Loretto, in Marble.

The inhabitants are still at work throughout the city, in repairing the Prussian devastations, particularly at the cathedral and imperial palace, which were both almost entirely demolished; these are situated on a high hill, facing that of St. Laurence.❞

DR BURNEY'S MUSICAL TOURS IN EUROPE, VOL. II,
PUB. OXFORD UNIVERSITY PRESS,
LONDON 1959

EM·PRAGUE

FOREIGN INFLUENCE

The writings of V. S. Pritchett (b. 1900), the British novelist and short-story writer, are full of shrewd observations of human nature and culture.

❝Prague, or more particularly old Prague, which is very large, is one of the noblest cities in Europe. Its hundred Gothic spires prick the sky, its medieval towers, its baroque belfries and cupolas bring their graces to the city panorama. One has an impression of another Paris of the Latin quarter. The broad river curves through the tree-lined embankments. One can see from the war between Gothic and Baroque that this city is marked at every corner by historical struggle. It is a difficulty for the Czech to admire the Baroque because it is the architecture of a foreign conqueror, though some of the art historians are beginning to weaken and point out that it was also the work of Czech artisans. One could see why L —— claimed that the Czechs had the highest level of political education in Europe; they have learned in the bitter school of oppression.❞

V. S. PRITCHETT, *FOREIGN FACES,* PUB. CHATTO & WINDUS, LONDON 1964

ARCHWAYS AND VAULTS

Patrick Leigh Fermor (b. 1915) describes the staircase leading to the citadel and King Vladislav's Hall of Homage.

❝The city teems with wonders; but what belongs where? Certainly that stupendous staircase called the Riders' Steps, and all that lay beyond them, were part of the great castle-palace. The marvellous strangeness of the late gothic vaults enclosing this flight must have germinated in an atmosphere like the English mood which coaxed fan-tracery into bloom . . . These vaults are almost impossible to describe. The ribs burst straight out of the walls in V-shaped clusters of springers. Grooved like celery stalks and blade-shaped in cross section with the edge pointing down, they expanded and twisted as they rose. They separated, converged again and crossed each other and as they sped away, enclosed slender spans of wall like the petals of tulips: and when two ribs intersected, they might both have been obliquely notched and then half-joggled together with studied carelessness. They writhed on their own axes and simultaneously followed the curve

of the vault; and often, after these contorted intersections, the ribs that followed a concave thrust were chopped off short while the convex plunged headlong and were swallowed up in the masonry. The loose mesh tightened as it neared the rounded summit and the frantic reticulation jammed in momentary deadlock. Four truncated ribs, dovetailing in rough parallelograms, formed keystones and then broke loose again with a wildness which at first glance resembled organic violence clean out of control. But a second glance, embracing the wider design, captured a strange and marvellous coherence, as though petrifaction had arrested this whirling dynamism at a chance moment of balance and harmony.

Everything here was strange. The archway at the top of these shallow steps, avoiding the threatened anticlimax of a flattened ogee, deviated in two round-topped lobes on either side with a right-angled central cleft slashed deep between the cusps. There had been days, I was told, when horsemen on the way to the indoor lists rode in full armour up these steps: lobster-clad riders slipping and clattering as they stooped their ostrich-plumes under the freak doorway, gingerly carrying their lances at the trail to keep the bright paint that spiralled them unchipped. But in King Vladislav's vast Hall of Homage the ribs of the vaulting had further to travel, higher to soar. Springing close to the floor from reversed and bisected cones, they sailed aloft curving and spreading across the wide arch of the ceiling: parting, crossing, re-joining, and – once again – enclosing those slim subdivided tulips as they climbed. Then they cast their intertwining arcs in wider

and yet wider loops with the looseness and the overlap of lassoos kept perpetually on the move, accelerating, as they ascended, to the speed of coiling stockwhips . . . Travelling the length of that arched vista of ceiling, the loops of the stone ribs expanded and crossed and changed partners, simultaneously altering direction and handing on the succession of arcs until the parabolas, reaching the far limit of this strange curvilinear relay-race, began to swing back. Nearing home and completing the journey in reverse, they rejoined their lost companions at their starting point and sank tapering and interlocked. The sinuous mobility entranced the eye, but it was not only this. Lit by the wintry chiaroscuro of the tall windows, the white tulip-shaped expanses that these stone ribs enclosed so carelessly seemed to be animated by an even more rapid and streamlined verve. Each of these incidental and sinuous facets reflected a different degree of white, and their motion, as they ascended the reversed half-cones of the vault and curled over into the ceiling, suggested the spreading and upward-showering rush of a school of dolphins leaping out of the water.**

PATRICK LEIGH FERMOR, *A TIME OF GIFTS – ON FOOT TO CONSTANTINOPLE, FROM THE HOOK OF HOLLAND TO THE MIDDLE DANUBE*, PUB. JOHN MURRAY, DATE?

NATURAL ATTRACTIONS

THE RIVER MOLDAU

Arthur Symons (1865–1945) was a British poet and critic and a leading spirit of the Decadent movement.

**The Moldau, which cuts Prague in two, is broad and swift, golden under sunlight, as it hurries under its five bridges, between the green banks and the quay. Long rafts of floating timber, on which men run to and fro with tall poles, pass slowly, hurrying as they shoot the weir. Boats cross from side to side, and one sees the slow, crossing gesture of men with long-handled scoops, dredging in a barge. A man stands on a heap of stones, in the very middle of the weir, fishing. Half-naked figures, or figures in bathing-gowns, move to and fro on the big brown floating baths, or swing out on a trapeze over the water. A sound of music comes from one of the green islands, where people are sitting at café tables under the trees. People drowse on the benches by the side of the river.

Warm, full of repose, heavy with happy sleep, at midday, at night the riverside becomes mysterious, a romance. The water silvers; with its islands, from which lights glimmer, it might be a lake, but for the thunder of the weir, which comes to you as you walk under the trees, or go out on a kind of platform beside a dusty mill, from which you see the water rushing violently towards the great wooden stakes by the bridge. Lights move on the opposite shore, at the foot of what seems a vast mountain, dimly outlined. The bridge, at first invisible, a detached line of lights, comes out gradually, as your eyes accustom themselves to the night-mist, in the palest of grey, like the ghost of a bridge. Beyond and above, the Hradčin emerges in the same ghostly outline, a long grey line against the sky, out of which the cathedral spire points upward. It is a view which seems to have been composed, almost too full of the romantic elements to be quite natural; and it has something of whatever is strange, placid, and savage in the character of the Bohemians.**

ARTHUR SYMONS, *CITIES*,
PUB. J. M. DENT & CO., LONDON 190?

PRAGUE IN THE SNOW

Karel Čapek (1890–1938), the Czech novelist and dramatist, decided to write this article about snow because he could no longer build snow men or snow castles.

❝When the snow comes down, Prague at once becomes a little old-world town; overnight we go back fifty or a hundred years and it is suddenly all countrified and old-fashioned, all quaintly baroque, straddling, naïve, and antique; for no reason at all one thinks of old women with seven petticoats, apples baked in their jackets, the smell of burning wood, old interiors, and flowered curtains. The folk in the street are happy, stamping their footprints in the snow, crunching it and waving their hands as they did a hundred years ago. And it is so still! the stillness of a little country town. Even the Vltava does not move; the tram tinkles like a sledge, and one would not be a bit surprised if motor cars began sounding little bells as sleighs used to once upon a time. Old world! Suddenly it is a world of old things and old dimensions. The charm of the quaint little town. The weather which brings old times back.

That is why, as you will understand, the only real snow is what we get on Malá Strana. That is why it lasts there longer than in other places; and when it is all blown away from other parts of the town (because there it is nothing special, just idle and good-for-nothing) on Malá Strana, thank God, it still lies in banks an drifts just wherever it can. For here it has a special right, here and up yonder round the Castle. . . .

Then when the moon shines on it all, what happens cannot even be expressed: Prague crouches down and makes hereself quite little; she holds her breath; the snow rings like glass under-foot, the roofs press themselves down to the ground, everything huddles together icily, and it is so light, so strangely light, that you are startled at the darkness within you.❞

KAREL ČAPEK, *INTIMATE THINGS*,
TRANS. BY DORA ROUND, PUB. GEORGE ALLEN & UNWIN LTD., LONDON 1935

LIVING IN PRAGUE

FOOD

Hester Piozzi (1741–1821) found that in Prague "everything seems at least five centuries behind-hand", but she was impressed by the food.

❝The eating here is incomparable; I never saw such poultry even at London or Bath, and there is a plenty of game that amazes one; no inn so wretched but you have a pheasant for your supper, and often partridge soup. The fish is carried about the streets in so elegant a style it tempts one; a very large round bathing-tub, as we should call it, set barrow-wise on two not very low wheels, is easily pushed along by one man, though full of the most pellucid water, in which the carp, tench, and eels, are all leaping alive, to a size and perfection I am ashamed to relate; but the tench of four and five pounds weight have a richness and flavour one had no notion of till we arrived at Vienna, and they are the same here.❞

HESTER PIOZZI, *OBSERVATIONS AND
REFLECTIONS MADE IN THE COURSE OF A
JOURNEY THROUGH FRANCE, ITALY AND
GERMANY*, EDITED BY HERBERT BARROWS,
PUB. UNIVERSITY OF MICHIGAN PRESS,
ANN ARBOR, 1967

CRIME

Czech novelist Jaroslav Hašek (1883–1923) describes the streetwise Cetlička, an outlaw who loves Prague.

❝Cetlička was banished from Prague . . . All went well in the daytime. He sauntered about Prague, no one recognised him, that is not until the terribly disastrous evenings.

Once when he was in *The Stars* he had wanted to run off with an overcoat; on another occasion he had wanted to slip away from the *California* without paying the bill. Then there were the fist fights in *The Wreath*. It all added up to a month of gaol for each incident because he had disobeyed the law.

Nevertheless, he loved his native Prague, because he as able to take full advantage of this city which had so much to offer.

No other city had as many skirts hanging outside the shop windows, nor did ne know any other town that had locks which were so easily pried open. Nowhere was it easier to steal than in Prague.

Whenever something happens on the streets, no matter how silly, a crowd of people will gather, all of them deaf and blind, jostling and elbowing their way to see for themselves that it was really a sparrow's egg that fell from the eaves of the roof right onto the hat of a respectable gentleman who was now indignantly showing his black bowler with a yellow stain on the crown to the inquisitive throng that had gathered about him.

Those were such opportune occasions for emptying pockets of overcoats, for hardly anyone ever carries wallets in breast-pockets as it saves them the trouble of unbuttoning jackets; to say nothing about the pleasure people get in being robbed.

Cetlička would plunge into the midst of a mob, they might be a horde of admirers watching a couple of monkeys race each other; wooden, mechanical monkeys in toyshops, in front of which adults would be pushing one another, although the display was meant for children who could not get near enough to see anything because of the hobbledehoy grown-ups.

He was among those who struggled to get seats in tramcars.

And wherever he went, he would reach down deep into people's pockets and depart unobserved.❞

JAROSLAV HAŠEK, *THE TOURIST GUIDE*, PUB. ARTIA, 1961

AN ANTIQUE ARMOIRE

Czech novelist Ivan Klima (b. 1931) writes of a travel courier observing his own city.

❝The repairs to the façades on the Old Town Square were almost finished, and the square gleamed with newness and colour like a grand Sacher cake; I liked it, and I got enormous pleasure out of just being able to wander about there. Before I found this job I came downtown twice a month at most, and then I was in a hurry to get back home and back to work. But now this job brought me here every day, and I could study the slow progress of repairs to the Týn Church, and peer into the exhibition room of the Town Hall. I could even have gone in, but felt reluctant to do so, for as long as I was moving through the streets with my pushcart in the general direction of my destination, I was working and no one could complain. But I had no business at an art show.

I stopped in front of the Town Hall tower. The first tourists of the morning were beginning to gather on the pavement below the astronomical clock. Tourists

from the West were still asleep or perhaps having breakfast, whereas those standing beside me, already burdened with parcels and waiting for the Twelve Apostles to appear when the clock struck the hour, were a group from the empire of our eastern neighbours. I likened to their soft speech, a language that had seduced some of our reckless and gullible ancestors into dreaming dreams of a brotherhood of the strong and the weak. But the conversation didn't seem to be about anything that made sense. The clock struck, the apostles paraded one by one past the tiny portals, but as always, they remained silent, telling us nothing and then vanishing into their darkness again.

I walked along Ironmonger's Street to Mustek where, in an antique store, I saw a Renaissance armoire costing 180,000 crowns. Doing the work I was doing now, this was the accumulated salary of ten years. I began to plan the story of a courier who decided not to eat, drink, live anywhere or even read so he could save all his money to buy this antique armoire. Several endings suggested themselves. The courier, who all that time had slept in a cellar and lived on the leftovers he picked off plates in the stand-up buffets, could die of exhaustion. Or he survives but meanwhile – and this was the most plausible outcome – the armoire is sold to someone else. Or, and this was my favourite: he finally drags himself to the shop, where he finds the armoire still waiting for him, but in the meantime the price has doubled. **99**

IVAN KLIMA, MY GOLDEN TRADES,
PUB. GRANTA BOOKS IN ASSOC WITH PENGUIN BOOKS, 1992

KAFKA'S DIARIES

Franz Kafka (1883–1924) wrote the following diary entries on November 18, 1911, and March 14, 1915, respectively

66 Yesterday in the factory. Rode back on the trolley, sat in a corner with legs stretched out, saw people outside, lights in stores, walls of viaducts through which we passed, backs and faces over and over again, a highway leading from the business street of the suburb with nothing human in it save people going home, the glaring electric lights of the railway station burned into the darkness, the low, tapering chimneys of the gasworks, a poster announcing the guest appearance of a singer, de Treville, that gropes its way along the walls as far as an alley near the cemeteries, from where it then returned to me out of the cool of

the fields into the liveable warmth of the city. We accept(ed) foreign cities as a fact, the inhabitants live there without penetrating our way of life, just as we cannot penetrate theirs, a comparison must be made, it can't be helped, but one is well aware that it has no moral or even psychological value, in the end one can often even omit the comparison because the difference in the condition of life is so great that it makes it unnecessary.

The suburbs of our native city, however, are also foreign to us, but in this case comparisons have value, a half-hour's walk can prove it to us over and over again, here live people partly within our city, partly on the miserable dark edge of the city that is furrowed like a great ditch, although they all have an area of interest in common with us that is greater than any other group of people outside the city. For this reason I always enter and leave the suburb with a weak mixed feeling of anxiety, of abandonment, of sympathy, of curiosity, of conceit, of joy in travelling, of fortitude, and return with pleasure, seriousness, and calm, especially from Zizkov. 99

66A morning. In bed until half past eleven. Jumble of thoughts which slowly take shape and hardens in an incredible fashion. Read in the afternoon (Gogol) in the evening a walk, part of the time the defensible but untrustworthy ideas of the morning in my head. Was in Chotek Park. Most beautiful spot in Prague. Birds sang, the Castle was its arcade, the old trees hung with last year's foliage, the dim light. 99

THE DIARIES OF FRANZ KAFKA, 1910–13,
ED. MAX BROD, TRANS. JOSEPH KRESH, PUB.
SECKER & WARBURG,
LONDON 1948

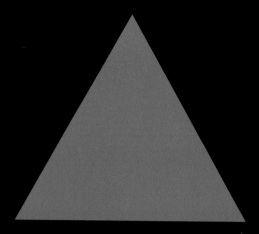

Itineraries in Prague

▲View of the Castle and the Vltava. The cupola of St Nicholas' Church and the tower on Charles B

▼ Prague by night, with St Nicholas' Church, Malá Strana in the foreground

▲ Church of Our Lady of Týn,   ▼ Statues on Charles Bridge

▼ "There are said to be as many churches here as there are days of the year." (Ingvalt Undset

▲ Černínská Street, Hradčany   ▼ Baroque façades in Old Town Square

▼ The old Jewish cemetery in Josefov

▲ The Nový Svet district   ▲ A Secession façade in the Old Town

▼ Kampa Island seen from Charles Bridge

▲ Archways near Loretánská Street

▲ Restaurant in the Town Hall   ▼ A road on Kampa Island

From Old Town Square to Charles Bridge

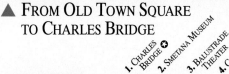

OLD TOWN SQUARE ★ ▲ 138

☑ One day
◆ B A4-B4-C4

The histories of Old Town (Staré Město)
and its Square (Staroměstské
náměstí) are closely inter-
related. Much of our
knowledge of the
city in its
earliest days
is based

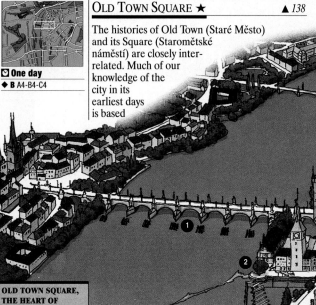

OLD TOWN SQUARE, THE HEART OF PRAGUE ✪
Old Town Square, an open space in the midst of narrow streets, is dominated by the soaring spires of the Church of Our Lady of Týn, Goltz-Kinský Palace and the statue of Jan Huss. It is worth climbing the clocktower of the Old Town Hall for the 360° view over Prague that it offers. From ground level, the performance of the Apostles in the astronomical clock is an entertaining spectacle. For a drink afterwards, avoid the cosmopolitan café terraces in the square in favor of the quieter ones to be found in Týn Courtyard.

on a document written by an emissary of the Caliph of
Cordoba, the diplomat and merchant Ibrahim Ibn Jacob. His
stay from 965 to 966 inspired him to write of his journey,
during which he came to realize that the city was an important
center of commercial exchange. The opening of the city to the
west and the development of commerce encouraged Soběslav
I (1125–40) to play a more active role in the commercial Týn
Courtyard (Ungelt) ▲ 160 behind the Church of Our Lady.
This was the start of Prague's role as an important
commercial center.

NEWCOMERS. New communities from Piedmont, Burgundy,
Germany and Flanders settled in Prague during the 12th
century, and their arrival increased the amount of business
transactions, already stimulated by the needs of the Royal
Court. At this time, the Germans occupied an area that was to
become Old Town Square; there, they founded a church
dedicated to St Nicholas ▲ 145, the patron saint of
merchants, and they also built a hospital, houses and shops.
The square began to look a little as it does today: the houses
on the north, east and south sides,
including Kinský Palace,
are aligned on axes
already determined in the
12th and 13th centuries.

**AIMING FOR MUNICIPAL
STATUS.** In 1230, Old Town
acquired the status of a
town, but it was not
entitled to have a Town

PRAHA
STAROMĚSTSKÁ RADNICE

Hall, the decisive symbol in the Middle Ages of city freedom. It was not for another hundred years, in 1338, that John of Luxemburg granted the right to erect a Town Hall in Old Town Square. With political and judiciary power now hand in hand, the bourgeoisie sought to install a prison inside the Town Hall and stocks in the square. As the town's political center, the square established itself as the economic and social epicenter, and it was inhabited by the wealthiest families. Apart from commercial activities, the square also hosted festive occasions, including tourneys.

An old engraving (above) showing the execution of rebel leaders in 1621.

Scenes of the liberation of Prague (below) in Old Town Square, May 1945.

HISTORIC EVENTS. Down through the centuries, Old Town Square has been the scene of momentous and bloody events: after his victory at White Mountain on November 8, 1620 ● *34*, Ferdinand II sent twenty-seven noble and bourgeois rebels to the scaffold (today marked by a rectangle of black stones). Twelve of the heads were hung on the tower on Charles Bridge and were not buried until 1631. On May 8–9, 1945, the partisans fought a ferocious battle here to liberate the city from the Nazis, and then on February 21, 1948, Klement Gottwald proclaimed the victory of Soviet Communism ● *39* from the balcony of Kinský Palace ▲ *143*. By 1968 the square had come to be known as "Hyde Park" and was soon the favorite venue for student meetings. Today, more people meet and walk here than in Wenceslas Square or any other square in Prague.

KINSKÝ PALACE. In a previous age, the Palace housed the German-language Imperial High School attended by German-speaking intelligentsia, notably Max Brod and Franz Kafka ▲ *110*. Today it houses the National Gallery collection ▲ *227*.

137

Kriz House. The building features an interesting window, or loggia, dating from 1520 and bears the inscription *Pragua caput regni.*

Historic Old Town Square (Staroměstské náměstí) is the very heart of the city. It also contains some of the finest examples of Prague's artistic riches; indeed, no other part of the city can boast such an extraordinary collection of architectural styles and periods. The square offers an amazing juxtaposition of different schools, mixing Gothic porches with Renaissance sgraffito, and Baroque pediments with classical monumental windows and Art Nouveau décor.

2

Town Hall Clocktower

This clock, built in 1410 by Mikuláš of Kadaň and renovated in the 16th century, has two faces. Above is the astronomical face whose operation is controlled by scientific theories of the 15th century, so that the Earth is in the middle and the planets circle round it. The face below, containing a calendar of months and signs of the zodiac, was painted by Josef Mánes in the 19th century; the original hangs in Prague City Museum. The calendar moves forward one day at midnight and completes a revolution once a year. When the hour strikes a mechanism above both of the faces is activated. First, Christ and the Apostles emerge one by one; then, when they have disappeared, the skeleton of Death inverts the hourglass. Finally, the cock flaps its wings and crows.

"Death pulled the cord, and rang by nodding its head. Other small statues stirred while the cock flapped its wings, and the twelve Apostles glanced impassively down at the street through the open window."

Guillaume
Apollinaire

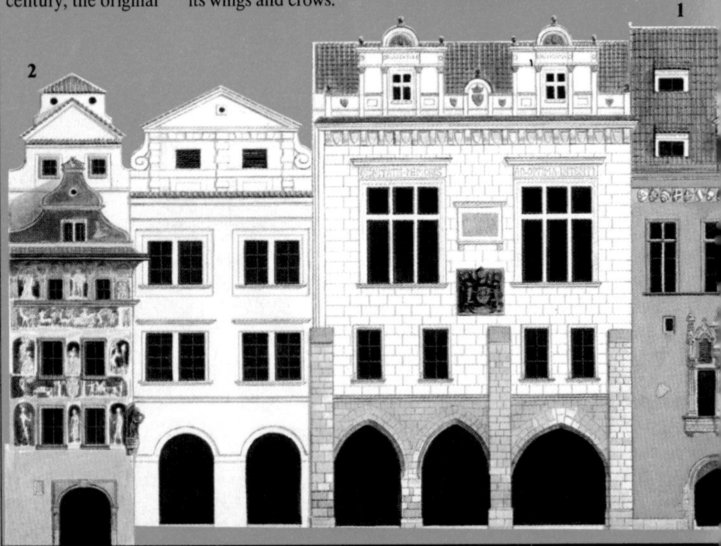

1

2

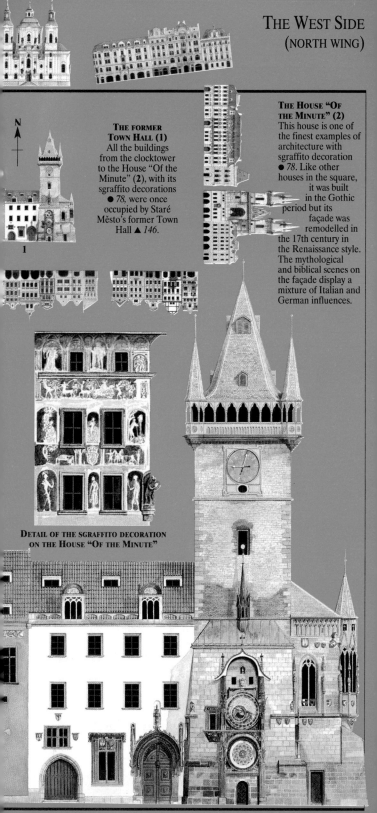

N

THE FORMER TOWN HALL (1)
All the buildings from the clocktower to the House "Of the Minute" (2), with its sgraffito decorations ● *78*, were once occupied by Staré Město's former Town Hall ▲ *146*.

1

THE HOUSE "OF THE MINUTE" (2)
This house is one of the finest examples of architecture with sgraffito decoration ● *78*. Like other houses in the square, it was built in the Gothic period but its façade was remodelled in the 17th century in the Renaissance style. The mythological and biblical scenes on the façade display a mixture of Italian and German influences.

**DETAIL OF THE SGRAFFITO DECORATION
ON THE HOUSE "OF THE MINUTE"**

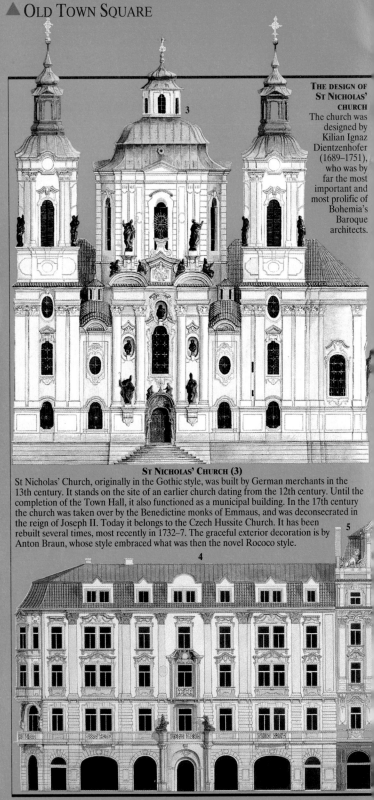

THE DESIGN OF ST NICHOLAS' CHURCH
The church was designed by Kilian Ignaz Dientzenhofer (1689–1751), who was by far the most important and most prolific of Bohemia's Baroque architects.

ST NICHOLAS' CHURCH (3)

St Nicholas' Church, originally in the Gothic style, was built by German merchants in the 13th century. It stands on the site of an earlier church dating from the 12th century. Until the completion of the Town Hall, it also functioned as a municipal building. In the 17th century the church was taken over by the Benedictine monks of Emmaus, and was deconsecrated in the reign of Joseph II. Today it belongs to the Czech Hussite Church. It has been rebuilt several times, most recently in 1732–7. The graceful exterior decoration is by Anton Braun, whose style embraced what was then the novel Rococo style.

Until the end of World War Two the elegant façade St Nicholas' was obscured by the Krenn House.

3. St Nicholas' Church (1732–7)
4. House at 934 Old Town Square
5 and **6.** Ministry of Internal Trade, 932 Old Town Square, built by the architect O. Polivka in 1900.
7. Former Pauline convent, 930, Old Town Square, built by the architect Giovanni Domenico Canevale in 1684.

THE INTERIOR OF ST NICHOLAS' CHURCH:
MAGNIFICENT SCULPTURES

St Nicholas' may well have the most beautiful church interior in Prague. It is impressively sculpted with architectural elements including tribunes, balconies, uneven cornices, arches, and curvilinear broken pediments set with scrolls. Such extraordinary complexity of design is quite unique. The high point of the decoration is Pater Asam's cupola fresco depicting the Life of Saint Nicholas and scenes from the Old Testament, notably *Joseph and Potiphar's Wife*. Asam's fresco in the small cupola in the choir recounts the Legend of Saint Benedict.

THE NORTH SIDE OF THE SQUARE

This part was substantially altered at the end of the 19th century when the Jewish quarter was pulled down. The neo-Baroque building on the left (**4**) has a fine door framed by columns surmounted by statues. The two central buildings in the neo-Baroque style (**5, 6**), occupying the site of three houses, are used by the Ministry of Internal Trade. They were built between 1898 and 1900 and their façades are not uniform. The former Pauline convent on the right (**7**) has Gothic foundations, the present Baroque construction dating from the late 17th century; it is linked to the Church of St Savior by a passageway.

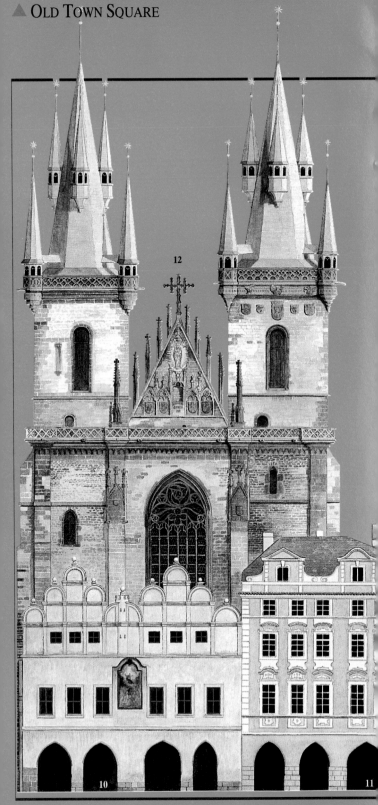

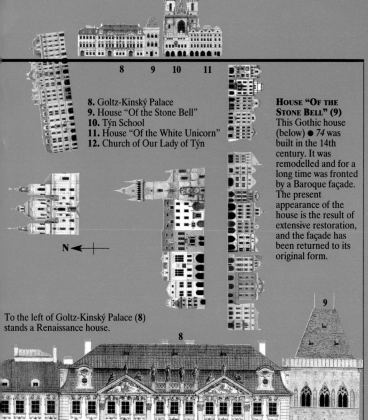

12

8   9   10   11

8. Goltz-Kinský Palace
9. House "Of the Stone Bell"
10. Týn School
11. House "Of the White Unicorn"
12. Church of Our Lady of Týn

HOUSE "OF THE STONE BELL" (9)

This Gothic house (below) ● *74* was built in the 14th century. It was remodelled and for a long time was fronted by a Baroque façade. The present appearance of the house is the result of extensive restoration, and the façade has been returned to its original form.

N ←—

To the left of Goltz-Kinský Palace (**8**) stands a Renaissance house.

8

9

GOLTZ-KINSKÝ PALACE (8)

The Rococo palace was built in 1755–65 by Anselmo Lurago for Count Goltz. It stands on the site of several Romanesque houses, some of whose cellars survive. The palace projects from the alignment of buildings on this side of the square, so that its monumentality is enhanced. It has a double-fronted façade and the arrangement of pediments, pilasters and doorways flanked by columns simultaneously emphasize the building's vertical axis and preserve the uniformity of the narrow façades that line the square.

TÝN CHURCH AND SCHOOL (12 AND 10)

Týn Church is the most important religious building in Prague after St Vitus' Cathedral. During the 10th century a church was built in the Týn courtyard ▲ *160*; it belonged to the foreign merchants' hospice. A new church in the early Gothic style was built in 1270 but was rebuilt from 1380. The roof was not completed until 1457 and the north gable only added in the reign of George of Poděbrady (1458–71). In front of the church stand Týn School (**10**), dating from the 14th and 16th centuries, and the House "Of the White Unicorn" (**11**), which was built in the 18th century.

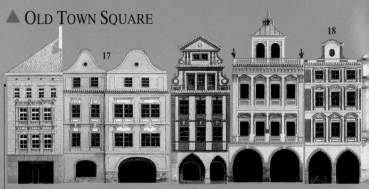

THE SOUTHWEST SIDE OF THE SQUARE

On this side of the square almost all the vaulted Romanesque cellars and Gothic doorways, vestiges of successive phases of rebuilding around the square ● *74*, survive. The façades, several times remodelled according to the style of the period, date mostly from the late 17th century. Although the Baroque style predominates, many Gothic and Renaissance details can be identified, as in Stepan House, with a Gothic doorway and Renaissance gables (**19**), and the former Servite convent (**20**), which has an early 17th-century Renaissance doorway.

THE SOUTHEAST SIDE OF THE SQUARE

Štorch House (**13**) was built in the neo-Renaissance style in the late 19th century on the site of a Gothic house. The architect Bedřich Ohmann decorated the façade with a representation of Saint Wenceslas on horseback. The

House "Of the Stone Sheep" (**14**) has an entrance dating back to 1520. The House "Of the Stone Table" (**15**) was built in the 14th century, although the façade was later remodelled in the Baroque style. The next building, which houses a

tavern, has well-preserved Romanesque foundations, although the façade was rebuilt in the neoclassical manner. The House "Of the Golden Unicorn" (**16**), which stands on the corner of Železná Street, has a 12th-century

Romanesque basement. It was converted into a tower house in the 14th century and was rebuilt in the Late Gothic style in the 15th century. Finally, Late Baroque alterations were added to the façade in the 18th century.

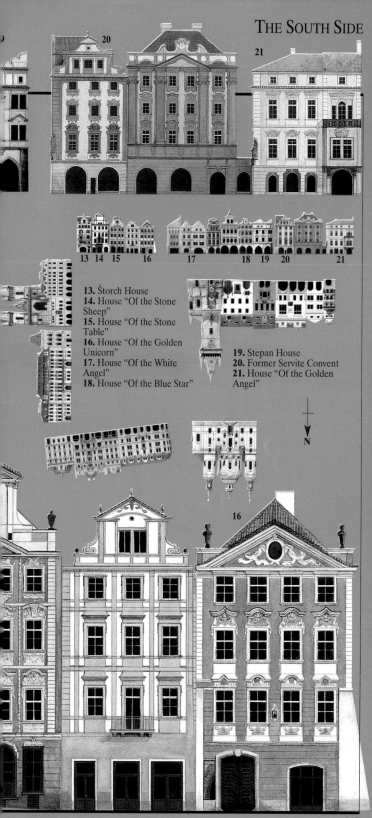

13. Štorch House
14. House "Of the Stone Sheep"
15. House "Of the Stone Table"
16. House "Of the Golden Unicorn"
17. House "Of the White Angel"
18. House "Of the Blue Star"
19. Stepan House
20. Former Servite Convent
21. House "Of the Golden Angel"

N

**MONUMENT TO
JOHN HUSS**
This statue by
Ladislav Šaloun
(1870–1946) ▲ *165,
176* was unveiled in
1915 to
commemorate the
quincentenary of the
death of John Huss
● *32*, by then a major
symbol of Czech
national identity. The
proximity of the
Marian Column ● *35*,
which recalls the
defeat of the
Habsburgs (it was
pulled down in 1918),
encouraged Šaloun to
use more horizontal
space so as to strike a
contrast with the
Column's height. The
power of the statue,
which owes much to
Rodin, shows the
great preacher
standing surrounded
by the fighters of
God, the Exiles and a
mother and child
expressing a wish for
national renewal.

OLD TOWN'S FORMER TOWN HALL

AN ANCIENT BUILDING. The heterogeneous complex of
buildings that now make up the Former Town Hall
accumulated only gradually. In 1338, the municipality
purchased WOLFLIN HOUSE on the corner, adding a belfry in
1364 and an oriel chapel by Petr Parléř in 1381. The Gothic
door, which is the main entrance, dates from the era of
Vladislav II Jagiello, as does the window in the vestibule,
while the surround of carved figures and floral decoration are
fine examples of the genius of the stonemason Matěj Rejsek
▲ *167*. Over the years, various houses have been added,
including KŘIŽ HOUSE with its lovely Renaissance window
(1520) and Baroque railing (1731) decorated with the
inscription *Praga caput regni*. The coats of arms are those of
municipal councillors of the second half of the 15th
century, except for the one in the middle which is
that of the town itself. COCK HOUSE,
connected to MIKEŠ HOUSE by a series of
broken arches, was integrated into
the Town Hall in 1835. The
HOUSE "OF THE MINUTE", with
its early 17th-century
sgraffito, was the last to be
added, in 1896, and the
Kafka family lived
there. Later, the main
development was to
the north wing,
when offices were
added. These were
destroyed during
World War Two
▲ *137*. The early
15th-century
astronomical clock
(left) dominates
the façade. Parts of
the building open to
the public include
the vestibule,
decorated with a
mosaic representing
Princess Libussa, the Old

"John Huss' long shadow stood out fleetingly
against the front of his bronze stake."

Sylvie Germain

Council Chamber (1470) and the meeting room, which was restored in 1879. The buildings left standing at the end of the war were not big enough to accommodate the various administrative services, which were transferred to another building ▲ 149. The Town Hall has been listed as a historic building and is now used for official receptions and exhibitions; the marriage parlor has not been removed.

CHURCH OF OUR LADY OF TÝN ▲ 145

After St Vitus' Cathedral, Týn Church (Týnský chrám) is the most important place of worship in Prague. There is evidence of there having been a church on this site since 1135, when it formed part of a hospice constructed by foreign merchants in Týn Courtyard ▲ 160. A new Early Gothic church was built here in 1220, but it was replaced in the 1380's; the roof was not completed until 1457 and the north pediment not added until the reign of George of Poděbrady (1458–71).

A MUSICAL VENUE
Týn Church had the finest organ in Prague in the 17th century; it was made by H. Mandl of Cologne. Josef Ferdinand Norbert (1716–82) was the church's most notable musical

A REFORMERS' CHURCH. The Church of Our Lady of Týn had links with the Hussite Movement, and early Reformers including Konrad Waldhauser, Jan Milíč of Kroměříž ● 26 and Matthew of Janov frequently preached here. Its successor continued the tradition and became the Utraquists' main church. Jan Rokycana, the only Hussite archbishop, was a priest here, and here the Utraquist King George of Poděbrady attended the first mass of his reign.

figure. His reputation as a contrapuntist was such that Joseph II asked him to be organist to the Royal Chapel in Vienna, but confirmation of his appointment arrived the day after he died. The funeral of Bedřich Smetana took place here on May 15, 1884.

BAROQUE RENOVATION. As Catholicism regained the ascendancy after 1626, the chalice which had adorned the pediment was removed and most of the early decoration destroyed. Baroque style was on the march. The finest elements of the new décor included the altars, many of them adorned with paintings by Karel Škréta (1610–74) ▲ 167, 220, the greatest Baroque painter in Bohemia; the high altar with an Assumption and a Holy Trinity; and the altars of Saint Barbara, Saint Joseph and Saint Adalbert. In the main nave, level with the third pillar on the right, is a fine altar of St John the Baptist (c. 1520). In contrast with the custom of the time, the reliefs were not painted, color being subtly suggested by the use of different materials. The artist has identified himself only with the monogram "IP". A fine canopy by Matěj Rejsek (1493) near the fourth pillar on the left decorates the tomb of the Hussite Bishop Augustine of Mirandola, and the tombstone of the astronomer Tycho Brahe is to be found on the fifth pillar

A MAJESTIC MADONNA
This wooden Madonna dating from 1420 is one of the many statues in the church.

ROTT HOUSE
The house was commissioned by the Rott steel company, and the façade is covered with representations of the various tools made in its factories; other motifs include allegories of skilled

artisans and agriculture. The decoration was executed after cartoons by Mikoláš Aleš.

Pharmacies have concentrated in Malé náměstí since the 14th century. The pharmacy on the corner of Karlova Square and Karlova Street is the best known in the city.

on the right. The oldest baptismal fonts in Prague (1414) are at the bottom of the south nave; the covers were not made until the 19th century. A curiosity of the church is a window in the south wall over the right-hand aisle and level with the third chapel. Our Lady of Týn is next door to a house in Celetná Street that was inhabited by a bigoted woman who insisted on the window being built. The Kafka family also lived here for a time.

AROUND MALÉ NÁMĚSTI (LITTLE SQUARE)

The HOUSE "OF THE TWO GOLDEN BEARS" (U dvou zlatých medvědů), a short walk from Old Town Square in Kožná Street, has one of the most beautiful Renaissance doors in Prague ● 76.
ROTT HOUSE ★. The center of the square is marked by a well dating from 1560, and decorated with a Renaissance railing surmounted in the 17th century by a gilt Lion of Bohemia. The House "At the sign of the Three White Roses" (or Rott House) at no. 3 has some remarkable Romanesque remains. In the 15th century, it belonged to a printer named Jan Pytlích who, with financial assistance from members of the Utraquist bourgeoisie in Old Town, published the first Bible in Czech in 1488. The house was then rebuilt in the Renaissance style and decorated with sgraffito ● 89 but, when it was restored in 1890, it was decorated in the neo-Renaissance manner ● 84. Today it houses a shop selling jewelry and cut glass. Visitors can look inside, admiring the interior, which dates from 1922–3, and the glass dome that covers the old interior courtyard.

KARLOVA ULICE. Karlova Street starts off at Jilská Street and ends at Cross and Red Star Square (Křížovnické náměstí), forming a direct link between Charles Bridge and Old Town Square via Small Square (Malé náměstí). It consists of three sections which protrude slightly one in front of the other. The street used to be part of the "Royal Route" or "Coronation Route" followed by the Kings of Bohemia when they were to be crowned at St Vitus' Cathedral. They went from Powder Tower to the Castle via Celetná Street, Old Town Square, Karlova Street, Charles Bridge, Mostecká Street, Malá Strana Square and, lastly, Nerudova Street. Many of the Gothic houses, including nos. 175/3, 156, 147, 452 and 451 which were renovated in the Baroque style, have preserved their Romanesque basements. Karlova ulice runs alongside the Clementinum, providing one of the many means of access to this building, and borders directly on the Italian Chapel and St Clement's Church. During the 16th and 17th centuries, it was known as Jesuit Street (Jezovitská ulice). One of the

most beautiful Renaissance houses is at no. 175/3: the House "OF THE GOLDEN WELL" (U zlaté studně) was renovated in the 17th century and further decorated in 1714, as the last plague to ravage Bohemia and Austria was finally dying out. The decoration consisted of stucco figures representing the two intercessors, Saint Roch and Saint Sebastian, the Virgin, and the country's two patron saints, Saint Wenceslas and Saint John Nepomuk. The first café in Prague ● 58 was opened in 1714 at no. 181/18, the House "Of the Golden Snake" (U zlatého hada), whose interior has only recently been renovated. From 1607 to 1612, Kepler lived at no. 188/4, a Renaissance building known as the House "Of the Crown of France", it was here that he wrote *The New Astronomy*, setting out the laws that bear his name.

CLAM-GALLAS PALACE. Clam-Gallas Palace is at 20 Husova Street on the corner of Marianské náměstí and Karlova Street. It is one of the most important buildings that the Viennese architect Johann Bernhard Fischer von Erlach produced for Prague; he designed it around 1700 for the Emperor's Ambassador Count Jan Václav Gallas, and it was built between 1713 and 1729 by Giovanni Domenico Canevale and Tomáš Haffenecker. The irregular groundplan is that of a building with several wings encircling two courtyards. The interior staircase is one of the most beautiful in the city, and Santin Bossi executed the stucco decoration in the hall. Since 1945, this palace has housed the city archives.

OLD TOWN'S NEW TOWN HALL. After passing the splendid Clam-Gallas Palace, enter Marianské Square with the Clementinum on the left, the Municipal Library (František Roith, 1924–8)

SCULPTURE AT CLAM-GALLAS PALACE
The atlantes flanking the entrance (1714) (below) and the sculpture decorating the pediment are the work of M. B. Braun ▲ *220, 224, 244, 276.* Three copies of the sixteen originals, Jupiter, Mercury and Venus, are there; the others are on display in the Lapidarium in the National Gallery ▲ *227.* The interior staircase is one of the most beautiful in Prague.

Layout of the Clementinum. Below: Karlova Street with the towers of the Italian Chapel and the entrance to St Clement's.

opposite and on the right, Old Town's new Town Hall built by Karel Osvald Polívka ▲ *176* between 1905 and 1912. It comprises a subtle blend of neo-Baroque and Secessionist elements ● *84, 86*. The decoration on the façade was the work of three of the greatest sculptors of the age: Stanislav Sucharda did the reliefs around the entrance and the two allegories on the right-hand cornice ('Bookkeeping' and 'Management Control'); Ladislas Šaloun sculpted the splendid Rabbi Löw ▲ *186* on the right and the Iron Knight, a character from ancient Prague legends, on the left; and Josef Mařatka ▲ *165* carved the groups on the balcony and the left-hand cornice.

THE CLEMENTINUM ★

The Jesuit Clementinum is an enormous complex built over the course of more than a century, between the end of the 16th century and 1726. It stands on the site not only of a former Dominican Monastery given to the Jesuits when they arrived in Prague in 1556, but also of three churches and over thirty houses. It has three entrances: two are main entrances, one of them giving onto Křížovnické náměstí and the other Marianské náměstí, and there is also a less important entrance in the very long wall that lines Karlova Street. The Jesuits entrusted the task of building their first college in Prague to Francesco Caratti. Today, it is the site of the National Library. The Clementinum Library has more than 4½ million works, of which 6,000 are manuscripts and 3,000 are incunabulae.

A room in the Clementinum Library.

REINFORCEMENTS. The Jesuits arrived in Prague in 1556, on the invitation of Ferdinand I of Habsburg, who wished to re-establish Bohemian Catholicism and minimize the influence of the University. The same year, they founded a school for the gentry to which Ferdinand sent his pages and his son, Prince Ernest of Bavaria-Munich. A Jesuit education suddenly became fashionable among the Czech aristocracy, but it was also a strategy for achieving a Catholic re-conquest. The Jesuits were soon granted the right to award doctorates, and this enabled them to compete with Charles University, which was Utraquist and therefore non-Catholic.

AN ARCHITECTURAL TREASURE SECOND ONLY TO THE CASTLE. The building consisted of four central wings organized around four interior courtyards with an observation tower where they intersected. In the first courtyard, there is a statue of a *Student* by Josef Max, erected in memory of the Prague students who, with the Jesuit Ferus, defended Old Town against the Swedes in 1648. **Libraries.** At the far end of this first courtyard is the former Jesuit College, now the National Library. In 1773, following the abolition of the Society of Jesus, the buildings were handed over to the Observatory and the Academy of Fine Arts and then, from 1800 onward, to Charles University. In 1924, the buildings began to be converted to house the National Library; these premises are also occupied by the University Library and Slav Library. Many of the rooms have preserved their Baroque magnificence: on the second floor, the vault of the former College Library, known as the "Baroque Hall", is decorated with frescos representing the arts and sciences, and in the center there is a remarkable trompe l'oeil by Johann Hiebl (1727); the Mozart Room in the wing that overlooks Platnéřská Street boasts elaborate Rococo ornamentation; the summer refectory is now a lecture room, and is adorned with paintings by Krištof Tausch dated 1710; the second courtyard has a Baroque fountain, and the Observatory tower, built in 1721, was renovated by Anselmo Lurago in 1778 and is surmounted by a statue of Atlas. The astronomer Joseph Stepling founded the Observatory in 1751, and the monument erected in his honor by Ignác Platzer stands in the third courtyard.

Ripellino describes the Clementinum as "[an] ill-tempered fortress, a protruding, provocative, haughty bastion, a mirror of supremacy and hard-line indoctrination."

Chapel of Mirrors
The Chapel of the Annunciation, also known as the Chapel of Mirrors owing to its stucco decoration incorporating mirrors, is in the third courtyard. It was built by František Maximilián Kaňka, who was also responsible for the Library. The Chapel is now used for concerts.

CROSS AND RED STAR SQUARE

The square (Křížovnické náměstí) takes its name from the convent of the Order that settled here. The building was raised to its current level only in the 16th century, and it did not acquire its present appearance until the 17th century. Although of only modest proportions, it is remarkable for its architectural unity. In the center of the square stands a statue of Charles IV erected by the University to commemorate the 500th anniversary of its foundation.

CHURCHES IN THE CLEMENTINUM

The Clementinum has three churches: St Clement's (Kostel sv. Kliment) and the Italian Chapel (Vlašská kaple), both accessible from Karlova Street through a Baroque portico executed by František M. Kaňka in 1715, and St Savior's (Kostel sv. Salvátora) which opens onto Cross and Red Star Square and Charles Bridge.

ST CLEMENT'S ★. St Clement's belonged to the Dominicans before it was handed over to the Jesuits when they first came to Prague, and the Clementinum took its name from this church. As it met neither the artistic criteria of the period nor the needs of the Jesuits, it was rebuilt between 1711 and 1715, probably by Kaňka to plans by Kilián Ignác Dientzenhofer. The sense of monumentality derives from the bays crowned by cupolas, and resembling huge canopies. The decoration includes pillars adorned with paintings of the saints by Ignác Raab ▲ *241*, and niches containing statues of the Four Evangelists and Fathers of the Church by Matthias Bernhard Braun (1684–1738). The statuary comes in the main from the workshop of Braun and his six companions which, in 1725, was the greatest in the city. Braun was also responsible for the sculptures of Saint Louis of Gonzaga, St Stanislas Kostka on the ALTAR OF THE CIRCUMCISION, the Prodigal Son and the group depicting the Plague. The high altar was painted in trompe l'oeil by Josef Kramolin, and the ceiling fresco recounting the life of Saint Clement is by Johann Hiebl. The building now belongs to the Greek Orthodox Church.

THE ITALIAN CHAPEL. This atypical building is sometimes known as the Italian Chapel of the Assumption of the Virgin Mary. It was built between 1590 and 1597 for the first Italians to settle in Prague, and has an oval groundplan, a

rarity in Bohemia. The designer was probably Ottavio Mascherino, a builder in the employ of the Pope.

St Savior's. This, the oldest of the three churches, has three Renaissance naves and dates from the years 1578–1601. It was restyled in the Baroque manner between 1638 and 1659 by the addition of a huge octagonal cupola by Carlo Lurago and Francesco Caratti, and acquired its present appearance in 1714 when František M. Kaňka added two towers. The church has fifty-five windows, the façade is decorated with fifteen statues by Jan Jiří Bendl and his workshop, and the beautiful and elaborate decoration in the interior includes stuccowork by Domenico Galli and Bendl. Bendl was also responsible for the wooden statues of the twelve Apostles that adorn the confessionals, and which are among the finest works of the period. The ceiling has a fresco by Kovář entitled *The Four Corners of the World* (1748), and the painting on the high altar is *The Transfiguration of Christ* by Hering.

CHURCH OF ST FRANCIS SERAPHIM

This belongs to the Monastery of the Brothers of the Cross, a Czech hospital Order founded in the 12th century by Agnes of Bohemia. Brunn's façade of the monastery overlooking the river (1850), to the left of the church, is classical; it gives onto Platnéřská Street, which is in the Art Nouveau style and was decorated by Josef Šakař ▲ *194* between 1910 and 1912. The church is the work of J.-B. Mathey (c. 1630– c. 1695) ▲ *141, 231, 272, 318* and is now used for concerts.

A MAGNIFICENT CUPOLA
The Brothers of the Cross were overawed by the overwhelming proximity of the Clementinum and, when they commissioned Mathey to build the Church of St Francis Seraphim, they asked him to rectify the imbalance. Accordingly, he designed a building on an oval, compact ground plan with a conspicuous cupola. This restrained structure is supported by giant pilasters which easily embrace the five horizontal registers, and even the concave corners cause the cupola to protrude even further through a compression of space. The interior, with its pilasters made of purple Slivenec marble, is superbly balanced. The cupola fresco of *The Last Judgement* by Reiner is quite remarkable for the twisting bodies which give a vivid impression of floating in space. The other paintings are by Michael Lukáš Willmann (including the one over the high altar) and Jan Kryštof Liška ▲ *241*.

Statue of Saint Francis Seraphim on Charles Bridge.

▲ FROM OLD TOWN SQUARE TO CHARLES BRIDGE

CHARLES BRIDGE ★

Charles Bridge has been a major thoroughfare ever since it was first built in the 14th century; until the 19th century, it was the only bridge across the Vltava, and is today a scene of constant animation. At night, the gaps between the street lamps create shadowy areas that encourage all manner of mysteries, mirages and surprises. When there is a mist, the whole place becomes magic or terrifying, according to one's temperament.

CHARLES BRIDGE AND ITS STATUES ✪
Supported by sturdy pilasters and protected by wooden ice-breakers, Charles Bridge gives an impression utter immobility. It is decorated with statues of richly garbed figures commemorating the triumph of the Counter-Reformation and it majestically links the banks of the Vltava. The statues are uncannily lifelike; according to legend, they engage in learned theological debates at midnight. The citizens of Prague will tell you that anyone who touches the statue of Saint John Nepomuk will have their wish fulfilled.

JUDITH BRIDGE. Prague's oldest bridge was made of wood and lay parallel to modern Charles Bridge. It is mentioned as far back as 1118. After it was destroyed by a flood in 1157, Vladislav I had a stone bridge built, which he named after his wife, Judith of Thuringia. It was completed some thirteen years later. At the time, it was the oldest stone bridge in central Europe after the bridge at Regensburg. It was destroyed again by floods in 1357.

CONSTRUCTION OF CHARLES BRIDGE. When Petr Parléř accepted Charles IV's commission to build Charles Bridge in 1357, he was only twenty-seven years old; work was not completed until 1402. It was known as the "Stone Bridge", and only took Charles' name in 1870. Charles Bridge was built with blocks of sandstone; it is 1,700 feet long and 30 feet wide, and rests on sixteen pillars. It was longer, wider and – above all – higher than Judith Bridge, and has survived numerous floods. Since being renovated in 1974, it has been restricted to pedestrians.

THE ROW OF SCULPTURES. The row of statues in front of the Jesuit College of Kutná Hora is reminiscent of the Ponte degli

The tower on the edge of the Old Town, guarding Charles Bridge.

154

> "Charles Bridge is disastrous to God's chosen ones."
>
> Roger Grenier

Angeli in Rome. The statues were brought together over a period of time. In the 17th century, the collection was limited to the Crucifix, Saint John Nepomuk, a Pietà and a Saint Wenceslas, the remaining statues dating from the first half of the 18th century, the high point of the Counter-Reformation; the most recent works were executed in the 19th century.

Many of the sculptures displayed today are copies of copies made in the 20th century.

CALVARY. The first Calvary adorned the bridge from its earliest days, but it disappeared at the time of the Hussite troubles. The present cross on the third pier is the fifth to be made, having been cast in Dresden in 1627–8. An inscription in Hebrew recalls a case of desecration in 1695 in which a Jew is alleged to have registered his contempt for the Calvary while he passed by; he was then ordered to pay for the gold-plated Hebrew inscription which reads "Holy, Holy, Holy God". The punishment is written below in German, Czech and Latin.

ST JOHN NEPOMUK. This bronze statue was the first statue to be placed on the bridge on the central pier on the north side. It was made in 1683 by Jan Brokoff, thirty-eight years before the saint was beatified ▲ *233*, but it lacks force and is of little stylistic worth. The bronzes on the pedestal recall scenes that are said to have happened during his life: the Queen's confession, and the moment when his body was thrown into the river. The second of these contains an allusion to the Massacre of the Innocents, with a soldier ill-treating a mother and her child.

THE TOWER ON CHARLES BRIDGE. For military reasons, Charles IV charged Petr Parléř with building a strong tower 130 feet high that closed the bridge off on the Staré Město side. By the early 15th century, it was already considered to be one of the most beautiful gates in

THE LEGEND OF THE BUILDING
Inevitably, Charles Bridge is surrounded by numerous legends. According to one, the masons were instructed to add egg yolk to their mortar so that the bridge was secure and, to make sure that there would be enough, carts loaded with eggs started to arrive in Prague from all the towns of Bohemia. Fearing that their eggs might break on the way, the inhabitants of Velvary sent hard-boiled eggs. The town was a

laughing-stock for years to come.

View of Charles Bridge crossing the Vltava and Kampa Island, and rejoining Staré Město at Malá Strana.

Europe, and Viollet-le-Duc referred to this Gothic masterpiece on a visit to Prague. The tower had carved decorations added by the workshop of Petr Parléř at the beginning of the 15th century. The west face was badly damaged by Swedish cannon in 1648, but the east face is still adorned with strikingly realistic figures of Charles IV (on the left) and Wenceslas IV brought from St Vitus' Cathedral.

THE TOWERS ON MALÁ STRANA BRIDGE. It was probably intended that there should be a similar tower on the left bank, but Wenceslas IV's indecisiveness, and the start of the Hussite Wars ● *32*, delayed the project. The complex consists of a Gothic gate (1410) and two towers, the smaller of which is the oldest as it formed part of the fortifications of Judith Bridge. The bigger of the two towers was built in the reign of George of Poděbrady in 1464, and imitates Parléř's masterpiece without the decoration.

SMETANA MUSEUM

NATIONAL OPERAS

After achieving some success with his opera *The Brandenburgers in Bohemia*, *The Bartered Bride* brought Smetana huge popularity. He then wrote *Dalibor* in 1868, a tragic opera recalling the struggles for national independence. But his style, considered to be too Wagnerian, attracted criticism and, by way of reply, he composed *Libuše* (1872), a glorification of the Czech nation. Smetana's writing was steeped in the folklore of Bohemia, and he devoted his genius to the six symphonic poems that made up *Má vlast*. His interest in chamber music is less well known but his compositions in this field no less remarkable.

Since 1936 the Bedřich Smetana Museum has been housed in a neo-Renaissance building of 1885 (below, left) on Novotný Lane (Novotného lávka), close to the end of the bridge. The exterior decoration ● *78* depicts battles against the Swedes that took place on Charles Bridge in 1648. The objects in the museum's collection are mostly the great musician's belongings. Bedřich Smetana (1824–84) ● *47, 50*, ▲ *195, 296* is a national figure and Bohemia's most representative composer. The whole country holds him in exceptionally high esteem, and every Prague Spring Festival opens with a performance of his *Má vlast* (*My Country*). Not only was he a composer of genius, he was also very active in the National Awakening after 1848 ▲ *296* and, in 1849, with the help of Liszt and Clara Schumann, founded a private music school where the use of Czech was compulsory. This was one of his methods of indicating his opposition to the official teaching of German. He also fought in an armed group called the "Concord", and there met Karel Sabina who was to be the librettist of his first two operas.

BALUSTRADE THEATER

The Theater "on the Balustrade" (Divadlo na Zábradlí) ● *55*, one of the most famous in Prague, is tucked away in discreet Anenské Square. Since it opened in 1958, the Theater has put on lively, unusual works, and Václav Havel worked there as a technician before becoming a prolific and talented playwright. The other great name in the theater's history is the mime artist Ladislav Fialka, a pupil of Marcel Marceau.

Around
Wenceslas Square

1. STAROMĚSTSKÉ SQUARE
2. CHURCH OF OUR LADY OF TÝN
3. TÝN COURTYARD
4. ST JAMES' CHURCH
5. BLACK VIRGIN HOUSE
6. CELETNÁ STREET
7. HOTEL PAŘÍŽ

☑ **Half a day**

◆ **B** C4-C5-D4-D5-D6-E5-E6

Celetná Street is pedestrianized and is one of the most popular streets in Prague. Mary Wortley Montague, who was staying there around 1715, complained of the lack of privacy, the overcrowding and the uncomfortable surroundings of the aristocratic houses.

CELETNÁ STREET

Celetná Street, one of the most important roads in the Old Town, leads out of Old Town Square toward Powder Tower. Like Karlova Street, it once formed part of a route taken by the Kings of Bohemia on their way to their coronations at St Vitus' Cathedral, and has been a major commercial thoroughfare since Roman times. The Gothic and Renaissance buildings that line Celetná Street are hidden behind façades dating from the Baroque period; some of them have preserved elements from earlier periods and offer lovers of architecture curious examples of stylistic superimposition. At basement level, many of the houses have retained vestiges of Roman times: the most interesting are the cellars at nos. 558–I/12, 53–I/12 and 603–I/12. Other houses incorporate passageways ● 82 linking them with Štupartská Street on one side and Kamziková Street and Ovocný Street on the other. At one end of Celetná Street is Sixt House ● 80, named after Jan Sixt of Ottersdof, a celebrated Old Town Chancellor who bought it in 1567. His son, Jan Theodor, a leader of the 1618 revolt ● 34, was one of the twenty-seven condemned to death in 1621. He was granted a pardon on the scaffold, but did not undergo religious conversion, and emigrated to Dresden in 1626. His house was then seized, and subsequently bought by the third person to be thrown out of the Hradčany window on May 23, 1618: the Aulic secretary, Filip Fabricius, thereafter known as "Long Drop". Since 1991, the premises have been occupied by a pleasant café named after

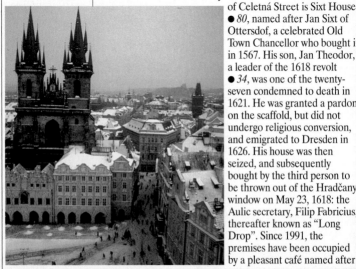

Egon Erwin Kisch, and by the "Sixt" restaurant in the basement. The building was restored in 1725; it contains a barrel-vaulted Romanesque room and Gothic elements in the courtyard.

HOUSE OF THE THREE KINGS. Opposite Sixt House is the House of the Three Kings (U tří králů), a building that has retained a number of Gothic elements including vaults, gables and framework. It was once inhabited by the Kafka family ● *110*, and it is likely that Franz occupied the room that overlooks the interior of Týn Church. Hrzán Palace (1702) at no. 12 is one of the most beautiful buildings in the whole street, and is the work of Giovanni Battista Alliprandi who was also responsible for Lobkowicz Palace ▲ *243* in Malá Strana (Lesser Town).

ARISTOCRATIC HOMES. In the 19th century, the former Caretto Millesimo Palace at no. 597/13 was a casino patronized by the Prague nobility. Although it was built in 1750 for Count Cavriani, whose coat of arms still adorns the main entrance, this house still boasts Gothic brick gables which are visible from the inner courtyard, and a Romanesque doorway. Buquoy House at no. 562/20 combines a Baroque façade, and a Mannerist doorway whose wreathed columns recall Ammannati's Florentine work. At no. 595/17 stands Menhart House which was rebuilt at the beginning of the 18th century; its outstandingly beautiful inner courtyard contains a wooden statue of Hercules and a Baroque statue of a saint. The building's superb vaulted chambers now house a fine

"Prague seemed . . . not only one of the most beautiful places in the world, but one of the strangest. Fear, piety, zeal, strife and pride, tempered in the end by the milder impulses of munificence and learning and *douceur de vivre*, had flung up an unusual array of grand and unenigmatic monuments. The city, however, was scattered with darker, more reticent, less easily decipherable clues. There were moments when every detail seemed the tip of a phalanx of inexplicable phantoms."
Patrick Leigh Fermor,
A Time for Gifts

Celetná Street derives its name from *calta* (from the German *Zelten*), a 14th-century plaited bun or flat cake made by the street's many bakers.

BERNHARD BOLZANO (1781–1848)
This philosopher, a disciple of Leibnitz, died at no. 25 Celetná Street. Bolzano supported the idea of a Czech nation in which Czechs and Germans lived side by side, and was accordingly dismissed from his professorship at the Carolinum ▲ 278 in 1819.

In the early 20th century, Celetná Street was lined with a large number of very fashionable shops.

Black Virgin House houses the Czech Museum of Cubism ● 106.

restaurant, the "U Pavouka" (At the sign of the Spider).
MORE MODERN COMPETITION.
A later addition to Celetná Street was Friedrich Ohmann's *U české orlice* (1897) at no. 567/30. This neo-Renaissance house has gables in the "Venetian" style and, on the other side overlooking Ovocný trh, a splendid oriel window. The polychrome sgraffito ● 78 is the work of Alois Drýak, who also designed the Evropa Hotel ▲ 174. This house is an excellent example of the "eclectic" or "historicist" style. More avant-garde is the newly renovated BLACK VIRGIN HOUSE on the corner of Celetná Street and Ovocný trh. Built by Josef Gočár in 1911–12, the façade is in the Cubist style. Since 1994, this extraordinary building has housed the Museum of Cubism along with collections of decorative art paintings and architectural projects. The polyhedral profiles of the dormer windows, the cut-off sections of glass and the form of the pillars at the main entrance are wholly Cubist in style. The house at no. 589/29, U Templu (In the temple), is what remains of restoration work carried out in 1801 when a small Baroque church and a hospice adjoining the façade were removed. Opposite is the front of the former Pachta Palace (1759), which includes a balcony with telamones and terms by Ignác Platzer. This building housed the mint from the 15th to late 18th centuries.

TÝN COURTYARD (UNGELT)

The entrance is in Malá Štupartská almost opposite St James' Church. From the 11th century, the courtyard was a shelter for foreign merchants to unload their carts and pay their taxes. It was also used as a warehouse, market and city toll until the 18th century. The original plan has been preserved. Most buildings around the Týn courtyard have now been restored: the most remarkable is Granovský House, built in 1560 on the model of an Italian Renaissance palazzo with an open loggia on the second floor. Chiaroscuro frescos on biblical and mythological themes are soon to be revealed.

ST JAMES' CHURCH

Access to St James' Church is along the passageway ● 82 belonging to the houses at no. 29 or no. 17, both of which over-look Štupartska Street. The Franciscan Friars Minor lived in the first St James' Convent on the invitation of Wenceslas I in 1232. The original church was not built for another hundred years, between 1335 and 1374.

THE FAÇADE. The façade was rebuilt after a fire in 1689, and is somewhat restrained in style: the main body of the church is set off by double columns with highly ornate capitals, and by the cornice and the superimposed pediments of the second level and the attic. This contrasts with extraordinary stucco compositions executed by Ottavio Mosto in 1695: on the left is Saint Francis, founder of the Friars Minor, in the center Saint James, and on the right St Antony of Padua. The walls have been hollowed out in places to heighten the effect of depth and chiaroscuro. Mosto introduced to Prague the artistry of Bernini, the brilliant sculptor who had been such an influential figure in the Roman Baroque. Mosto's period of creativity was short-lived, but his influence was considerable mainly thanks to his great expressiveness and the vivacity of his works. Overall, the church exudes magnificence without excess, and the pulpit (1738) is a fine example of this; it is well worth comparing with the pulpit in St Nicholas' Church in Malá Strana. The nave and choir are punctuated by tall, browny-red pilasters topped by opulent, gold capitals, and the eye is drawn to the "guard of honor" that these pilasters form. No less impressive is the effect of perspective which takes the eye from the cornice, at the bottom of the windows, to the upper part of structure framing the altar. Jan Šimon Pánek's

THE ENTRANCE TO ST JAMES' CHURCH
An extraordinary feature of Mosto's Group of St Francis is how quickly the initial impression of disorder, even of

overcrowding, disperses on close examination. Each group is executed with simplicity, and benefits from the effects of symmetry; only the little angels flying over the saints create any confusion. Unquestionably, the swarms of plump children are the fruit of a powerful imagination: two of the putti are embracing passionately, another is flying downward head first, while yet another is searching for something beneath a coat of arms.

ST JAMES' CHURCH
St James' Church has superb acoustics, and the organ recitals are not to be missed. The church is frequently used for recordings, and is also noted for its magnificent masses at Christmas time.

Bar-Vinárna. Otevřeno od 8ʰ več.
Franc. kuchyně ⚭ Grill ⚭ Koncert

The Hotel Pařĺž was built in 1907 by Jan Vejrych (1856–1926), who also designed several buildings in Pařĺžka Avenue ▲ *190.*

"I SERVED THE KING OF ENGLAND"
The narrator has just obtained a job at the hotel, and describes his arrival: "The Hotel Pařĺž was wonderful to behold – so beautiful, in fact, that I almost fell over. The mirrors on the walls, the copper banisters, the door handles, the impeccably polished chandeliers. . !You would think you were in a golden palace, what with all these red carpets and glass doors!"

Baroque restoration of 1689–1702 did not totally conceal aspects of the building's original Gothic structure such as the height of the nave and the length of the choir.

THE HIGH ALTAR. The ceiling was painted by František Maxmilián Voget in 1736; the life of the Virgin covers the nave, while the glory of the Holy Trinity is over the choir. The light yet warm colors suit the overall harmony admirably well. The painting over the high altar, and a Martyrdom of Saint James (1739) by Václav Vavřinec Reiner ▲ *285,* all but disappear next to the opulent frame by the Tyrolian Matthias Schönherr. The high altar is a truly monumental composition which sweeps upward toward the vault, where angels lift up a hanging to reveal the monstrance for all to contemplate.

TOMB OF COUNT VRATISLAV MITROWICZ. This tomb (1714–16) is situated in the left aisle, level with the choir; it is the work of the Viennese architect Fischer von Erlach. The sculpted figures are by Ferdinand Maxmilián Brokoff (1688–1731), the most beautiful piece undoubtedly being the figure of Chronos, identified by an hourglass. Brokoff trained in the workshop of his father Jan, and during this time worked on groups adorning Charles Bridge. He completed his studies in Vienna in the workshop of the Strudel brothers, where he appears to have been introduced to Italian art. Ferdinand Brokoff inherited the style of Bendl and, with Braun, represented the apogee of Bohemian Baroque sculpture.

ST JAMES' CONVENT. This convent stood adjacent to the church and was once one of the major musical centers in Bohemia. Unfortunately, few scores survived the fires of 1689 and 1754 to tell us of the convent's impressive musical activity. However, some musicians of the period are known: they include Bernard Artophaeus (died 1721), Česlav Vaňura (died 1736) and Bohuslav Černohorský (1684–1742). Works by these composers are available on a compact disc on sale throughout Prague entitled "Music at Prague's St James' Church".

HOTEL PAŘÍŽ

This is one of the most famous hotels in Prague. Stylistically, it is a mixture of Secession (the awning over the entrance), neo-Gothic (particularly the corner gable) and highly elaborate architectural style in general. The interior has been renovated and is worth a visit: the restaurant is decorated with Art Nouveau mosaics and the café boasts splendid paneling and furniture of the utmost refinement.

BOHUMIL HRABAL AT THE PAŘÍŽ. The writer Bohumil Hrabal, who was born in 1914 in Brno and who has recently died, was one of the most popular Czech writers. He immortalized the "Pařĺž Hotel" in his novel *I Served the King of England*

Hotel Paříž
LVOVSKÁ ULICE

(1981). After an eventful life as a student, Hrabal, the son of a brewery manager, managed to obtain a doctorate in law in 1946, before embarking on a series of jobs including railway worker, commercial traveler, steel worker, packer of old papers, and property master in a theater. He had keen powers of observation, and his experiences provided the inspiration for his works, although they were not published for many years due to censorship. In 1963 he came into the public eye with *A Pearl in the Background*. It was a success: critics and readers alike saw him as the true successor to Jaroslav Hašek; the brewery anecdote, a minor genre of story closely associated with Prague folklore, forms an important element in the work of both writers. Hrabal also had exceptional skill with words, combining literary language, neologisms, the spoken language and slang. His best-known works include *Closely Watched Trains*, *Dancing Lesson for Adults and Advanced Pupils* (1969), *Sacrificed Head of Hair* (1987), *Tender Barbarian* (1988), *Wedding in the House* (1990) and his masterpiece *Too Lonely a Solitude*.

The restaurant and bar of the Hotel Paříž, which are nowadays situated on the corner of Oberního domu and Králodvorská streets, were enormously popular in the early part of the 20th century.

KOTVA SHOPPING CENTER

Jakubska Street leads away from St James' Church toward Králodvorská Street and the Kotva shopping center. It was constructed and internally designed between 1972 and 1974 with the help of Swedish capital by Vera and Vladimir Machonin, and is one of the biggest of its type in eastern Europe. When the foundations were being laid, relics were found. They throw interesting light on the locality's history. This includes a palace in the Middle Ages, a church of the Order of St Benedict dating from the Roman era, and a 13th-century monastery of Teutonic Knights.

ST JOSEPH'S CHURCH

St Joseph's Church, which stands in náměstí Republiky (Republic Square) opposite the Kotva shopping center, dates from 1636–53 and is one of Prague's earliest Baroque churches. It was built as the chapel for a Capuchin convent, and its sober decoration recalls that Order's love of simplicity. The statue of Saint Francis (1708), overlooking the square, is by František Preiss ▲ *293* and originally stood on Charles Bridge. It was brought here in 1855, and the angels that once flanked it are now in the courtyard. The statue of Saint Jude Thaddeus (1741) is traditionally surrounded with tokens of thanksgiving, and inside the church, by the side altars, there are two paintings of Saint Anthony and Saint Felix by Karel Škréta.

ST JOSEPH'S CHURCH The main entrance is surmounted by the Questenberg coat of arms (above). The former Capuchin monastery next to the church was pulled down in 1795 and, at that time, only the hospital was restored. This, too, was eventually demolished and replaced by the military barracks where Josef Kajetán Tyl ▲ *280* composed the Czech national anthem *Where is my home? (Kde domov jůj?)* in 1834.

A table at the Hotel Paříž (left).

EXTERNAL VIEW OF OBECNÍ DŮM
The mosaic on the central pediment, *Homage to Prague*, was the work of Karel Špillar who had acquired Puvis de Chavannes' taste for subdued, stilted scenes during his stay in Paris. Ladislav Šaloun's Baroque-inspired allegories above the metal awning represent the nation's Despondency and Uprising.

INTERIORS
Despite objections from his colleagues, Alfons Mucha was given the task of providing painted decorations for the Mayor's Room (below) ● 88.

TOWN HALL

AN UNUSUAL DECISION. In many ways, the construction of the Obecní dům between 1905 and 1911 was one of the high points in the history of Prague's architecture and decorative arts. It was also a hugely demanding task. The municipal authorities wanted a prestigious building which could accommodate not only the everyday public services, but also various cultural events. In particular, it had to comply with the complex limitations of an irregular lozenge-shaped area of land which had been the site of a former royal palace pulled down in 1903–4. The palace had been badly damaged by fire in the 17th century and had been rebuilt, but now housed only a military academy. The members of the jury selecting the final plan argued long and hard, and in the end agreed to award the prize to two architects: Antonín Balšánek, who was made responsible for the exterior, and Karel Osvald Polívka ▲ *176*, who was commissioned to do the interior. Such a decision risked an element of disparity in the design, and the construction of a building that lacked unity of style. However, it is now difficult to identify which parts were done out by which architect, although a comparison with Antonín Balšánek's other work suggests that he was responsible for the overall design, and that Osvald Polívka concentrated on conceptualizing the dominant forms and executing the interior design. In building the façade, Balšánek, who had the benefit of historicist training, used traditional decorative styles and adapted them to modern tastes. The overall result is somewhat neo-Baroque. By contrast, the interior is

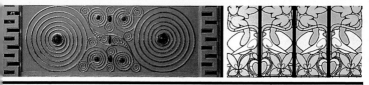

completely Art Nouveau: it consists of the ceremonial rooms including the Mayor's Room with its allegory of Prague just above the line of chairs painted by Alfons Mucha (facing page, bottom), the exhibition halls, a concert hall (the Smetana Hall), a café (opposite, top right) and a restaurant with a mixture of decorations.

AN ARTISTIC MELTING-POT. As with the National Theater ▲ *294*, decorating the Town Hall succeeded in mobilizing all the artistic talent that Prague could muster. This included the painters Mikoláš Aleš, Alfons Mucha, Karel Špillar, Jan Preisler and Maxmilián Švabinský, and the sculptors J. Mařatka, Bohumil Kafka, František Úprka and Ladislav Šaloun. However, unlike the National Theater, where esthetic and political plans had gone hand in hand, the construction of *Obecní dům* relied on a wide range of decorative styles. Careful examination reveals signs of the exuberant inventiveness that characterized Prague in the early years of the 20th century and that is best appreciated by a close attention to the detail. There are two trends here that exist side by side: elegant Art Nouveau plant décors ● *86*, and geometrical designs inspired by the Secession and the Wiener Werkstätte (Viennese Arts and Crafts Workshops). The lift cars, for instance, comfortably combine naturalistic floral motifs and strict geometrical designs, but are nonetheless able to incorporate the subtlest of transitions and echoes. The result is one of the many astounding interplays of form that Prague abounds in. In the restaurant, the characteristically Secessionist clock combines well with the botanical stucco on the archway where a plump young woman appears to be using her generous endowments to challenge the flat, frontal bodies of the other painted allegories. As luck would have it, as soon as the Town Hall was finished it seemed out-of-date to the new generation of artists, and it was opened in 1912 in an age which was already being swept along by new currents such as Cubism ● *89* and Viennese rationalism. Perhaps the décor was too severe. The geometry of the elegant iron awning over the entrance, which has been further embellished by the renovation work on the whole building, and many of Osvald Polívka's decorative motifs do not, however, clash with the new, modern works.

A THWARTED GENIUS. Of all the artists involved in the decoration of the Town Hall, the most controversial by far was Alfons Mucha ▲ *232* who, fortified by his successes in Paris, wanted to do all the interior decoration himself. His colleagues saw things differently and rebuked him for placing his talents so rarely at the service of his own city.

Decorative details from the Mayor's Room (Primátorské salon). Above, from left to right: a stucco scroll, part of the railing of the reception room and a blue stained-glass window.

TOWN HALL
Detail (above) of the ceiling of the Mayor's Room painted by Alfons Mucha between 1910 and 1911, after he returned from the United States.

165

PRAGUE SYMPHONY ORCHESTRA
Václav Smetáček (1906–86) was a frequent conductor of the Czech Philharmonic but from 1942 to 1972 he devoted much of his career to conducting the second of Prague's three orchestras, the

Prague Symphony Orchestra, the third one being the Czech Radio Orchestra. Smetáček also taught at the Conservatory and the Academy of Music.

THE SMETANA HALL. The second floor of the Town Hall houses one of Prague's largest concert halls, the 1,500-seater Smetana Hall. On either side of the stage are two sculpted groups by Ladislav Šaloun, one of them symbolizing Smetana's *Má vlast* (*My Country*) and the other representing Dvořák's *Slavonic Dances*. Statues of Czech composers adorn the escutcheons decorating the boxes, and the paintings on the walls and ceilings are the work of Karel Špillar. In the small, second-floor ceremonial rooms at the front of the building, music takes pride of place in Maxmilián Švabinský's frescos, a testament to the crucial role that music played in the nation's rebirth. The vestibule contains busts of the conductors Václav Talich (1883–1961) and Václav Smetáček, both of them key figures in the history of Czech music.

THE CZECH PHILHARMONIC ORCHESTRA. The Czech Philharmonic Orchestra (CPO) and the National Theater are the most important institutions in the musical life of Prague ● *46, 48*. The CPO regularly performs in the Smetáček Hall although its official home is now the Rudolfinum ▲ *194*. Founded in 1894, it was originally made up of musicians from the National Theater, but became independent in 1901. As a private organization, times were sometimes difficult and the orchestra performed many concerts and undertook a large number of tours to survive. Later on, under the first Republic, the government came to appreciate its importance as an ambassador of Czech culture, and the Czech Philharmonic was nationalized by Edvard Beneš' government in 1945. Under Václav Talich, who was conductor from 1917 to 1954, the CPO became one of the world's great orchestras; Talich proudly promoted the music of Otakar Ostrčil, Josef Suk, Vítěslav Novák, Bedřich Smetana and Antonín Dvořák, and also of Bohuslav Martinů, the first performance of whose opera *Juliette* he conducted in 1938. Talich was also involved in the formation of the Slovak Philharmonic Orchestra in 1952.

POWDER TOWER

This tower (PRAŠNÁ BRÁNA) was built in honor of Vladislas Jagiello II on the site of one of the gates that had formed part of the old fortifications. Work was commenced in 1475, but this was abandoned when the king transferred his residence to the castle in 1484. It was not finished until the 19th century. The decorations by Matěj Rejsek (c. 1450–1506) have been well preserved, thanks to the integrity of Josef Mocker (1835–99) who was also responsible for St Vitus' Cathedral ▲ 214 and rebuilt the Church of St Peter and St Paul at Vyšehrad ▲ 325. Mocker completed the upper story, raised the roof and decorated the net vault, and enthusiasts will enjoy guessing which parts were done by Rejsek and Mocker respectively. The depictions of the Kings of Bohemia on the east and west walls are the work of sculptors invited by Mocker: Čapek, Seeling and Šimek ▲ 290.

NOVÉ MĚSTO

AMBITIOUS TOWN PLANNING. Nové Město (New Town) stretches beyond Republic Square. The Old Town was no longer large enough to contain the growing number of inhabitants and, on his ascent to the throne, Charles IV ● 66 combined the various districts that stood outside the Old Town into a "new" town which was founded in 1347 and designed in accordance with his ideas of breadth and space. It was the biggest piece of town planning in the Middle Ages, and included streets 60 to 70 feet wide and a main thoroughfare 200 feet wide and 5 miles long. Furthermore, the building plan was notable as much for its insistence on the rules and time constraints of construction as for the geometrical structures of the streets.
ENORMOUS MARKETS. The plan for the New Town included three vast areas which adjoined the former districts and were designed as markets: they were the cattle market (later to become Charles Square ▲ 308), the horse market (later renamed Wenceslas Square ▲ 172) and the hay market (Senovážné náměstí).
CAPITAL OF BOHEMIA AND THE EMPIRE. It was Charles IV's ambition to make Prague into a second Rome, and he went some way to achieving this aim by founding the University ▲ 278 by a decree of April 7, 1348. By 1355, he had become Holy Germanic Emperor and was at the height of his powers, and Prague had become the imperial capital. In 1378, the last year of Charles' reign, Prague had a population of forty thousand and was one of the biggest cities in Europe.

FORMER U HYBERNŮ CHURCH
The "Hibernians" were Irish Franciscan monks who came from "Hibernia" (the classical name for Ireland) in 1629; Their church was built between 1652 and 1659, almost certainly by Giovanni B. Orsi; it was rebuilt in the Empire style between 1808 and 1811 by the Viennese architect Georg Fischer (1768–1828) and used as a customs office. The convent has retained its Baroque appearance.

"We wish and command that a town shall be built called New Town, and that its inhabitants shall be the owners of the entire area between the Old Town and the walls with which we shall encircle the New Town. We also command that they shall be free to build houses and outhouses . . ."
Decree announcing the foundation of Nové Město (New Town), April 3, 1348.

POWDER TOWER
Up until the 17th century gunpowder was stored in this tower.

FAÇADE OF THE CENTRAL HOTEL
A short walk along Hybernská Street, past what was once the U Hybernü Church, leads to the former Central Hotel. The hotel was built between 1899 and 1902 (that is the Corso Café) to plans by Friedrich Ohmann; the whole building has been recently restored, with the exception of the second floor.

SWEETS-SPORCK PALACE
This building at nos. 3–5 Hybersnká is in fact two Baroque buildings combined. It has a façade built by Antonín Haffenecker c. 1780, and the doors and the roof statuary are by Ignác Platzer. In 1912, it hosted the 6th Conference of the Russian Social Democratic Party where the Bolsheviks, led by Lenin, founded an independent party. For many years, the Sweets-Sporck Palace housed a Lenin Museum.

FORMER CENTRAL HOTEL

THE EARLY DAYS OF ART NOUVEAU. Art Nouveau, with its floral motifs that proliferated in the Central Hotel, was characterized by its French-style naturalism; there are many examples of this in Prague, particularly in buildings of overwhelmingly large proportions. However, Prague's version of Art Nouveau took as long as ten years to develop, and did so on the basis of ideas which had been developed by Ohmann but which were only to find truly Baroque vigor beyond simple neo-Baroque styles. Not far away, on the corner of Havlíčkova Street, is the neoclassical Masaryk Station; it was Prague's first railway station, and was built in 1845.

FORMER CAFÉ ARCO

MAX, FRANZ & CO ... For many years at the beginning of the 20th century, the Café Arco ● 58 at no. 16 Hybernská Street was the meeting place for the great names of German-language Czech literature. Max Brod (1884–1968) made the acquaintance of Kafka ● 110 here while still a student; he used to go to the Café Arco in his university days, and it was also there that he met the younger Franz Werfel (1890–1945), and became one of his supporters. Werfel, too, was a student at the Carolinum and a habitué of the Arco, and in this way he became friends with Jan Urzidil, Ernst Pollak, Kornsfeld and Haas. In 1911, thanks to Brod, he published his first, and highly successful, novel, *Friend of the World*.

FORMER LEGIO BANK

This curious building, which was built in 1922–5, stands in Na Poříči Street, and is approached along Havlíčkova Street. It is the work of Josef Gočár (1880–1945), who was a student of Kotěra and became the first President of the Group of "Plasticians". It is an astonishing mixture of the spirit of Cubism and of local tradition, and the enormous doorway with pilasters recalls entrances to many Renaissance and Baroque buildings. The decorated frieze and the telamones depict the world of work and industry, fields of endeavor that the bank did much to foster.

FORMER MORTGAGE BANK

Dlážděná Street leads into Senovážné Square, the former hay market. The former Mortgage Bank at no. 13 is a building in the neo-Renaissance style. Kafka was employed here.

A DYNAMIC BANKING CENTER. From 1860 onward, Prague was gripped by a fever for investment, with mechanical industries and banking establishments in the forefront, and the Czech middle classes were particularly active in the economic development of Bohemia. Initially, all the major financial operations were in the hands of the Viennese banks that had branches in Prague, but this period also saw the establishment of the first Czech banks; these included the Discount Bank (1863) and the Mortgage Bank (1864). In one corner of the square, in Jeruzalemská Street, stands the JUBILEE SYNAGOGUE which was built in 1906 in a half-Art Nouveau, half-Moorish style. At right angles to the synagogue is ST HENRY'S CHURCH; it is one of the biggest churches in the New Town and was restored during the Baroque period.

FRIEDRICH OHMANN (1858–1927)
The architect trained in Vienna and became a professor of the second "special class" at the Academy of Fine Arts. Otto Wagner, who was working in the first "class", was therefore a colleague of his. Ohmann taught for ten years at Prague's School of Arts and Crafts before returning to Vienna in 1899. There, he became a leading architect although, as the years went by, his style tended toward bombast. This led him to embrace historicism, and his work of this period includes the neo-Gothic Štorch House (1896–7) in Old Town Square and the Czech neo-Renaissance *U české orlice* house (1897) in Celetná Street ▲ *160*. However, it also includes examples of Art Nouveau which he introduced to Prague, particularly the Corso Café (1897–8), which has now been pulled down. In the view of K.B. Madl, a leading critic of the Secession, Ohmann was the "John the Baptist" of Modernism in Prague.

PRAGUE CITY MUSEUM

Prague City Museum lies about five minutes away, on the edge of the New Town and on the other side of the ramparts now replaced by the city's internal freeway. It is unjustly ignored by visitors – a visit here is an excellent introduction to the Czech capital. The Museum is opposite the Jan Šverma Gardens (Sady Jana Švermy, Prague 8), and occupies a neo-Renaissance building (1895–8) designed by Antonín Wiehl and Antonín Balšánek. The rooms on the ground floor contain Gothic and Roman statues, frescos and illuminated manuscripts, along with models and objets d'art; these are displayed chronologically and trace the city's history. The museum's most important piece, however, is on the top floor: a huge model of

COMMERCE AND CRAFT INDUSTRY BANK
This neo-Renaissance building stands at no. 20 Na příkopě Street. It was built in 1894 by Polívka ▲ 176

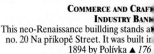

EARLY 20TH-CENTURY HOUSES
Dorfler House, (above), at no. 7 Na příkopě Street, has retained elements of the Secession despite its "modernized" floors. Also known as the "Pelikan Building", it was designed by Blecha and Justice. Koruna House, which stands opposite between nos. 4 and 6, probably has the narrowest façade in Prague. Like Koruna Palace ▲ 174, Koruna House was built by Antonín Pfeiffer and is notable for its marked Art Nouveau decoration.

Prague made by Antonín Langweil between 1826 and 1834. A proper examination requires at least half an hour and the use of binoculars is recommended; the model shows the city limits and its architectural styles during the 19th century, and it is quite possible to visualize what the Jewish quarter, Na příkopě Street, Wenceslas Square and Masaryk Quay looked like during that period. The room also contains an old map of Prague which makes study of the model even more intriguing.

NA PŘÍKOPĚ

This pedestrianized shopping street has some wonderful buildings, and a superb panorama of styles stretching from 1860 to today. It actually goes back further than that as it was initially built in 1760 after the ditch which surrounded the Old Town's ramparts was covered over. This is the origin of the name of the street, which means "over the ditch".
NATIONAL BANK. The imposing building that houses the Bank of the Czech State (1936–8) at nos. 24–8 is the work of František Roith (1876–1942), who also designed the Municipal Museum (in Marianské náměsti.). After studying under Otto Wagner in Vienna, Roith settled in Prague where his taste for monumental and restrained styles revealed the influence of his Austrian teacher's principles.
SLAV HOUSE. Czech Communists held meetings of the Central Committee in the Přichovsky Palace between 1945 and 1948. The neoclassical façade designed by Filip Heger (c.1734–1804) conceals an earlier Baroque façade dating from the late 17th century, but in 1873 the building was turned into a casino which became popular with Germans. As a reaction to this, the building was renamed "Slav House" (Slovanský dům) after the war. Prague's first Art Nouveau building was constructed opposite; it was designed by Friedrich Ohmann, and the Corso Café occupied the first floor.

FORMER INVESTMENT BANK. The Živnostenská (Commerce and Craft Industry Bank), which opened in 1868 at no. 20, was the leading financial institution of the Czech bourgeoisie, and many of its administrators played key political roles. The present building was constructed in 1894–6 for the National Bank: the monumental staircase and the enormous hall on the second floor are well worth a visit.

SYLVA-TAROUCCA PALACE. This extremely beautiful example of Rococo architecture at no. 10 Na příkopě is the work of the architect K. I. Dientzenhofer and was built between 1743 and 1751. It was intended for Prince Ottavio Piccolomini whose family had settled in Bohemia after the Battle of White Mountain ● 34. All the carved decoration is from the workshop of Ignác Platzer, while the frescos on the ceiling over the staircase were executed by V. B. Ambrozzi. The Savarin Palace Casino can be found on the second floor.

STATE BANK. At nos. 3–5 Na příkopě, there is another building belonging to the Czech National Bank; this is clad in beautiful polished granite. It represents an early 20th-century example of a form of re-discovered and refined classicism inspired by Viennese styles, and the powerful influence of Otto Wagner in particular. Another instance of this is the extraordinary Adria Palace ▲ 291 by Joseph Zasche, a German architect who lived in Prague. Franz Metzner's massive and severe sculptures in marble marry very well with the architecture. Opposite Adria Palace, at no. 4, is the FABRIC HOUSE, the oldest of Prague's big department stores, built in 1870. From the roof terrace of the Universal building on the corner of Na můtsku there is a lovely view out over the neighboring districts.

ALFONS MUCHA (1860–1939) Mucha started out as a theater designer.

He then entered the service of Count Karl Khuen-Belasi, whose Emmahof Castle he decorated, before being sent to Paris to complete his training. After his patron committed suicide, Mucha earned his living through contributions to various illustrated magazines, including La Vie Parisienne. His career took off in 1894 thanks to a fortunate meeting with the celebrated actress Sarah Bernhardt for whom he created some famous posters. The one above was designed for Lorenzaccio (1899).

▲ Around Wenceslas Square

VÁCLAVSKÉ NÁMĚSTÍ
MANY YEARS AGO
This photograph
dated 1876 shows the
square after the
Horses' Gate was
pulled down and
before the National
Museum was built.
The square had been
a popular and busy
area since the
beginning of the
19th century, and
gradually the royal
vines planted behind
the gate were
removed to make way
for the new buildings
which make up the
Vinohrady district.
On either side, large
magnificent buildings
replaced the small,
low houses at the top
of the square, and
elaborate street
lamps were erected

MUCHA MUSEUM

Housed in Kaunicky Palace at no. 7 Panská Street, behind
Wenceslas Square, the Mucha Museum opened in February
1998. Dedicated exclusively to the unique works of Alfons
Mucha (1860–1936), the famous Art Nouveau Czech painter
▲ *171*, it was created in cooperation with the Mucha Foundation
▲ *232*. More than eighty items, including decorative panels,
posters, charcoal drawings, pastels, lithographs and personal
objects, are on display. The prestigious Parisian period
(1887–1907) is particularly well represented, and Mucha's
workshop, with its original furniture and the artist's own
photographs, has been reconstructed as part of the exhibition.

WENCESLAS SQUARE

ORIGINS OF VÁCLAVSKÉ NÁMĚSTÍ. This former horse market
is the longest of the three huge squares that Charles IV ● *25*
planned for his New Town. It forms a cross with the others
(Senovážné and Karlovo náměstí) which are in turn linked by
roads at right angles: Jindřišská Street and Vodičkova Street.
The square was originally closed off at one end by the Horses'
Gate, which formed part of the city's fortifications; in 1885–90,
the gate was replaced by the monumental National Museum.

down the middle
from 1868 onward.
The city fortifications
and the gates began
to be removed in
1875.

THE STATUE OF WENCESLAS. The original statue of the patron
saint of Bohemia was executed by Jan Jiří Bendl in 1680, and
it was situated in the middle of the square before being taken
to Vyšehrad in 1879. The modern statue of the saint on
horseback is the work of Josef Václav Mylsbek and was
erected in 1912; this Wenceslas is surrounded by five patron
saints of Bohemia: saints Ludmila, Procope, Adalbert, Vojtěch
and Agnes. The words of a piece of 13th-century choral music
are written on the plinth: "May we and our descendants not
perish." Czechs have always sung this piece in difficult times
and at important moments in their history.
DOWN THROUGH HISTORY. Wenceslas Square has played an
important role in the history of the people of Prague. It was
during the Revolution of 1848 ● *28* that the square received
its current name, symbolizing the identity and durability of
the Czech nation. In 1918, the square was the scene of huge
demonstrations in favor of national independence, and then,
in August 1968, it was where the inhabitants of Prague tried to

> "We have lived too long in the dark."
>
> Alexander Dubček
> November 23, 1989

PRAGUE SPRING ● *40* On August 21, 1968, the five countries of the Warsaw Pact invaded Czechoslovakia, and in Prague, Soviet tanks took up positions in Václavské náměstí. Opponents of the invasion made the square into a symbol of national resistance, some of them opting for confrontation and others remaining seated at the foot of the statue of Saint Wenceslas.

THURSDAY NOVEMBER 23, 1989 Not even the bitter cold prevented hundreds of thousands of inhabitants of Prague from coming to hear Václav Havel speak. The following day, excitement reached new heights when Dubček appeared on the balcony, and the great mass of people surged forward to hear the great Slovakian reformer continue a speech that had been interrupted back in August 1968. On this day twenty-one years later, many people were in tears and Wenceslas Square proved far too small to accommodate all those who yearned for freedom.

stop Russian tanks advancing into their city. In January 1969, a student, Jan Palach, set fire to himself at the foot of the statue of Saint Wenceslas ▲ *198*. To prevent groups of people gathering there, the authorities reacted by building the new innercity motorway (*magistrala*) which runs between the National Museum and the statue; the statue was also surrounded by chains to stop people approaching. All demonstrations during the 1980's either began or finished in Wenceslas Square. It was also here that May Day marches took place during the forty-one years of Communist rule.

FOCAL POINT OF THE VELVET REVOLUTION ● *40*. The savage suppression of the first demonstration of November 19, 1989 – it commemorated a demonstration that had taken place on November 19, 1919 – followed by the setting up of the Civic Forum, led to several consecutive days of demonstrations. It attracted up to a million people on November 23 and 24,

173

Right:
the National Museum

LUCERNA
Lucerna Palace is the
work of a well-known
architect and former
resident, Václav
Havel, grandfather of
the President. The
drawing room is used
for concerts, and
famous musicians
including Chaliapin,
Bronislaw Huberman,
Pablo Casals and
Toscanini have all
played here. Prague's
younger generations
also come to learn the
waltz and the tango in
the vast rooms with
their parquet floors.

PETERKA HOUSE
Peterka House at 12
Václavské náměstí
was the first building
that the architect Jan
Kotěra (1871–1923)
designed in Prague; it
signaled the start of
the geometrizing
phase of the Prague
Secession. Kotěra
studied in Vienna
under Otto Wagner,
and his arrival in the
capital of Bohemia
was warmly welcomed
by the supporters of
Modernism.

when workers and young people addressed the well organized
and peaceful crowd from the balcony of the Melantrich
publishing house; they were flanked by the dissident priest
Václav Malý, the politicians Havel and Dubček, other
representatives of the Civic Forum, and even the Archbishop
of Prague.

KORUNA PALACE

Koruna Palace ● 84, 86, a former commercial and
administrative building on the corner of Na příkopě Street,
was designed by Antonín Pfeiffer. It is a good example of the
buildings of "Babylonian" inspiration that were constructed at
the end of the 19th century in the wake of the new,
widespread interest in eastern civilizations. Archeological digs
in Mesopotamia started in 1899, and discoveries made there
encouraged a fashion for so-called "Babylonian" monumental
motifs. Sucharda's sculptures are most impressive.

EVROPA HOTEL

This hotel, which is unquestionably the most famous in
Prague, was built by Bendrich Bendelmayer and Alois Drýak
▲ 288 between 1903 and 1906. It embodies the
best of Prague's Art Nouveau ● 86, 92,
particularly the plant motifs and
geometrical design. The entire gamut of
Art Nouveau devices are to be found
here, both on the exterior and inside:
they include carved balconies,
mosaics, ornamentation
characteristic of Kotěra, and gilt.

WIEHL HOUSE

In 1896, the architect
Antonín Wiehl built
himself a large four-

tory house on the corner of Wenceslas Square and Vodičkova treet. It is one of Prague's finest examples of neo-Renaissance style. The façade is decorated with sgraffito ● 78 nd frescos depicting national stories and legends; they were ainted by L. Novák and F. Urban after cartoons by Mikoláš Aleš and Josef Fanta.

EVROPA HOTEL
The café has an oval gallery. The restaurants are curiously outdated but extremely refined.

NATIONAL MUSEUM ★

The only way to reach the National Museum is by crossing the motorway that runs through the city or by walking through the underpass. Like the National Theater, the National Museum embodies the nation's rebirth ▲ 194. It was founded in 1818 ollowing encouragement from Czech patriots spurred on by Count Kašpar Šternberk and the philosopher Josef Dobrovský ● 28, ▲ 267; since then, many leading figures in Prague life including the historian František Palacký, the philologist Josef Jungmann and the naturalist Jan Evangelista Purkinjě ▲ 308 have contributed to its continued success. The modern building, which dates from 1885, was constructed at the top end of Wenceslas Square to designs by the architect Josef Schulz. The fountain at the foot of the slope incorporates a number of sculptures by Antonín Wagner, including an allegory of Bohemia towering above personifications of the Rivers Elbe and Vltava. The interior has a main staircase consisting of four flights leading up to the pantheon, a vast room crowned by a dome decorated with statues of leading figures in Czech artistic and intellectual life. The museum comprises three departments including an immense library that contains precious medieval manuscripts. Some of the displays on the second floor deal with the region in prehistoric times, as well as modern history and popular traditions; there are also sections on mineralogy and petrology, and a particularly interesting collection of precious and semi-precious stones. The third floor consists of sections devoted to zoology and paleontology. There is a delightful café at the far end of the entrance hall, and concerts of classical music are regularly given on the main staircase.

NATIONAL MUSEUM ★
The imposing façade of the national museum, set with statues, conceals great riches within. The lobby, grand staircase and galleries are graced with works glorifying the evolution of the arts and sciences. As well as an extensive library, the museum contains collections devoted to mineralogy, anthropology and natural history. The busts in the dome of the pantheon depict famous Czech artists, scholars and writers. After so absorbing so much information, the little café at the back of the lobby provides visitors with very some welcome refreshment.

Much of the artistic endeavour of Karel Osvald Polívka (1859–1931) took place in Prague. He was a student at the Polytechnic School and then an assistant to Josef Zítek, the architect of the National Theater and the Rudolfinum, before collaborating with Antonín Wiehl, who designed the Prague City Museum. After forsaking historicism, Polívka established himself as a leading representative of Art Nouveau architecture, and threw all his energies into this form. His best works include the interiors of the Town Hall, the U Nováku building, the former Praha Insurance building and the Topíč publishing house.

"PRAHA"

The building occupied by the former "Praha" insurance company is at 7 Národní třída and dates from 1905–7; it stands next to one of Polívka's later works, the Topíč publishing house (1910). The ornamentation on the Praha Insurance building, particularly Ladislav Šaloun's allegorical and figurative designs, recalls Viennese Secession styles. It was through this free and inventive use in both subject matter and form of façade stucco that Art Nouveau in Prague retained links with the Baroque.

ČELDA KLOUČEK

This sculptor and interior designer was one of Polívka's more important collaborators; he also taught at the School of Applied Arts in Prague between 1888 and 1916. Klouček was one of the first interior designers in Prague to use naturalistic formulas for his ceramics. A measure of his importance can be gained from the warm welcome accorded to his students at the International Exhibition in Paris in 1900.

WORKING WITH POLÍVKA

Polívka demanded that collaborators employed on decorative work took the greatest of care. He was able to gather around him the most talented artists in Prague but, as a result, this occasionally went too far in the direction of another form of abundance typical of the florid style associated with Symbolism.

STATUES AT THE MINISTRY OF INTERNAL COMMERCE
This building, dating from 1900, is at 7 Old Town Square, and is one of Polívka's best examples of neo-Baroque design. Particularly noteworthy are the monumental doorway, the characteristic undulation of the façade, and the mock-Baroque stucco ornamentation. Even the statues framing the mosaic, the sole concession to Art Nouveau, recall the roof statuary of Baroque palaces.

The Praha building avoids this because of the care that Polívka took to mark out the ornamental motifs. He seems to have harbored a positively jealous concern that the almost Wagnerian signature of the façade should not be compromised.

COMMERCE AND CRAFT INDUSTRY BANK
(20 Na příkopě)
Here, Czech neo-Renaissance style combines with an upper level decorated with mosaics by Mikoláš Aleš, Čelda Klouček and Stanislav Soucharda; they depict allegories of technology, commerce, industry and agriculture. The main hall is decorated with frescos by Maxmilián Švabinský.

STATE OPERA

THE FRUITS OF RIVALRY. When the national movement culminated in the building of the National Theater ▲ *294* with the help of donations from all over the country, the powerful German bourgeoisie did not want their choice to be limited to the Estates Theater ▲ *281*, which was a hundred years old and smaller than the Theater of the Czechs. This conflict led to the building of a new theater, the "German Theater", on the site of the New Town Theater on the ramparts, and between Wilson Station and the National Museum. This theater, which opened in 1888, is still the biggest in Prague and is an exact, though smaller, replica of the Vienna Opera.

DISTINGUISHED MUSICAL DIRECTORS. The first director was the celebrated Angelo Neumann. The first conductor was Karel Muck, and he was followed by Gustav Mahler, Leo Blech, Georges Szell, Bruno Walter, Erich Kleiber and Richard Strauss. The opera house traditionally opted for a German repertoire, but it changed direction under Alexander

CENTRAL STATION
Built between 1901 and 1909 to plans by Josef Fanta (1856–1954), the Central Station is a fine example of unity of design. The towers and the central arcade give the whole building an unusual strength. The carved decoration is by Šaloun.

GUSTAV MAHLER (1860–1911)
For a time, this great musician was second-in-command at Prague's German Theatre.

Zemlinsky (1911–27), who was not only a fine conductor but also a composer of operas including *The Dwarf* and *The Florentine Tragedy*. He also promoted Richard Strauss' operas and Mahler's symphonies. His time in Prague was noted for appearances by some of the greatest exponents of German opera including Alfred Piccaver, Leo Slezak, Richard Tauber, Lotte Lehmann and Max Laurenz, and a number of Czech singers including K. Burian. The theater was partly destroyed in 1945 and when it reopened it was named the "Smetana Theater", and became the country's second most important theater. It was restored between 1968 and 1973 but, with the rebuilding of the National Theater, it has again achieved independence. Its new name, the State Opera (Státní Opera Praha), acknowledges that it is the only theatre in Prague to perform opera exclusively. The State Opera has an international repertoire, while the National Theater concentrates on the Czech repertoire.

From the Na Františku Quarter to Josefov

1. OLD TOWN SQUARE
2. ST NICHOLAS' CHURCH
3. PARIS AVENUE
4. MAISEL SYNAGOGUE

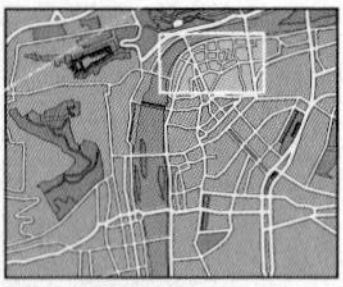

Half a day

◆ B A2-A3-A4-B2-B3-B4-C2-C3-C4

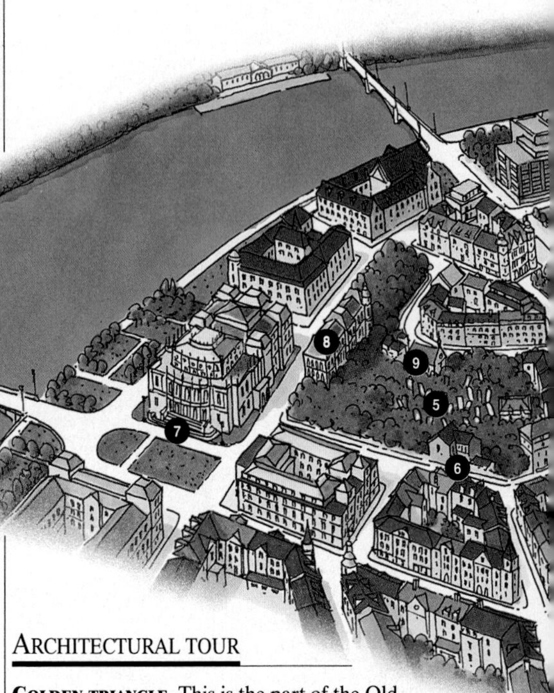

6 VĚŽEŇSKÁ STREET The entrance to this building in Věžeňská Street is one of the most remarkable in the whole district.

ARCHITECTURAL TOUR

GOLDEN TRIANGLE. This is the part of the Old Town which, from 1892 onward, was most affected by the rebuilding program usually referred to as the "clean up". Here, as elsewhere in Prague, architecture enthusiasts can walk along street after street and marvel at the extraordinary beauty of so many of the houses. Two of the city's main attractions are Masaryk Quay ▲ *300* and Paris Avenue ▲ *186*. Some of these fine constructions, which include entire roads in the Secession and Art Nouveau ● *86* styles, such as Vinohrady Street, are not very well known because they are some distance from the city center; but there are others, very close to Old Town Square, that are still hardly known at all. Dlouhá, Kozí and Haštalská streets form a triangle made up of 19th- and early 20th-century buildings with wonderfully imaginative façades.

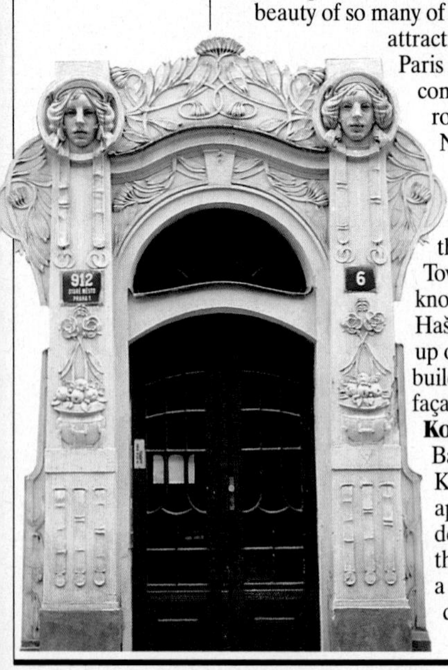

KOZÍ ULICE. The designer of the neo-Baroque building on the corner of Kozí Street and V. Kolkovně Street appears to have been obsessed with a desire to include every component of the Baroque repertoire. The result is a house topped by an onion-shaped dome, a pediment pierced with a bull's-eye window, masks and

SECESSION STYLE
In the early years of the 20th century, Art Nouveau was the art form that encapsulated modernity and supplanted the neo-Renaissance and neo-Baroque styles that had dominated the previous decades. As Petr Wittlich has remarked, "During the characteristic period of the neo-Renaissance, the architect played a representative role; by contrast, and in a complex manner, the Secession took control of the very functioning of the city itself." Polívka ▲ *176* made the greatest contributions to the Secession movement in his role as Prague's official architect; he

was involved in the design of banks and other official buildings, as well as districts, such as Vojtěšská, Karlova and Haštalská streets, that were being "cleaned up" but whose architecture looked back to the neo-Baroque.

garlands.
s this
neo-Baroque? Perhaps it is
more neo-Rococo as, apart from the
doorway, this façade lacks the monumental proportions of so
many others. The next two buildings are quite different. No. 7
is an imposing structure which recalls the period of sgraffito,
and is also decorated with busts of medieval architects. No. 9,
which was built in about 1907, is a minor Art Nouveau
masterpiece; the fine, curvilinear pediment is elaborately
ornamented and pierced by a bull's-eye window, and the
whole structure is a free creation containing innumerable
allusions to Baroque architecture. Ornamentation on the
lower floors combines two aspects of Secession style: the rich
floral décor of the pediment and the window frames
contrasting with geometric elements. Significantly, the
roughcast stops short at the windows, and the "brutalist"
appearance thereby achieved recalls certain Modernist
theories of Kotěra, Novotný and Bílek dating from the second
decade of the century. On the other side of the street, the
façade of no. 4 Haštalská Street is in the Secession style, and
is the work of Polívka (c. 1907).
ŘĚŽEŇSKÁ ULICE. This street is as richly decorated as Kozí
Street. Of particular interest is the Secession façade by
A. Stárek at no. 6 decorated with a statue of Saint Wenceslas.

**CHURCH OF
ST HASTAL**
A Gothic church with
two naves was added
to this 14th-century
building in 1375. The
sacristy walls are
adorned with frescos.

ST AGNES' CONVENT
Below are the
archways of the
cloister, and to the
right is one of the
convent's two
churches; the Church
of St Francis which
was in ruins until
1981 and is now a

popular concert hall.
The Convent is
attached to the
National Gallery and
houses collections of
art of the medieval
era (1200–1550).

The patron saint's presence may partly account for the
Gothic form of the narrow windows and the consoles
suggesting covered ways. The doorway is the most beautiful
in the whole street.

V. KOLKOVNĚ. The contours of the building at no. 6, which
dates from 1905, are almost pure in this setting. The house
next door has more in common with neo-Baroque styles.

ST AGNES' CONVENT

A TROUBLED HISTORY. St Agnes' Convent (ANEŽSKÝ
KLÁŠTER) comprises two churches: a convent belonging
to the Poor Clares and a Franciscan monastery. It was
founded in 1233, and was one of the first religious buildings
in Prague constructed in the Gothic style; the architecture,
like that of St Giles' Church ▲ 285, is clearly inspired by
Cistercian Burgundian art. Building work on the whole
convent lasted from 1233 to 1280, and the Franciscan
monastery founded by Agnes of Bohemia was completed
in 1240. In time, the Convent was to become an extremely
important place of worship and, in the 14th century,
consisted of as many as seven churches. However, the
occupants were forced to leave at the time of the Hussite
troubles ● 32, and the complex then remained empty until it
was handed over to the Dominicans. They had been living in
the Convent of St Clement, which stood on the site of the
Clementinum and had been given to the Jesuits in 1556.
The Poor Clares returned in 1627. The Convent was then
dissolved and, in 1782, during the reign of Joseph II, was
turned into workshops and a refuge for
the poor. A Union for the Restoration of
St Agnes was established in 1892 and it
paid for plans to rebuild both churches;
the work was begun by A. Cechner. After
a long interruption, work was resumed in
1940 under Oldřich Stefan until
archeological digs in 1941, and later in
1953–5, revealed the original remains.
This allowed a more thorough program
of restoration work to begin in 1960.
**MUSEUM OF ANCIENT BOHEMIAN AND
CENTRAL EUROPEAN ART** Laid out
in the Convent at the end of 2000,
the museum presents a magnificent
collection of paintings and sculptures
that were formerly on display in St
George's Convent, as well as pieces that
were newly restored for the opening of
the museum.
MUSIC AT AGNES'. Today, the Convent
houses a splendid and well-appointed
arts complex. During the time that the buildings that had
been handed over to the National Gallery were undergoing
restoration, the chapel was turned into a concert hall, work
having been done to improve its acoustics. This charming
room is a great favorite with chamber music lovers. It is
notable for a sculpture entitled *Music*, by Josef Václav
Myslbek, which originally stood in the foyer of the National
Theater ▲ 294.

THE GREAT MASTERS OF BOHEMIAN GOTHIC ART

The Convent's collection includes works by three important painters: the Masters of the Vyšší Brod and Třeboň altarpieces, and Theodoric. The *Madonna of Roudnice* (left) is attributed to the Master of the Třeboň Altarpiece, an anonymous painter who was active in Prague in the 1380s and who's exquisite work marks the apogee of Gothic painting in Bohemia. He is named for an altarpiece painted for the Augustine Convent at Třeboň and which is now on display at St Agnes'. *Saint Vitus* (below, left) was painted by Theodoric, from whom Charles IV commissioned a series of portraits for the chapel at his castle at Karlštejn, not far from Prague.

AGNES OF BOHEMIA

Agnes of Bohemia, daughter of Přemysl Otakar I and sister of Wenceslas I, brought the Poor Clares and the Franciscans to Prague and founded the Crusaders of the Red Cross. Her letters are kept in the Church of St Clare of Assisi. According to legend, her canonization, which took place one week before the Velvet Revolution in 1989, would shower Bohemia with blessings.

HOSPITAL OF ST SIMON
In 1761, this famous hospital was the first medical lecture theater in Bohemia to be equipped with a display of anatomical specimens. By 1780, it was acknowledged to be one of the finest in Europe.

SPANISH SYNAGOGUE
This synagogue was originally built to cater for the descendants of Spanish Jews. The interior is in a neo-Moorish style directly influenced by the Alhambra in Granada.

CHURCH OF ST SIMON AND ST JUDE

A short walk from St Agnes' Convent along U milosrdných Street and past the hospital leads to the Monastery of the Brothers of St John of God (U milosrdných). The 18th-century façade is by Jan Josef Hrdlička, but the church itself goes back to 1615–20. It was built by the Union of Czech Brethren on the site of a chapel belonging to the Gothic hospital, but alterations in the Baroque style dating from 1751 have obscured its original Renaissance features. Both Haydn and Mozart played the organ here.

SPANISH SYNAGOGUE

Further down Dušní Street, on the corner with Bílkova Street, stands a building with three extraordinary atlantes in the Babylonian style by František and Václav Kavalír (1910–11). Dušní Street itself is the center of one of the oldest Jewish colonies in Prague. The Spanish Synagogue (ŠPANĚLSKÁ SYNAGÓGA) was built in 1867–8 to plans by Vojtěch Ignác Ullmann (1822–97) ▲ 289 on the site of the Old School, Prague's oldest synagogue, which had been pulled down in 1867. It was in the Old School in 1837 that the Reformed Service had been introduced to Prague, and Jewish liturgical music first performed: the composer František Škroup ▲ 281 was organist there for ten years and made important contributions to the development of this music. The land occupied by the synagogue is separate from the ghetto and defines the boundary of the Sephardic community. An exhibition on the history of Jewish emancipation between the 18th and 20th centuries is currently planned. Almost opposite is the Church of the Holy Spirit (Kostel sv. Ducha) constructed in the Gothic style (1346) and later restored in the Baroque manner (1689). It contains Jan Jiří Heinsch's *Saint Joseph*.

CHURCH OF ST SAVIOR

At the bottom of Dušní Street is the Church of St Savior. It was originally built in 1611–14 in the Renaissance style as a temple for German Lutherans. According to a 17th-century chronicle, eleven of the conspirators executed in 1621 ● 35 were buried here after their heads had been exhibited on one of the towers at the end of Charles Bridge ▲ 154.

FORMER GHETTO

Kostečná Street leads directly into Paris Avenue, the boundary of the former ghetto.
SITUATION. Geographically, the ghetto was bound by Elišky Krásnohorské Street to the east, 17 Listopadu Street to the north and northwest (parallel to

> "Prague rivals Vienna for its palaces,
> Dresden for its gardens and
> Cracow for its ghetto."
>
> Paul Morand

the river), and Kaprova Street in the south. It was one of the oldest in central Europe and of great importance to other communities in Bohemia. A Jewish community is referred to in the year 965 by the merchant Ibrahim ibn Jacob, but at that time it stood at the foot of the Castle. Another colony settled there around 1091 on the road to Vyšehrad. A third colony appeared no later than the 12th century close to Old Town Square on the Josefov site.

AN ENLIGHTENED SOVEREIGN. Despite the early pogroms and the anti-Jewish interdictions issued by the Lateran Council of 1215, Jewish people did receive some protection from certain sovereigns. One of these was Přemysl Otakar II who, in an edict in 1254, accorded them privileges, banned anti-Semitic violence and slanderous suggestions, forbade forced baptisms, and guaranteed freedom of worship, administration and justice. In spite of this royal protection, several sovereigns abused their power, confiscated goods and made scant efforts to put down pogroms; the 1939 Easter pogrom in Prague left 3,000 dead. It was not until the reign of Joseph II that the Jews were able to enjoy rights and participate fully in Bohemia's cultural and economic life, particularly agriculture and industry.

DESTRUCTION OF THE GHETTO. In the early years of the 19th century, the more prosperous Jews slowly began to settle in the immediate vicinity of the former ghetto, but complete equality throughout the Empire was not granted until 1867. In the meantime, the ghetto became Prague's fifth district in 1861; it was called Josefov after Joseph II, and was restricted to the poor

ŠTENC HOUSE
The printworks and former graphic art establishment at 931/8–10 Salvátorská Street is the work of the architect Otakar Novotný. The building is made of brick and is one of the earliest examples of the Rationalist style. The first floor is punctuated by enameled pillars, and the windows are arranged asymmetrically. The right-hand façade in the neo-Baroque style is by Polívka ▲ 176.

Prague's sense of magic and the fantastic finds one more echo in the memories of its ghetto. The Jews are said to have come here after the destruction of the Temple in Jerusalem but, whether or not that is the full story, they have always been an essential component of the cultural mix that Prague boasts. Until it was pulled down, the Fifth District was a labyrinthine skein of narrow, sombre lanes crammed with tumbledown houses. That was how Gustav Meyrink described it in his novel *The Golem* which linked the Jewish legend for ever to the Prague of Emperor Rudolph II.

"The hidden nooks and crannies, the secret passageways, the blind windows, the grubby courtyards, the noisy taverns, the sinister inns live on inside us . . . The insalubrious Jewish Old Town is a lot more real than the hygienic new town that surrounds us."

Franz Kafka
(Letter to G. Janouch)

ŠIROKÁ STREET
The most famous of Prague's Jews lived at no. 90 of what used to be Josefovská Street, a road that followed the course of modern Široká Street almost exactly. He was Jehuda Liwa ben Bezabel ben Chaïm, known as Rabbi Löw, born at the beginning of the 16th century and at one time a Rabbi in Mikulov in Moravia. Legend links him closely with Rudolph II. Some see Rabbi Löw as a Jewish Faustus, a conspirator who brought to life a creature made of mud (i.e. the Golem); He was still the first Jew in Prague to have an audience with the King, when Rudolph received him at the Castle on February 16, 1592 and promised to give protection to the Jewish community.

THE GOLEM

This giant, made by Rabbi Löw ▲ *190* out of a mixture of earth and clay is still legendary in Prague. The Golem, who was intended to protect the Jewish community and became the Rabbi's devoted servant, came to life through a *chem*, a parchment marked with a holy sign which his master placed in his mouth. One evening, however, on the eve of the Sabbath, the Rabbi forgot to remove the talisman and the giant angrily went round the ghetto terrifying everybody. Löw eventually retrieved the *chem* and managed to mollify the monster, who turned back into a mound of mud. Opposite: a still from Paul Weneger's film, *The Golem* (1920).

OLD TOWN SYNAGOGUE

Legend has provided many accounts of the origin of Prague's oldest synagogue. Some people believe it was built with the stones of the Temple that Jews brought over from Jerusalem; others say that the stones were transported by protecting angels. Another version claims that an old man showed the elders of the community a mound under which the synagogue had already been built.

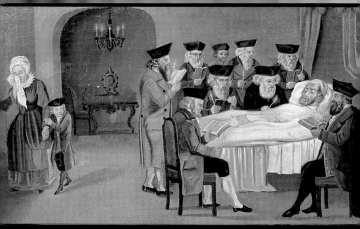

Members of the burial society attend the dying man during his last moments.

The undertakers carry the body, while the man in the black gown collects gifts.

The cortège arrives at the new cemetery where the minister gives a funeral eulogy.

THE HOLY COMPANY OF PRAGUE
A cycle of fifteen paintings illustrates the
activities of this religious charitable
organization. They are by an anonymous artist
and were probably executed in about 1780.

The new Jewish cemetery with its broad, well-kept avenues was situated outside the city.

Some Jewish men gather in front of the funeral monument of Maharal, the Rabbi Löw.

The leader of the burial society was elected by his peers at the annual dinner.

PAŘÍŽSKÁ TŘÍDA
The many fascinating buildings in Paris Avenue include a neo-Baroque structure by Jan Koula (1902) at no. 1; a group of houses by Jan Verych , the architect of the Hotel Pařiž, at nos. 7, 9, 10 and 13; and, at no. 17, a strange corner building (below) by Weyr and Klenska, two designers with a strong interest in the unexpected.

Interior of the Klaus Synagogue, which now houses one of the collections of the National Jewish Museum.

of all denominations. However, the maze of tiny lanes and courtyards and backyards was insalubrious, and they began to be pulled down in 1892, although many years passed before the level of the land could be raised, water piping installed and new streets built. By the beginning of the 20th century, all that remained were six synagogues, the cemetery and the Jewish Town Hall. The demolition of the ghetto was not the only change to Prague's layout: the quarter round St Adalbert's Church ● *303* and the Na Františku and Podskálí districts were rebuilt, and the area near the quays was renovated.

PARIS AVENUE

MODERN TIMES. Paris Avenue (Pařížská třída) is one of the most famous streets in Prague. It starts in Old Town Square level with St Nicholas' Church ▲ *145*, runs down to the Vltava and offers a view over to Letra ▲ *316*. The neo-Baroque and Secession buildings are unusually elegant, and the Avenue is a favorite place for walks. A corner building at 14 Bílkova Street by Otakar Novotný (1917–18) is one of the finest examples of Cubist architecture ● *89* in Prague. Paris Avenue was built at the end of the 19th century, and its construction was considered to be a matter of exceptional prestige.

OLD-NEW SYNAGOGUE

This Gothic synagogue (STARONOVÁ SYNAGÓGA), which was constructed in 1270–5, is the oldest building in the ghetto and is the center of the district. This synagogue was originally called the New School but when other places of worship were built, it became the Old-New. Unlike the ghetto's other religious buildings, the Old-New Synagogue was never closely surrounded by houses, and in that way avoided any fires that broke out. It was not until the late 19th century that any rebuilding work was done, and this was carried out in the "purist" style by Josef Mocker. Further restoration took place after 1920 and in 1966–7. The interior decoration is restrained. The synagogue has always been an active place of worship, even under Communist rule.

"RABBI LÖW". As this has always been the Jewish community's most important synagogue, its Rabbis have always been selected from amongst the most brilliant candidates. The most famous of these was the erudite Jehuda

Liwa ben Bezabel ben Chaïm (1512–1609), who was known as the Rabbi Löw and created the legendary Golem ▲ *187*.

KLAUS SYNAGOGUE

This synagogue (KLAUSOVÁ SYNAGÓGA), which is in U starého hřbitova Street (At the Old Cemetery) and very near the old cemetery, was built in the late 17th century. Today, the former Burial Guild Ceremonial Hall (obřádní síň Pohřebního bratrstva) houses an exhibition of Jewish festivals and traditions. At one time, Prague boasted the oldest Jewish printing center north of the Alps, and its workshops were famous throughout Europe. The first Hebrew print works opened at the beginning of the 16th century; it belonged to Gershom Kohen and ran for almost three hundred years. The collection contains manuscripts done by copyists in the 18th and early 19th centuries. There are many old books in Hebrew on sale in the bookshops along Celetná Street ▲ *158*.

FORMER BURIAL GUILD CEREMONIAL HALL. This neo-Romanesque building dates from 1906, and contains a number of works of art in addition to documents, particularly children's drawings, from Terezín. Before the war, Terezín was a fortified garrison town with 6,000 inhabitants; it lay some 38 miles to the north of Prague. In 1941, the Nazis expelled the inhabitants and replaced them with Jews from Czechoslovakia, Germany and Austria with the aim, so they said, of building a "thermal spa" ghetto. They also allowed musicians to put on symphony concerts, operas and chamber music recitals, thereby seeking to persuade international opinion of the benefits that they were providing the detainees. Goebbels himself went so far as to organize a visit from the Red Cross, and the place was swept, repainted and smartened up for the occasion, inmates in poor health being sent off to the concentration camps. The Reich's propaganda department even produced a film entitled *The Führer gives the Jews a Town*. In fact, Terezín was a transit camp from which prisoners were sent to the death camps. Food shortages and dysentery killed up to 150 people a day, and altogether about 140,000 people, including 15,000 children, passed through. In 1945, there were only 17,000 survivors. Buses bound for Litoměřice depart from the Na Florenc bus station and pass through Terezín.

FORMER JEWISH CEMETERY

LAYERS OF GRAVES. This cemetery (STARÝ ŽIDOVSKÝ HŘBITOV) dates from the 15th century. Earlier cemeteries on

The tympanum over the doorway of the Old-New Synagogue, with fig-leaf carving (below).

THE JEWISH CEMETERY ✪
The old Jewish cemetery, set in the heart of the former Ghetto and encircled by a great wall, contains some 12,000 tombstones. In use from 1439 to 1787, it is one of the oldest in Europe, and is a testament of the Jewish community's great influence on the history of Prague. It is reached via the Pinkas synagogue, then by following the path that meanders between the tombstones, which seem to be planted in the ground like so many crooked teeth. According to legend Rabbi Löw's golem wanders about the cemetery at night. On Starého Hřbotova Street, just outside the cemetery, street stalls offer an interesting range of local handicrafts.

חברא קדישא

"The hands
of the clock
in the Jewish quarter
go backward
And so you slowly
draw back
in your life
Climbing up
to Hradčany, and
in the evening
listening
To the singing of
Czech songs
in the taverns."
Guillaume
Apollinaire

the same site disappeared after the Middle Ages. This is true of a cemetery which lay where Spálená and Jungmannova Streets now stand in Nové Město, and where the bodies of people of all faiths were laid to rest. The cemetery took up a very small amount of land, and soon there was no more room for any new graves. Where a religion permitted bodies to be exhumed, they were placed one on top of the other, sometimes ten deep.

ELABORATE DECORATIONS. From the early 17th century onward, important people were entitled to graves with four walls, and these were covered in texts that glorified the lives of the deceased. Examples of this practise are the tombs of Mordechaï Maisel (1528–1601) and Rabbi Löw. Over the centuries, these inscriptions became more elaborate and varied: a few words were deemed sufficient in the Middle Ages, but by the 15th century the texts detailed the dead person's profession and celebrity. Later, the Baroque period saw the introduction of lengthy texts which included poems, rhetoric and quotations from the Bible.

ŠIROKÁ STREET

Maislova Street runs downhill from the cemetery, and the first turning on the right, Široká Street, is notable for a wide range of the most interesting buildings. They include a neo-Gothic building at no. 11 (1906) by Matěj Blecha which is visible

MAISELOVA ULICE
This street in the Jewish quarter is named after Mordechai Maisel, a former mayor of the old city. It contains two buildings that the Rabbi commissioned: the Town Hall and the Maisel Synagogue. The pink outline of the Jewish Town Hall is at no. 18; the present building by Josef Schlesinger dates from 1763–5, and replaced the former Town Hall built in 1580 by Pankrác Roder and destroyed by fire in 1754. The tower contains a clock adorned with Hebrew figures, on which the hands turn from right to left. The new Town Hall is now the home of a number of official institutions in the Jewish community, and houses the Sefer publishing house and an important library.

גומלי חסדים

from the climb up Paris Avenue, neo-Baroque designs at nos. 12 and 14, and a house in the Secession style at no. 7 by František Weyr (1867–1939). In sharp contrast is no. 5, a fine building by a student of Otto Wagner ▲ *170*, the Rationalist designer Antonín Engel (1879–1958).

HIGH SYNAGOGUE

This synagogue (VYSOKÁ SYNAGÓGA), which lies at the back of the Town Hall in Cervená Street, was built in the 16th century by Pankrác Roder. Restoration work to the building was carried out a few years ago. The fine collections of Jewish textiles, including thousands of curtains, fabrics, mantles, bindings for the Torah, and other draperies from all the Jewish communities of Bohemia and Moravia,

covering a period extending from the 16th century to the present day, are no longer held here. Some items are temporarily on display at the Maisel synagogue and others are in the Klaus synagogue. The most interesting pieces are curtains that are hung inside the Arks in front of the Torah scrolls.

JEWISH TOWN HALL

(ŽIDOVSKÁ RADNICE). The Jewish community in Prague had administrative and legal independence for many years, but there is no documentary evidence of there being a Town Hall on this site until 1541. In 1648, after Jewish people had played an active part in the defence of the city against Swedish troops, Ferdinand III showed his gratitude by granting them the right to build a clock tower over their Town Hall. This was a very considerable privilege as only Christian buildings were allowed to add towers.

MAISEL SYNAGOGUE

Nearby, at 10 Maislova Street, is the Maisel Synagogue (MAISELOVA SYNAGÓGA), which was completely remodeled in neo-Gothic style between 1893 and 1905 by Alfred Grotte. In 1591, Rudolph II had granted the Jewish leader, Mordechaï Maisel, permission to build a synagogue. According to David Gans, it was a magnificent building with twenty pillars; unfortunately it was destroyed, together with 316 ghetto houses, the synagogues and the public buildings, in a fire in the Old Town started by French emissaries in 1689. The synagogue now houses a permanent exhibition on the history of Bohemian and Moravian Jews (from Czechoslovakia) from the 14th to the 18th centuries.
RABBI MAISEL. Mordechai Maisel was considered to be one of the richest men of his time. He died in 1601. He is almost as famous as Rabbi Löw, and is the subject of numerous legends; he is also one of the main characters in Leo Perutz's *By Night under the Stone Bridge*, a novel set in Prague in the time of Rudolph II. This great financier negotiated terms with

PINKAS SYNAGOGUE
(Široká ulice)
This synagogue was originally built in 1535 in the Late Gothic style. Despite alteration in 1625, the vault's Flamboyant Gothic design has

survived. Since 1959, the synagogue has been a memorial to Bohemian and Moravian Jews murdered in Nazi concentration camps, and the walls are covered with almost 80,000 names together with dates of birth and the dates on which they died. After restoration work on the building, the names were carefully re-copied on the walls (above).

ŠIROKÁ ULICE
The house at no. 9 has a Secession façade decorated with allegorical statues of two plump women carved by Karel Vítězslav Mašek in 1908.

The exterior is decorated with statues of composers (Palestrina, Orlando di Lasso, Vittoria, Handel, Cherubini, Auber, Bach, Gluck, Mozart, Haydn, Beethoven, Schubert, Mendelssohn and Schumann), sculptors, painters and architects (Bramante, Della Robbia, Masaccio, Brunelleschi, Donatello, Ghirlandaio, Apelles, Phidias and Ictinus).

Emperor whereby he would improve the living conditions of Jewish people in Prague; in return, half of his fortune would revert to the King on his death. The day after he was buried, bailiffs came to take away his goods, but the amount of money that they found was considered to be insufficient. This led to a civil action against Prague's Jewish community, who were asked to pay up what Maisel owed. The content of this action, which lasted for over 180 years before it was officially closed during the reign of Joseph II, is held in the Vienna Archives.

RUDOLFINUM

Jan Palach Square is dominated by three important buildings. They are Josef Sakar's FACULTY OF PHILOSOPHY (1929), which is at the end of Široká Street and also overlooks Kaprova Street; the SCHOOL OF DECORATIVE ARTS (1884), to the left, in the neo-Renaissance style by F. Schmoranz the Younger and J. Machytka; and the Rudolfinum to the right, also known as the House of Artists (Dům umělců). The latter is a neo-Renaissance building conceived as a "Temple to Beauty" by its architects Josef Zítek ▲ 294 and Josef Schulz, who were also responsible for the National Theater ▲ 294. It was built between 1875 and 1884 to a commission by the Czech Savings Bank to celebrate their fiftieth anniversary. It was then renamed the Rudolfinum after Crown Prince Rudolph, the tragic hero of the Mayerling episode of January 1889.
DVOŘÁK HALL. This large concert hall, noted for its fine colonnades and magnificent decoration, is situated on the south side of the Rudolfinum. It has an organ by the Rieger Brothers of Krňov which replaced the original instrument made by the Frankfurt-an-der-Oder firm of Sauer. Behind the Dvořák Hall is a

maller concert hall used for chamber recitals. The
orth end of the building used to be reserved for the
plastic arts and exhibitions and, until restoration
work in 1990–2, also housed the Conservatory and
he Academy of Music. The exterior is notable for
graffito executed after cartoons by the painter
Petr Maixner. The Rudolfinum is also the home of
he Czech Philharmonic Orchestra ▲ 166. During
he time of the Third Republic, the concert hall
and the rest of the buildings housed the National
Assembly, and the Academy of Music had to find
quarters in Na Slovanech (Emmaus Monastery
▲ 312). Since the recent work, the Academy has
been accommodated in Liechtenstein Palace
▲ 250, and the Conservatory has been in Palffy
Palace ▲ 262, in Valdštejnské Square.

PRAGUE SPRING. The House of Artists has become the home
of the Prague Spring International Music Festival ● 48,
founded in 1946 to celebrate the fiftieth anniversary of the
Czech Philharmonic. The Festival traditionally opens on May
12, the anniversary of the death of Bedřich Smetana, with a
performance of *Má vlast* (*My Country*), and closes on June 3
with Beethoven's *Ninth Symphony*. It is a choice that
underlines both the durability of Bohemia and its place in a
fraternal world. The Festival's scope and reputation go way
beyond the boundaries of the Czech Republic.

ARTISTS NO LONG WITH US. No visit to the Rudolfinum is
complete without a moment's thought for the musicians who
were deported to Terezín Camp ▲ 191. The most celebrated
were the composers Viktor Ulmann (born 1898, died at
Terezín), Gideon Klein (1919–45), Pavel Haas (1899–1944),
and Hans Krase (1899–1944) who composed the famous
children's opera *Brundibar*. The singer Karel Berman and the
conductor Karel Ančerl (1908–73) both survived.

MUSEUM OF DECORATIVE ARTS

Prague's Museum of Decorative Arts (Uměleckoprůmyslové
muzeum – UPM), built by Josef Schulz between 1897 and

HOUSE OF ARTISTS
This poster by Jan
Konůpek was for the
Krásná Praha
exhibition at the
Rudolfinum in 1906.

"Fortunately, it was
enough simply to wait
at the top of the
Rudolfinum's grand
staircase, one's back
relishing the gentle
murmur coming from
the brightly lit rooms,
and one's face turned
to the other side of
the square toward the
trams . . ."

Petr Král

▲ MUSEUM OF DECORATIVE ARTS

JOSEF CHOCHOL
Drawing-room
armchair (1910–11)

Prague's Museum of Decorative Arts houses fine collections of glassware, furniture, posters and jewelry, besides large numbers of precious and other assorted objects. Glass objects from the Middle Ages to the 19th century are currently displayed in rows in glass cases as enticing as Ali Baba's caves. Other collections, including splendid Art Deco and contemporary glassware, can only be seen in temporary exhibitions.

PENDANT (1909)
This pendant by Marie Křivánková was influenced by the geometrical and spiraliform styles which, in that period, also characterized the paintings of Klimt. This style claims to imitate Byzantine and Egyptian forms.

JOSEF GOČÁR
Secretaire made in 1913. Gočár was one of Prague's leading representatives of the Cubist movement.

"AT THE WINDOW" (1932)
This Art Deco glass object is the work of Josef Drahonovský. It is 10½ inches high and consists of three panels of engraved glass. Drahonovský (1877–1938) opened his own workshop in 1904 and started teaching at Prague's School of Decorative Arts in the same year. He was one of the few 20th-century artists to devote his career to the revival of glass engraving. Some of his work is in the Cabinet des Médailles of the Bibliothèque Nationale, Paris. At the Paris Exhibition of 1925, he won the "Grand Prix" for glassware.

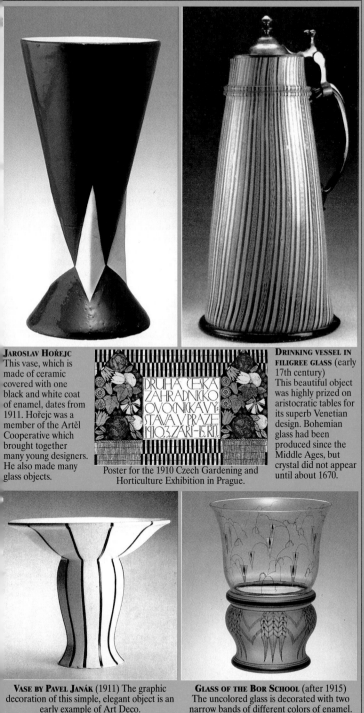

"After functionalism comes thought and abstract expression."

Pavel Janák

JAROSLAV HOŘEJC
This vase, which is made of ceramic covered with one black and white coat of enamel, dates from 1911. Hořejc was a member of the Artěl Cooperative which brought together many young designers. He also made many glass objects.

Poster for the 1910 Czech Gardening and Horticulture Exhibition in Prague.

DRINKING VESSEL IN FILIGREE GLASS (early 17th century)
This beautiful object was highly prized on aristocratic tables for its superb Venetian design. Bohemian glass had been produced since the Middle Ages, but crystal did not appear until about 1670.

VASE BY PAVEL JANÁK (1911) The graphic decoration of this simple, elegant object is an early example of Art Deco.

GLASS OF THE BOR SCHOOL (after 1915)
The uncolored glass is decorated with two narrow bands of different colors of enamel.

197

MUSEUM OF DECORATIVE ARTS

On entering this museum, visitors are immediately struck by

the monumental stairway, the ceiling (above), and the windows designed by the architect Josef Schulz.

Before his death, Jan Palach wrote, "My action has achieved its aim, but I do not want anyone to imitate me . . . The living must keep up the fight." When he was buried, students led by the Rector, Dean and Professors of the Faculty of Philosophy marched through Prague holding up photos of their friend who had died for freedom.

1901, houses fine collections of glassware, furniture, posters and jewelry, besides large numbers of precious objects. Glass objects from the Middle Ages to the 19th century are displayed in rows in glass cases as enticing as Ali Baba's caves.

Other collections, including splendid Art Deco and contemporary glassware, can only be seen in temporary exhibitions. **COLLECTIONS IN THE MUSEUM OF DECORATIVE ARTS.** The museum's very extensive collection consists of more than 250,000 pieces of glassware, pottery and porcelain, graphic art and photographs, furniture and other wooden artefacts, metalware, jewelry and textiles. The permanent displays trace the history of the decorative arts in Europe from antiquity to the 20th century. The techniques of glassmaking go back a long way in Bohemia's history, the earliest examples of local art forms dating from the 14th century. Bohemian glassmaking began to achieve widespread fame in the reign of Rudolph II, who invited to his court Kaspar Lehman, the most celebrated gem engraver of his day. The museum also mounts temporary exhibitions focusing on a single material, technique or period.

JAN PALACH SQUARE

Until 1989, this square (Jana Palacha náměsti) was dedicated to the soldiers of the Red Army; it was then renamed after Jan Palach, a martyr of the Prague Spring ● 40.

A TRAGIC END. On the afternoon of January 16, 1969, a twenty-one-year-old student tried to commit suicide in the manner of Vietnamese bonzes, at the foot of the statue in Wenceslas Square. A tram conductor managed to put out the flames, but the young man was in a critical state by the time he reached hospital. He was suffering from 85 percent burns, and died on January 19. Jan Palach was one of fifteen students who had decided to protest against the invasion of Soviet troops by setting fire to themselves; Palach's name had been drawn by lot. His death sparked off tumultuous reactions throughout Europe, and the Czech people gave him a national funeral.

The Castle

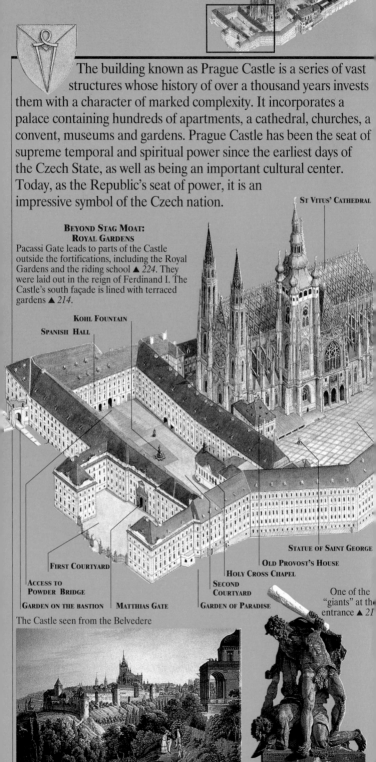

▲ PRAGUE CASTLE

The building known as Prague Castle is a series of vast structures whose history of over a thousand years invests them with a character of marked complexity. It incorporates a palace containing hundreds of apartments, a cathedral, churches, a convent, museums and gardens. Prague Castle has been the seat of supreme temporal and spiritual power since the earliest days of the Czech State, as well as being an important cultural center. Today, as the Republic's seat of power, it is an impressive symbol of the Czech nation.

ST VITUS' CATHEDRAL

BEYOND STAG MOAT: ROYAL GARDENS
Pacassi Gate leads to parts of the Castle outside the fortifications, including the Royal Gardens and the riding school ▲ 224. They were laid out in the reign of Ferdinand I. The Castle's south façade is lined with terraced gardens ▲ 214.

KOHL FOUNTAIN

SPANISH HALL

STATUE OF SAINT GEORGE

OLD PROVOST'S HOUSE

FIRST COURTYARD

HOLY CROSS CHAPEL

ACCESS TO POWDER BRIDGE

SECOND COURTYARD

GARDEN ON THE BASTION   **MATTHIAS GATE**

GARDEN OF PARADISE

One of the "giants" at the entrance ▲ 21

The Castle seen from the Belvedere

200

THERESIAN BUILDINGS

During the reign of Maria Theresa (1740–80), the architect Niccolo Pacassi erected the buildings in the First Courtyard and transformed those around the second and on the south side of the third into a three-story building in the Viennese Rococo style, giving them a stylistic uniformity. Above, left to right: the buildings seen from the Garden "Over the Ramparts", the Garden of Paradise and the Garden on the Bastion.

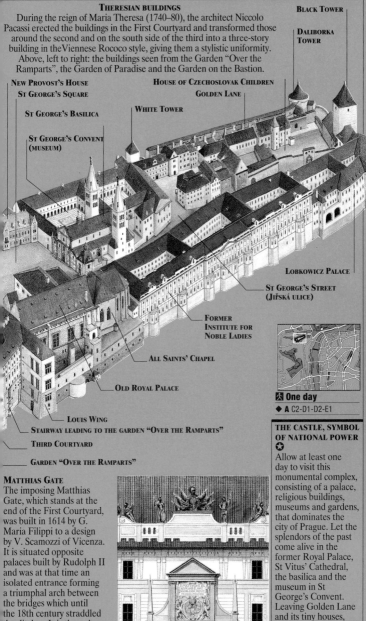

NEW PROVOST'S HOUSE
ST GEORGE'S SQUARE
ST GEORGE'S BASILICA
ST GEORGE'S CONVENT (MUSEUM)
HOUSE OF CZECHOSLOVAK CHILDREN
GOLDEN LANE
WHITE TOWER
BLACK TOWER
DALIBORKA TOWER
LOBKOWICZ PALACE
ST GEORGE'S STREET (JIŘSKÁ ULICE)
FORMER INSTITUTE FOR NOBLE LADIES
ALL SAINTS' CHAPEL
OLD ROYAL PALACE
LOUIS WING
STAIRWAY LEADING TO THE GARDEN "OVER THE RAMPARTS"
THIRD COURTYARD
GARDEN "OVER THE RAMPARTS"

🚶 One day
◆ A C2-D1-D2-E1

MATTHIAS GATE

The imposing Matthias Gate, which stands at the end of the First Courtyard, was built in 1614 by G. Maria Filippi to a design by V. Scamozzi of Vicenza. It is situated opposite palaces built by Rudolph II and was at that time an isolated entrance forming a triumphal arch between the bridges which until the 18th century straddled the ditches. It is the only Mannerist work that preceded the Baroque period. It also marked the Castle perimeter, and helped transform the western section of building into a residence that was worthy of a king.

THE CASTLE, SYMBOL OF NATIONAL POWER ✪

Allow at least one day to visit this monumental complex, consisting of a palace, religious buildings, museums and gardens, that dominates the city of Prague. Let the splendors of the past come alive in the former Royal Palace, St Vitus' Cathedral, the basilica and the museum in St George's Convent. Leaving Golden Lane and its tiny houses, walk through the terraced gardens laid out below Lobkowicz Palace toward Wallenstein Square, taking the opportunity to admire the red rooftops of Malá Strana.

201

The Rose Window

The rose window covers an area of 1066 square feet, and depicts the creation of the world. It was constructed in 1927–8, based on cartoons by František Kysela, and in collaboration with the glass artist, Josef Vlasak, who used 26,740 pieces of glass. Beneath the window are reliefs by Stanislav Sucharda representing the builders of the cathedral.

A Belated Completion

The vaulting over the nave, the final bays, the west front with its ornate rose window, the triple entrance with its three great bronze doors and the twin towers, 270 feet high, were completed in 1929. This put the finishing touches to the cathedral while also respecting the building's original Gothic conception.

Plan and Elevation of the Choir

The chevet of the cathedral bears the mark of the first architect, Matthew of Arras, whom Charles IV called Matthew of Avignon in 1344. By the time he died in 1352, Matthew had only managed to build as far as the triforium; he also completed the polygonal choir with five radiating chapels, the north and south side chapels and the ambulatory.

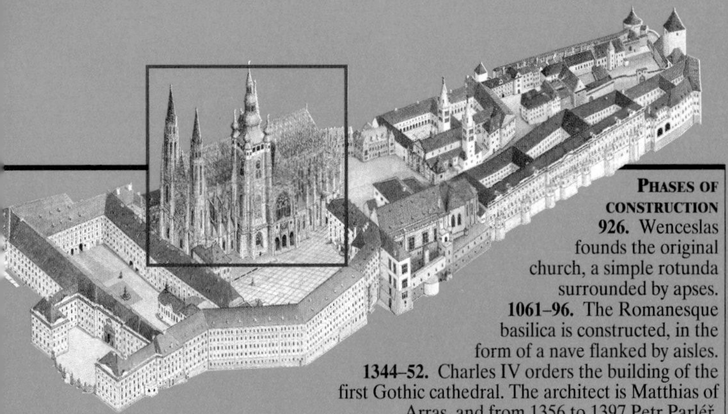

PHASES OF CONSTRUCTION

926. Wenceslas founds the original church, a simple rotunda surrounded by apses.
1061–96. The Romanesque basilica is constructed, in the form of a nave flanked by aisles.
1344–52. Charles IV orders the building of the first Gothic cathedral. The architect is Matthias of Arras, and from 1356 to 1397 Petr Parléř.
1861–1929. The western part of the cathedral is finally completed by Josef Kranner, Josef Moker and Kamil Hilbert.

DISASTERS STRIKE
The Hussite rebellion of 1420 hampered the progress of the building program. Work resumed in 1509, when the foundations of the Black Tower were laid. Construction of other parts of the cathedral also went ahead, although none reached completion. The cathedral was damaged by several fires, including a major one in 1541.

CATHEDRAL TOWER
The main tower, which reaches a height of 325 feet, was covered by a Renaissance dome in 1560–2, but this was replaced in 1770 by an onion-shaped Baroque roof by Pacassi. It is illuminated through a window decorated with an extremely beautiful Renaissance railing ● 68. The tower contains two rows of bells.

PHASES OF CONSTRUCTION
12th century. Original Romanesque royal palace.
1370–87. The Chapel of All Saints is built by Petr Parléř in the Gothic style.
1493–1509. Benedikt Ried builds the great rooms of the Old Palace in the Late Gothic style.

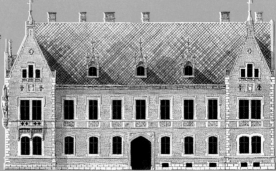

THE PROVOST'S HOUSES
The Old Provost's House (right) is Romanesque and has a façade dating from the 1660's. The New House (above) is neo-Gothic and was built between 1878 and 1881 on the site of several old houses.

ALL SAINTS' CHAPEL (5)
The chapel's complex vaulting was removed during rebuilding that took place in the 14th century.

THE OLD ROYAL PALACE
The foundations of this palace, which served as a residence for the Kings and Princes of Bohemia until the 16th century, date from the 12th century. Gothic structures were built over Soběslav's old Romanesque palace, but Vladislav II Jagiello's reconstruction in 1430 included the first Renaissance elements, as well as a new story dominated by a Hall called after the King himself.

Top to bottom: the Vladislav Hall, the Riders' Staircase and the Vladislav Room.

THE VLADISLAV HALL (1)

The vault above the Banqueting Hall has no central supporting structure, and comprises five areas resembling flat cupolas; the surface consists of a network of intermeshed ribbing which creates an extraordinary sense of space.

THE RIDERS' STAIRCASE (2)
AND THE VLADISLAV ROOM (3)

The Riders' Staircase ● 90 features a highly complex pattern of interlaced ribbing (right). The Vladislav Room above it is decorated with deeply sculptured motifs.

LOUIS WING (4)

This transverse block in the Renaissance style was built in 1502. It housed the Chancellery of Bohemia, famous for being the site of the Defenestration of Prague. It was this event that sparked off the Thirty Years' War.

PRAGUE CASTLE: ST GEORGE'S CONVENT AND GOLDEN LANE

GOLDEN LANE

A line of houses of Lilliputian dimensions are backed up against the wall between White Tower and Daliborka Tower. Some of them have stories less than three feet high and used to be inhabited less well off. At the end of the 19th century the appearance of the lane changed, living conditions improved, and artists arrived. Franz Kafka lodged at no. 22 in 1917, and Jaroslav Seifert, winner of the Nobel Prize for Literature, lived here in 1929.

ST GEORGE'S BASILICA

By the end of the 19th century, the appearance of this Romanesque basilica had been completely distorted by a series of renovations, and a decision was taken that it should revert to its original style. The only features retained were the Baroque façade decorated with statues of Vratislav and Abbess Mlada (the statue of the latter had its original red, ocher and white polychromy restored).

ST GEORGE'S CONVENT

Founded in 973, the Benedictine convent was the earliest religious establishment in Bohemia. It was rebuilt or remodelled several times, and now has a double cloister. Closed in 1782, the complex was converted into barracks. Restoration began in 1962, and today it houses the Museum of Czech Art.

PHASES OF CONSTRUCTION

912. A wooden church is built.
1142. The Romanesque church is built.
End of the 14th century. A Gothic chapel, built by Petr Parléř, is added.
1657–1680. The Baroque façade is added.

THE BASILICA

The Baroque façade obscures one of the oldest Romanesque buildings in Bohemia ▲ 220. Twin towers frame the basilica. The three-tiered nave, flanked by aisles, leads up to a choir built to a square plan and crowned with a dome. The barrel-vaulted apse is raised over a crypt.

THE BASILICA'S SIDE ENTRANCE

The side entrance, dating from the early Renaissance, has a relief depicting St George and the Dragon.

THE LEGEND OF GOLDEN LANE

According to an 18th-century legend, Rudolph II ordered the construction of alchemists' laboratories and workshops for artisans working in gold and making elixirs of life. These were to be near the Castle in a mysterious lane with tiny houses, known as Golden Lane. In Rudolph II's time, this lane was inhabited by archers and the less well off ▲ 223, but legend has it that it was known for activities relating to the occult sciences. It was indisputably the site of esoteric practices and became the city's "soul", giving Prague that "devilish" aura which it has never shaken off. Many 19th-century writers sought to perpetuate the legend. One of them, Gustav Meyrink, states in Golem ▲ 187: "I was in the Street of the Goldsmiths where, in the Middle Ages, those who were skilled in alchemy burnt the philosopher's stone and poisoned the moonbeams."

**WORK STARTS ON A
NEW CATHEDRAL**
Work on St Vitus'
Cathedral was begun
during the reign of
Charles IV (opposite,
left), and under the
direction of Matthias
of Arras (opposite,
right) who endowed
the building with the
classical form of a
French Late Gothic
cathedral. However,
St Vitus' mainly bears
the hallmarks of Petr
Parléř, the church's
architect from 1356 to
1399.

A THOUSAND YEARS OF HISTORY

A statue of the
Přemyslid Princess
Eliška in the
Triforium of St Vitus'.

Prague in the late
15th century.

DISPUTED ORIGINS. Recent research by archeologists and
historians somewhat contradicts the view expressed by
Kosmas (in the oldest Czech chronicle dating back to the 11th
century) that the first residence of the Dukes of Bohemia was
at Vyšehrad. In fact, the Castle was probably founded earlier,
between 880 and 890; at all events, we know for sure that it
was built by the Přemyslid Prince Bořivoj. The Castle's oldest
church, the small stone chapel to the Virgin Mary founded by
Bořivoj and Saint Ludmila, has disappeared.

ROMANESQUE FOUNDATION. The second church built within
the Castle walls was dedicated to Saint George (905) ▲ *220*,
but this was supplanted by the Rotunda of St Vitus erected in
the middle of the Castle by Duke Wenceslas in 925. Around
973, St Vitus' became the cathedral of Prague's new bishopric.
The Castle was where dukes were elected and monarchs
crowned, but it was also a cultural center of great importance
because of the Chapter Choir and St George's Convent.

EARLY FORTIFICATIONS. It was not until after 1041, during the
reign of Břetislav I (1034–55), that a stone rampart was built,
and a new ducal palace, also made of stone, was constructed
in the Roman style. Between 1060 and 1074, Spytihněv turned
St Wenceslas' Chapel into a magnificent Ottonian-Roman
basilica 250 feet long. Vratislav I, the first King of Bohemia,
was crowned here in 1085, and the rebuilding of the Castle

> "Above us, wherever we happen to be in the town, the Castle is omnipresent and omnipotent. Not just a building built on a hill, but a miniature city overhanging this city."
>
> Dominique Fernandez

was completed with the construction of a new palace for Soběslav I (1125–40). The palace fell into disuse after the fire of 1303, and particularly when the Přemyslid dynasty died out in 1306.

ARCHITECTURAL BRILLIANCE IN THE REIGN OF CHARLES IV.
After his coronation in 1347, Charles IV undertook the construction of a superb residence on the model of a French palace. The result was a castle that became the center of power of the King of Bohemia and the Holy Roman Emperor. The most remarkable feature was St Vitus' Cathedral, the foundation stone of which was laid on November 21, 1344.

Charles IV's son, Wenceslas IV (1378–1419), felt that the palace did not have the capacity to deal with the new administrative tasks and had it rebuilt; meanwhile, he went to live in a new royal residence in Old Town. The Castle became the fortress of the Anti-Hussite party, and in July 1420 Emperor Sigismund had himself crowned King of Bohemia there. After Prague was taken in 1421, though, the Castle passed into the hands of the Hussites but, respected and protected by both sides, it came to represent the State. As a result, it was preserved. The castle once again became a royal residence in 1483 when Vladislas Jagiello (1471–1516) abandoned his palace in Old Town.

UNDER THE HABSBURGS. The Habsburgs' accession to the Czech throne marked the beginning of a new era in the life of the Castle. Ferdinand I was crowned in the cathedral on October 24, 1526; he did not live in Prague permanently, but was responsible for having important building works carried out. However, the idea

SAINT WENCESLAS
The cathedral remained unfinished for no good reason. It richly deserved to be the country's main church, the repository of the Crown Jewels and the burial place of its founder.

In fact, the remains of Saint Wenceslas were buried in the south apse, while those of Bishop Vojtěch (Adalbert) are in the west chapel. The statue of Saint Wenceslas (left) stands in the chapel dedicated to him ▲ 216, and depicts him as a knight wearing a princely crown. It is made of calcareous tufa (1373) and still bears traces of the original polychromy. Although the mark of Parléř's workshop is on the plinth, the statue is attributed to Jindřich Parléř.

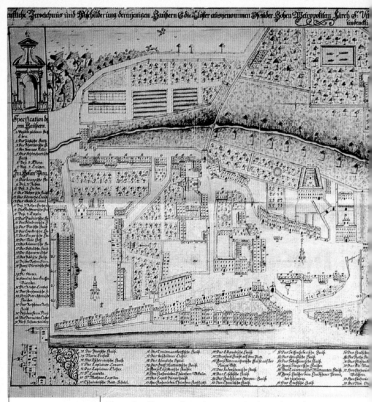

BAROQUE SPLENDOR
At the height of the
Baroque period in the
reign of Charles VI,
both the Castle and
the cathedral were
the scenes of
magnificent
ceremonies. The
coronation shown
here in 1836 recalls
the pomp that dated
back to the 16th and
17th centuries.

of turning Prague into the sovereign's main and permanent
residence was abandoned following the fire in Malá Strana of
June 2, 1541. After his victory over the revolt of the Estates of
Bohemia in 1547, Ferdinand appointed his youngest son
Viceroy, and the time he spent in Prague witnessed some
major cultural advances. The Castle was rebuilt and
modernized, and once again became a residence that was
actually lived in; the architect, Bonifác Wohlmut, placed the
building containing the Bohemian archives next to the palace.

**ARCHITECTURAL ACHIEVEMENTS DURING THE REIGN OF
RUDOLPH II.** Prague properly became the capital when, in
1583, Rudolph II chose to make his permanent residence
there. The Castle was soon the home of immense Imperial
collections as well as the King's stables of Spanish horses, and
the last decade of Rudolph's reign saw the high
point of the castle's renovation under the
architect, Giovanni Maria Filippi. A new
entrance, known as the Matthias Gate and
completed during the reign of Rudolph's
successor, marks the Castle's present-day
boundary. However, Emperor Matthias
(1611–19) went back to live in Vienna, and
thereafter none of the Habsburgs ever returned
to live in Prague permanently.

THE "WINTER KING". In 1618, the Castle was
the scene of an event which sparked off the
Thirty Years' War ● 34. For a year, the Castle
had become the seat of the "alternative"
Calvinist King Frederick, who was made Elector
Palatine by the rebellious Diet in 1619. From
1634 to 1637, the future Ferdinand III (1637–57)
lived at Prague Castle as Viceroy, and had
alterations carried out both in the so-called

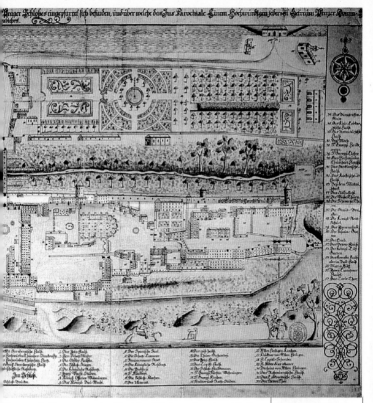

Empress's Rooms overlooking the third courtyard and in the north-south wing between the second and third courtyards. The "New Way", which later became Nerudova Street and linked Prague and the castle, was built after 1640.

BEGINNINGS OF A DECLINE. The Castle was renovated after the Peace of Westphalia in 1648 ● *27*, and following the departure of the Swedes, who had mercilessly pillaged it. The accession of Leopold I marked the beginning of the Imperial residence's decline. Maria Theresa (1740–80) was responsible for a major administrative reorganization and by attempting to turn the castle into a modern, up-to-date residence. The modernization work changed the building's appearance substantially ▲ *201*, but after 1775 the Castle was unable to find an appropriate role for itself; it simply lay on the side of the hill like a kind of fossilized enclave amidst a rapidly expanding city.

20TH-CENTURY REVIVAL. After the creation of the Czechoslovak Republic in 1918, Prague Castle acquired a new lease of life as the Head of State's residence. Renovation work during 1920–34 was entrusted to the Slovenian architect, Josip Plečnik ▲ *213, 327*. The Castle escaped damage during World War Two, and was accessible even during the time it served as the residence of Communist presidents. Building works, which continued between 1950 and 1980, mainly involved the transfer of some of the National Gallery's collections to St George's Convent and the establishment of a historical museum in Lobkowicz Palace ▲ *223*. Václav Havel was solemnly proclaimed president here during the "Velvet Revolution". Building and renovation work has been resumed, and the most recent has taken place in the grounds.

PLAN OF THE CASTLE AND GROUNDS IN THE 18TH CENTURY
The royal gardens were laid out in the reign of Ferdinand I (1526–64).

COMPLETION OF ST VITUS'
The construction of St Vitus' Cathedral was resumed after 1860 by an association of Czech patriots led by Josef Kranner. The cathedral was completed under the Czechoslovak Republic in 1929 to celebrate the saint's thousandth anniversary.

THE FIRST COURTYARD

The first courtyard adjoins Hradčanské Square, and is separated from it by monumental railings bearing the monogram of the Empress Maria Theresa and eight carved groups; the most imposing of these are on the entrance columns. This courtyard is the newest part of the castle, having been built over the moats during the 18th century and used as the main courtyard; the buildings lining it are in the Viennese Rococo style. Fresh from renovating Rožmberk Palace and houses in Jiřská Street, the architect Niccolo Pacassi effectively joined the buildings to the west of the palace into a uniform grouping as far as the first courtyard. In this way, Prague Castle lost the picturesque charm that the Renaissance and medieval buildings had provided and at a stroke, the Castle's development over a thousand years came to an end. A side entrance to the Castle on the left of the main courtyard leads to the "NA BAŠTĚ GARDEN" (Garden over the Bastion), which takes its name from the bastion that formed part of Vladislas Jagiello's fortifications.

THE SECOND COURTYARD

Access to this courtyard is through the Matthias Gate ▲ 207. It was built in the second half of the 16th century, but its current appearance dates from the end of the 18th century. The southern end contains buildings that belonged to the new Imperial palace in Matthias' time, while the northern end consists of the remains of a Renaissance wing from the reign of Rudolph II; it includes the Renaissance stables which now house the Picture Gallery, the Spanish Hall and Rudolph's Gallery. The two ends are linked by a central structure put up during the reign of Ferdinand III around 1645.

THE PRAGUE CASTLE PICTURE GALLERY. This is on the first floor in the north and west wings, in what were once the royal stables. The collection derives from previous royal collections, although it now comprises only a very small part of them. After Rudolph II's superb collection was pillaged by the Swedes in

"ZÁMECKÉ SCHODY"
Two stairways lead up to the castle. The stairway on Thunovská Street climbs the hill, reaching the royal residence near Hradčanské Square and the garden over the ramparts.

The Changing of the Guard takes place every day at noon. This slightly uninspiring ceremony is improved by the bright new uniforms designed by Pišťěk, the costume designer who won an Oscar for *Amadeus*, which was filmed in Prague by Miloš Forman.

THE GIANTS
The entrance to the castle is decorated by pairs of statues representing Čeněk Vosmik's early 20th century "Fighting Giants". They are copies of statues made by Ignác Platzer the Elder in 1768.

> "The leaves of gold which Charles IV used to cover the roof
> of his castle have long ago been taken away and melted down.
> But the fame they brought the city lives on."
>
> Jaroslav Seifert

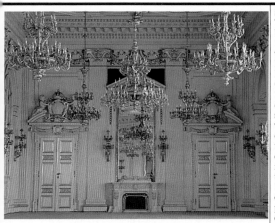

1648, it was replenished by Ferdinand III before being dispersed by the Habsburg Charles VI; the most valuable paintings were transferred to Vienna and Dresden, and the rest were sold by auction in 1782. Inventories of the period described the remaining paintings as merely anonymous items, and it was not until the 1960's that art historians were able to establish the exact identities of the artists responsible for many dozens of them.

THE SPANISH HALL AND THE RUDOLPH GALLERY. These reception rooms are situated on the second floor of the north wing. The Rudolph Gallery, formerly known as the German Room and ultimately the home of the royal collections, dates from 1586. Lit by a thousand candles placed in gold chandeliers, it is as long as the Spanish Hall but not so wide.

THE THIRD COURTYARD

This courtyard is completely overlooked by St Vitus' Cathedral and the Royal Palace. Various 10th- and 11th-century remains, including ramparts, roads and houses, were preserved beneath a concrete framework constructed by the architect Josip Plečnik between 1925 and 1928. The granite monolith, the work of the same artists, was erected in memory of those who died in World War One.

THE NEW PALACE. This huge building brings together a number of constructions that were gradually

SPANISH HALL
This magnificent banqueting room is 160 feet long, 80 feet wide and 40 feet high. It was built in the Renaissance style by G. Filippi between 1601 and 1606, and is decorated with stucco, mirrors, and with bronze chandeliers bearing three thousand candles. The most recent alterations to the décor date from 1865; they were carried out in preparation for the coronation of Franz-Josef as King of Bohemia, which did not ultimately take place.

HOLY CROSS CHAPEL
This chapel, situated in the south wing and protruding into the courtyard, was built between 1756 and 1763 by Anselmo Lurago. It is richly decorated with paintings and neo-Baroque sculptures and is the site of the castle's information center. It once housed the major part of the St Vitus' Cathedral Treasury (a unique collection of liturgical objects and ecclesiastical and secular jewelry; this was assembled by Charles IV, who was passionately keen on holy relics). The collection of jewelry has now moved to the Cathedral Treasury.

The belltower, dating from the Renaissance, is sometimes open to visitors, offering a breathtaking view over Malá Strana.

THE DOORS
Today, the main entrance consists of three porches on the west side which incorporate bronze doors (below, top). The Golden Door, which was the cathedral's main entrance for five hundred years, includes a beautiful, decorative railing made by J. Horejc in 1954.

turned into a single residential palace. It now houses the office of the President of the Republic and some reception rooms. A staircase in the southeast wing leads to the garden "Over the Ramparts" (Na valech), and from the terrace in the Garden of Paradise (Rajská zahrada) there is a fine view over the city.

ST VITUS' CATHEDRAL (CHRÁM SVATÉHO VITÁ) ★

After succeeding in making Prague the seat of an archbishop, Charles IV undertook the construction of a new cathedral ● 68 on the site of the rotunda put up by Wenceslas and the early Romanesque basilica. Work was commenced by the French architect Matthias of Arras in 1344, and was continued by Petr Parléř, the greatest Gothic builder in central Europe, and his sons; however, the building was not completed for another five hundred years. First, work was held up by the Hussite Wars, and it was not resumed afterward through lack of money; although consecrated in 1385, St Vitus' Cathedral was not actually finished until 1929. In the course of this work, the earlier Gothic part was restored and the non-Gothic furnishings removed, while the newer neo-Gothic part was decorated as it is today. The church is 400 feet long, 200 feet wide and 110 feet high; the vault is supported by twenty-eight pillars.

THE WEST FAÇADE. This was the last façade to be finished, and it was only in 1929 that the West Door became the main entrance. The new neo-Gothic façade is adorned with fourteen statues of saints and Charles IV, and busts of the later architects. The three bronze doors were executed in 1927 by Otakar Španiel, and are decorated with carvings: the story of the cathedral over the central entrance, the life of Saint Adalbert (Vojtěch) over the right-hand door, and the life of Saint Wenceslas over the left-hand door.

THE SOUTH FAÇADE AND THE GOLDEN DOOR. In 1406, the completed part of the cathedral was simply shut off by a wall at the level of the Golden Door. For five hundred years, then, the south façade was the main façade, and the Golden Door gave access to the cathedral. The door takes its name from the red and gold background of the mosaics depicting the Last Judgement. Charles IV and his last wife, Elizabeth of Pomerania, may be seen kneeling in the tympana of the central arch, their hands joined in solemn supplication. Parléř's main tower is 300 feet high, and is topped by a cupola by Pacassi dating from 1770.

THE VAULT. The cathedral has three naves, a transept, an ambulatory and radiating chapels. The ribbed vault is Petr Parléř's masterpiece. On returning to the site where he was to remain for almost fifty years, Parléř reworked the plan originally produced by Matthias of Arras, but when he came to the vault, he opted for innovation. He was no longer content with a simple ogive with crossed ribs. Instead, he prolonged the arch which was punctuated with windows, and the ribbing then formed new ogives which became entangled; they project over the shortest ribs as far as the

STATUE OF SAINT GEORGE
This is a copy; the original is kept in St George's Convent.

It was made by Jiří and Martin of Cluj in 1373. When it was damaged by the fire of 1541, parts of it were recast in the Renaissance style by the celebrated metal caster, Tomáš Jaroš of Brno.

St George's Square in 1830, showing the apse of St Vitus', the old Royal Palace on the left, and the beginning of Vikářská Street on the right.

ROYAL MAUSOLEUM
(1566–89)
This is the work of the
Flemish artist
Alexandre Colin de
Malines. The
recumbent statues
represent Ferdinand I,
his wife Anna Jagiello,
and his son
Maximillian II, all of
whom were buried
here. Ferdinand I,
who ruled Bohemia
from 1526 to 1564, is
considered to be the
founder of the
Habsburg dynasty
in Bohemia and
Hungary.

Below: the tomb of
Saint John Nepomuk.

keystone which is in turn transformed into the middle of a
magnificent star. It would be difficult to list all the priceless
objects to be found in the cathedral; we shall confine
ourselves to the most important. A visit begins with the
various chapels, including the Chapel of St Wenceslas (below)
shortly before reaching the choir.

THE HIGH ALTAR. This neo-Gothic altar by Josef Kranner
dates from 1868–73. The Renaissance pulpit dates from the
17th century, and the sides contain wooden reliefs made by
Jan Jiří Bendl between 1625 and 1650. The relief on the left
shows the flight of the "Winter King" ● *34*, while that on the
right depicts a fascinating view of Prague dating from 1620.

TOMB OF SAINT JOHN NEPOMUK. Two tons of silver were
required to complete this tomb (1733–6) to plans by the
architect Josef Emanel Fischer von Erlach, the sculptor
Antonio Corradini and the Viennese goldsmith Johann
Joseph Würth. The paving of this section of the ambulatory
covers the tombs of fourteen bishops of Prague.

ROYAL VAULT. From the HOLY CROSS CHAPEL (last chapel in
the right-hand aisle), a staircase leads down to the vault
where there are remains of the original Rotunda of St Vitus.
The royal vault contains the tombs of Charles IV, his four
wives and his children, King Wenceslas IV, Vladislav,
Wenceslas' son who was born after his father died, George of
Poděbrady and Rudolph II, and Maria Amelia, the daughter
of Maria Theresa. Their remains were placed in new
sarcophagi during the 1930's.

ROYAL ORATORY. Vladislav Jagiello's oratory, which was
designed by Benedikt Ried in 1493, is one of the finest
examples of Flamboyant Gothic in the whole cathedral. The
gallery rests on vaults adorned with stylized branches forming
ribs which incorporate the coats of arms of the countries
conquered by Vladislas. The oratory is linked to the Royal
Palace by a covered way.

ST WENCESLAS' CHAPEL. This is the most impressive
and most venerated of all the chapels. It is an
undisputed Gothic masterpiece of the period
1362–7 and is an example of the impressive esthetic
standards attained by Czech artists. The chapel was
constructed by Petr Parléř on the site of the 10th-
century Romanesque rotunda where the martyr
prince was interred. The decoration, which consists
entirely of murals from 1509 and comes
from the workshop of the so-called
Master of the Litoměřice Altar, is
appropriate to its function as a
reliquary. The upper parts of
the walls are devoted to the life
of Saint Wenceslas; the lower part
includes a cycle of the life of Christ,
and ornamental sections consisting of
more than 1,000 semi-precious Czech
stones (jasper, amethyst, chalcedony and
chrysoprase) set in gilded plaster. The
main altar, whose walls were renovated at
the beginning of the 20th century and
which are also covered with precious
stones, lies on the site of the saint's tomb.
On the door to the chapel there is a heavy

> "These ancient wrongs must have lost much of their bitterness in the baleful light of modern times when the only evidence to survive is an heirloom of luminous architectural beauty."
>
> Patrick Leigh Fermor

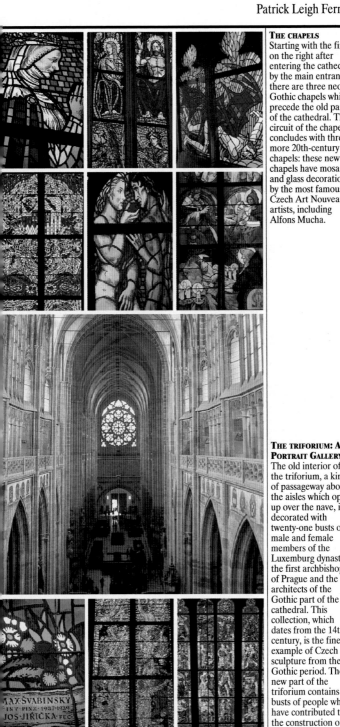

THE CHAPELS
Starting with the first on the right after entering the cathedral by the main entrance, there are three neo-Gothic chapels which precede the old part of the cathedral. The circuit of the chapels concludes with three more 20th-century chapels: these new chapels have mosaic and glass decoration by the most famous Czech Art Nouveau artists, including Alfons Mucha.

THE TRIFORIUM: A PORTRAIT GALLERY
The old interior of the triforium, a kind of passageway above the aisles which opens up over the nave, is decorated with twenty-one busts of male and female members of the Luxemburg dynasty, the first archbishops of Prague and the two architects of the Gothic part of the cathedral. This collection, which dates from the 14th century, is the finest example of Czech sculpture from the Gothic period. The new part of the triforium contains busts of people who have contributed to the construction of the cathedral.

Opposite: the walls of the Land Registry Hall decorated with the coats of arms of magistrates who held positions there.

"Terrified, you see yourself portrayed in the rubies of St Vitus'. You saw yourself mortally sad the day you saw yourself there. You look like a beggar frightened by the daylight."

Apollinaire, *Zone*

STOVES
The castle was heated by large stoves (opposite) which were supplied with fuel from a corridor or a neighboring room. They were usually covered with green, glazed bricks.

knocker which bears a symbol: legend has it that, when Wenceslas was murdered at Stará Boleslav on the orders of his brother Boreslav, he hung on to the door knocker and stayed upright even after he had died. The knocker was later found and placed in the chapel.

ROYAL TREASURY. A stairway in the St Wenceslas Chapel leads to the Royal Treasury. The door has seven locks, the keys to which are held by seven different institutions. The Treasury has housed the Czech Crown Jewels since 1791, but unfortunately the collection cannot be seen although facsimiles of the most important pieces are on view in the Historical Museum at Lobkowicz Palace ▲ *223*.

THE OLD ROYAL PALACE

The entrance to the Old Royal Palace (Starý Královský palác) ▲ *202* is underneath the balcony at the far end of the courtyard. The palace was a residence of princes and kings from the 12th century onward, but the Habsburgs deserted it in the mid-16th century for the newer parts of the castle. The Old Palace continued to be occupied by central State organizations until the late 18th century, but is now only rarely used.

VLADISLAV HALL. This room, the largest secular hall in Europe, was built by Benedikt Ried of Piesting between 1493 and 1503. It occupies almost the entire second floor of the palace and is 200 feet long, 50 feet wide and 40 feet high. The interior, and the vault's complex ribbing ▲ *203* in particular, are good illustrations of the vitality of Gothic architecture in the late Middle Ages; the exterior, the entrances, and the huge windows, announce the Renaissance.

ALL SAINTS' CHAPEL. At the far end of the Vladislav Hall, a rood screen overlooks the interior of All Saints' Chapel. It was originally built by Petr Parléř in 1370, but was destroyed by fire in 1541 and not restored until the end of the 16th century. At that point, it was joined to the Vladislav Hall. The painting of All Saints on the high altar is by Václav Reiner (c. 1732).

THE LOUIS WING. After completing the Vladislav Hall, Benedikt Ried started work on a Renaissance transverse block sometimes known as the "LOUIS PALACE", after Vladislav's son ▲ *201*.

DIET HALL. Although this room was constructed by Benedikt Ried toward the end of the 14th century, its current appearance dates from the mid-16th century by Bonifác Wohlmut. The 19th-century furnishings are faithful copies of the original 17th-century pieces, and they give an idea of how the sessions were organized: the royal throne, with the archbishop's seat to the right of the King's and just behind the prelates' bench; then, along the walls, places reserved for senior functionaries; and lastly, opposite the throne, the bench occupied by lords and knights. Near the right-hand window is a gallery for representatives of the royal cities.

THE NEW LAND REGISTRY HALL. A stairway beside the knights' bench leads to this hall. The registers contained information relating to land ownership, and detailed all the property rights of the Superior Estates (or Orders) of the Diet as well as decisions handed down by the Court of Justice and the Diet itself. They were destroyed in the fire of 1541. A beautiful chest in one of the rooms dating from 1562 contains a few of the registers.

RIDERS' STAIRCASE ▲ *202*. This ramp opens into the Vladislav Hall through an accoladed gateway; its broad steps enabled knights to climb it on horseback.

GOTHIC PALACE OF CHARLES IV. The same ramp also gives access to the Gothic Palace situated under Vladislav Hall. The new tiles of the so-called CHARLES HALL are imitations of the original paving stones, while the walls are decorated with copies of busts from the cathedral triforium.

VLADISLAV HALL Banquets and jousts were once held in this ceremonial hall. It was also used for important meetings of the Diet. Since 1935, the results of Presidential elections have been announced from here.

The spines of the country's registers were adorned with drawings – distinctive signs that could be recognized by the illiterate staff who looked after them.

Wonderful sketches tracing the various stages of construction tell the story of how the area has changed since work began.

ST GEORGE'S SQUARE

Despite its restricted size, St George's Square (JIŘSKÉ NÁMĚSTÍ) was the Castle's central area throughout the Middle Ages. As can be seen from old engravings ▲ *214*, the square had numerous shops and wash houses until about 1870.

ST GEORGE'S BASILICA ● *68*

Beneath the Baroque façade (below) of St George's Basilica (Bazilica sv. Jiří) lies the façade of a real Romanesque church. Apart from the archeological remains of the tiny Church of the Virgin of Bořivoj and St Vitus' Chapel, this is the oldest monument from the Romanesque period in Bohemia. It was originally built of wood, and was founded in 912 by Prince Vratislav I. It was enlarged in 973 and, in 1142, following a major fire, was rebuilt in a late Romanesque style with two towers. In 924, the church had received the remains of Saint Ludmila, Saint Wenceslas' grandmother; it subsequently housed the remains of other 10th- and 11th-century members of the Přemyslid family, including the church's founder, Vratislav I, and the founder of the nearby convent, Boleslav II.

BUST OF A YOUNG GODDESS
Fragment of the attic decoration of Clam-Gallas Palace, executed by Matthias Bernhard Braun in 1716.

RESTORATION. The basilica was renovated during the Gothic period by the workshop of Petr Parléř, and later during the Renaissance and Baroque periods; it was then restored during the 19th century ▲ *206*. The interior has been frequently redone and dates from the second half of the 12th century; the exception is the Gothic Chapel of Saint Ludmila to the right of the choir, where there is a late 14th-century tomb hewn out of the limestone by the workshop of Petr Parléř.

THE CRYPT. Beneath the stairway leading to the choir is the crypt (1142) which is covered by a vault resting on pillars with cubic capitals. It contains the tombs of the convent's first abbesses, including that of Mlada; it was Mlada who obtained from Pope John XIII a letter making Prague the seat of an archbishop. To the right, on the altar table, is a statue of Saint Bridget (*Vanitas*), with her entrails full of snakes and lizards; this is a Baroque naturalist allegory of vanity. According to legend, an Italian stone-cutter called Spinetti carved it in

penance for an act of violence he committed in the church. Between 1718 and 1722, the ST JOHN NEPOMUK CHAPEL was built by František Maxmilián Kaňka and the Dientzenhofers, beside and adjoining the basilica.

ST GEORGE'S CONVENT (KLÁSTER SV. JIŘÍ) ★. This, the earliest religious establishment in Bohemia, was founded according to the Benedictine Rule by Mlada, the sister of Prince Boleslav II, in

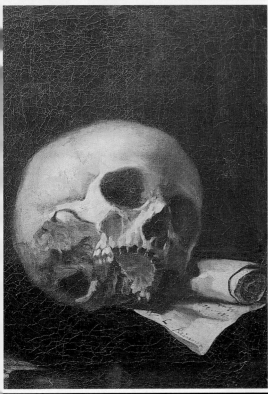

The simple, narrow, long nave is connected to the square, semicircular apsidal choir by a beautiful Baroque staircase. Unusually for Prague, the 10th- and 11th-century arches are made of splendid light-colored stone that has not been decorated.

MASTERS OF CZECH BAROQUE PAINTING IN ST GEORGE'S CONVENT
The collection of paintings on display in St George's Convent certainly deserves a visit. It includes works by such major artists as Karel Škréta, P. Brendl, M.B Braun, M. Brokof and Václav Vavřinec Reiner (1689–1743), one of the greatest Czech exponents of the Baroque style. Among his works on display in the Convent is *Still Life with Skull*.

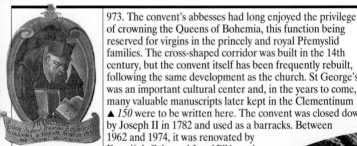

VIKÁŘSKÁ ULICE
Vicars' Street is situated between the fortifications and the north side of the cathedral. In the middle is the Powder Tower, an artillery bastion built in the 15th century by Vladislas Jagiello. The Castle's information office is at no. 2, the house of the Old Dean: the ceiling of this house is decorated with portraits of the Deans of St Vitus'.

HISTORICAL MUSEUM
This 2nd–1st-century BC man's head made of stone was found at Msecke Zehrovice. It is considered to be one of the most accomplished pieces of Celtic art.

973. The convent's abbesses had long enjoyed the privilege of crowning the Queens of Bohemia, this function being reserved for virgins in the princely and royal Přemyslid families. The cross-shaped corridor was built in the 14th century, but the convent itself has been frequently rebuilt, following the same development as the church. St George's was an important cultural center and, in the years to come, many valuable manuscripts later kept in the Clementinum ▲ 150 were to be written here. The convent was closed down by Joseph II in 1782 and used as a barracks. Between 1962 and 1974, it was renovated by František Cubr and Josef Pilár and underwent alterations before becoming the MUSEUM OF CZECH ART. The exhibits, from the basement to the top floor, span the centuries from the Mannerist period, and the work of painters active during the reign of Rudolph II, to the Baroque era of the 17th and 18th centuries.

AN ESTABLISHMENT FOR NOBLE LADIES. This building at the beginning of St George's Street (Jiřská ul.) was originally the Rožmberk family's palace (1545). In 1600, the owner exchanged it with Rudolph II for Schwarzenberg Palace in Hradčanské Square. The palace was then rebuilt by Tomáš Haffenecker between 1723 and 1731 and, on the orders of Maria Theresa, became an Institute of Noble Ladies for the benefit of female members of poor aristocratic families.

GOLDEN LANE (ZLATA ULIČKA)

Golden Lane is approached by going halfway down Jiřská Street and turning left into a passageway called U Daliborky. Rudolph II's name, and the fashion for occult sciences during his reign in the 18th century, inspired a legend surrounding this lane of alchemists ▲ 207. In fact, Golden Lane derived its name rather more simply from some craftsman gold-beaters who took refuge there after the Malá Strana fire of 1541. After that, Rudolph had wooden houses built for his archers who somehow found space to live there with their families. The situation deteriorated during the succeeding centuries as some of them built a first floor less than four feet high, and houses sprang

up on both sides although the lane was no more than four feet wide. In the 18th century, Maria Theresa ordered the inhabitants to replace their slums with houses made of brick, or at the very least cover them with roughcast. Between 1952 and 1955, the street was entirely renovated to plans by Pavel Janák; the choice of colors for the houses was entrusted to Jiří Trnka, a painter well known for his animated cartoons, and the street subsequently became popular with tourists.

WHITE TOWER AND DALIBORKA TOWER. These towers, which are situated to the east and west of Golden Lane respectively, were built as artillery bastions under Vladislas Jagiello in 1485. Both were used as prisons until the 18th century. The second tower takes its name from Dalibor of Kozojedy, who was imprisoned here in 1498 and whose story inspired a famous opera by Smetana.

JIŘSKÁ ULICE

After Golden Lane, St George's Street (Jiřská ul.) on the left leads to the Black Tower.

LOBKOWICZ PALACE. This palace (Lobkovický palác), at no. 1/3 on the right, was built after 1570 by Vratislav of Pernštejn. It came into the possession of the Lobkowicz family in 1651 and has remained there until the 20th century. The late Renaissance interior is well preserved, although the façade was redone in 1791 in order to merge with other parts of the castle. In 1973, the palace was turned into a department of the NATIONAL MUSEUM dealing with Czech history.

FORMER PALACE OF THE BURGRAVES. This building stands opposite, and contains the "House of Czechoslovak Children". In the 16th century, it was the home of the Chief Burgrave, chosen from among the great aristocratic families of Prague; he was the leading citizen in the country after the king, and his official representative in the latter's absence.

THE BLACK TOWER. Jiřská Street is closed off by a huge ogival door flanked by a high, square courtyard, the Black Tower. It formed part of the castle's system of fortifications during the first half of the 12th century; then, Wenceslas I had the tower walled up and he opened the present door in the 13th century. It had been given a golden roof during the reign of Charles IV, and it was known as the Golden Tower; it was damaged by the fire of 1541, which blackened it completely – hence its current name. Through the door is an observation terrace from which it is possible to take in all of Malá Strana.

The small houses in Golden Lane are now souvenir shops.

DALIBOR THE KNIGHT
Dalibor of Kozojedy was imprisoned in the Castle for supporting an uprising by a neighboring knight's serfs. To ease the boredom, Dalibor used to play the violin; according to legend, his music cast a spell over the whole town, and the people pleaded that he be set free, but he was later beheaded.

Above: the Powder Tower and gateway to the former Palace of the Burgraves with nobles' coats of arms.

223

REAL TENNIS ★
This Renaissance structure in the Royal Garden was built by Bonifác Wohlmut between 1567 and 1569. It was used as a

real tennis court, then as a royal stable, and finally as a military store. It was destroyed during World War Two, but an identical copy was then put up; this now serves as an official building. In front of the house is a carved group by Anton Braun, the nephew of Matthias Bernhard Braun. The façade is decorated with allegorical sgraffito of the sciences, virtues and earthly elements. Concerts are sometimes given here.

The Belvedere.

BEYOND POWDER BRIDGE

From the second courtyard, POWDER BRIDGE (PRASNÝ MOST) leads to those parts of the castle outside the fortifications that were added in the reign of Ferdinand I after 1526.

RIDING SCHOOL. The riding school (JÍZDÁRNA), to the right of the bridge, is a fine example of utilitarian architecture in the heyday of the Baroque style. It was designed by Jean-Baptiste Mathey in 1694. After being partly rebuilt by Pavel Janák, it was turned into an art gallery in 1948–9.

THE ROYAL GARDENS. These gardens (Královská zahrada) were laid out for Ferdinand I by G. Spatio and the court gardener, Francesco, and are one of the most beautiful examples of Renaissance art. Exotic trees like fig and grapefruit were grown here, and tulips were also introduced. Destroyed by the Swedes and the Saxons, they were redesigned in the 18th century. After being devastated yet again by the French army of occupation in 1743 and by Prussian bombardment in 1757, they were once more laid out during the 19th century, and then abandoned, before being restored by the architect Pavel Janák after 1918. The pathways in the park are adorned with statues from the workshop of Matthias Bernhard Braun.

THE ROYAL SUMMER PALACE (KRÁLOVSKÝ LETHORÁDEK). This huge one-story building with a curved roof, also known as the "Belvedere" (Belvedér), was commissioned by Ferdinand I for his wife Anna, and built in 1535–64 to designs by Genoese architect Paolo della Stella and completed by Bonifác Wohlmut. It is considered to be an example of the purest Renaissance architecture to be found outside Italy ▲ *80*. The first floor is bordered with a gallery of arcades with elegant columns supporting seventy-four reliefs. Nearby is a statue of Victory (above, right) by J. Stursa, dating from 1921. In the small garden, there is a bronze, "singing" fountain: a few moments spent beneath its basin suffice to justify its name.

From Hradčany
to Malá Strana

▲ From Hradčany to Malá Strana

1. Strahov Monastery ✪
2. Černin Palace
3. Church of Our Lady of Loreto
4. Loretánská Street
5. Toscan Palace
6. Martinic Palace

⏱ Half a day

◆ **A** A2-A3-B2-B3-C2-C3

Coat of arms of the Archbishopric of Prague.

Archbishop's Palace.

The Hradčany district is relatively modern in that it did not become a "town" until 1320 during the reign of John of Luxemburg. It was built on the orders of Berka of Duba, Burgrave of Prague. Originally, the district only consisted of what is now Hradčanské Square (Hradčanské náměstí) and a group of houses scattered round present-day Kanovnická and Loretánská streets; only in 1598 did Hradčany benefit from the royal privileges that other royal towns enjoyed, and it remained under the monarchy's strict control for many years. In June 1541, a fire destroyed Malá Strana and spread as far as the Castle and Hradčany, and the land thereby made available enabled the Church and the aristocracy to build fine Renaissance, and later Baroque, houses and palaces. Hradčany is probably better known than any other part of Prague for its peaceful atmosphere, its gardens and its exceptionally well preserved 17th- and 18th-century architecture. For the writer, Jiří Karásek, a visit to Hradčany is like a walk into times gone by; the past "blows over you from green shadows in the huge gardens with their thick foliage. It envelops you from the shade of a doorway and the depths of a palace hallway."

ARCHBISHOP'S PALACE

Hradčanské Square is lined with several palaces; the Archbishop's Palace (ARCIBISKUPSKÝ PALÁC) is at the bottom near the Castle. The architectural history of this building is complex because it has been added to and redecorated on many occasions. It was designed by Bonifác Wohlmut and built by Udalrico Aostalli between 1562 and 1564. A century later, between 1675 and 1694, it was renovated by Jean-Baptiste Mathey, and the façade is the work of Jan Josef Wirch (1732–87) although the main entrance is attributed to Mathey. The palace is now the most beautiful in the whole square. The decoration on the piano nobile (the third level) is a superb example of balance. It is articulated not only by the

8. OLD TOWN HALL · 9. HRADČANSKÉ SQUARE · 10. CHURCH OF ST JOHN OF NEPOMUK · 11. ARCHBISHOP'S PALACE · 12. SCHWARZENBERG PALACE · 13. CASTLE · 14. VLAŠSKÁ STREET · 15. LOBKOWICZ PALACE · 16. SCHÖNBORN-COLLOREDO PALACE

slight projection of the lateral wings and the central body of the building, but also by the display of half-columns and pilasters; the balconies, bull's-eye windows and pediments are in the Rococo style.

STERNBERG PALACE (ŠTERNBERSKÝ PALÁC)

NATIONAL GALLERY. Access to Sternberg Palace is by a passageway that runs along the left-hand side of the Archbishop's Palace. From what remains today, we can see that it originally formed part of a more ambitious, yet never completed, project on which a number of celebrated architects collaborated. These included Domenico Martinelli of Lucca, the workshop of Krištof Dientzenhofer and, in the final phase, Giovanni Battista Alliprandi. The building is remarkable for the elliptical pavilion overlooking the garden. Today, Sternberg Palace houses the National Gallery's collections of European art. The majority of its collection comprises works from the Italian and northern European schools ▲ 228. The fine collection of 19th- and 20th-century French art, which was exhibited, up to 1995, in an annexe of the Palace, is now housed in the Museum of Modern Art at Veletržní Palace ▲ 317. The museum also houses the collection of the art critic and collector, Vincenc Krámář (1877–1960).

RESTORED TO THEIR RIGHTFUL OWNERS. At one point, the collection was threatened by the 1990 Law of Restitution. This law gave people whose goods had been seized by the Communists after February 1948 the right to repossess them. But it proved to be very difficult to implement these rights in the art world. Krámář's heirs claimed a right to sixteen Picassos, two Braques, two Derains and a dozen Czech Cubist painters, but the Curator of the National Museum relied on correspondence from Krámář to show that the great collector, an ardent Communist, had knowingly donated his paintings to the State.

THE NATIONAL GALLERY COLLECTIONS
Six museums in Prague have a permanent exhibition of part of the collection of the National Gallery. The Convent of St Agnes ▲ 182 houses the collections of medieval Bohemian and Central European art. St George's Convent ▲ 220 exhibits the works of Bohemian artists from the reign of Rudolf II to the end of the Baroque period. The Sternberg Palace exhibits European art from the 14th to the 18th centuries. The Veletržní Palace ▲ 317 houses art of the 19th and 20th centuries. Asiatic art is exhibited at the Zbraslav Convent ▲ 328. The Kinský Palace ▲ 137 houses the information center of the National Gallery, as well as temporary exhibitions.

227

At the end of the 18th century, Prague was quite unlike Vienna, Munich or Dresden in that it did not have an art gallery worthy of the name. Count František Josef Šternberk decided to rectify this sorry state of affairs by founding the Society of Patriotic Friends of the Arts in Bohemia in 1796, with the aim of creating a public art gallery. Gifts flowed in immediately both from the aristocracy and from the enlightened bourgeoisie and, during the 19th century art collections were further enhanced by bequests from Dr Josef Hoser, particularly paintings of the Dutch School. In 1937, the gallery was acquired by the Czechoslovak State, and since 1945 it has been part of Prague's National Gallery.

«PORTRAIT OF ÉLEONORA OF TOLEDO»
This portrait by the Florentine Agnolo Bronzino (1503–1572) depicts the daughter of the Viceroy of Naples.

"FEAST OF ROSE GARLANDS"
This is the Sternberg Museum's greatest work. It was painted in 1506 by Albrecht Dürer and was hung in the Church of St Bartholomew. It was later purchased by Rudolph II and transported across the Alps. The work escaped the ransacking Swedes, but was sold in 1782, then bought back by the abbey of Strahov in 1793. In 1934 it was bought by the state.

«JASPER SCHADE VAN WESTRUM»
Frans Hals (c. 1582–1666)
A masterly work from the Dutch school.
The painter has captured the haughty
personality of this young Utrecht
nobleman with ingenious
subtlety. The highlights on the
costume also highlight the vanity
of the wearer, and give the painting
a nervous vitality.

«ST BRUNO»
Antony van Dyck (1599–1641)
one of the most influential painters of the
XVII century. A prolific portraitist, he
also executed a number of mythologicial
and religious works, such as this
St Bruno. Here we can see the
elegant touch of the great
master. The work is characterized
by a sentimental piety.

«CHRIST»
Doménikos
Theotokópoulos
(1541–1614), who
was born in Crete,
acquired the name
El Greco (the Greek)
after he settled in
Toledo in 1577.
It was in the Spain of
the late 16th century,
imbued with religious
mysticism, that his
genius reached its
height. This *Christ*,
painted around
1595, was one of
the most important
acquisitions made by
the National Gallery
while it was under
the direction of
Vincenc Kramář
in the years
1919–39.

The square has hardly changed in two hundred years. In the center stands Ferdinand Macmilián Brokoff's Column of the Plague erected in 1726 to commemorate the end of the 1679 epidemic. At the far end of the square is Toscan Palace, which served as headquarters for Marshal Count de Bellisle, commander of the French army that occupied Prague in 1741–2.

FORMER SCHWARZENBERG PALACE

This building is opposite the Archbishop's Palace and once formed part of Lobkowicz Palace. Today, it houses the Swiss Embassy. The palace was built by František Pavíček (1776–1861) between 1795 and 1810, and its design is in the Empire style which was so popular at the beginning of the century.

SCHWARZENBERG-LOBKOWICZ PALACE

Schwarzenberg-Lobkowicz Palace (1545–63) easily makes a big impression beside its somewhat insipid neighbor. It was built by Augustin Vlach to a commission by Prince Johann Lobkowicz, and is a magnificent example of Czech Renaissance style. Vlach invested the palace's grandeur and refinement with great originality, while the gables, the cornices with their curious lunettes, and the sgraffito ● *78* established Schwarzenberg-Lobkowicz as an architectural touchstone when Czechs began to rediscover their architectural heritage in the 19th century. There are many neo-Renaissance buildings in Prague that include elements that are characteristic of this building. It now houses a military museum ▲ *231*.

CONVENT OF THE DISCALCED CARMELITES

"ST MICHAEL"
This carving by Ottavio Mosto (1693) adorns the façade of Toscan Palace on the corner of Loretánská Street.

Next to Schwarzenberg-Lobkowicz Palace stand a number of buildings that made up the former Barnabite Convent in the 17th century. It was closed down in 1786 and handed over to the Discalced Carmelites in 1792. The Church of St Benedict, once Hradčany's parish church and restored in the 16th, 17th and 18th centuries, is in the middle. In his *Magic Prague*,

Angelo Ripellino quotes from *A Gothic Soul* (1900), a novel by Jiří Karásek, in which the hero is a hypochondriac terrified at the prospect of going mad. The Convent of the Discalced Carmelites, with its myriad legends, particularly attracted him: "At midnight, before taking his vows," each novice "had to remove the ring from the crushed hand of the mummified Saint Elekta . . . During the ceremonies, the voices of the living dead could be heard singing psalms, as if from the depths of an abyss". Today, the palace is used to accommodate visiting dignitaries.

TOSCAN PALACE

The west side of Hradčanské Square consists of Thun-Hohenstein Palace, otherwise known as "Toscan" Palace (TOSKÁNSKÝ PALÁC) and originally owned by the Grand Dukes of Tuscany who bought it in 1718. The palace, built in 1689–91, is attributed to Mathey and is a skilful combination of Romanesque architecture and French classicism. The decoration of the impressive façade consists of two belvederes projecting from the balustraded attic story. The statues of the seven liberal arts are from the workshop of Jan Brokoff.

LORETÁNSKÁ STREET

There are some interesting buildings in this lesser known street. The first is the FORMER HRADČANY TOWN HALL (1601–4), built in the Czech Renaissance style, and notable for its sgraffito ● 78, some pieces of Imperial armor, and a representation of Justice. At no. 4 is Martinic Palace by Bartolommeo Scotti, who worked to plans by the architect, Carlo Fontana; it is one of Prague's rare examples of design influenced by Roman styles. At the end of Loretánská Street, there are steps leading to Nerudova Street ▲ *254*.

Above left: the magnificent Schwarzenberg Palace seen from Nerudova Street, details of the façade decorated with sgraffito decoration in diamond point. Right: sgraffito of biblical motifs on Martinic Palace.

"The broad façade of the old Royal Palace . . . is the most powerful. The family castle of the princes of Schwarzenberg and another building . . . stand on the other side [of the square] as if regarding them with perpetual reverence."
R. M. Rilke,
Histories from Prague

In the 19th century, Hradčanské Square was lit by street lamps in the form of candelabra.

MILITARY MUSEUM
An interest in military matters is not essential to enjoy a visit to this museum. The ceilings are splendidly frescoed, and the magnificent collections of arms and uniforms are fascinating. Left, *The Battle of Solferino* (1859). The museum is currently closed for renovation.

● 78

MARTINIC PALACE

This fine Renaissance building (MARTINICKÝ PALÁC), somewhat restrained in appearance despite its sgraffito decoration employing biblical and mythological themes, has an entrance dating from 1560; the gables date from the 17th century. The part of the building overlooking the courtyard is also decorated with sgraffito. The palace was once the property of Jaroslav Bořita de Martinic, one of the Councillors thrown from the Hradčany in 1618 ● *34*.

MUCHA'S HOUSE

Alfons Mucha's old house, one of the most beautiful buildings in Prague, is situated at 6 Hradčanské Square, and abounds in evidence of the painter's lyricism and refinement ▲ *171*. Today it houses the Mucha Foundation. Visits are only by request, via the Mucha Museum ▲ *172*.

LEADING FIGURE IN PRAGUE ART NOUVEAU. Mucha had unparalleled skill at adapting the heady convolutions of modern design to the language of drawing and posters, and he managed to revive the genre with his peerless command of color, his placement of figures and his decorative arrangements. His success was limited, however. A trip to the United States in 1904 did not live up to his expectations, and his return to Bohemia was only moderately successful ▲ *165*, as a new, more radical generation was already guiding Czech painting in new directions. Nonetheless, his best posters are true masterpieces, and many less well-known works are interesting, particularly the pastels he completed in the early 1900s.

Poster from 1898

MUCHA FOUNDATION. Jiří Mucha has faithfully recaptured the atmosphere of his father's house. Nearly all of the works that took Paris by storm – and made the actress Sarah Bernhardt such a famed beauty – are now mostly in the Mucha Museum ▲ *172*. However the Foundation still houses a few gifts from friends, including

AMADEUS
Opposite Martinic Palace (Hradčanské náměstí 7) is a handsome building which Miloš Forman selected as Mozart's Viennese house in his film *Amadeus*.

A TOUCH OF 1900
The lyrical, turn-of-the-century world of Alfons Mucha is much in evidence in the painter's house, one of the most beautiful in Prague.

somewhat risqué sculpture of two women from Rodin, and a harmonium from Gauguin. Alfons Mucha died in 1939. His works were miraculously spared during the period of Communist rule, but his son, Jiří, a celebrated writer, spent many years in prison. He later divided his time between Paris and Prague tracking down his father's works. In 1991, ten years after Jiří's death, his son and his widow created the Mucha Foundation with the support of the Minister of Culture. The Foundation organizes exhibitions of the painter's works.

CHURCH OF ST JOHN OF NEPOMUK

Kanovnická Street leads to this church, which was built between 1720 and 1728 by Kilián Ignác Dientzenhofer to a commission by the Ursuline nuns. Inside, Václav Vavřinec Reiner's frescos (1728) depict the legend of St John of Nepomuk, a leading figure in central European culture and one of the patron saints of Bohemia.

JOHN OF POMUK. In 1393, the Vicar-General of the diocese of Prague, John of Pomuk, was arrested and tortured on the orders of King Wenceslas IV following a violent argument between the king and Archbishop John of Jenzenstein. He died under interrogation, and his body was thrown into the Vltava under cover of darkness. Legend has it that stars began to sparkle round the body on the surface of the water, and this is the origin of the crown of stars that statues of St John always wear. He was later buried at St Vitus' Cathedral.

CONFUSION. Around 1450, the Viennese chronicler Ebendorfer claimed that the reason for the Vicar-General's death had been his refusal to reveal to the king what his wife, the queen, had said in the confessional. This new version was somewhat embellished and became the basis of the legend of St John of Nepomuk. A confusion of dates that came to light in the 15th century had him dying in 1383, and Václav Hájek's *Kronika Česká* (*Czech Chronicle*) of 1541 ▲ *324*, which drew freely on contradictory sources, even recounted the death of two characters, St John of Nepomuk and John of Pomuk, despite the fact that the Vicar-General died in 1393. However, it was the former, the supposed martyr of the confessional, who was beatified in 1721 and canonized in 1729. Veneration of Saint John of Nepomuk was widespread in the 17th and 18th centuries. A number of versions of his legend were published in the 17th century: the most famous, by the Jesuit Bohuslav Balbín, appeared in the *Acta Sanctorum*, published by the Bollandists of Louvain in 1680.

A SYMBOL OF SILENCE. On April 15, 1719, when Saint John's tomb was opened up, something was found which was thought

ST JOHN NEPOMUK
"The tongue's . . . burning ruby rising out of . . . the house of verses burns with constancy/from the divine depths spared by the all-powerful dust."
J. Zahradníček

ČERNIN PALACE
The 500 feet-long façade includes an impressive line of thirty huge columns; they are in two rows and rest on a crepidoma decorated with diamond-head bosses.

to be his tongue, although it was subsequently established in 1980 that it was nothing more than a piece of dried out brain. Back in 1725, this scrap of moistened organic tissue had been examined by experts charged with the task of instituting the process of canonization, and the "tongue", the martyr's symbol of silence, became his emblem; this emblem is now found in all the churches in Prague dedicated to Saint John of Nepomuk. Nowadays, John of Pomuk is no longer thought to have been the queen's confessor, and it seems that it is his more legendary double who has been canonized.

ČERNIN PALACE ● 8

From the Church of St John of Nepomuk, Nový Svět Street and then Kapucínská Street on the left lead into Loreto Square (Loretánské náměstí). The formidable Černin Palace (ČERNÍNSKÝ PALÁC) (1669–79) is the main work of Francesco Caratti. The interior decoration (1717–23) was by F. M. Kaňka ▲ 274, also responsible for the Baroque garden; the main entrances were executed by Anselmo Lurago in 1747–9. Count Humprecht Černin of Chudenice, who had commissioned the palace, hoped his residence might vie with Prague Castle: in his favor, only a few modest buildings stood between it and his palace, the area having been laid waste during the Thirty Years' War.

IMMODERATE TASTES. The Count originally asked Bernini to design his residence, but he subsequently chose another architect, Francesco Caratti. His time as ambassador in Venice

eems to have turned his head, and he wanted to have his
alace built on an elevated spot so as to make an even more
triking impression. The count's monumental architectural
astes almost cost him his fortune; particularly as his son,
Iermann Jacob, was having yet another palace built in
/ienna. In his Prague residence, the latter amassed such a
agnificent collection of paintings that it was thought to be
ne of the finest in the Empire.
UICIDE OR ACCIDENTAL FALL? In 1779, by which time the
alace had fallen into a state of considerable decay, it was
ffered for sale but did not find a buyer. It was turned into a
ospital during the Napoleonic Wars, and then a barracks in
851. In 1919, it became the headquarters of the Ministry of
oreign Affairs, and it also housed the Nazi "protectorate"
uring World War Two. Tragedy again visited the palace on
Iarch 10, 1948, when the body of Jan Masaryk (1886–1948),
on of the first President of the Republic and then Minister of
oreign Affairs in the Gottwald cabinet, was found nearby. It
·sa never established whether he had committed suicide
·r had been pushed out of a window.

NOVÝ SVĚT ★
Nový Svět (New
World) Street is one
of the most delightful
in Prague. The
surrounding area was
originally very poor
(it was where Castle
staff used to live) and
was frequently
ravaged by fires, but
it was later rebuilt in
the Renaissance style
and often renovated.
Today, it is home to
many artists and
writers.

CHURCH OF OUR LADY OF LORETO ● 71

**LORETANSKÉ
SQUARE ★** is bound
by Černin Palace to
the west, the Church
of Our Lady of
Loreto to the east,
and the former
Capuchin Monastery
to the north.

his church (LORETA) is both an important religious
uilding and a highly regarded example of architectural
esign. It is constructed around a *Casa Santa* (Holy
Iouse), a replica of an Italian sanctuary at Loreto, near
ncona in Italy, which, according to legend, was a house
f the Virgin Mary that had been transported there by
ngels in 1294.
ASA SANTA. The Prague replica is not the only one
1 Bohemia, where there are about fifty altogether.
he Casa Santa was built to celebrate the Catholic
ictory at the Battle of White Mountain ● 34 by
enerating the Virgin Mary and is the architectural
nd ideological center of the Church. Of the
uildings left standing, it was the first to be
onstructed. It was built between 1626 and 1631
y Giovanni Battista Orsi with money

The slope in front of the Loreto Church is decorated with statues of *putti*.

PRINCESS LOBKOWICZ
After a visit to the "Casa Santa" in Mikulov, Moravia, the Princess built a similar shrine in Prague. It later became the most famous in Bohemia.

provided by Princess Benigna Catherine of Lobkowicz. The façade is articulated by sixteen columns with Corinthian capitals, which also include niches containing statues of prophets and sibyls; the reliefs recount the life of the Virgin Mary. Inside, the silver altar and the limewood statue are dedicated to the Virgin. The rest of the church was completed shortly afterward, and the courtyard was surrounded by cloisters before 1664; an extra floor was built above them by Kilián Ignác Dientzenhofer in 1747–51.

THE FAÇADE. Krištof Dientzenhofer, Kilián's father, started the façade shortly before he died in 1722, and it was completed by his son, who added the terrace. This consists of two side pavilions and a central structure with a bell tower topped by an onion-shaped dome. The décor, which resembles that of a carved reredos, features the theme of the Annunciation; Mary is kneeling on the left-hand gable and there is an angel on the right-hand gable. They are accompanied by statues of the saints and evangelists on the balustrade and above the main entrance.

CHURCH OF THE NATIVITY. This is the largest chapel in the church, and one of the best examples of Baroque style in Prague. In 1734, Jan Jiří Aichbauer (1685–1737) enlarged the church which the Dientzenhofers had also worked on, Václav Vavřinec Reiner ▲ *162, 184, 285* painted his fresco, *The Presentation in the Temple*, over the choir, while Jan Adam

Schöpf (1702–72) painted more frescos in the nave. The paintings in the side altars are by Antonín Kern (1709–47), a leading exponent of the Rococo, whose works can also be seen in St George's Convent in the Castle ▲ 220. The abundant statuary is beautifully situated and gives the church a slightly theatrical air.

CHAPEL OF OUR LADY OF SORROWS. This chapel is situated in the southeast corner of the cloister. A side chapel dating from 1730, which is dedicated to a Spaniard, Saint Wilgefortis, depicts a curious scene. According to legend, this virtuous princess asked God to save her from a marriage that her father had arranged with a pagan. God obliged by giving her a magnificent beard, but the father was so furious that he had the unfortunate woman crucified. This Spanish saint has never been significantly worshiped in Bohemia any more than other imported saints like Saint Felix and Saint Marcia whose remains are kept in the side chapels of the Church of the Nativity. Popular tradition replaces this picture of Saint Wilgefortis with one of the medieval Czech saint, Saint Starosta, who boasts an identical legend.

The Casa Santa the high altar of the Church of the Nativity, and a general view of the church.

FORMER CAPUCHIN CONVENT

Loreto Square also contains the former Capuchin Convent, the Order's first monastery in Bohemia. It was built between 1600 and 1602 on land donated by the powerful Lobkowicz family; the adjoining Church of the Virgin and Our Lady of the Angels is designed in the restrained style that the Capuchins particularly favored. The cycle of fourteen Gothic paintings that once adorned the church are now in the National Gallery. At Christmas, the convent is home to the biggest crib in Prague; it dates from the 18th century.

STRAHOV MONASTERY ★

The Premonstratensian Strahov Monastery (STRAHOVSKÝ KLÁŠTER) is not far from Loreto Square. This is no longer Hradčany, but the Malá Strana district to which the monastery properly belongs. It is more pleasant to walk through the maze of passageways than along noisy Pohořelec Street. The Premonstratensians occupied the convent from the 12th century until 1952, the year when religious orders were abolished by the Communists. The monastery was returned to the order after the Velvet Revolution.

THE PREMONSTRATENSIANS. The order was founded in the 12th century, at a time when a sense that the Church had strayed too far from the spirit of the Gospels encouraged a number of individuals to seek reforms. One of these was Saint Norbert; born in 1080, this aristocratic chaplain to the German Emperor was a key political figure, and he participated directly in the dispute over Investitures. He abandoned temporal struggles in 1115 and, like many

STRAHOV MONASTERY AND ITS BAROQUE TREASURES ✪
Strahov Monastery, which crowns Pétřín Hill, is one of the largest in Bohemia and seems to rival the nearby Castle. Its finest features are the Church of the Assumption, with its profusion of Baroque decoration, the picture gallery and the library (visits by arrangement). Not only does the library contain 130,000 volumes and illuminated manuscripts; it is also notable for its Theology and Philosophy Rooms, which impress by their size and their magnificent ceilings. Afterwards, it is worth going out onto the terrace behind the church, which overlooks orchards and commands a panoramic view of the plain of Prague.

Ever since its foundation in 1143, Strahov Monastery has been famous for its library. The collections have been frequently ruined, but on each occasion they have been built up again, and in the 17th and 18th centuries respectively, the Theology and Philosophy Rooms were added to house extra books. The library continues to receive gifts and bequests: in 1950, it contained 130,000 volumes, including 3,000 manuscripts and 2,000 incunabula, a remarkable number for an abbey library.

SAINT JOHN THE EVANGELIST
Fifteenth-century wooden statue.

LECTIONARY FROM STRAHOV
The oldest manuscript in the Monastery (left), is a fine example of Ottonian art. This 9th-century document contains illuminations which probably come from the *scriptorium* of Saint Martin of Tours.

THEOLOGY ROOM (1671)
This room contains 16,000 books, many of them bibles, including the famous Kralice Bible (1579–93), and writings of Fathers of the Church and leaders of the Counter-Reformation. It was enlarged in 1721 and redecorations by a local monk, Siard Nosecký, consist of seventeen large scenes depicting the thoughts of the then Abbot, J. Hirnhaim.

PHILOSOPHY ROOM (1783)

This room contains 50,000 volumes including philosophy, history and philology, and which include Diderot's *Encyclopédie*. Following Joseph II's decision to close down the monasteries, the Abbot, J. Mayer, managed to save his house from secularization and acquired the wonderful carved wood cabinets from the Monastery at Louka. Abbot Mayer's intention was to recreate the room at Louka by employing the same painter, the Austrian master Franz Anton Maulbertsch. The theme chosen expressed the optimism of the Age of Enlightenment: the upward journey of humanity under the guidance of Providence toward philosophical and religious knowledge.

MOZART AT STRAHOV
Music has never been far from this spiritual shrine, whether in the library itself or in the Baroque Church of the Assumption (right). It is said that Mozart visited the church, and improvised an organ sonata which was partly noted down by one of the priests, Norbert Lehmann. The Abbey organist at the time was J. B. Kuchař, who was known as the "second Seger"; he was one of Mozart's greatest admirers and helped in the preparation of the scores of operas performed in Prague.

members of the nobility, took Holy Orders and became a priest, and embarked on his career as a reformer. He founded his first abbey in 1120 at Prémontré, near Laon in northern France. More monasteries were opened, and in 1126 Norbert was elected Archbishop of Magdeburg; he subsequently became Chancellor of the Empire and died in 1134.

A NOTABLE HISTORY. The year 1140 saw the foundation by Prince Vladislav II of the Premonstratensian monastery at Strahov; this came about at the suggestion of Jindřich Zdik, Bishop of Olomouc. The monastery was ideally situated close to the commercial route that ran between Nuremberg and Krakov. It is also the oldest Premonstratensian monastery in Bohemia, and is known as "Mount Sion" because the layout of the town on the hill is reminiscent of Jerusalem. The first occupants of Strahov Monastery came from Steinfeld Convent, and the wooden buildings rapidly gave way to stone

Strahov Monastery seen from Petřín Hill ▲ 269.

structures, beginning with the primitive church which was completed in 1150 and dedicated to the Assumption. The monks enjoyed a certain degree of comfort: water, for example, came from springs on Petřín Hill along an ingenious system of wooden canals. At the end of the 16th century, Rudolph II ordered the construction of a votive church, and work took place between 1603 and 1612 on this sanctuary dedicated to SAINT ROCHE. The church was built next to the main entrance, and is often attributed to Giovanni Maria Filippi ▲ 271; it manages to combine elements of both Gothic and Renaissance styles. Substantial additions were made during the 17th and 18th centuries; these included the

Abbot's Library, the present-day Theology Room (1671–9) by
Giovanni Domenico Orsi, Jean-Baptiste Mathey's summer
refectory (1679–90) decorated with a brilliant trompe l'oeil
fresco (1728–31) by Siard Nosecký, and the new library's
Philosophy Room (1782–92) by Ignaz Johann Palliardi. The
Philosophy Room's ceiling fresco, the Austrian painter F. A.
Maulbertsch's last great work ▲ *239*, depicts the upward
advance of humanity based on the Old and New Testaments,
symbolized respectively by Moses and Aaron before the Ark
of the Covenant and by Saint Paul before the unknown god in
Athens. Special cupboards covered with wire mesh and placed
above the doors contained prohibited publications, the *libri
prohibiti*. Strahov Monastery had little to fear from the
secularization of religious orders decreed by Joseph II; he was
greatly impressed by the Order's way of life and, in the event,
it was only closed briefly toward the end of his reign.

The
Premonstratensians
followed the Rule of
Saint Augustine.
Their main aims were
to propagate solemn
liturgy and a life of
penance, and to
devote their lives to
the apostolate.

MAIN ENTRANCE. The majestic doorway, a Baroque
masterpiece by Johann Anton Quitainer made in 1742 on
plans by Anselmo Lurago, is surmounted by a statue of
Saint Norbert.

CHURCH OF THE ASSUMPTION. What
survives of this Romanesque building
(right) dates from 1758. The Assumption
of the Virgin at the main entrance (1744)
is one of J. A. Quitainer's greatest works.
Leading figures of 18th-century
Baroque art took part in the
decoration of the church.

ABBEY BUILDINGS. These are
situated to the right of the
courtyard, and take the form of

LOBKOWICZ COAT OF ARMS. The Lobkowicz family has been well known since the 14th century. In the 16th

century, they became one of the most important houses of the Czech aristocracy through their great wealth and political activity. Members of the family still live in the Czech Republic; some continued to live there during the period of Communist rule, and others returned from abroad after 1989. Some of their property has been returned to them, and several family members hold important posts.

four wings surrounding a closed yard known as the Paradise Courtyard. The buildings are predominantly Baroque in style, and were built over Roman foundations which had in turn replaced earlier wooden constructions. They were discovered in the course of archeological digs which are still in progress.

MUSEUM OF CZECH LITERATURE. The main door leads to the various second-floor rooms belonging to the library ▲ *238*. Another door situated behind the Abbey Church gave access to the Museum of Czech Literature, founded by the Communists, that presented a historical perspective of Czech literature. The library and its archives are now open to the public and temporary exhibitions are organized on a regular basis.

VLAŠSKÁ STREET

Vlašská Street (Italian Street) leads down the hill away from Strahov Monastery; about halfway down, there are some benches where the visitor may rest, admire the view and enjoy the countryside.

A HOSPITAL AT THE FOOT OF PETŘÍN HILL. This is an enormous building. At one time, there were vines and bourgeois homes here but, between 1851 and 1864, the Sisters of Charity of St Carlo Borromeo had a hospital built to plans by A. Gudera. The Empire style building was enlarged during the 19th century and modernized in 1970; today, it is a university hospital. The Church of St Carlo Borromeo (1855), which forms part of the hospital, is in the late Empire style. It is decorated with paintings by V. Kandler and sculptures by V. Lev, and now also houses a medical library.

VLAŠSKÝ ŠPITAL AND THE ITALIAN HOUSE. A large colony of Italians emigrated to Prague during the second half of the 16th century, and an Italian religious order was founded in 1573. At the beginning of the 17th century, it had a hospital built on the site of a number of old houses; the architect was Domenico de Bossi. Today, the buildings are used by the Italian Cultural Center.

LOBKOWICZ PALACE ● *80*

Slightly further down and to the right is Lobkowicz Palace, now the home of the German Embassy and one of the most beautiful Baroque buildings in Prague. It was built between 1703 and 1713 by Giovanni Battista Alliprandi, and another floor was added in 1769 by Ignaz Johann Palliardi. Altogether, the building offers a curious contrast between the almost severe façade that overlooks the street and is very classical in style, and the other façade overlooking the gardens which was influenced by Bernini's project for the Louvre (1655). The garden was laid out at the same time as the palace on plans by J. J. Kapula; it covered land where vines had once grown. After 1793, it was converted into a natural English Garden, and this is how it has remained to the present day. The landscape gardener J. V. Skalnic, already noted for his work on the gardens at Marienbad, established the first alpinum in Bohemia. The gardens are not open to the public, but a few feet further up the street, visitors can turn left into an overgrown garden, and walk along behind the palace gardens. The railings are decorated with two beautiful sculptures depicting the abductions of Persephone and Oreithyia. The protruding, rounded central building houses frescoed halls. On leaving the palace, Šporkova Street leads into a charming little square with a large number of trees and some delightful houses.

Top, left to right: a general view of Lobkowicz Palace; painted entrance hall with stucco decoration; on the façade, the coat of arms of the Lobkowicz family, owners of the property since 1753. Above: statue in the Church of St Carlo Borromeo.

SCHÖNBORN-COLLOREDO PALACE

Further still along Vlašská Street is Schönborn-Colloredo Palace, now occupied by the United States Embassy. The palace was commissioned by General Count Rudolph Colloredo (1587–1657), whose family settled in Bohemia during the Thirty Years' War. He amassed a fortune after 1620 and inherited a vast Renaissance residence, entrusting its entire restoration to Carlo Lurago. This palace, with beautiful wooden doors and huge grounds, was renovated by Jan Blažis Santini-Aichl in 1715, but is not open to the public.

Lobkowicz Palace and grounds in 1740.

"Úvoz Street" by Vincenc Beneš
This splendid work shows a clearing toward the south, the Strahov orchard in the foreground, and then Petřín Hill. This oasis of complete calm in a quite unexpected rural setting is only a few minutes from Charles Bridge.

Above: entrance to Vrtba Palace garden. Right: bust of the Moon decorating "Stone Column House" in Úvoz Street, where there is also a Sun.

Vrtba Palace

Vrtba Palace is at the end of Tržiště Street, but the entrance is in Karmelitská Street. It is on the site of two Renaissance houses joined together by Sezima of Vrtba around 1631, and was rebuilt in the late Renaissance style which it has retained to this day. The house originally belonged to Kryštof Harant of Polžice (1546–1621). He was one of Bohemia's most important composers and also one of the leaders of the rebellion against the Habsburgs. He was beheaded in 1621 in Old Town Square ▲ 136. His house was seized, and later given to Sezima of Vrtba. The painter, Mikoláš Aleš, also lived here from 1886 to 1889. The old road that separated the two houses is still there, and is now the passageway that leads to the garden. The grounds, which are adorned by an Atlas, were laid out by F. M. Kaňka in 1720; they comprise some of

the most beautiful Baroque gardens (Vrtbovská zahrada) in Prague ▲ 274. The statues are the work of Matthias Bernhard Braun, and the paintings on the first floor are by Reiner.

Úvoz ulice

Úvoz Street is an alternative, and very pleasant, road to Strahov Monastery. The southern side of the road is shut off by the wall running along the monastery garden, while the northern side is lined with attractive houses as well as house signs ▲ 264. The end of Úvoz Street marks the beginning of the panoramic route that goes to Petřín Hill. Vines were once grown on these slopes; later, gardens such as Na Nebozízku, Seminářská zahrada and the Kinsky Gardens (Kinského zahrada) were laid out, but after 1945 they were joined up to the gardens of Petřín Hill.

Malá Strana 1: at the foot of the Castle

HISTORY

THE EARLIEST INHABITANTS.
There is archeological evidence
that there were people living in what is now
Malá Strana in prehistoric times; it is also thought that,
no later than the 8th century, there were a number of markets
down the hill from the Castle, the oldest of which extended
over the site of present-day Sněmovní Street. The first major
medieval exercise in town planning was carried out by
Vladislav I who, after 1157, began the construction of Judith
Bridge ▲ *154*; the effect of this was the creation of a new
thoroughfare now known as Mostecká Street. Around this
time, the Knights of St John of Jerusalem erected a hospital
and the Church of Our Lady Under the Chain ▲ *272,* and the
Premonstratensians established their monastery on the hill at
Strahov ▲ *237.* Bishop Jindřich Břetislav, the King's nephew,
also had his residence transferred to a palace built on the site
of what is now Dražikého Square. There were already

**MALÁ STRANA: OFF
THE BEATEN TRACK
✪**
Renowned for its
churches and palaces,
Malá Strana has a
self-contained
atmosphere, so that it
seems to be quite
separate from the
Castle and even the
river. The district's
houses, lanes and
taverns, their names
imbued with legend,
make it certainly the
most charming and
magical of Prague.
A walk through
carriage gateways and
along narrow passages
will reveal delightful
gardens and many
secret courtyards. A
day's exploration of
Malá Strana will
invariably end with a
tankard of Pilsen,
savored in one of the
district's many beer
cellars.

Half a day

◆ **A** D2-D3-E2-E3

fourteen churches
in Malá Strana by the middle of
the 13th century. In 1257 King Přemysl
Otakar II founded the royal town of Malá Strana and
drove the existing inhabitants out into neighboring villages,
replacing them with German settlers, and merchants and
artisans attracted by tax and legal benefits; the new arrivals
remained subject to the laws of their town of origin,
Magdeburg. He also had the Archbishop's Palace and the
JOHONITES COMMANDERY fortified, and completed the
ramparts started by his father, Wenceslas I, in 1253: these now
extended from the Castle to the river, and were later altered
during the reign of Charles IV in the 14th century.

A TIME OF WAR AND RECONSTRUCTION. The Hussite Wars ● *32*
were the cause of widespread devastation: Malá Strana was
burnt down, the Archbishop's Palace was destroyed, a
Carthusian monastery near Ujezd Gate was razed to the
ground, and many other buildings were badly damaged.
Worse, the battles between Hussites and royal troops by the
Castle walls caused the destruction of one third of all of Malá
Strana. After being rebuilt at the end of the 15th century, the
Lesser Town (Malá Strana) was laid waste once again in 1541
by a fire that also reached the Castle and the site where the
Cathedral was being built. The Gothic buildings were
replaced by architecture in the Renaissance style, and
numerous Italians – masons, architects and stuccoists – came
to Malá Strana and settled in Vlašská Street and the
surrounding area. Former Hrzán Palace in Velkoprěvorské
Square and the House "At the sign of the Golden Swan"
▲ *259* in Sněmovní Street both date from this era.

LEADING FAMILIES
After the Battle of
White Mountain
● *34*, aristocratic
Catholic families, and
others that had
converted to
Catholicism and
rallied to the
Habsburgs, bought up
plots of land from
Protestants cheaply
and built their palaces
on them. Malá Strana
owes much of its
reputation as the
Baroque jewel of
Prague to the
magnificence of these
and later buildings.

247

"Although the Castle is turned toward Malá Strana lying at its feet, Malá Strana itself does not seem to be looking at the Castle; it is not even looking at the river. Its buildings adorned with belvederes, roof decorations, towers, garrets and chimney stacks are deep in slumber, turned in on themselves, and as dour as strongboxes; its narrow lanes resemble green spaces, poky recesses and mysterious passageways. . ."

Angelo Ripellino,
Magic Prague

HOUSE "AT THE SIGN OF THE GOLDEN LION" ● 77
This house (U zlatého lva), in a pure Renaissance style, once housed an oast house whose façade is at 14 Tržiště Street; under the arcades is At Maecenas (U mecenáše), an old bar named in connection with from Václav Trost, a noted defender of the arts.

A PERIOD OF INERTIA. Following the Battle of White Mountain and throughout the 18th century, Malá Strana was the scene of much building work: the aristocracy enthusiastically had palaces and gardens built and the Church was only slightly less energetic. Malá Strana's building expansion came to a halt toward the end of the 18th century, something the visitor may well be grateful for. Prague's four main towns were brought together administratively by Joseph II in 1784, but Malá Strana continued to be inhabited by the lesser folk, most of them Czechs. For most of the year, the palaces of the aristocracy stood empty; most aristocrats lived near the Emperor in Vienna, even though the institutions and offices of the Government of Bohemia remained in Prague. During the second half of the 19th century, architectural activity on the other side of the river increased. The closing years of the century saw plans for a railroad and building works that included the ghetto, but only the Straka Academy at the foot of Letná Hill ▲ *316* was actually built.

MALÁ STRANA SQUARE

Malostranské náměstí lies on the route followed by the Royal Way between Mostecká Street and Nerudova Street, a road that climbs up toward the Castle; the square is laid out around St Nicholas' Church. From the 10th century, a Romanesque church dedicated to Saint Wenceslas has stood in the square, along with a few other buildings. In 1283, a Gothic parish church dedicated to Saint Nicholas bisected the square dividing it into an upper part and a lower part. In the 16th century this division was emphasized by the construction in the

century of a Jesuit college on the site of St Wenceslas' 16th
Church; then, in the 18th century, the monumental Baroque
St Nicholas' Church was built on the site of an earlier church
of the same name that had been handed over to the Jesuits in
1625. The houses and palaces lining the square form a
wonderful blend of Renaissance and Baroque styles; most of
them were built after the fire of 1541.

COLUMN OF THE PLAGUE. This monument was erected in 1715
by F. W. Herstorfer on a plan by architect Giovanni Battista
Alliprandi. Standing in the middle of the Square, it
commemorates the end of the plague epidemic that
decimated the population of Prague between 1713 and 1714.

FORMER TOWN HALL

Malá Strana's former Town Hall (Malostranská beseda)
stands at the end of the east side of the square, and partly
gives onto Letenská Street; built in 1478, it was remodeled in
1617–22 on plans by Giovanni Campione de Bossi. The
interior was then altered in 1660, and the third floor fitted out
as a chapel. It was not until the 19th century that the
characteristically Renaissance corner towers were removed.
The building is now used for concerts, exhibitions and plays.

THE "CZECH CONFESSION". In 1575, the evangelical Estates of
the Diet of Bohemia presented to Maximilian II a document
that had been drawn up in this Town Hall by representatives
of the various currents of Czech Reform: the Union of Czech
Brethren, the Lutherans and the Utraquists. It had been
modeled on the Confession of Augsburg which, on
Charles V's initiative, allowed Protestants to produce their
own statement of belief, and now claimed freedom of
confession on behalf of non-Catholics in Bohemia. The
Emperor, who was also King of Bohemia, undertook to
observe the terms but refused to sign the document.

PALACES IN MALÁ STRANA SQUARE

SMIŘICKÝ-MONTÁGŮ PALACE. This palace, which stands at
no. 18 on the corner of the square and
Sněmovní

GRÖMLING PALACE
This palace (no. 28)
was built behind the
church about 1772,
and is usually known
as the House "At the
sign of the Stone
Table" (*U kamenného
stolu*) ▲ *143*; on the
second floor there is a
café called
Malostranská kavárna
where Kafka ● *110*
and writer Urdizil
used to go. Until
1918, it was known as
the *Radetsky Café*.

**THE SMIŘICKÝ
PALACE PLOT**
It was within the walls
of Smiřický Palace
that opponents of the
Catholic League met
on May 22, 1618
before going up the
hill to the Castle to
meet the Imperial
Governors. The
episode sparked off
the famous
Defenestration
of Prague
● *34*.

▲ MALÁ STRANA 1:
AT THE FOOT OF THE CASTLE

Street, was built in 1606 and is one of the best preserved from Renaissance times; the façade was renovated in the Baroque manner in 1763 by František Josef Jäger ▲ 267, 272. The owner, Albrecht Smiřický, was head of one of the richest families in Bohemia; he had studied at the Calvinist University of Heidelberg and was a fierce opponent of Ferdinand II. He died in 1618. After the Battle of White Mountain ● 34, his house was seized and Wallenstein gave it to one of his relatives, Maximilian of Valdštejn.

STERNBERG PALACE. This palace, at no. 19, is situated to the right of Smiřický Palace. Architect Giovanni Battista Alliprandi built it in 1720 on the site of three Romanesque houses.

KAISERSTEIN PALACE. This palace, built by Alliprandi in 1700 on the grounds of two houses, is also known as the *U Petzoldů* house. The rear overlooks Josefská Street and dates from 1536; the attic is decorated with allegories of the seasons by Ottavio Mosto.

LIECHTENSTEIN PALACE

This enormous palace at no. 13 takes up the entire west side of the upper part of Malá Strana Square. Until the beginning of the 17th century, the site was occupied by five separate houses that the Liechtenstein family gradually acquired after the Battle of White Mountain, and had turned into a palace after 1638. The fifth house, the largest of all, was purchased in 1598 by Václav Popel of Lobkowicz, a *hejtman* (captain) of the Old Town. Karl von Liechtenstein, who lived in the palace until his death in 1627, was known as the "Bloody Governor": as Governor of the Kingdom and, Steward Extraordinary, the King's representative, he ordered the execution of the leaders of Ferdinand II's representatives on July 21, 1621 ● 34. On the orders of Ferdinand II, he also found himself, together with Wallenstein, at the head of the Confiscation Commission set up in the aftermath of White Mountain playing a major role in the redistribution and sale of the rebels' goods to the Emperor. He had previously received the hereditary title of Prince from the Emperor Matthias. The palace was renovated in 1791 by Matthias Hummel who was responsible for the neoclassical façade executed in the style of Niccolo Pacassi's work at Prague Castle ▲ 201. Philosopher Josef Dobrovský, who was prominent early on in the National Awakening Movement ● 28, lived in this palace. Subsequently it was closely linked to significant moments in the city's history: these include the military element of the coup d'état that took place when Czechoslovakia ● 36 was created in 1918.

ACADEMY OF MUSIC. The Academy of Music has been housed in Liechtenstein Palace since the House of Artists (Rudolfinum ▲ 194) was rebuilt; it is difficult to dissociate it

ACADEMY OF MUSIC
The Academy's reputation rests on its trumpet and horn classes. It has also produced violinists of the caliber of Ševčík, Kubelík, Ondříček, Kocián and Suk, and pianists including Jan Hermann, Rudolf Firkušný and Josef Páleníček. Other artists, specializing in ancient music, include Vachulka and Veselka, and Venhoda who has formed the Prague Madrigalists' Ensemble.

View of Charles Bridge and Malá Strana.

from the Conservatory, which was based in Palffy Palace in Valdštejnské Square ▲ *262*. Until the 19th century, musical education was mainly provided by churches and convents, or simply by village schools under the direction of teacher-cantors ● *46*. The Prague Conservatory, the oldest in central Europe, which had been founded in 1808 and open to students since 1881, was nationalized following the creation of Czechoslovakia in 1918. Founded in 1948, the Academy of Music is more recent. Even though the standard of teaching is the same as that available at the Conservatory, the Academy appears to offer opportunities for more advanced study and research. Students wishing to transfer to the Academy from the Conservatory have to pass an entrance examination. The current director of the Academy is cellist Chuchro, while his opposite number at the Conservatory is composer Jaroslav Neumann. The roster of composers who have graced these institutions either as a students or as teachers is impressive. Since the days of Dvořák ● *46*, composers who have taught at the Academy have included Suk, Hovák, Foerster and Hába, and the great historian Otakar Šin.

St Nicholas' Church ★ ● *72*

In 1625, shortly after the Battle of White Mountain ● *34*, the Jesuits received from Ferdinand II of Habsburg the Church of St Nicholas (Kostel sv. Mikuláše), a Gothic parish church founded in 1283. The followers of Saint Ignatius of Loyola maintained it in good condition and in 1653 commissioned Italian architects Giovanni Domenico Orsi, and then Carlo Lurago, to rebuild it. The east, north and east wings were completed at the end of the 17th century.

A FAMILY OF ARCHITECTS. Starting in 1704, three architects from the same family were involved in this major building project: Krištof Dientzenhofer, who did the nave, and probably the magnificent façade adorned with sculptures from the workshop of Hieronymus Kohl; Kilián Ignác Dientzenhofer, who succeeded his father in 1722 and was responsible for the choir and cupola; and Anselmo Lurago, Kilián's son-in-law, who added the clocktower in 1755 and took charge of the interior design.

INTERIOR. The interior of St Nicholas' emphasizes the dynamism of the exterior; this is largely due to the oblique positioning of the pillars.

The ceiling is decorated with an *Apotheosis of St Nicholas* and scenes from his life by Austrian artist Johann Lucas Kracker (1717–79). Covering almost 1,800 square yards, it is not only the largest painting in Prague but also one of the most interesting of the whole period: Kracker's skill at achieving detail in the plaster enabled him to give his characters a sharpness and plastic freshness that were most unusual in the 18th century.

FRESCO OF ST CECILIA. The organ case is surmounted by a trompe l'oeil fresco that seems to add an extra level to the church. The main scene depicts an *Apotheosis of St Cecilia* by Silesian artist, Franz Xaver Palko (1724–67). Palko, who had studied in Italy, initially had difficulty in making a name for himself as Bohemian painters distrusted foreign ideas; however, they were eventually obliged to give way to this artist who brought the Viennese style to Prague, and who

CUPOLA OVER THE CHOIR
According to legend, while Franz Xaver Palko was painting his *Glory of the Holy Trinity*, he demanded that no one should see his work until it was finished. A Jesuit ignored this request, and when the painter caught him, he promised that his curiosity would be punished. When the painting was unveiled, the priest saw, to his considerable embarrassment, that his face had been given to a fisherman, one of the characters in the fresco, for all posterity to see.

ST NICHOLAS' CHURCH, THE APOGEE OF BAROQUE ✪
Seen from the Castle, the verdigris dome of St Nicholas' Church resembles a clover leaf floating on a sea of red roofs. The interior is stunning; let the eye be taken in by the vertiginous detail of the trompe l'œil statues, the Rococo angels and the paintings that cover the ceiling. The summer concerts (of music by Mozart, who performed there to great acclaim) are unforgettable.

> "St Nicholas' is a thanksgiving service . . .
> in which everything is peace, joy and
> bursts of laughter."
>
> Paul Claudel

even rivaled the great Reiner. Nonetheless, when he collaborated with sculptor Ignác Platzer, he opted for a more restrained approach to art that pervades all the works he executed for St Nicholas' Church. Palko also did a *Death of Saint Francis Xavier* for one of the chapels: on this occasion, there are no little angels, celestial clouds or dazzling flashes of lightning. The walls of the main nave present a glorification of the life of Saint Nicholas. They were painted between 1761 and 1770 by Johann Lucas Kracker.

CHOIR. The choir is of a more restrained, more classical, appearance. Built by Kilián Ignác Dientzenhofer, it is topped by a cupola decorated with a fresco by Palko, the *Glory of the Holy Trinity* (1752). The four sculptures of the Fathers of the Church (1768–9) by Ignác Platzer are in a neoclassical style and are the best of the statues decorating the choir. The pulpit, made in 1765 by Richard Georg Prachner, is adorned with elegant motifs and small angels; the absence of a staircase underlines the sense of lightness.

SIDE CHAPELS. Most of the sculptures are by Platzer, while the frescos are by J. Hager, Johann Lucas Kracker and Josef Kramolin. Each of the paintings in the chapels relates to an aspect of the Counter-Reformation: they include a scene of charity (*Saint Thomas of Villeneuve Giving to Charity*) in the first chapel on the left after entering the church, and a Crucifixion by Karel Škréta.

MOZART. Wolfgang Amadeus Mozart played on the organ of this church when he was staying in Prague in 1787 ▲ *322*. His death in extreme

STATUES IN THE CHOIR
The four statues made by Platzer represent four Fathers of the Church whose names appear clearly on each pedestal: they are Saint Basil, Saint Cyril, Saint John Chrysostom and Saint Gregory of Nazianzus. All of them were Greek Fathers who left the Eastern Church before the Great Schism.

Interior of St Nicolas' Church in Malá Strana.

Commemorative plaque of Jan Neruda.

JAN NERUDA (1834–91)
Jan Neruda, the author of *Tales of the Malá Strana*, was born in this quarter of Prague and lived in the house "Of the Two Suns". He published numerous collections of poems and short stories, and was a masterful journalist. It was out of admiration for his work that Pablo Neruda, winner of the 1971 Nobel Prize for Literature, chose his name as his pseudonym.

penury in Vienna is well documented, but his passing was greatly lamented in Prague: a few days after his death, over four thousand people gathered at St Nicholas' Church in Malá Strana, and his friend Josefina Dušková sang a Requiem in his memory. Another fifty years were to pass before Vienna accorded Mozart similar honors.

NERUDOVA STREET ★

Nerudova Street, which starts in Malá Strana Square, is one of the most famous in Prague. It also contains a marvelous group of Baroque houses. The house at no. 2 "Of the Tomcat" (*U kocoura*) has Renaissance doors and stucco decoration; the brewery sells a beer of which writer Bohumil Hrabal and film director Miloš Forman have sung its praises. At no. 4, the house "Of the Golden Anchor" (*U zlaté kotvy*) has an 18th-century façade adorned with a bust of Saint John Nepomuk, while no. 10, known as Švab, belonged to Bartholomew Spranger, one of the most important Mannerist painters in the Court of Rudolph II ● *31*. The house at no. 12 "Of the Three Little Fiddles" (*U tří housliček*) is one of the best known: according to Angelo Ripellino in his *Magic Prague*, "The charming sign of the Three Violins in Nerudova Street could easily stand as a symbol for the doleful music-making of Malá Strana". It was originally in the Gothic style, but was then rebuilt in the Renaissance manner and renovated in the 18th century. The sign of the three violins is a reminder that, between 1667 and 1748, the house was inhabited by the Edlinger family of instrument makers. Valkoun House at no. 14 was built by Krištof Dientzenhofer, and then by Jan Blažis Santini-Aichl, who renovated it in the early 18th century; the same architect also worked on the neighboring house "Of the Golden Goblet" (*U zlaté číše*). The house "Of St John Nepomuk" (*U svatého Jana Nepomuckého*), at no. 18 was built in 1556 and still bears the original sgraffito.

MORZIN PALACE. This palace stands next to the House "At the sign of the Golden Goblet" and today houses the Romanian Embassy. Architect Santini-Aichl, one of the greatest in Prague's Baroque period ● *80*, made the plans and built the façade. The palace combined four separate houses, and work began in 1713–14; the balcony is supported by two Moorish

atlantes carved by Ferdinand Maxmilián Brokoff, the doors depict Day and Night and the roof statuary represents allegories of the four corners of the world.

THUN-HOHENSTEIN-KOLOVRAT PALACE. Thun-Hohenstein-Kolovrat Palace is at no. 20 and stands opposite Morzin Palace. It is decorated with a range of sculptures made by Santini-Aichl who, at the time, lived at no. 14. The House "Of the Golden Crown" (*U zlaté koruny*) has a Renaissance façade that was altered during the Empire Period.

CHURCH OF OUR LADY OF PERPETUAL SUCCOR OF THE GAETANI. (*Kostel Panny Marie ustavičné pomoci u Kajetanů*) This church, also known as the Church of the Theatines, a religious order that settled in Prague in 1665, is also the work of Santini-Aichl; it was originally entrusted to the Italian Guarino Guarini and then to J. B. Mathey, but it finally fell to Santini-Aichl in 1797. He was also responsible for the exterior decorations. The church was consecrated in 1717, and contains a painting by Jacques Callot depicting a Virgin with Saint Gaetano. THE FORMER MONASTERY OF THE THEATINES stands at no. 24. Following secularization under Joseph II, it was bought in 1793 by Count Morzin, who opened up a passageway that connected to steps leading up to the Castle; the passageway can still be seen to this day. Between 1835 and 1837, the refectory was used as a Czech Theater under Josef Kajetán Tyl. A number of writers including Mácha and Sabira acted here in an amateur capacity.

FROM NO. 27 TO NO. 47. The House "Of the Golden Key" (*U zlatého klíče*) is at no. 27, while the House "Of the Golden Wheel" (*U zlatého kola*) at no. 28 boasts a rich façade in the Baroque style. Former Bretfeld Palace at no. 33 is attributed to Jan Josef Wirch (1765): during the 18th century, it was a very fashionable place and the cream of Prague society, including Casanova and Mozart, were invited to balls held there. The sign of Wenceslas on horseback at no. 34 identifies a former pharmacy that may have been the first in Malá Strana. The House "Of the White Beetroot" (*U bílé repý*) at no. 39 was originally Gothic, but has been altered since. Its name derives from an owner who cultivated the market

THUN-HOHENSTEIN-KOLOVRAT PALACE
This building, which now houses the Italian Embassy, dates back to the period 1715–25. The entrance is adorned with two eagles holding the Thun-Hohenstein coat of arms. These sculptures are by Matthias B. Braun.

"... of the palaces on sloping Neruda Street, the one belonging to Count Morzin stands out with its two thick-lipped, frizzy-haired atlantes. Two black men, or perhaps two Moors."
Dominique Fernandez
Le Banquet des anges

gardens on Strahov ▲ 237. Sculptor Johann Anton Quitainer lived here for many years before he died in 1765. The next two houses, no. 41 "Of the Red Lion" (*U červeného lva*) and "Of the Green Lobster" (*U zeleného raka*), were rebuilt in the early 18th century and combined in 1968. Over the House "Of the Black Lion" (*U černéo lva*) at no. 45, is a representation of a lion gripping a tankard between its paws; this is an amusing way of indicating a tavern. The House "Of the Two Suns" (*U dvou slunců*) ● 80, at no. 47 has one of the most appealing façades in the whole street; it dates from 1673–90.

St Thomas' Church ★

ENTRANCE TO ST THOMAS'
The most magnificent part of the façade consists of the elements framing the main entrance, which itself dates from the Renaissance (1617); the broken pediment resembles a pair of pincers. The dynamism of the curved lines is sufficient to save the monumentalism of the doorway from a complete lack of expression. Another feature is the elegant embrasures.

HISTORY. St Thomas' Church (Kostel sv. Tomáše) belongs to the Augustinian Hermits who were brought to Prague by Wenceslas II in 1285. The Augustinians were adversaries of the Hussites, and their monastery was burned down in 1420. It was rebuilt at the end of the 15th century but was destroyed again in the fire of 1541. The present church is in the Baroque style and was built by Kilián Ignác Dientzenhofer (1723–1731). In the monastery (*U sv. Tomáše*, 12 Letenská Street) beer was first brewed in 1358; today, in the old monastery vault, a famous dark beer is still sold.
FAÇADE. St Thomas' Church has one of the most spectacular façades in the whole of Prague. It overlooks a narrow, one-way street, and has an extremely powerful, sculptural appearance, in every way worthy of Kilián Ignác Dientzenhofer, on whose plans it was based. The statue of Saint Augustine over the entrance (1684) and the statue of Saint Thomas over the south door are both by Kohl.
INTERIOR. Like the interior, the exterior lies halfway between the monumental and the elegant. The archways in the nave and the pilasters articulate the space with authority, but in the galleries Dientzenhofer introduced gold Corinthian capitals, cartouches, delicate stucco work and richly molded pediments. The vaults are decorated with paintings by Václav Reiner and his workshop (1728–30) depicting the life of Saint Augustine. The

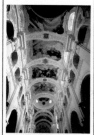

INTERIOR DESIGN
The numerous altars in the nave and aisles are decorated by different artists. Karel Škréta ▲ 164, 220 painted the reredoses of the Holy Trinity and the Assumption (in the choir, 1644), and a portrait of Saint Thomas on the right of the nave.

sculptures include works by Quintainer, father and son: the father, Andreas Philipp (1679–1729), was responsible for a sculpture of Saint Vitus over one of the altars in the left-hand aisle that incorporates a cock as an emblem. On the same altar, there are representations of Saint Augustine, Saint Adalbert and St Wenceslas, all dating from 1720–1. The statues are made of limewood and are models of

the silver statues that once adorned the high altar; they were melted down in 1729 to pay for alterations to the church, and the wooden models have stood on the altar ever since. At the entrance to the nave, there are two glass coffins containing the remains of Saint Just and Saint Boniface; such representations of death exemplify the sensitivity characteristic of the Counter-Reformation.

HIGH ALTAR. The overall design of the high altar is by Kilián Ignác Dientzenhofer. The *Martyrdom of St Thomas and St Augustine and the Child* by Rubens are copies; the originals (1638–40) are kept in Sternberk Palace ▲ *229*. Johann Anton Quitainer, the son, was responsible for the two angels that flank the main reredos. The patron saints are from the workshop of Brokoff and were completed by his collaborator, Ignác Müller. *St Augustine and the Child* is a comment on the inadequacies of scholarship; it represents one of the most common legendary iconographies applied to this saint from the Renaissance onward. In this painting, he is seen walking along the seashore, and meeting a child who with the help of a shellfish is pouring seawater into a hole hollowed out of the sand. The saint seems surprised but the child, who is in fact an angel, replies: "It would be easier for me to pour all the water into this hole than for you to explain the tiniest part of the mystery of the Trinity."

ST THOMAS' CLOISTER. The entrance to the cloister is on the left of the main entrance of the church. This tranquil spot contrasts with the hubbub of nearby Malá Strana Square. The Monastery's ancient buildings once incorporated a retreat house. A halt on one of the benches placed in the middle of the cloister provides an opportunity to admire the pure lines of this white building; it is possibly most restful place to be found

anywhere in this increasingly busy city. Architecture enthusiasts may manage to get inside St Barbara's Chapel; the entrances, identifiable by Renaissance doors made by Bernardo de Alberto in 1596, are situated in the middle of the cloister's east wing. The chapel escaped renovation in the Baroque manner, and the original Gothic style has survived. The beautiful reredos by Josef Heintz the Elder (c. 1600) depicts the Virgin with Saint Barbara, Saint Catherine and some angels.

"U Zlatého Jelena"
The façade of the house "At the sign of the Golden Stag" is decorated with a group of Saint Hubert and the Stag carved by Brokoff. This bourgeois house rivals the aristocratic residences of Malá Strana.

The Lion of Bohemia. The lion, the emblem of Bohemia, appears in the Vyšehrad Codex ● *43* as early as 1085. Prince Wenceslas is seated on a curule chair decorated with the head and paws of a lion.

Sněmovní ulice
In this part of Malá Strana, the narrow streets are beautifully laid out, and peace and tranquility prevail. Sněmovní Street has some superb Baroque façades. Part of the street is in the form of a small square called "Fünfkirchen Square" until the 19th century. At the time, the population of Prague was mixed, with Germans and Czechs living side by side.

House "At the sign of the Golden Stag"

Near St Thomas' Church, standing on the corner of Letenská Street and Tomášská Street, is Schnell House (*U Schnellů*), a well-known restaurant and tavern at one time frequented by many famous people including Tsar Peter the Great of Russia. Next to it is the House "Of the Golden Stag" (*U zlatého jelena*), which was designed by Kilián Ignác Dientzenhofer in 1725–6. The 18th century was a time when the bourgeoisie acquired confidence in architectural matters, and took over from the aristocracy and the clergy the task of reconstructing old buildings. The House "Of the Golden Stag" is one of the more successful examples from this period.

St Joseph's Church

Only a few steps from St Thomas' Church in Josefská Street stands a Carmelite church, whose curious façade and simple, serene interior the busy tourist could easily miss.
Baroque Rubens-style. The façade of this Baroque church, which was built between 1683 and 1693, was more influenced by Flemish models than by Romanesque buildings. Most unusually, the building is constructed on a central plan with a cupola, and there is altogether little subtlety of balance with the double columns overwhelming the chapels, and the obelisk-shaped pilasters in opposition to the feeling of space in the cupola. It is nonetheless a captivating church with an inconspicuous pulpit, but a complete absence of sculptures, frescos and any other dramatic decoration. The high altar

> "The inexhaustible charm of Malá Strana, hanging on to the side of the Castle. This totally Baroque quarter is as big as a Parisian arrondissement."
>
> Dominique Fernandez

is decorated with a painting of the *Holy Family* (1702) by Petr Brandl; another, also by Brandl, showing a vision of St Theresa is to the right of the pulpit. The importance in Baroque art of pictorial and plastic representations of ecstasy is well established, and it is easy to agree with Émile Mâle that, from the 17th century onward, they became the "seal of holiness". One of the altars on the left is decorated with limewood statues by Matěj Václav Jäckel (1696). They include a beautifully crafted Saint Ludmila on the right, holding a crown of martyrdom in one hand and her sash in the other; the movement of the drapes and the saint's swaying gait and proud air make for a wonderful combination of elegance and large scale. The other statue is of Saint Wenceslas.

THUN PALACE

A short journey from St Joseph's Church takes the visitor to this palace; it involves walking in the direction of St Thomas', then going to the end of Tomášská Street, turning left into Thunovská Street, and then right into Sněmovní Street (Diet Street). Thun Palace occupies the whole length of the righthand side of this street. It was built by Santini-Aichl between 1696 and 1720 and, from 1861 onward, housed the provincial Diet; it was also here that the deposition of the Habsburgs from the Bohemian throne was announced on November 14, 1918, the date that also marks the creation of the Czechoslovak Republic and the election of Masaryk as President. The Senate sat in the palace from 1918 to 1940, and was followed by the Czech National Council from 1968. It now houses the British Embassy. The main decoration on the façade is a lion, the symbol of Bohemia.

THOMÁŠ GARRIGUE MASARYK ● *36.* Masaryk was born into a very humble family, but became Professor of Philosophy and Sociology at the Czech University in Prague in 1882. As a member of the Sokols and a Slavist, he founded the *Athenaeum* review, and his political career was established when he was elected to the Reichsrat in 1891. He soon set up the Realist Party and, in his writings, synthesized and proposed a model of Czech identity that turned Czechs into democratic humanists, and heirs to the traditions of Hus, Kmujkés and the Enlightenment. From 1915, in France, and later on in the United States, he was among those putting forward the idea of a Czechoslovak state. He became the first President in October 1918.

AROUND THUN PALACE. At no. 5 Sněmovní ul. is LAZANSKÝ PALACE, built by Francesco Caratti in 1670 and then renovated by F. M. Kaňka in 1712. Next is the House "Of the Golden Swan" (*U zlaté labutě*) at no. 6. At

ST JOSEPH'S CHURCH
The three statues decorating the façade are the work of Matěj Václav Jäckel: they represent Saint Joseph, Saint Theresa and Saint John of the Cross.

THOMÁŠ G. MASARYK
Masaryk (1850–1937) devoted much of his energy to a number of major works, including *The Czech Question* (1895) and *The Social Question* (1898), in which he rejected Marxism and the theory of class struggle. His originality lies in his scientific analysis of Czech society.

no. 13 is BYLANDT-RHEIDT PALACE, designed by J.-B. Mathey: while it was under construction, the Romanesque Church of St Michael had to be pulled down to make way for it. Sněmovní Street terminates at the blind alley "Of the Golden Well" (*U zlaté studně*): the façade of the "Painters' House" (U malířů) house at no. 3 has a mural by Karel Klusáček (1897), and at no. 4 is the House "Of the Golden Well".

WALLENSTEIN PALACE

Several palaces line Wallenstein Square (Valdštejnské náměstí). AUERSPERK PALACE, at no. 1, is in the Baroque style going back to 1751; LEDEBOUR-TRAUTTMANSDORFF PALACE, at no. 3, was built by Palliardi in 1787.

THE BIGGEST PALACE IN PRAGUE. The square is closed off by the façade of Wallenstein Palace (Valdštejnsky palác), the entrance to which is through the gardens in Letenská Street. It was built between 1623 and 1629, and covers a site once occupied by twenty-six houses. Wallenstein entrusted the project to Italian architect Andrea Spezza (died 1628), who had been very active in Cracow; he was succeeded by Niccolo Sebregondi, but it was Giovanni Pieroni who designed the huge *sala terrena* of the grounds. The interior of the palace, generously endowed with marble, stucco and frescos, is in keeping with the first owner's ambitions, and the palace's chapel by Ernst Heidelberger (c. 1630) contains one of the best Baroque altars in Prague.

DUKE OF FRIEDLAND. Albrecht Václav Eusebius was born in Bohemia in 1583; his mother was from the Smiřický family, an old Czech aristocratic family. He was brought up according to the teaching of the Union of Czech Brethren, and studied in Prague and Germany before fighting for the Imperial Army against the Turks. After converting to Catholicism, he returned to Prague and in 1608 married a rich widow, the owner of huge estates in Moravia. About the same time, a Prague banker, Hans de Witte, became his administrator. Wallenstein was then widowed in 1614 and he was sole heir to his deceased wife's fortune. His second marriage

WALLENSTEIN DEIFIED
The large banqueting-room is two stories high, and because of the way the mirrors are placed appears to be even larger. The ceiling was decorated by Baccio del Bianco with a representation of Wallenstein, Duke of Friedland, as Mars, God of War in Roman mythology.

introduced him to the corridors of power, his father-in-law, Count Karl von Harrach, being an influential member of the Viennese Catholic Party and a future Private Councillor to Ferdinand II. Wallenstein was ambitious and in 1617 put together an armed force, which he put at the service of Ferdinand, then at war with Venice. His valor earned the future Emperor's gratitude. On his return, he was not directly involved in the Battle of White Mountain although his private regiment took part. His wealth continued to grow as he appropriated the estates abandoned by Albrecht Smiřický, who had no heir. By dint of skilful acquisitions, Wallenstein increased his lands around Jičín, the fief of the Smiřický family: these included mines. Within a few years, his property became the most prosperous in all Bohemia, and also the best administered. As master of a quarter of the land in Bohemia, and in his capacity as Duke of Friedland and Prince of Sagan, he ruled what was virtually a principality of over three hundred subjects. He also became one of the Emperor's biggest creditors; this was a relatively easy ambition to achieve as, with Hans de Witte, he was a member of the financial consortium charged with minting coins. The privilege lasted for no more than fourteen months, but it was quite sufficient to enable the two men to amass fortunes. At the height of his powers, Wallenstein was in a position to place a 24,000-strong army of well-paid, well-fed men, the only force worthy of the name of "army", at the disposition of an Empire devastated by the Thirty Years' War. However, the story had a sad ending. Too much power all too easily leads to trouble, and the Emperor began to fear his subject; matters came to a head when Ferdinand learnt that Wallenstein was negotiating secretly with the Saxons and the Swedes, and demanding absolute loyalty from his officers. The Emperor had him assassinated in his bed at Cheb in 1634.

THE GARDENS ★ A visit to the gardens is a must; the grotto, the *sala terrena* (1623–7) and the statues bring an element of animation to the otherwise static setting. The SALA TERRENA is the most beautiful part of the palace. It is an immense loggia inspired by Italian models like the Loggia dei Lanzi in Florence and is the finest architectural achievement of the

LEDEBOUR AND PALLFY PALACE GARDENS. The Baroque terraced gardens of the Ledebour-Trauttmansdorff and Pallfy palaces, with their loggia, *sala terrena* and statuary, are carved into the southeastern slopes of Prague Castle where once grew vineyards but are now derelict. They are being restored by the Prague Heritage Fund set up by President Václav Havel and the Prince of Wales. Above, left to right: Ledebour-Trauttmansdorff Palace, the *sala terrena*, the fountain in the grounds of Wallenstein Palace; the statue of Hercules fighting the dragon (above) is by Adriaen de Vries, sculptor to Rudolph II.

View of the lake in Wallenstein Palace.

MALÁ STRANA 1:
AT THE FOOT OF THE CASTLE

period. The paintings and stucco work by Baccio del Bianco recall the Trojan War and the *Aeneid*.

PALACES IN VALDŠTEJNSKÉ SQUARE

KOMENSKÝ MUSEUM. No. 20 Wallenstein Square houses the fascinating Komenský Pedagogical Museum. JAN ÁMOS KOMENSKÝ, or Comenius (1592–1670) ● *43*, maintained the momentum of Czech reform and humanist thought, and proposed the idea of nursery schools, insisting on the importance of play in education. After becoming a Bishop in the Union of Czech Brethren at the age of twenty-six – he was to be the last – Komenský became one of the great Czech writers of the 17th century; he wrote in both Czech and Latin. On being exiled in 1624, he threw his inexhaustible energies into "federating" the dispersed communities, and emphasized pre-school education: as he said later, "It is easier to educate than to re-educate". In *Didactia Magna* (1632) particularly, he urged the use of music at school, together with experience and images. His manuals, *Orbis Pictus* and *Janua linguarum reserata*, were used in Jesuit education in the country of his birth. Even today, a number of private schools in Prague that have been opened since 1900 have adopted some of the teaching principles set out in his pedagogical texts.

KOMENSKÝ OR COMENIUS
Jan Ámos Komenský was a Humanist and cultural pioneer, and a contemporary of René Descartes.

LEDEBOURG AND PALFFY GARDENS. (no. 3) These elegant terrace gardens, designed in the 18th century and recently restored, lead directly to the castle's gardens in the summer, enabling the visitor to avoid the busy Nerudova Street. Concerts and plays are put on in these enchanting surroundings.

PALFFY PALACE. This palace at no. 14, built in the early 18th century on the ruins of two old houses, now contains the CONSERVATORY OF MUSIC. The Conservatory was founded in 1811 on the initiative of the Association for the Encouragement (or the Renaissance) of Music in Bohemia, and initially it was based in the Dominican Monastery near St Giles' Church ▲ *285*: instrumental lessons were given with a view to turning out orchestral players. In the late 19th century, the Conservatory merged with the Academy of Music, which was housed in Liechtenstein Palace ▲ *250*. Antonin Dvořák ● *46* was Director at the end of the 19th century. Upstairs there is a pleasant restaurant, and the terrace commands a lovely view over the gardens of the SMALL CZERNIN PALACE at no. 12.

KOLOWRAT PALACE
This palace was the residence of the Presidents of the Czechoslovak Republic from 1918 to 1940.

KOLOWRAT-CZERNIN PALACE. Like its neighbors, this house at no. 10 was built on land previously covered by gardens. Ignaz Johann Palliardi, who laid out these gardens in the Late Baroque style in 1784, had also designed the remarkable gardens on the terrace ▲ *274*.

> "You gagged me and bound my eyes in vain.
> I trust in God that you will not
> bind my reason and my thought."
>
> Jan Ámos Komenský

FÜRSTENBERG PALACE. Fürstenberg Palace at no. 8 was built in 1743–7 in a style that has survived to the present day; it also has some beautiful Baroque gardens. The palace now houses the Polish Embassy.

KLÁROV

Valdštejnská Street runs into the Klárov crossroads, which are lined with several Empire-style buildings.

KLÁR INSTITUTE. The Klár Institute at no. 6 was designed by Alois Klár (1763–1833) and built by his brother between 1836 and 1844. This two-story building once gave shelter to blind people; a relief shows Tobias giving sight to a sick man.

RICHTER HOUSE. Karel Emanuel Richter had this house at no. 3 rebuilt in 1832. An inscription on the façade recalls that the actor E. Vojan died here in 1920.

LETENSKÁ STREET. VRTBA PALACE at no. 5 was built between 1707 and 1725 for František Vrtba. It was built in the High Baroque style, and today houses the Union of Architects.

LUSACE SEMINARY STREET

VOJAN PARK. In the 17th and 18th centuries, Lusace Seminary accepted Catholic students from Protestant Germany, and particularly from Lausitz (Lusace); U lužického semináře Street passes through a more popular quarter of Prague. To the right behind a high wall is Vojan Park (Vojanovy sady) where the Archbishop's Palace was built. The garden, dating from the late 1800's belongs to the Discalced Carmelites.

PROLETARIAN MILITANTS. Several houses once belonged to individuals prominent in working-class movements and strikes of the late 19th century ● 28. The HOUSE "OF THE THREE GREEN CROSSES" (*U tří zelených křížků*) at no. 16 was the headquarters of the trade union magazine *Dělnici* (The Workers), while no. 12 housed the offices of another magazine, *Budoucnost* (The Future) founded by Ladislav Zápotocký (1852–1916) and Josef Boleslav Pecka (1849–97), the two founders of the Czechoslovak Workers' Social Democratic Party. The party adopted the ideas of Karl Marx, and in 1889 joined the Second International.

"VENICE IN PRAGUE". This is the name given to a district overlooking a stretch of the Vltava called Čertovka ▲ 266. Several houses were built on the remains of the former Judith Bridge; the last house, near Charles Bridge, is the House "Of the Three Ostriches" (U tří pštrosů), now a restaurant.

GROTTO IN VOJAN PARK
The main building in this garden is the curious St Elias Chapel, which resembles a grotto. It is formed of numerous stalactites and stalagmites. The paintings on the ceiling relate the legend of the prophet Elijah.

View from the Castle over the tile roofs of Malá Strana and Charles Bridge.

House signs are now ornamental, but in the Middle Ages they indicated which house was which. In those days, houses were not numbered.

Malá Strana 2: from Kampa to Petřín Hill

▲ Malá Strana 2: from Kampa to Petřín Hill

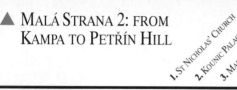

1. St Nicholas' Church
2. Kounic Palace
3. Maltese Square
4. Turba Palace
5. Church of Our Lady of the Victory
6. Church of Ou Lady Un

⏱ Half a day
◆ A C5-C6-D3-D4-D5-E4-E5-E6

RELAXING ON KAMPA ISLAND ✪
Separated from Malá Strana by the Devil's Channel, this island has many watermills, and a park and lawns that are ideal for a relaxing stroll. The new museum also merits a visit. Leave Kampa Island by Most Legií Bridge to rejoin Střelecký Ostrov Island.

KAMPA ISLAND

Kampa Island nestles between the Vltava and the Čertovka, a cut-off known as the "Devil's Channel" and once an important mill-race. In 1159, King Vladislav I gave a large amount of land, including Kampa, to the Sovereign Order of the Knights of Malta, and they built a fortified commandery, Malá Strana's first monastery and numerous bourgeois houses on it. This autonomous territory was known at the time as the Jurisdiction of Malta.

NA KAMPĚ NÁMĚSTÍ. This square, where a pottery market is held each year, is lined by some enchanting dwellings. The House "Of the Painting of the Virgin" (no. 9) gives onto Charles Bridge; legend has it that the picture on the façade drifted this far during a flood. It was once the home of Adolf Kaspar (1877–1934), the famous painter and illustrator. The House "Of the Golden Lion" at no. 7 was built by Giuseppe Bartolomeo Scotti (1685–1737) in 1732, while at no. 13, the House "Of the

Golden Boot" has a beautiful Rococo façade attributed to František Josef Jäger (1731–93). The House "Of the Blue Fox" (opposite, right) at no. 1 dates from 1696: this dwelling, originally called the House "Of the Three Golden Goblets", was built in 1605 for the Flemish jeweler to the Court of Rudolph II, L. Steward and reconstructed in 1664; the relief fox dates from the same period.

Martinů's house. Bohuslav Martinů (1890–1959) ● 47 lived at no. 11 while a student at the Conservatory 1906–1910, but soon moved to France. While second violin in the Czech Philharmonic Orchestra he discovered the works of Debussy, Ravel, Dukas and Roussel. He performed the latter's *Poème de la Forêt*, and became his pupil in 1923. Martinů was one of the most important members of the Paris School, most of whom were central European. To escape the Nazis he fled to the United States, where the conductor Sergei Koussevitsky got him a chair at Princeton. Despite his exile, Martinů was still inspired by Czech and Moravian themes, and *Julietta* and *Recké pasije* (*The Greek Passion*) are works of homage to his homeland.

Kampa Museum. Na Kampě Square runs into a lane called U Sovových mlýnů. At no. 2 is a new gallery of modern art, opened by the Mladek Foundation. It exhibits the major Czech artists of the 20th century, including Kolar ● 102, Guttfreund ● 107 and Kupka. At no. 4 is the former Liechtenstein Palace, built in the Baroque style by G. B. Alliprandi, and later redone in the late Empire style, although the Baroque gate was retained. Opposite is a villa (1797) which was once the property of

Josef Dobrovský (1753–1829)
Dobrovský was a philosopher of rationalist tendencies, a writer on Czech literature, a philologist and a prominent figure in the forming of the Slav identity. He was also a key protagonist in the "national awakening" ● 28. Unlike Josef Jungmann, who based his conception of the nation on its linguistic identity, Dobrovský wrote in Latin and German as he did not believe that Czech had a future as a scientific language.

Count Nostitz; it has been the home of Josef Dobrovský (his bust is only a stone's throw from the villa) and, in the 20th century, the poet Vladimír Holan and the writer Jan Werich. Near these houses, there is a park which is particularly popular with local residents.

ŘÍČNÍ STREET

At the end of U Sovových mlýnů, there is tiny Říční Street which leads off Kampa Island. The short trip passes a lavishly neo-Renaissance construction, the JECHENTHAL BUILDING at nos. 1 and 3

THE HUNGER WALL (Hladová Zed')
Charles IV is thought to have had this wall built to provide work for the poor who were dying of hunger during the famine of 1360 and who, as a result, were being driven to steal. It is also called Chlebova Zed' (Bread Wall), the crenelations allegedly serving as a reminder that the teeth of the poor have to have something to bite on.

Malostranské nábřeži (quay); it was built by Josef Schulz, who also worked on the Rudolfinum ▲ 194 and the National Theater ▲ 294. For a long time, this building has been one of the most opulent in Prague.

CHURCH OF ST JOHN OF THE WASH HOUSE. The Church of St John of the Wash house, one of the oldest foundations in Malá Strana, stands on the corner of Říční Street and Všehrdova Street. After being rebuilt in the 13th century and having the choir added during the Renaissance, it was secularized in 1784 and turned into a wash house. During the Middle Ages, it was the parish church of the town of Újezd, part of which was handed over to Malá Strana in 1360, the remainder staying where it was. In 1935, it reverted to the Czechoslovakian Church, now known as the Czech Hussite Church. To the west of the church, at 6 Říční Street, stands Malá Strana's former hospital which was built in 1662 by G. de Capauli.

MICHNA OF VACINOV PALACE (MICHNŮV PALÁC)

EARLY BAROQUE. Visitors may reach this palace, which is also called Tyrš House, by climbing up Všehrdova Street. It is a large building on the corner of Karmelitská Street; the oldest wing, decorated with sgraffito ● 78 and looking onto Všehrdova Street, dates from 1580. The palace was enlarged by Francesco Caratti (1631–44) ▲ 234, and opens onto the main courtyard which was largely covered with gardens in the

Československo

Michnovský palác, Praha Malá Strana

MICHNA PALACE
This was the first example of the Baroque in Prague ● 80 based on Roman Baroque. The façade is articulated with pilasters, and is decorated with a wide variety of pediments, *oculi* and balconies with a loggia.

A walk on Petřín Hill.

18th century. During the Thirty Years' War, Caratti worked for Pavel Michna of Vacinov who, with Wallenstein, Liechtenstein and Cardinal Dietrichstein, was one of the members of the financial consortium that ruined Moravia after the Battle of White Mountain ● *34*. The banqueting room has stucco decoration by Domenico Galli, who was additionally responsible for the stucco on the exterior. The building was never completed and, after being turned into a barracks and then an arsenal in the late 18th century, it was finally purchased and restored in 1921 by the Association of Sokols and equipped as a gymnasium. It now houses the Sports Faculty of Charles University (Carolinum ▲ *278*) and the Museum of Physical Education.

The Sokols. The spread of associations during the second half of the 19th century provided Czechs with ample opportunity to fight for their national cause. The Sokol ("Falcon") Gymnastics Association, founded by Miroslav Tyrš and Jindřich Fügner in 1862, became a real mass movement which advocated values of equality and fraternity that were close to the ideals of the Union of Czech Brethren ● *43*. Clubs sprang up not only in Bohemia and Moravia, but in other Slav countries, and meetings of gymnasts were attended by thousands of people. In 1914, there were 128,000 members, and by 1947 there were over a million, or one Czech in every fourteen! The rules of the Sokols stated: "Through the education of the body and mind, through physical energy, through art and science, through all moral means: rebuild the fatherland!" The Association has been re-forming since 1990, and is likely to recover the many goods confiscated in 1948. After the period of Nazi rule, the Communists banned the Sokols and imprisoned its leadership.

Miroslav Tyrš (1832–84)
This philosopher and writer on Czech art history is best known for *Laocoon, a Work of the Roman Era* (1872) and *Of the Gothic Style* (1881).

Below: Petřín Tower or belvedere.

PETŘÍN HILL

A huge forest once extended from Petřín Hill to the site of the Battle of White Mountain. The area has been laid out as gardens and vineyards since the 12th century and, with the addition of interesting monuments, is now a delightful place for walks.
Petřín Park (Petřinské sady). The best way to Petřín Hill is by the

funicular railway from Na Újezdě Station: from Michna Palace, cross the Karmelitská-Újezd crossroads and continue straight on.

THE BELVEDERE. The Petřín belvedere, a miniature copy of the Eiffel Tower, was erected for the Jubilee Exhibition of 1891 and moved to the top of the hill during the 1930's. The belvedere offers wonderful views over the city, and Malá Strana in particular.

ST LAWRENCE'S CHURCH. This Baroque church, which was designed by Ignác Johann Palliardi and built between 1735 and 1770, was constructed over the remains of a Romanesque building referred to as early as 1135. Some vestiges are still visible in the south wing of the present building. St Lawrence's Church is recessed in the Wall of Hunger (Hladová zed). Beside it is the Calvary Chapel (1735), the façade decorated with sgraffito (1936) ● *78* depicting the Resurrection.

KINSKÝ GARDENS. The Kinský Villa (Vila Kinských) and gardens are further to the south, in the direction of Holečková Street. The charming Villa in the Empire style is the work of the architect, Jindřich Koch (1827–31), and the grounds contain a statue of Psyche by Antonio Canova (1757–1822). In the 19th century the house was leased to the heir apparent Archdukes Rudolph and Francis Ferdinand of Habsburg ● *31*. It later housed the Ethnology Section of the National Museum ▲ *175*, but is now closed. More exotic is the Carpathian Church of ST MICHAEL OF PETŘÍN

St Lawrence's Church on Petřín Hill.

CHURCH OF OUR LADY OF THE VICTORY
The Baroque altars of this church are notable for restrained decoration highlighted by touches of gold and black combined. The high altar (above) is by Johann Ferdinand Schor ▲ *314*, and includes a statue of the Virgin by Josef Čapek.

(below). This old Orthodox church from the High Tatra Mountains in the Carpathians is made of wood and dates from the 18th century. The church was passed to Czechoslovakia under the Treaty of Trianon (June 4, 1920), but in 1929 it was transferred from Medvedovce (in Subcarpathian Russia, an area which belonged to Hungary until 1918) to Prague. It is in this way that the culture and traditions of this minority have been represented in Prague.

MONUMENT TO KAREL HYNEK MÁCHA. This commemorative monument, which is reached by walking along the wall of the old fortifications, occupies an important place in the Czech national conscience. Mácha (1810–36) was the greatest and most authentic of Czech Romantic poets, and there are many people who know *Máj* (*May*), his most famous poem and a true hymn to love, by heart. It is a custom, every May 1, for young lovers to lay flowers at the foot of the statue and to embrace as evening comes.

CHURCH OF OUR LADY OF THE VICTORY

To reach the Church of Our Lady of the Victory (Kostel Panny Marie Vítězné), go down Petřín Hill to Malá Strana, pass Michna Palace, and up Karmelitská Street. The Church is at no. 9. It was originally a German Lutheran temple dedicated to the Holy Trinity, but in 1624 it was handed over to the Spanish Discalced Carmelites who had only recently arrived in Bohemia. The name of the church recalls the Battle of White Mountain ● *34*; according to legend, the Catholic victory was due to the actions and prayers of the Superior General of Carmelites, Dominique a Santa Maria. The church door was paid for by one of the leaders of the Imperial Armies, Don Baltazar de Marroas. The whole building was constructed in 1611 on plans by Giovanni Maria Filippi ▲ *240*, and then it was completely redesigned in 1636–44, thereby laying claim to be Prague's first Baroque ● *70* church; it was the first example in the city of a three-part façade with pilasters and scrolls. All that now remains of this Protestant church is the door on the

THE LITTLE JESUS OF PRAGUE
The main attraction of the Church of Our Lady of the Victory is probably the "Little Jesus of Prague". In 1628, Princess Polyxěna of Lobkowicz, the wife of the Grand Chancellor of Bohemia, offered the church this wax statuette which her mother, Doňa María Manrique de Lara, had brought in her trousseau when she came from Spain in 1555 to marry Vratislav of Pernštejn. The statue of the "Little Jesus of Prague" has been said to have miraculous properties since the 17th century, and has always attracted a large number of pilgrims. It owns a fine wardrobe which is changed for each feast of the year. In 1742 the Empress Maria Theresa ● *31* had a costume of gold brocade made for it after the French troops who had been occupying Prague departed; she did this to thank the statue for saving the city from being pillaged.

271

NOSTITZ PALACE
Poster showing the façade of Nostitz Palace, one of the main centers where musical events took place during the "Prague Spring" Festival ● 48.

OUR LADY UNDER THE CHAIN
The name of this church comes from a legend that says the bridge was closed off by a golden chain. The task of protecting Judith Bridge ▲ 154 was given to the Order of the Hospital of St John of Jerusalem whom Vladislav I had encounteredduring his expedition to the Holy Land in 1147. When the Malá Strana fortifications were being built in 1253, the end of the bridge was connected to the monastery by the ramparts.

right-hand side of the façade and the marble baptismal fonts. The paintings of Saint Joseph, Saint Joachim and Saint Anne on the third side altar, and the painting of Saint Simon on the left, are by Petr Brandl and date from the early 18th century. The crypt has a number of open coffins containing the exceptionally well preserved corpses of eminent Carmelites and benefactors to the Order. At no. 8, on the corner of Harantova Street and level with the Church of Our Lady of the Victory, is ROHAN PALACE built by Josef Zobel in 1796; it is now the premises of the Czech Ministry of Education.

CONVENT OF ST MARY MAGDALEN

The Convent and Church of St Mary Magdalen used to be at nos. 2, 4 and 6 Karmelitská Street. This early building, consecrated to the Madeleinites, and dating from the beginning of the 14th century, was destroyed during the Hussite Wars ● 32. A convent was then rebuilt between 1656 and 1677 under the direction of the Dominicans and with money largely provided by Pavel Michna of Vacinov ▲ 268. The plans for the church were supplied by Francesco Caratti, and by Krištof Dientzenhofer who is said to be buried there with his son, Kilián Ignác. After the abolition of the Orders, the convent was put to many other uses: the buildings served as a post office from 1791 to 1849, then as a police barracks until 1945 since when it has been used to store State archives.

MALTESE SQUARE

Maltézské náměstí is reached by turning off Karmelitská Street into either Prokopská Street or Harantova Street.
STRAKA PALACE. This palace at no. 14 was probably designed by Jean-Baptiste Mathey around 1690.
TURBA PALACE. The façade of this palace built by František Josef Jäger in 1767–8 is framed with pilasters, the pediments alone betraying any sign of Rococo imaginativeness. Since it was restored in 1990, this palace has become one of the most elegant in Prague. It now houses the Japanese Embassy.
NOSTITZ PALACE. The right-hand side of the north end of Maltese Square consists of Nostitz Palace at no. 1. It is attributed to Francesco Caratti, who probably built it in the 1660's; it is in a style commonly referred to as "Primitive Baroque", which is here set off by an order of huge capitals. The façade was redone during the 18th century; the balustrade and the corner towers on the roof, and subsequently the door with a balcony and the stucco decoration, helped to soften the building's overall severity. Caratti was also responsible for the enormous Černín Palace ▲ 234.

CHURCH OF OUR LADY UNDER THE CHAIN

The Church of Our Lady under the Chain is in Lázenská
Street, off Maltese Square.

CENTER OF THE COMMANDERY. This church, known as Kostel
Panny Marie Pod Řetězem, is the oldest foundation in Malá
Strana; the Romanesque church was discovered between 1169
and 1182. King Vladislav II ● *30* had it built for the Sovereign
Order of the Knights of Malta. There were plans in the 14th
century to pull the entire building down and replace it with a
new church, but the idea was abandoned some time after
work was started. The present building still has fine
Romanesque remains between the two towers of 1385. The
new church dates from the early 17th century, except for the
choir, redesigned by Carlo Lurago in
1640–50. The high altar is decorated by
Karel Škreta's *The Virgin, St John the
Baptist and the Battle of Lepanto*, while
the pulpit is probably the work of Johann
Georg Bendl, who made the statues of St
Gerhard and St Ubal-deska. The marble
statue is of Rudolph Colloredo-Waldsee,
Prior of the Order which defended
Prague against the Swedes in 1648.

DEFENDING THE BRIDGE. The 12th-
century Judith Bridge ▲ *154* was guarded at either end by
two fortified churches: in Staré Město by St Clement's
▲ *152* (now rebuilt and integrated into the Clementinum),
and in Malá Strana by Our Lady under the Chain.

MALTESE PALACE

The Maltese Palace, or the Palace of the Grand Priors, which
stands against the right-hand side of the church, was built by
G. B. Scotti in 1724–8. Until 1990, it housed the Museum of
Musical Instruments. The restrained façade still has three
lunette windows surmounted by stone masks; the highest of
these is to be found in the bay of the entrance where
the elaborate decoration is concentrated. To the
left of the church is another property
belonging to the Knights of Malta, a
former monastery rebuilt by Tomáš
Haffenecker in 1728–31. Opposite,
at no. 11, is the HOUSE "OF THE
GOLDEN UNICORN"
(U ZLATÉHO JEDNOROŽCE), a
hotel at one time patronized by
Beethoven and Mozart.

MALTÉZSKÉ NÁMĚSTÍ
The area round
Maltese Square is full
of palaces, and this
well-preserved
quarter provided a
natural backdrop for
Miloš Forman's film
Amadeus.

**HOUSE "AT THE SIGN
OF THE BATHS"**
This used to be a
hotel patronized by
Peter the Great and
also by Chateau-
briand while on his
mission to
Charles X, during the
latter's exile in
Prague in 1833.

**HOUSE "AT THE SIGN
OF THE PAINTERS"**
This building at 11
Maltese Square dates
from 1531. Its name
(*U Malířů*) and sign
(below) recall that
the painter Jiří Šic
lived here during the
second half of the
16th century. It now
contains a restaurant.

FRANÇOIS RENE
DE CHATEAUBRIAND
BYDLIL V TOMTO DOMĚ
V HOSTINCI NAZVANÉM V LÁZNÍCH
24–30. KVĚTNA 1833.

The Baroque triumphed in Prague during the 17th century and the early part of the 18th century and at that time the arts flourished through a synthesis of architecture and decorative design which found its quintessential expression in the landscaping of gardens. The 1541 fire in Malá Strana made a lot of land available and this enabled the nobility to erect Baroque palaces with terraced gardens close to Prague Castle and on the steep hillsides of Petřín Hill. The unevenness of the land inspired complex solutions which, in a manner totally appropriate to the "genius of the place", were a treasury of fascinating proportions and perspectives. These "theaters of greenery" were organized around an axis but, away from the center, they encouraged walkers to abandon themselves to the gardens' intimate charms and secrets. After many years of neglect, they are now being restored.

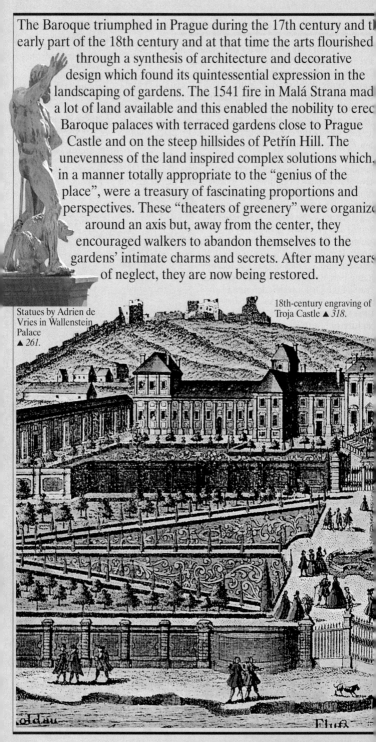

Statues by Adrien de Vries in Wallenstein Palace ▲ 261.

18th-century engraving of Troja Castle ▲ 318.

"All of a sudden, I was lost in wonderment. It was a sort of open-air theater hewn out of the hillside, tiered with curved terraces and adorned with magnificent statues. . ."

Dominique Fernandez

GARDENS THAT INSPIRE THE SENSES

A *sala terrena* (or loggia), decorated grottos and summer houses (above). The architecture of the gardens of Prague is best enjoyed walking along tranquil paths, or climbing up sometimes rather steep steps which lead to porches, unfamiliar passageways and terraces with balustrades.

Everywhere there is an intertwining of plants and foliage, unexpected glimpses into the countryside, sweet-smelling flower beds brimming over with arabesques and festooned with topiaries, fine Baroque statues and fountains gurgling away musically.

HOMAGE TO LENNON
This gave citizens of Prague a way of articulating their dissidence.

KOUNIC PALACE
Situated at no. 15 this is considered to be one of the most beautiful buildings in Mostecká Street. It was constructed by

Anton Schmidt in 1730–75, and houses the Embassy of the former Yugoslavia. The attic statuary comes from the workshop of Ignác Platzer (1717–87).

View of Mostecká Street, with St Nicholas' Church, Malá Strana, in the background ▲ 251.

VELKOPŘEVORSKÉ SQUARE

BUCQUOY-VALDŠTEJN PALACE. The most beautiful building in the Square of the Grand Prior (Velkopřevorské náměstí) is the Bucquoy-Valdštejn Palace, designed by Jean-Baptiste Mathey around 1632; the façade was redone in 1719 by F. M. Kaňka. The stucco decoration comes from the workshop of Matthias Bernhard Braun, Kaňka's favorite collaborator. Bucquoy Palace now houses the French Embassy.
HRZÁN PALACE. This palace at no. 1 has preserved its door and Renaissance gables. The Baroque wing on the left, restored in 1760, overlooks Čertovka Street. The composer Josef Bohuslav Foerster (1859–1951) ● 47 was born here.
JOHN LENNON IN PRAGUE. The wall of the garden of Maltese Square opposite is covered with tokens of homage to John Lennon. During the "normalization" period, young people gathered in front of the "John Lennon Wall" on the anniversary of his death, and sat waiting in silence until the police brutally moved them on. Large numbers of letters addressed "John Lennon Monument, Prague" used to arrive here, and the postmen simply attached them to the wall. But normalization is history now, and the singer's portrait, partly obliterated by the weather, now attracts only tourists.

MOSTECKÁ STREET

Lázenská Street leads into the busy Mostecká Street (Mostecká ulice). The courtyard at no. 16 still has remains of the Gothic Archbishop's Palace, destroyed by the Hussites at the beginning of their uprising ● 32; at no. 3 is SAXONY HOUSE, an old Gothic residence whose façade was rebuilt in the late 1700's. The road is closed off by the towers of the bridge and by MALÁ STRANA GATE. The smallest tower, which dates from 1166, formed part of the fortifications of the former Judith Bridge ▲ 154; it was decorated with gables and sgraffito ● 78 in 1591. The tallest dates from the late 1600's.

From the Carolinum to the National Theater

THE CAROLINUM ★

FOUNDED BY CHARLES IV.
After Wenceslas II (1278–1305) failed in his attempt to establish a *studium generale* in the capital, Charles IV founded the University of Prague in 1348. It was modeled on the Sorbonne in Paris and the University of Bologna, and was central Europe's first university, before even Cracow (1364) and Vienna (1365). The education of the élites of the Kingdom of Bohemia and of neighboring countries no longer depended solely on Italian and French universities. In medieval times, there were four faculties: Arts, Law, Medicine and Theology.

THE BUILDINGS. The Carolinum's hub was the Gothic house belonging to the financier Rothlev, who presented it to the institution. The Baroque elements were introduced at the time of F.M. Kaňka's late restoration in 1718. The Carolinum is still part of the university, although it is used mainly for official ceremonies; the fine vaulted rooms on the ground floor, on the right by the entrance, house exhibitions of contemporary art.

Below: Tapestry from the Great Hall in the Carolinum, depicting Charles IV and Wenceslas.

ONE OF EUROPE'S INTELLECTUAL CENTERS.

The university was established by Charles IV primarily to serve the needs of the Kingdom of Bohemia, and then those of the Empire. From 1363 until 1470, it was organized into four nations: Czech (a group that embraced the Moravians, Hungarians and southern Slavs), Polish (including the Silesians and their German neighbors), Bavarian, and Saxon (together with the Swedes, Norwegians and Danes). In practice, the student population, which was extremely numerous from the outset, was divided into Czechs and Germans. The University enjoyed productive relations with the Universities of Paris and Oxford, and counted theologians of renown such as Matthew of Cracow among its number.

The only remains of the original Carolinum building are the first-floor arches and the oriel window of the chapel overlooking Ovocný trh.

SEAL OF CHARLES IV
The University developed rapidly and, by the late 14th century, was the most important in central Europe.

JOHN HUSS, RECTOR OF THE UNIVERSITY. From the early 15th century, John Huss ● 32 taught the ideas of John Wycliffe, as did most of his Czech colleagues who supported his notions of realism. This led to a revival of Pelagianism, a 14th-century heresy that had been resisted by Saint Augustine. At that time, the German teachers at the University were nominalists and rejected Wycliffism, but their authority was sorely undermined when, on January 18, 1409, Wenceslas IV reformed the University's statutes, giving three votes to the Czech teachers and only one to the other three "nations". "Human laws, divine law and natural instinct all insist that Czechs have priority in Bohemia," wrote Huss, who became Rector in 1409. The Germans left the University on May 16, 1409 and re-established a university in Leipzig in Saxony. John Huss was burned at the stake in 1415. After some hesitation, the University teachers declared in 1417 that communion was essential for good health. Henceforth, the university was to play an important role in the development of the conservative Hussite program, and it was also there

"TRACTATUS DE PESTILENTIA"
A page from a 15th-century manuscript in the Carolinum Library.

JOSEF KAJETÁN TYL (1808–56) ▲ 163.
The Estates Theater was once known as the Tyl Theater, after one of the most prolific popular dramatists of his time. The future Czech national anthem, "Where is my home?", was taken from one of Tyl's plays entitled *Fidlovačka* (1834). Tyl was also one of the organizers of public balls ● 52 called "Czech Balls"; the first of these took place in the concert hall in the former Jesuit College ▲ 288.

that the celebrated "Four Articles of Prague", a more moderate version of this programme, were drawn up in 1419. In 1420, the University supported the legitimacy of the uprising against the King to defend God's cause, and round 1430 teaching almost came to a halt. In the reign of George of Poděbrady ● 30, the University was Utraquist and remained so until the Battle of White Mountain ● 34. At that time, teachers promised allegiance to the King and the chalice, and foreign Catholic students no longer applied to come. Lutheran reforms in the 16th century made it possible to re-establish contact with countries that had turned Protestant, and Prague students completed their educations in Wittenberg, and then in Basel and Geneva. The university was vitally important for Bohemia and, during the 16th century, all schools in the towns and provinces except for the one run by the Union of Brethren came under its control. Following the fall of the Protestant Estates of Bohemia, the university was closed down and handed over to the Jesuits in 1622. The Faculties of Law and Medicine were closed until 1654, the year in which the University took the name of Charles Ferdinand, a title it retained until 1918. At the time, Law and Medicine came under the State, while Philosophy and Theology were in the hands of the Jesuits. However, a series of reforms began to be introduced in 1747 ensuring that all subjects remained strictly under the control of the State until the end of the 18th century. In 1784, German supplanted Latin as the medium of instruction but, by 1848, in spite of everything that had gone before, the Faculty of Letters became one of

the centers of the Czech national rebirth. The reforms of 1848–50 followed and, in 1882, the University divided on the one hand into a German University, and on the other into a Czech University attended not only by Czechs but also by Slovaks, Slovenes, Serbs and Croats. In 1918, when the State of Czechoslovakia was established, it became known as Charles University, a name it has retained to this day.

A MUSICAL TRADITION ● 46. Under the reign of Charles IV, the Court, the University and the Church found both *Ars Nova* and Gregorian Chant both competing fiercely for favor, and there were also assertive claims being made by more localized schools and by the resurgence of the traditions of the Slav liturgy. One of the university's duties was the training of singers for the Chapter of St Vitus' Cathedral ▲ *214*. The religious ceremonies and music of the court also took on a new luxuriance following polyphonic advances and an expansion in the realm of musical instruments. These developments were halted when John Huss denounced the irrelevant and perverse opulence of church music and condemned the use of musical instruments in liturgical rituals.

ESTATES THEATER

The plans for this theater were provided by the architect, Antonín Haffenecker, in 1781. The building was subsequently redone when an extra floor was added in 1859; then, in 1881, the theater was given a metallic structure and decorated in the neo-Renaissance style ● *84*. Restorations were commenced in 1983, and it re-opened its doors in 1989.

NATIONALIST SENTIMENT. The construction of Count Nostitz's theater also marks a date in the Czech "national awakening" ● *28*. Although most of the works were German, there were performances in Czech as early as 1785.

ESTATES THEATER
It was in this famous Prague theater, that Mozart's *Don Giovanni* and *La Clemenza di Tito* were given their first performances in 1787 and 1791 respectively. The director, Miloš Forman, filmed the opera scenes here for his 1984 film *Amadeus*.

FRANTIŠEK ŠKROUP
The composer František Škroup ▲ *184*, who died in 1862, was active in the National Awakening Movement, but did not get involved in sectarianism. He used his position as Head of German Opera at the Estates Theater to introduce Liszt, Wagner and Berlioz to Prague audiences.

The Estates Theater is also been known as the Nostitz Theater, the National Theater, the German Theater and the Tyl Theater. It was commissioned at the end of the 18th century by Count František Nostitz-Rienek, Chief Burgrave of the Kingdom of Bohemia.

The St Havel Market
The St Havel district is now one of the most delightful in all of Prague, with its colorful daily market.

Uhelný trh
A number of Renaissance houses with arches have survived in the southwest of St Havel. Until 1807, there was a forge here where it was also possible to buy coal; the square then came to be known as Coal Market, although this was changed to Green Market and later to Vegetable Market. One of the old buildings in the square is the House "Of the Golden Lion", a Gothic construction which was renovated in the Baroque style in the 17th century. At the end of the 17th century, it belonged to the composer František Dušek; his friend Mozart stayed there in 1787.

The earliest works in the Czech repertory to be given at the Nostitz Theater included Klicpera's *The Magic Hat* and *Hadrian in the Cornice* (these pieces are still performed) and the first modern Czech opera, František Škroup's *The Tinker* (1826). In 1786, a group of actors persuaded the Emperor to open a theater made of wood called "The Shed" (Bouda) not far from the Nostitz Theater in Wenceslas Square ▲ *172*, where they would put on Czech plays. "The Shed" disappeared in 1789, and in 1797–9 Count Nostitz sold his theater to the Diet (or Estates) of Bohemia for 60,000 florins; this is the origin of the name that it bore for many years, and which it adopted once more in 1990.

St Havel

Royal Privilege. Not far from the Estates Theater, Havelská, V. Kotcích and Rytířská streets form what was once the old town of St Havel. This early township, which began to grow in Romanesque times as Old Town, too, began to expand, was situated between Ovocný trh "fruit market" and Uhelný trh "coal market". Then, in 1232, Wenceslas I granted it the status of city and also had the first enclosure of Prague's ramparts raised, thereby protecting an area of approximately

> "One evening at home, as he removed his irksome wig,
> Mozart looked at this charming little square from the
> window of a nearby house."

Jaroslav Seifert

100 acres. New districts were built, and the completely new city of St Havel was constructed. It was a lively place, attracting mainly German colonists, and was soon providing competition for Old Town Square ▲ *136*.

ST HAVEL'S CHURCH (KOSTEL SV. HAVEL)

NOTABLE CONTRIBUTION FROM SANTINI. St Havel's Church (also called St Gall) was founded in 1232 at the same time as the city of the same name, but it was rebuilt in about 1330 and then substantially redone around 1671–80 by Carlo Lurago and Domenico Orsi. The façade was not erected until 1723–38 on plans by Jan Blažej Santini-Aichl (1677–1723) ● *80*. The most valuable item in the church is a crucifixion with four evangelists by Brokoff. The convent buildings adjoining the church, once occupied by Discalced Carmelites, were restored by private individuals following secularization of religious orders by Joseph II. Neither the cloister nor the refectory, which is elaborately decorated with stuccowork, have survived the ravages of time.

Jakoubek of Stříbro took communion in both kinds for the first time at St Martin's Church in October 1414.

A REFORMING PREACHER. Konrad Waldhauser (c. 1326–69) used to preach at St Havel's. Widely considered to be the initiator of the Hussite Movement ● *32* in Bohemia, he settled in Prague in 1363, after spending over ten years as an itinerant preacher, and made his name denouncing the clergy's corrupt lifestyle and simony. John Huss also preached here from 1402 to 1414.

CHURCH OF ST-MARTIN-IN-THE-WALLS

From St Havel's Church, Havelská Street runs into the market, Uhelný trh, which then connects with Martinská Street, the site of the Church of St-Martin-in-the-Walls (Kostel sv. Martina ve zdi). This church, probably founded in the 12th century, has a coffered ceiling dating from 1610 and a door from 1779. A plaque on the church wall states that the sculptors Brokoffs, father and son, are buried in St Martin's cemetery. Access to the interior is only possible for concerts.

UTRAQUISM. Jakoubek (c. 1373–1429), a disciple of Matthew of Janov, was the author of a voluminous theological work comparable to that written by John Huss. According to Jan Lavička, "Of all the Czech teachers, he was the one who came closest to the Protestants through his loyalty and new ideas about worship. However, the scholastic dryness of his Latin written style and the fame that John Huss enjoyed after his death consigned him to oblivion." Communion was to be in both kinds (*sub utraque specie*), that is, take bread and wine. The choice of the chalice as the Reformation's symbol stems from this; so do the words "Calixtine" and "Utraquist" to designate Protestants of the Reformation.

BRETHREN OF BOHEMIA. From now on, St Martin's Church belonged to the Union of Czech Brethren, a community born in 1457 out of the reunification of radical Hussites. Many Brethren emigrated after 1620 ● *32*, but the Union re-formed in the early 18th century at Herrnhut in Saxony under the new

ST-MARTIN-IN-THE-WALLS
The south wall was incorporated into the fortification wall of Old Town in the 13th century; this explains the phrase "in the Walls." Below: Interior of the Gothic Church of St Martin.

283

name of Moravian Brethren, and with quite different statutes and doctrines from the Brethren's original Church. The Herrnhut Brethren were missionaries and established themselves throughout the world, in particular the United States where they still own a university in Baltimore. Some of those who stayed behind in Bohemia and Moravia concealed their views until 1781; in 1918, they chose to take once more the name of the church of Comenius and their ancestors, and finally renamed themselves the Evangelical Church of Czech Brethren.

FORMER VRATISLAVSKÝ HOUSE

Skořepká Street leads to Jilská Street where, between 1813 and 1817, the composer Carl Maria von Weber lived at no. 16. This was once known as Vratislavský House, named after Count Vratislavský, its owner in the 18th century. When Count Nostitz's theater ▲ 281 was taken over by the Diet of Bohemia and the influence and power of Italian theater began to wane, Weber was appointed its Director; it had by now become the Estates Theater and was situated in Václav Müller Square. Weber's task was to reorganize opera with the support of the music-loving aristocracy including members of the Nostitz, Pachta and Lobkowicz families. Despite his successes and his desire to raise artistic standards and expand the repertoire the new Director, who was in poor health, was not able to tolerate the hostility of the people of Prague. They were not prepared to accept that an Italian director could be replaced by a German instead of a Czech. This was an early sign of the spread of the ideas and influence of both the Awakeners ● 28 and the general public.

"FISHERMAN'S HOUSE"
This statue adorns the façade of the "Fisherman's House" (Na rybarně) at 10 Betlémské náměstí. It is probably the work of the architect Alliprandi, who rebuilt the house in the Baroque style around 1704. Today, it is occupied by a tavern famous for wines known as the "Wines of the Kings of Bohemia".

BETLÉMSKÉ NÁMĚSTÍ
This early 20th-century view of Bethlehem Square shows Náprstek Museum in the background and, in the foreground, the Savings Bank of Bohemia building (details are shown at the top of the opposite page).

ST GILES' CHURCH

CISTERCIAN INFLUENCE. The entrance to St Giles' Church is in Husova Street, a thoroughfare noted for its galleries of contemporary art. Jan Milíč of Kroměříž ▲ *147*, a precursor of Huss, preached here from 1365, and St Giles' is one of the churches in Old Town to have preserved their Gothic exteriors. It was started in 1310 during the lifetime of John of Dražice, Bishop of Prague. This well-traveled prelate had lived at the Papal Court in Avignon and had the opportunity to savour French Gothic architecture, which he then introduced to Bohemia. That is why Bohemian Gothic sometimes draws on Cistercian Gothic styles prevalent in Burgundy; it also explains the restrained design of the façade, and the addition of a porch and a flat chevet.

VAULTED CEILING. The interior of St Giles' is based on a Baroque renovation undertaken by František Spacek in 1733. Václav Vavřinec Reiner (1689–1743) executed the frescos in the vaults, including the most successful section, the *Triumph of the Dominicans over Heresy* (1733–4), over the central nave. Reiner ▲ *162, 184, 220, 236* a native of Prague, brought mural painting to the same lofty standards that sculpture had attained some time before. He is particularly noted for his ability to compose huge scenes without allowing the dramatic tension to lapse.

ST GILES' CHURCH
The most beautiful decorations in this church are the vaulted ceilings with their trompe l'oeil frescos. The high altar (1734–8) has wooden sculptures by František Ignác Weiss.

BETHLEHEM SQUARE ★

On leaving St Giles' Church, the visitor should take Husova Street on the left; the first turning to the right then leads into Bethlehem Square (Betlémské náměstí). The square takes its name from the chapel of the same name, although it also used to be known as the Chapel of the Holy Innocents. A Prague tradition has it that this was the site of a fountain into which unworthy mothers are

JOHN HUSS
His university work at the Carolinum ▲ 279 and his didactic work at the Bethlehem Chapel, where he preached from 1402 from 1414, were the two priorities of John Huss' life.

AT THE STAKE
After his arrest, John Huss was found guilty by the Council of Constance and burned at the stake on July 6, 1415.

said to have thrown their unwanted children. On the pediment of the Baroque house at no. 10, the birthplace of the painter Jaroslav Čermák (1830–78), is a bust of the Emperor Joseph I; this is also where the first meeting of the Czech political group first known as the "Slav Eagle", and later called the "Slav Linden", took place. The square is now full of antique shops, book shops and pleasant restaurants.

BETHLEHEM CHAPEL

THE FOUNDATION. The Bethlehem Chapel was founded by a courtier, Hanuš of Mühlheim, and a merchant by the name of Křiž, and was built between 1391 and 1402. It was constructed in a very sober style similar to a barn-like church, and from its earliest days it was devoted to preaching in Czech. At the time, the chapel was situated in a popular quarter of town that was incessantly exposed to flooding. It was also a huge building – it held up to three thousand people – and was the first whose layout responded to the sensitivities of the Reformation. The Chapel was pulled down at the end of the 18th century, but rebuilt in 1950–2 by the Communists in memory of the egalitarian ideas espoused by Czech Reformers. The reconstruction seems to be a faithful one; this is born out by the permanent exhibition on the second floor. The church is organized around three exterior walls that have been preserved and integrated into neighboring houses. To the right of the Chapel, is John Huss' house, now known as the PREACHER'S HOUSE.

HUSSITE SERMONS. John Huss preached in the Bethlehem Chapel every day from 1402 to 1414, to packed congregations of artisans, workers, small business people, and clerics whom he urged to return to practises set out in the Gospels. He never let himself be distracted by interdicts from the Archbishop; indeed, his ideas spread all the more easily as the 1,200 poor clerks made up a substantial part of the city's population of 40,000.

HUSSITE HYMNS. Preaching in the Bethlehem Chapel in the vernacular language of Czech was the implementation of one of the basic principles of the Hussite Reformation, and this linguistic revolution went hand in hand with the composition of popular hymns with Czech texts which Huss himself had often written or adapted. A great tradition of hymns was born in Bohemia with the rise of Hussism, and it was to have a major influence on Czech music. The Hussite leader Jan Žižka included the singing of hymns in the struggles of the Taborites against the troops of the Pope or the Emperor. The most popular, "We who are God's

The interior of this church is remarkable for its austerity. The walls are decorated with a few paintings, but these are copies of medieval illuminations which recall, in particular, the opulence of the Church and the life of John Huss ● 32. Two other walls are hung with texts of Huss and Jakoubek of Stříbro; these were discovered and completed when the Chapel was restored during this century.

combatants", was often used by composers, particularly Smetana ● 47 in his opera *Libuše* ▲ 296 and his symphonic suite *Má vlast* (*My Country*), and by Janáček ▲ 296 in the second of *Mr Brouček's Excursions*. A large number of Hussite songs are collected in the *Jistebnice Songbook* (1436).

NÁPRSTEK ETHNOGRAPHICAL MUSEUM

The Náprstek Ethnographical Museum is on the corner of Náprstkova and Betlémská Streets; it is located in U Halánků House, a building reconstructed in the late 18th century. Vojtěch Fingerhut-Náprstek (1826–94) was a noted Czech patriot: a disciple of Josef Jungmann ▲ 290, he was particularly active in the balls organized by Josef Kajetán Tyl ▲ 280 and took part in the 1848 Revolution ● 28 before emigrating to the United States.

OPENING A MUSEUM. When he returned to Prague in 1858, Náprstek brought with him a large quantity of souvenirs, including his earliest ethnographical and technological

287

▲ From the Carolinum to the National Theater

objects. By 1863, with the devoted support of numerous women friends in Prague, including Princess Taxis, he was able to open a proper industrial museum. The collections that filled this museum have now been integrated with the items housed in the National Technical Museum in Kostelní Street. Náprstek was also deeply involved in the struggle for women's votes and their rights at work. Náprstek's other passion, ethnology, took shape in the museum in U Halánků House, and various explorer friends of his including Holub, Hloucha, Kořenský, Frič and Vraz gave him large quantities of masks, arms and costumes; these now make up the collections in the present-day ethnological museum.

Former Trade Union Building

Průchodní Lane leads out of Bethlehem Square into Bartolomějská Street. Here stands the former Trade Union Building constructed by Alois Dryák (1872–1932) ▲ 174 in 1925. It was the venue for meetings of members of the Czech Communist Party from 1945 onward. Klement Gottwald ● 39 prepared for his accession to power here in 1948; the building then became the headquarters of the security authorities, and many opponents of the régime were subjected to severe interrogations there.

Former Jesuit College

At no. 11, opposite the Trade Union Building, is a former Jesuit College that occupies the length of Průchodní Lane. Although this was a red light district in the Middle Ages, the Cistercians built a monastery here, and the Jesuits then bought it in 1660.

Former concert hall. The monastery buildings are currently being restored. In the 1920's, it was turned into a movie theater, and the old walls pitted with saltpeter once again echoed to the sound of music, the College having been Prague's leading concert hall in the mid-19th century. Beethoven came here in 1798, and Václav Tomášek wrote that he gave a warmly received performance of his Concerto No. 1 in C, Op. 15 and the Adagio and Rondo in A, Op. 2, and improvised on the theme of an aria from Mozart's *Clemenza di Tito*. He then repeated the concert and started something of a trend. This concert hall eventually lost out to the hall on Slav Island (1836) ▲ 302, but it was still used until the beginning of the 20th century by eminent musicians including Hans von Bülow, Rubinstein and Weniavsky, and the Czech violinists Ondříček and Laub. Josef Suk ● 47 also wrote his piano cycle, *Between Life and Death*, for this hall. The first "patriotic" Czech ball was held at the College in 1840, and 1859 saw the

COLLECTIONS
The Náprstek Ethnological Museum contains numerous objects brought back from Africa. Above: A mask from new Guinea. Top of page: Drums, also from New Guinea.

"Old Prague has its narrow alleyways, houses that open out onto two or three streets, and passageways that are so cleverly connected that it is possible to pass through entire districts without setting foot on an uncovered footway."
Roger Grenier

first concert given by the Männergesangverein; in 1861, this group was renamed the Česká beseda as most of its members were Czechs. The concert hall was housed in the former refectory of an establishment with another claim to fame. It was once the famous Organ School which replaced the School of Composition, as the Music Conservatoire founded in 1811 was devoted exclusively to instrumental playing. The majority of Czech composers from the time of Smetana onward worked here.

ROTUNDA OF THE HOLY CROSS ★

Bartolomějská Street runs into Karoliny Street, a road that takes its name from the writer Karolina Světlá who was born in the House "Of the Three Kings"(U tří králů) (no. 3) in 1830. She was a great admirer of George Sand, and was influenced by the city of Prague, and later by northern Bohemia. The Rotunda of the Holy Cross is also in this street. This 12th-century church, one of the few Romanesque buildings left in Prague ● 68, was saved from demolition and was restored between 1864 and 1876 to plans by Vojtěch Ignác Ullmann ▲ 184; the interior was decorated around the same time by Waschmann, and contains vestiges of Gothic mural paintings.

FORMER TRADE UNION BUILDING
The bas-reliefs on this building recall the inspiration of Proletarian Realism that was fashionable around 1920.

ST BARTHOLOMEW'S CHURCH
This church is attached to the former Jesuit College, and was built by Kilián Ignác Dientzenhofer between 1725 and 1731. It is currently being restored. The lavishly decorated main façade overlooks the College courtyard. The church was pulled down after 1773, but was restored in 1854 on the instructions of the Grey Sisters. The paintings on the vaults are by Václav Vavřinec Reiner.

289

JUNGMANN SQUARE

CHURCH OF OUR-LADY-OF-THE-SNOWS. This church where Jan Želivský ▲ *308* once preached was one of Charles IV's foundations. It is also the tallest building in the city, and yet is no more than the choir of a building constructed between 1379 and 1397 specifically to be the venue of Charles IV's coronation. Religious wars delayed the construction of both the nave and the façade, which were never ultimately built, although the vault of the choir was redone in the 16th century. The south face of the convent is marked by a very pleasant garden which belongs to the Franciscan monastery to which the church is attached.

MONUMENT TO JOSEF JUNGMANN. Jungmann Square (Jungmannovo náměstí) This square contains not only a remarkable Cubist street lamp (opposite) but also a monument to the memory of Josef Jungmann. This sculpture, executed in 1878 by Ludvik Šimek, commemorates one of the major figures of the National Awakening Movement ● *28*. Jungmann was convinced that Czech could establish itself as a language for poets and intellectuals, just like French and German, and in 1835 published a five-volume *Czech-German Dictionary* which was to become an essential tool for anyone seeking to understand and use the Czech language. For each word, Jungmann and his team produced a literary history which referred to medieval and Baroque usage, and when there was no word to express an idea, they looked for one in Polish or Russian or in other Slav languages. Similar linguistic research was also adopted by many mathematicians, philosophers and physicians.

URBÁNEK HOUSE

This building at no. 30 Jungmannova ul. belonging to the Urbánek publishing house used to be called the "Mozarteum"; it was constructed by Jan Kotěra between 1911 and 1913. Although the architect only used quite modest bricks, he managed to bring the façade to life by means of a number of subtle decorative touches. In the 1920's, the large concert hall was used for conferences that were addressed by specialists in Functionalist architecture including Oud, Gropius, Le Corbusier, Ozenfant and Loos, and by Jan Kotěra, the leading representative of this trend in Prague.

ADRIA PALACE

This building by Joseph Zasche ▲ *170* and Pavel Janák (1923–5) ▲ *197, 223* is a fine example of the inventiveness of Prague's architects at the beginning of

Above: Mosaic on the door to the Church of Our-Lady-of-the-Snows, and an interior view of the church which contains the biggest high altar in Prague.

JOSEF JUNGMANN (1773–1847) Jungmann believed that the great expressive powers of the Czech language placed it on a par with the monuments of world literature. Accordingly, he translated Shakespeare, Molière, Voltaire, Schiller and Goethe, in addition to his greatest successes, Chateaubriand's *Atala* and Milton's *Paradise Lost*.

> I am sitting in the café next to the window; outside the snow is falling. Národní Avenue is decorated with swastikas, ... the police are there, and in the street the German motorized army parades past."
>
> Jiří Mucha

the 20th century. They took their inspiration directly from the Venetian palazzi of the Italian Renaissance. It was commissioned by an Italian insurance company, the Riunione Adriatica di Sicurtà.

SECESSION GALLERY ★ ● 82. The Adria Palace's Secession gallery is lit up at night, and is probably one of the most beautiful in Prague. The mosaics on the floor are in the three colors of Czechoslovakia: red, blue and white.

ZA BRANOU II THEATER. Nowadays, the Adria Palace hosts a wide range of activities, including a terrace café and the ZA BRANOU II THEATER. The owner and director, Otomar Krejča, has been a prominent figure in Prague theater life since the 1950's. The theater was closed down by the authorities in 1972, but it resumed business with the return of democracy and, by way of celebration, was renamed Za Branou II.

HLÁVKOVY DOMY
The backs of the neo-Renaissance houses in Vodičkova Street are adorned with sgraffito ● 79. The drawings (above), on a black background, depict allegorical themes of work.

NÁRODNÍ AVENUE

For many years, Národní Avenue (Národní třída), or National Avenue, was known as "Ferdinandstrasse". Since 1781, it has marked the boundary between Staré Město and Nové Město, and it follows the route of one of the town's former defensive moats.

MAJ STORE. The building occupied by the Maj Store was designed in 1970 by Miroslav Masák, Johnny Eisler and Martin Rajniš, a group of architects working under the name "Sial 02". Since the Velvet Revolution, Maj has belonged to the American chain, K-mart.

ALBATROS PUBLISHING HOUSE. Albatros, a publisher of children's books, is opposite the Maj Store. This building has replaced a neoclassical structure which once housed the CAFÉ UNION ● 59 on the second floor. Albatros was very well known at the beginning of the 20th century, and attracted many writers, artists and scientists. In particular, members of the "Devětsil" Group used to go there. As the writer Jaroslav Seifert has so aptly put it, "We spent hours on end in cafés that overlooked the street, and we neglected neither circuses nor panoptics. It was all in line with our new artistic program – when art had ceased to be art, when Malevich brought figurative art to an end with his square abstract paintings."

ZA BRANOU THEATER
The entrance to the Za Branou Theater in the gallery of Adria Palace has adopted the forms and decorative devices of the Secession ● 88.

Of all the commissions given to the architect Osvald Polívka ▲ 176 by the city of Prague, the Praha Insurance Company building is the most successful. With a skilful use of symmetry, Polívka articulates the façade with windows and balconies, and the colored decoration of the surface is adorned with masterful attic sculptures by Ladislav Šaloun. Above: architect's plan (1903).

KAŇKA HOUSE

This small building at 16 Národní Avenue is without question one of the oldest in the road. Kaňka House – it takes its name from the architect who designed it – dates from 1730 and boasts a Baroque façade lavishly adorned with stucco decoration. Beneath the recently restored arches (opposite, right) is a plaque commemorating the great demonstration of November 17, 1989 which, in the course of the few days that followed, led to the Velvet Revolution ● 29 ▲ 173.

ST URSULA'S CHURCH

URSULINE CONVENT. St Ursula's Church, which was built by Marcantonio Canevale (1652–1711) between 1702 and 1704, once belonged to an Ursuline convent built thirty years earlier to plans by the same architect.
INTERIOR. Before the Dientzenhofers ▲ 251 carried out their great

works, the nave of St Ursula's was the first example of the type of nave with pilasters that was to become extremely popular in Prague's High Baroque period ● 70. A number of statues, particular those of Saint Jude Thaddeus and Saint Philip and the statues on the high altar (1709–10), are by FRANTIŠEK PREISS. Preiss (c. 1660–1712) ▲ 163, a pupil of Jan Kohl, was among the first to welcome Roman art when it was brought to Prague by Ottavio Mosto. To the left of the high altar, there is an *Assumption of the Virgin* by Petr Brandl (1668–1739), the painter who conclusively represented the high point of Baroque painting in Bohemia.

FORMER PRAHA INSURANCE COMPANY BUILDING

This building at 7 Národní Avenue was designed by Osvald Polívka for the Praha Insurance Company. The façade is, for once, significantly influenced by the Viennese Secession, and is decorated with complex figurative motifs and sculptures by Ladislav Šaloun. Šaloun (1870–1946) was a member of the Mánes Society ▲ 303 and one of the most active representatives of the Secession Movement ● 86 in Prague. He executed the decoration depicting the three stages of life on the façade of the Praha Insurance Company building, but he was also responsible for the monument to John Huss ▲ 146 and the reliefs framing the entrance to the new Town Hall in Old Town ▲ 149.

TOPÍČ HOUSE

Topíč House, at 9 Národní Avenue, is also the work of Osvald Polívka (1910). These two buildings, which stand side by side, express two contrasting visions of the Secession, with Topíč House presenting a more geometrical, more Germanic, version. Between the two world wars, it was owned by Borový, a celebrated publisher who specialized in French literature and who brought out editions of the work of all the great writers from the first few decades of the 20th century.

ST URSULA'S CHURCH AND CONVENT
The church itself is a place of worship, but the convent buildings in Národní Avenue are occupied by a

celebrated "Klášterní vinárna". The whole complex was handed back to the Ursulines in 1990, together with modern ancillary buildings belonging to the National Theater including administrative offices, a tavern and a restaurant. This restitution of goods has created a legal imbroglio and controversy that has taken Prague by storm.

"I went straight round to the French Pommeret Library and got out four volumes of Verlaine poems, as well as a selection of his poems that I unearthed in the Topíč shop window."
Jaroslav Seifert

JOSEF ZÍTEK (1832–1909)

Josef Zítek was a celebrated exponent of neo-Renaissance style and, in his day, was one of the most highly regarded architects in Prague. The Rudolfinum is one of his greatest achievements ▲ *194*.

"The passengers ended up by getting off the trams which had come to a halt, and rejoining the procession which turned off at the corner by the National Theater. On the different floors of the Theater, and framed from head to foot in the golden light of the glass bays, the usherettes in their black dresses . . . waved their hands as a sign of their complicity."
Sylvie Germain

NATIONAL THEATER ★

This deeply symbolic building both represented and crowned the struggles of the Czech people to have their national culture recognized. Any music lover with a sense of Czech history will be as keen to see the National Theater as the Vltava.

PAID FOR BY THE PEOPLE. Theaters had been presenting shows in Czech since the end of the 17th century, but they had been few and far between. It followed that Czech people felt a profound need to have a theater they could call their own. In 1849, a decision was taken to build a National Theater, and donations came in from both Prague and the provinces – and, what is more, from all social classes. The German-dominated Estates of Bohemia refused to fund the project.

FOUNDATION STONE. In 1868, the "Committee for the Construction of the National Theater", the body charged with managing the money collected, felt that work could begin on the plans provided by Josef Zítek. The preparations aroused extraordinary collective enthusiasm and, on May 16, 1868, 50,000 people formed the procession that marched before the foundation stones brought from all the historic sites of Bohemia and Moravia. The first stone, which was laid by František Palacký ● *28*, came from Říp Hill where Čech, the Czech people's legendary ancestor, is said to paused in his travels. Jan Masaryk, the son of President Masaryk, once said of Čech, "That fool! Why did he have to set us down between the Germans and the Russians?"

A FIRE. However, the theater had hardly been completed when it burned down in July 1881 after only a dozen performances. The Czech people once again mobilized and, within two months, a subscription campaign collected enough money to

rebuild the theater in two years. This time, the design was by one of Zítek's collaborators, Josef Schulz (1840–1917), architect of the National Museum ▲ *175* and the Museum of Decorative Arts ▲ *195*. Schulz's masterpiece combines monumentalism and a range of other effects, the first level being decorated with bosses, while the remainder are punctuated with Corinthian pilasters and crowned with a dome. Each façade is designed with the setting and the angles in mind: for instance, the loggia overlooking Národní Avenue is decorated with statues of Apollo and the nine Muses by Bohuslav Schnirch.

THE "NATIONAL THEATER GENERATION". The job of decorating the interior of the National Theater enthused Prague's artists to such an extent that they came to be known as the "National Theater Generation". They included MIKOLÁŠ ALEŠ (1852–1913), the most celebrated of the group, who executed the scenes inspired by Smetana's *Má vlast* on the fourteen lunettes in the Grand Foyer. He was held in contempt by official institutions run by the Germans and, in a bid to stir up a polemic, was elected President of the Mánes Society ▲ *303*. His interest in popular art gained him much credibility among the younger artists of the Secession. VOJTĚCH HYNAIS (1854–1925) was greatly inspired by French Symbolism – he studied at the School of Fine Arts in Paris from 1878 to 1880 – and went on to enjoy an international career; he also taught

MAGIC LANTERN
In this production at the National Theater, the lively performance given by actors, singers and dancers is accompanied by music, kinetic scenes and projections, including film. The result is a unique spectacle.

ANTONIN DVOŘÁK
RUSALKA

National Theater poster advertising Dvořák's *Rusalka* ● *46*.

"LIBUŠE"
Poster for Bedřich Smetana's famous opera.

V sobotu dne 11. června 1861.
OTEVŘENÍ NÁRODNÍHO DIVADL
by pwrd
Thitsr past.
J. J. CÍS. KRÁL. VÝSOSTI
Nejjasnějšího korunního prince BEDŘIŠE A Nejjasnější korunní princezny STEFANIE.
Národní hymna a hymna belgická.
Po první
LIBUŠE.
Hlasovitaí zasivrkou vo 3 belsiteh.

Above: the small sitting room of the Presidential Box at the National Theater.

"Prague's National Theater has a history of long struggles, untiring perseverance, and the final triumph of a nation for which it symbolizes art and literature."
Louis Léger

NÁRODNÍ DIVADLO
Today, Prague boasts over twenty theaters, but the National Theater is still without question the best in the country. The repertoire includes operas and plays as well as ballet and concerts.

many Secession artists. For the National Theater, he painted the four allegories of the Seasons in the ladies' restroom and the décor on the main curtain ● 55. Other members of the "Generation" were less well known; they included Václav Brožík, another artist trained in Paris, who executed the historic compositions in the men's restroom, and Julius Mařák, who did the paintings of towns that adorn the corridors. The sculptures are by Myslbeck, Antonín Wagner ▲ 175 and Bohuslav Schnirch.

BEDŘICH SMETANA AND THE NATIONAL THEATER.
Smetana's life was intimately linked to that of the National Theater. On his return from Sweden in 1861, Smetana ● 47 threw himself into the political and musical struggle surrounding it. When the foundation stone was laid on May 16, 1868, the very date on which his national opera *Dalibor* was first performed, Smetana announced that "the future of the Czech people is in music. . ." and "Father of the Fatherland" historian František Palacký ● 28 declared that, with its National Theater, the nation truly existed and would never die. Work was started on the site of a former saltworks where the Provisional Theater (1862) had already been built. The two buildings merged in 1883 and they were officially opened on November 18. For the foundation stone ceremony, Smetana composed a solemn *Prelude* and a chorus dedicated to the Czech peasantry as a tribute to the villagers who, in the darkest hours for the Czech language and music, had put up most of the money for the theater and its maintenance. The National Theater was reopened on November 18, 1983 and, just as a century earlier, the occasion was marked by a performance of Smetana's historical-cum-mythological opera *Libuše*.

LEOŠ JANÁČEK. The National Theater's repertoire permitted the great Czech composers to give full voice to their lyric inspiration. One of these, Leoš Janáček (1854–1928), was not a citizen of Prague, but he was nonetheless recognized as a great Czech musician. While in the capital during 1874–5, he spent all his time at the School of Organists, but otherwise lived most of his life in Brno. However, it was at the National Theater that his opera *Jenufa*, written in 1903 and poorly received in Brno, was first performed in

> "The theater . . . must be the spiritual home of the period."
>
> Václav Havel

1916. Having finally achieved recognition at the age of sixty, Janáček now worked without pause and, in the space of a dozen years, produced some of the most important works in the Czech canon. They include *Taras Bulba* (1915–18), the *Sinfonietta* (1926), the *Glagolithic Mass* (1926), and his operas *Kat'a Kabanova* (1919–21), *The Makropulos Affair* (1923–5) and *From the House of the Dead* (1927–8) after Dostoievsky. Janáček's music struggles relentlessly to express emotions as directly as possible, a risky strategy as the libretti are often extremely dramatic. His orchestration demands from musicians the suppleness and veracity in which the orchestras of Prague are unrivaled.

DÉCOR AT THE NATIONAL THEATER
As a member of the "National Theater Generation", František Ženíček decorated the auditorium and the main foyer with allegories of the arts; the exceptions were the lunettes. Above: The ceiling of the theater.

MAGIC LANTERN. For its centenary, the National Theater was completely restored and modernized, and it was also provided with a new stage called the "New Stage". It houses the famous Magic Lantern where musical performances are occasionally given. The Magic Lantern is very well known abroad, and enjoyed considerable success at the Universal Exhibition in Brussels in 1958, and then in Montreal. Its performances are based on a wide range of artistic genres, and it makes use of all the technical possibilities offered by drama and cinematography. Magic Lantern programs are devised in such a way as to appeal to, and be comprehensible to, foreign audiences.

OPERA TO THE FORE. As the National Theater concentrates on the Czech repertoire, the practise is for the company to alternate with a resident company. Famous names from the world of opera to have performed here include Ema Destinnová, Karel Burián, O. Mařak, Antonín Vávra, Josef Lev and Karel Strakatý, and directors and conductors such as Karel Kovařovic, Otakar Ostřcil and, in particular, Václav Talich, who conducted triumphant performances of Bohuslav Martinů's *Julietta* ▲ 267 in 1938. Star performers since World War Two have included Ivo Žídek, Karel Bermann, Karel Pruša, Vilém Přybil, Beno Blachut, Věra Soukupová, Gabriela Beňáčhová and Peter Dvorský, and the conductors Břetislav Bakala, Jaroslav Krumholc, Bohumil Gregor, Zdeněk Košler and František Jílek. The Estates Theater is administratively and artistically linked to the National Theater and, for the most part, concentrates on a theatrical repertoire.

BEDŘICH SMETANA
Smetana's name is more closely associated with the National Theater.

Center: costume for Smetana's opera, *The Devil's Wall.*

THE PERENNIAL CAFÉ SLAVIA ✪
On the corner of Národní Street and Smetana Quay, opposite the National Theater, is the Café Slavia. Once the favorite haunt of the intelligentsia and of artists, it has seen the passing of many years, the very air imbued with memories of the past. Its newly restored Art Deco interior is an attraction in itself (the toilets are especially worth seeing). The green lighting and the painting on the far wall pay tribute to all the absinthe that is consumed there. Meals are served at all hours, although the simple pleasure of enjoying a pastry is as you watch the river flow by is equally attractive.

Right: the Café Slavia, the 1992 student stronghold, and below: decoration detail.

LAŽANSKÝ PALACE ★

At no. 3 Národní třída is the Czechoslovak Academy of Sciences, a neo-Renaissance building by Vojtěch Ullmann (1858–61) ▲ *184, 289*, who was also responsible for the Lažanský Palace at no. 1. This neo-Renaissance palace in the French style was built between 1861 and 1863 for Count Prokop Lažanský to plans by Ullmann on land occupied by baths in the 14th century and then by a hospital belonging to the Brothers of the Cross. Between 1863 and 1869 it was the home of Bedřich Smetana ● *47*, and it was here that he composed two of his most famous operas, *The Bartered Bride* (1866) and *Dalibor* (1868). The building now houses the Academy of Fine Arts, and for many years the famous Café Slavia was on the first floor.

CAFÉ SLAVIA. Prague has innumerable cafés ● *58* and, in 1910, around the time of the National Awakening, it is estimated that there were as many 1,500. During that period all polemical texts, manifestos and speeches were written in cafés. From the 1930's onward, the Café Slavia became the favorite haunt of the progressive intelligentsia, and later of the dissidents. Closed for a long time, it was restored at great expense and reopened in 1997. Its décor has not been altered much and is still a favorite with the people of Prague.

Around Charles Square

1. CHARLES SQUARE
2. TOWN HALL
3. TRINITY CHURCH
4. DIAMOND HOUSE

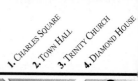

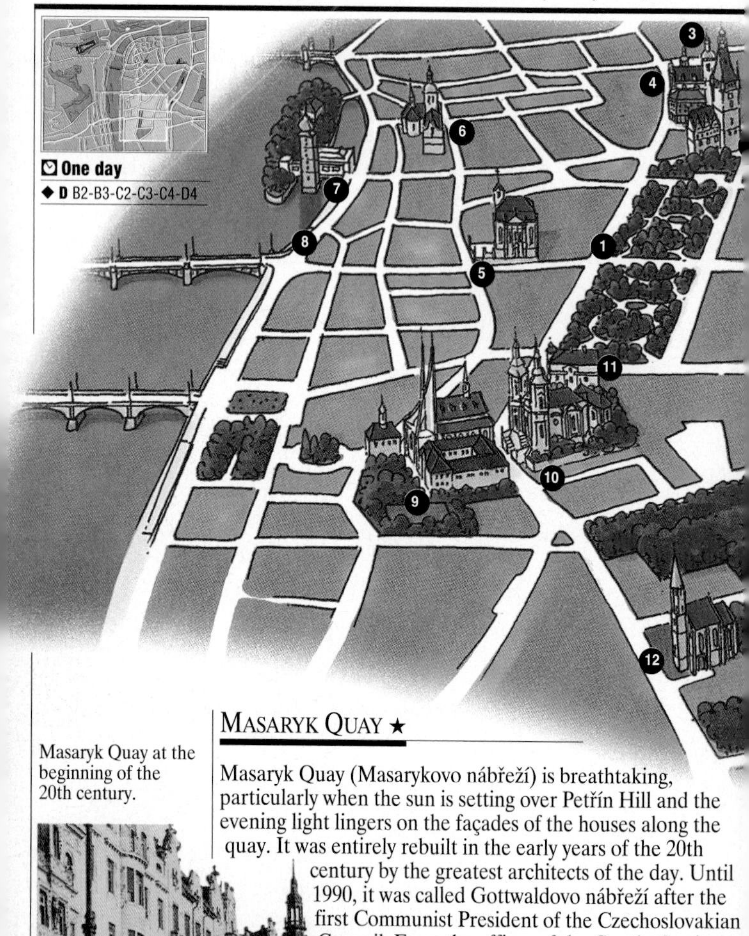

One day
◆ **D** B2-B3-C2-C3-C4-D4

MASARYK QUAY ★

Masaryk Quay (Masarykovo nábřeží) is breathtaking, particularly when the sun is setting over Petřín Hill and the evening light lingers on the façades of the houses along the quay. It was entirely rebuilt in the early years of the 20th century by the greatest architects of the day. Until 1990, it was called Gottwaldovo nábřeží after the first Communist President of the Czechoslovakian Council. From the offices of the Goethe Institute at no. 32 as far as the neo-Baroque building on the corner of the quay and Jiráskovo náměstí, there is not a single façade that is not outstanding in one way or

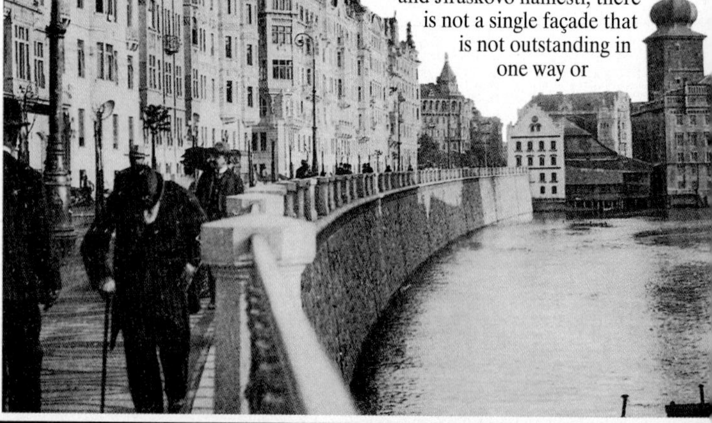

Masaryk Quay at the beginning of the 20th century.

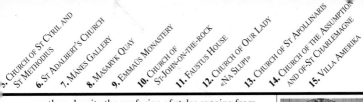

5. CHURCH OF ST CYRIL AND ST METHODIUS   **6.** ST ADALBERT'S CHURCH   **7.** MÁNES GALLERY   **8.** MASARYK QUAY   **9.** EMMAÜS MONASTERY   **10.** CHURCH OF ST-JOHN-ON-THE-ROCK   **11.** FAUSTUS HOUSE   **12.** CHURCH OF OUR LADY «NA SLUPI»   **13.** CHURCH OF ST APOLLINARIS   **14.** CHURCH OF THE ASSUMPTION AND OF ST CHARLEMAGNE   **15.** VILLA AMERIKA

another, despite the profusion of styles ranging from neo-Renaissance and neo-Baroque to Art Nouveau. Strictly speaking, these are not historic houses as such; the Quay is simply a magnificent architectural complex overlooking the Vltava.

No. 32. This fine structure, built for a bank by Jiří Stribal in 1905, marries Secession and neo-Baroque styles and is adorned with external

The façade of the Goethe Institute.

MASARYK QUAY, AN ARCHITECTURAL DELIGHT ✪
This quay is named in honor of the first President of the Czech Republic. The extraordinary diversity of the façades and the contrasting colors of the houses that line it do not detract from the striking harmony of the whole, so that a walk along the quay is a visual treat. On Slav Island, a little way off the center of the quay, is the renowned Mánes Gallery, specializing in modern art. For a rest after visiting the gallery, there are benches along the Vltava or the pleasure of a peaceful boat ride on the river.

decorations by Ladislav Šaloun. It was the site of the East German Embassy until 1990, and has since been turned into the Goethe Institute.

NOS. 30, 28, 26 AND 22. No. 30 is another neo-Baroque building dating from 1905 but, with its strange pediment, is not entirely lacking in Baroque elements. The figurative panels depict modern scenes. The unusually elegant house at no. 28 is by Matěj Blecha (1904–5) ▲ *175*, *192*, *310*; no. 26, by Kamil Hilbert, has a fine entrance with stained-glass windows; and no. 22 recalls the Renaissance with two distinct kinds of windows: Czech designs on the fourth and fifth floors, and Italian for the sixth floor with arches resting on small columns.

No. 16. A plaque states that the building was constructed on plans by Josef Fanta for Hlahol, a celebrated Czech singing club that played a key role in the nationalist politics of the late 19th century. The club's conductors included Smetana in 1863, Bendl from 1865 to 1877, and Knittl from 1877 to 1903. The mosaics and the entrances are very elegantly worked. Hlalol soon merged with the Circle of Artists (Umělecká beseda), a body founded in 1863 to represent Czech music and to counter the Deutsches Casino (1862).

Façades on Masaryk Quay.

General view of Slav Island.

SLAV ISLAND (SLOVANSKÝ OSTROV, ŽOFÍN)

A MUSICAL ISLAND. Originally known as Sophia Island, after the Archduchess Sophia, the mother of Franz Joseph, Slav Island has always been famous for the society balls and the concerts that were held in its 400-seater hall after 1840. Many great soloists and composers have performed there, including Berlioz in 1846, and later Liszt. An Academy of Music founded here in 1840 by Alois Jelen was inaugurated by a rendering of Václav Tomášek's *Coronation Mass* and, on his return from Sweden, Smetana conducted a performance of his three symphonic poems, *Richard III*, *Wallensteins Lager* and *Hakon Jarl*. The city of Prague purchased Sophia Island in 1884, and since then it has been used for dances and sporting and folk events. It declined in importance after the opening of the Rudolfinum ▲ *194* in 1885 and even more so after the Town Hall ▲ *164* was built.

SLAV CONGRESS. The hall is currently being restored. The island's modern name is a reminder that this was the venue of the pan-Slav Congress of June 1848 ● *28*; the meeting was cut short by an uprising in the city that was brutally put down by the Austrian General Windischgrätz.

ZDENĚK FIBICH. It was here, in the late 19th century, that the composer Zdeněk Fibich ● *47* met Anežka Schulzová, a woman of letters who became his pupil and librettist. The famous *Poems of Fibich* is a testament to their love affair.

RODIN EXHIBITION
The Mánes Gallery organized an important Rodin retrospective in 1902. The exhibition was to have a remarkable impact, if only because it established Rodin as a major figure in Prague, and opened up a new world for Czech artists ▲ *304*. It was most enthusiastically received. Rodin exhibited ninety-eight sculptures, including his superb *Balzac*, and seventy-five drawings. Above: the gallery's former home, and Auguste Rodin surrounded by Czech artists, including Alfons Mucha standing to his right.

MÁNES GALLERY

The design of this Functionalist building seems slightly anachronistic in a locality abundant with the splendors of so many neo-styles and the Secession; the explanation is that it was built very late. The Mánes Gallery was constructed in 1923–32 by Otakar Novotný ▲ *185*, an adherent of Rigorist Modernism. The first gallery was situated in the Kinský Gardens at the foot of Petřín Hill, but was pulled down shortly before World War One and replaced by the present building. The tower has nothing to do with the gallery: it is part of the Šítkovsky Water Tower (opposite). The building is now the premises of the Union of Artists, and a café and a restaurant on the side facing the river offer lovely views.

MÁNES SOCIETY. This society was founded in 1887, and brought together those teachers and students from Prague's Academy of Fine Arts and School of Applied Arts who yearned to disturb the slumber into which official art had fallen. The society's organ was a monthly review called *Volné Směry* (*Free Trends*) that first appeared in 1896; it was an important forum for ideas and became very well known. The Mánes Society also played a key role in the opening up of Czech art to modernist thinking and to cosmopolitan currents, and its major exhibitions ▲ *304* were very important events.

A SECOND MAJOR EXHIBITION
The Edvard Munch exhibition of 1905 was also held at the Mánes Gallery. It was the occasion of another "esthetic" revolution ▲ *304* which produced an entire generation of Czech Expressionists.

ST ADALBERT'S CHURCH

St Adalbert's stands in Vojtěšská Street, and was built in the 13th century; it was given two naves in 1370, renovated in the Baroque manner in 1720–30, and then restored in 1885–91. The church is of little interest except for the fact that it is dedicated to one of Bohemia's most important patron saints and, in the 19th century, was the scene of great music-making.

SAINT ADALBERT. Adalbert (Vojtěch) was born into the Slavník family, one of the most powerful in eastern Bohemia. He became Prague's first bishop in 973, but was forced into exile in Rome after his entire family was murdered. He was

ŠÍTKOVSKY WATER TOWER
This is one of four water towers which supply Nové Město's public fountains and taverns with water. This Gothic construction was redesigned in the Renaissance style; the onion dome was added only at the end of the 18th century.

SOPHIA PAVILION
The Sophia (Žofín) Pavilion, a dance and concert hall, was built on Sophia Island in 1837. It became an important center of the city's social and cultural life and, from 1841 onward, was the venue for the most celebrated of the Czech patriotic balls ● *52*.

At the beginning of the 19th century, Prague was in rebellious mood under the influence of the Viennese Secession. At the same time the city was straining to adapt Secession to its own traditions and myths. Furthermore, Prague was trying to thwart Austria's cultural domination by seeking models elsewhere in Europe, particularly in France. After the Great War, German Dadaism and Italian Futurism had a certain impact on the formation of an emerging Czech artistic consciousness. However, Paris remained t source of all innovation; only Moscow, the symbol of the October Revolution and of bold experimentation in all the arts, represente any form of counterweight to the influence wielded by Paris.

PARIS: THE SOURCE OF ARTISTIC REVOLUTION

Auguste Rodin's major retrospective organized by the Mánes Society in 1902 was the first of a series of events establishing the predominance of French creativity. Czech Cubism was born in 1910, and the "Plasticians", a group that included artists and architects, launched their *Art Monthly* around the same time. The "Plasticians" included Picasso, Friesz,

DEVĚTSIL

PRAHA 1922

Derain, Braque and Gris in their 1912 exhibitions, and the Paris School in their 1914 exhibition.

THE EMERGENCE OF SURREALISM

The arrival of Josef Šima in Paris in 1921, and of other Czech artists shortly afterward, strengthened links with André Breton's group and with circles that grew out of Surrealism. The Czech Surrealist group was formed in May 1934 even before translations of Breton's books went on sale in Prague.

THE AVANT GARDE

Both the tragedy of war and national independence brought about huge changes in the artistic and literary life of Prague's intelligentsia. The Tvrdošijní (Obstinate group came out boldl against established values; the "Devětsil" Group was founded i 1920 ● 59.

SOUBORNÁ
VÝSTAVADĚL
SOCHAŘE
RODINA
(PARIŽ)

10.V.-15.VII.1902

PRAZE.
KINSKÉHO
ZAHRADA.
OTEVŘ.9-7 HOD.

VSTUPNÉIK.V.RONDEI

EDVARD MUNCH

Prague's more creative artists were never going to be satisfied with an influence as exclusi as that of the Frenc They were overwhelmed with enthusiasm for Edvard Munch's paintings in 1905, a later on observed the developments of Expressionism in Germany with passionate interest. Czech Cubism owes its originality to its Expressionist past which counterbalanced Cézanne's formalism.

Poster for an exhibition of the Independents in Prague in 1910.

BOHUMIL KUBIŠTA *Self-portrait March 17 1910* by the best-known exponent of Czech Cubism.

MOSCOW: THE OTHER SOURCE OF INSPIRATION

When Roman Jakobson was sent to Prague with the Soviet Legation as Press Attaché, he sought to build bridges between the Czech capital and the capital of the fledgling USSR. He became the propagandist of Russian Futurism. In 1921, he published *New Russian Poetry. First Sketch* in Prague, although not in Moscow, and introduced the works of Mayakovsky and Khlebnikov. He was close to the group of Poetists and, in Karel Teige, the instigator of the Czech Surrealist Group, he found a fervent supporter of Constructivism. Teige tried hard, but with little success, to convince his painter, sculptor and architect friends to follow the path of Malevich and Rodchenko.

ST ADALBERT'S CHURCH
Views of the interior and exterior. The vaulting is Gothic.

martyred while on a journey to convert Prussians in 997. Saint Adalbert is also the patron saint of Poland and Hungary.

A MUSICAL CHURCH. St Adalbert's Church is well known to musicians for its associations with the composers Josef Foerster and Antonín Dvořák. In the 19th century Foerster (1833–1907), the church's choirmaster and organist, introduced Gregorian chant and the music of Palestrina in the 19th century, and foreign musicians, including Saint-Saëns, never failed to come and listen when they were passing through. Dvořák, too, worked here: between 1874 and 1877, while still poor and little known, he earned small sums playing the organ. Josef Bohuslav Foerster (1859–1951), ● 47, ▲ 276, also a composer, succeeded his father from 1882 to 1888.

FOERSTER MUSEUM. The presbytery at 17 Pětrossová Street is a fine Baroque building, and the staircase is worth a visit for the trompe l'oeil painted by Johann Hoffmann in 1778. The building now houses the Foerster Museum. Josef Bohuslav Foerster was a very active man: he was a composer, a noted critic and the organist at St Adalbert's and choirmaster at Our-Lady-of-the-Snows. After teaching for a few years in Vienna, he returned to Prague where, from 1919 onward, he taught at the Conservatory. He wrote a large number of symphonies and concertos, but his greatest skill lay in choral compositions and in operas, the best remembered of which is *Eva*.

Late 15th-century Gothic statue of the Virgin of Zderaz on an altar in St Adalbert's Church.

U FLEKŮ TAVERN ★

Of Prague's innumerable taverns, the U Fleků (Křemencova 11) is undoubtedly the most famous. Its reputation also extends far beyond the boundaries of the Czech Republic. Since 1499, the U Fleků has dispensed a famous dark beer called *flekovský ležák* ● 61.

CHURCH OF ST CYRIL AND ST METHODIUS

This Baroque church (Kostel sv Cyrila a Metoděje), initially dedicated to Saint Carlo Borromeo, was built by Kilián Ignác Dientzenhofer (1730–6). Pavel Ignác Bayer painted the ceiling fresco depicting the life of Carlo Borromeo. The church served as a place of worship for those who lived in the adjoining house, a group of old priests who had retired from diocesan work in Bohemia. This had been founded in 1681, but it was pulled down by Joseph II in 1783. The church was not used during the first Republic until 1935, when it was handed over to the Czech Orthodox Church and rededicated to Cyril and Methodius. These two holy men first came to Grand Moravia from Thessalonika in 863, translated liturgical books into Old Slav and developed a Glagolithic alphabet.

ASSASSINATION OF HEYDRICH. This church has the unhappy distinction of being the last hiding place of the members of the Resistance who killed Reichsprotektor Reinhard Heydrich

"The great brewer handed me a pint of orange beer,
a pint overflowing with a rush of steam bubbles."

Bohumil Hrabal

U FLEKŮ
All the buildings that make up the tavern, together with the dining rooms and the garden lined with

arches, are carefully looked after. The rooms are decorated with frescos and carved wood, and each one has a different name.

(below) on May 26, 1942 ● *39*. This led to violent reprisals, including the seizure of 10,000 hostages and the annihilation of the inhabitants of the village of Lidice and the tiny hamlet of Ležáky (all the men were murdered and the women and children were deported). Heydrich's assassination had been ordered by the government-in-exile in London as a way of establishing the Czech Resistance's identity; the Nazis threatened to murder one Czech in ten and promised to reward anyone who would denounce Heydrich's killers. The parachutists responsible for the assassination took refuge in the crypt, and eventually died there. The Czech orthodox Bishop Gorazo, who had given them shelter, was also executed by the Germans.

MEMORIES OF THE RESISTANCE
A commemorative plaque and innumerable bullet marks on the façade

ST WENCESLAS' CHURCH

St Wenceslas' (sv. Václav na Zderaze) is close to the Church of St Cyril and St Methodius, but the main door opens onto Dittrichova Street. It is extremely old, founded before 1180, and was a parish church by the late 13th century. In the nave and tower are Romanesque remains. Mělnický's 16th-century vault and the choir were redone in the 17th century by the Augustinians.

of the Church of St Cyril and St Methodius recall the tragic events of 1942.

FIRST DEFENESTRATION OF PRAGUE
On July 30, 1419, Jan Želivský ▲ *290* delivered a particularly telling sermon which so inflamed those listening that serfs from the countryside were persuaded to take up arms against their feudal lords

● 26. When the sermon was over, the crowd marched behind the preacher to Nové Město Town Hall to call for the release of citizens imprisoned for their Hussite sympathies. When they were refused, three councillors and seven members of the Prague bourgeoisie were thrown from the windows by the people of Nové Město.

CHARLES SQUARE (KARLOVO NÁMĚSTÍ)

THE CENTER OF NOVÉ MĚSTO. This square, the largest in Prague, is 1,700 feet long and 490 feet wide. When it was opened in 1348, it was effectively the center of New Town (Nové Město), which had been founded by Charles IV, and it was the site of the livestock market, one of three markets in the town. In May of each year, Charles had the Crown Jewels displayed in the middle of the Square, and then, after 1382, in the Corpus Christi Chapel, a church modeled on the Palatine in Aix-la-Chapelle, which was destroyed in 1791.

LAID OUT AS A GARDEN. Between 1843 and 1863, the Square was turned into a public park divided into two sections by Ječná Street, a wide thoroughfare served by trams. It was dotted with statues of famous people, including V. Strunc, a scientist who discovered the uniqueness of fingerprints, the poet Vítězslav Hálek, Karolina Světlá and Eliška Krasnohorská, both women of letters, the naturalist Jan Evangelista Purk, and the botanist B. Roezl; lastly, there is the statue of the revolutionary Hussite priest, Jan Želivský, which dates from 1960.

ZDE ŽIL
A ZEMŘEL
JAN EV· PVRKYNĚ

VĚNOVÁNO
SP·Č·LÉKAŘŮ
A VM·BESEDOV·

NOVÉ MĚSTO TOWN HALL

This building occupies the entire north side of the square, but a distinction needs to be drawn between the east section (the old part of the Town Hall) and the west section (today the Law Courts). New Town's Town Hall (Novoměstská radnice) was founded before 1367 and built in 1377, and it was then rebuilt and enlarged between 1411 and 1418 under the supervision of Martin Friček and Master Kříž. The hall, on the first floor, with columns and two naves, dates from this period; it was turned into a marriage parlor in 1957. The tower was erected in 1452–6 and bears the Gothic emblems of Nové Město. After being frequently damaged by fire, the Town Hall was renovated in the 16th century when three pediments in the Renaissance style were added. After 1784, the year in which the towns of Prague were united in a single city, it was used as the Law Courts, offices and a prison. In 1905–6, Antonín Wiehl and Kamil Hilbert tried to restore the building's original appearance.

FOUNDING OF NOVÉ MĚSTO
The founding of New Town (Nové Město) was a key element in Charles IV's intention to develop the city. His plan was quite unique for the time, and is admirable even by today's standards. It is encircled by ramparts 2½ miles long and covers 890 acres, three times the size of Old Town, and for five hundred years, it was deemed large enough to contain the town's population. The old roads were retained, but new ones between 60 feet and 85 feet wide were constructed, forming crossroads at the huge market places. These were the livestock market and the horse market, both in Charles Square, and the hay market in Senovážné náměstí.

ST IGNATIUS' CHURCH (KOSTEL SV. IGNÁCE)

In 1623 Ferdinand II gave the Jesuits the Gothic Church of Corpus Christi in the center of Charles Square, along with the neighboring houses and land, on which they were to build a seminary. This Baroque building was constructed by Carlo Lurago from 1665 to 1670, then by Pavel Ignác Bayer to plans by Giovanni Domenico Orsi and modeled on the Gesù in Rome. The protruding, monumental façade is adorned with stucco decoration on the surfaces and various figures in the portico, and crowned with a radiant statue of Saint Ignatius, the founder of the Jesuit Order.

JESUIT COLLEGE

This college (Jezuitská kolej) was the third building that the Jesuits had constructed in Prague. A Baroque structure, and older than the church, it was built between 1658 and 1667 on the site of twenty-three houses and thirteen gardens. The restrained façade punctuated by pilasters is most impressive, and the two doors, which date from the 1760's, were designed by Jan Josef Wirch ▲ 226. In 1773, when the Order was abolished on the Pope's instructions, the College was closed and turned into a hospital. It was partly destroyed in an air raid in 1945, but was later meticulously reconstructed.

A FINE INTERIOR
Jan Jiří Heinsch's painting over the high altar is a glorification of Saint Ignatius; the vaulting of the first side chapel is frescoed with themes of the Last Judgement.

CUBIST ARCHITECTURE
"Blecha's little summer house – possibly designed together with Pfeiffer – contains an 18th-century statue of Saint John Nepomuk, just next to Diamond House. The symbiosis between the Cubist summer house and the Baroque sculpture is so subtle, so happy, that it proves that the relationship claimed by Cubists with the *genius loci* is sincere and viable."
Luca Quattrochi
The Secession

RUDOLPH II, A TORMENTED SOUL
Certain aspects of the King's behavior, which involved magic, were so extreme that many believed he was possessed by the devil. It was said that the very sight of the Cross provoked him to fits of hysteria.

SPÁLENÁ STREET

DIAMOND HOUSE. Just before the other side of the square is Spálená ulice; a few yards along, on the corner with Lazarská Street, stands Diamond House, a Cubist building designed by Ladislav Sřívánek, Matěj Blecha and Antonín Pfeiffer in 1910–12. The monumental proportions and the stylization of the carved figures on the fourth floor recall the Babylonian elements that Blecha ▲ *175* used to such brilliant effect. The entrance is framed by two massive pilasters (above). Diamond House is connected to the Baroque Church of the Holy Trinity by a strange Cubist arch beneath which stands a statue of Saint John Nepomuk.

OLYMPIC BUILDING. This building, dating from 1923–7, was the first Functionalist construction to be seen in Prague. It brought its architect Jaromir Krejcar (1895–1949) immediate fame. Krejcar had started his career as a builder and site foreman, before studying under Kotěra ▲ *174*; he then worked for the Gocá agency until 1923 before launching his own business. As a member of the "Devětsil" Group ● *59*,

PRVNÍ
ČESKÁ VZÁJEMNÁ
POJIŠŤOVNA
(ZAL. R. 1827)

...e played an important role in the diffusion of Purist and Constructivist theories around Czechoslovakia.

Mosaic in the insurance company Česka Pojistovna in Spálená Street.

U Nováků House

Vodičkova Street is on this side of the square and leads directly to U Nováků House. This neoclassical building was entirely renovated in the Art Nouveau style by Polívka ▲ *176* between 1902 and 1904. It was originally a large shop, but now contains a restaurant.

Faustus House

This house (Faustův dům) was renovated for the Mladotat ze Solopysk family in 1740–70 and is not unrelated to the mysterious Renaissance residence which, according to legend, was inhabited by no less a person than Dr Faustus (opposite). It is more than likely that the Devil would have come to look for him here, and there are even claims that it is still possible to see the hole in the roof through which he carried off one of his disciples. There are several Faustus Houses in Prague. On a more everyday level, the house was inhabited by several alchemists including the celebrated English adventurer, Edward Kelley. While in the employ of Rudolph II, he undertook to discover the philosopher's stone but, although the Emperor made him a "Knight of Imana", he nonetheless suffered a sorry fate. The King grew tired of waiting and threw him into prison (Kelley had already had his ears cut off in England after being found guilty of forgery). On his release, he died of poisoning.

PRAGUE, A CITY OF FANTASIES. Prague is enormously popular with writers of fantastic stories, both Czech and foreign. Many factors have contributed to the development of this trend over the centuries. The reign of Rudolph II (1576–1611) particularly enhanced the magic reputation of the city. The Emperor was prey to profound melancholia and even fits of madness, and sometimes actually figured in fantastic stories: an example is Mikhail Bulgakov's *The Master and Margarita* in which Rudolph is among the guests invited to Satan's Ball. A society as strange as that which surrounded Rudolph II, one in which astrologers, witches and alchemists mingled with truly learned men and practical jokers, was bound to have its Dr Faustus. Although he had lived in Germany in the late 15th and early 16th centuries, legend allows its hero to move freely in both time (by permitting him to live in two centuries) and space.

U Nováků House
The façade is adorned with stucco, a profusion of wrought iron, and an immense mosaic representing an allegory of commerce and industry made after cartoons by Jan Preisler ● 87. The first floor still has its glass canopies and splendid stained-glass windows. Apart from Novak establishments on two of the floors,

this house was the home of the Liberated Theater ● 54 from 1924 to 1938. The U Nováků gallery links with the Lucerna and Rokoko galleries, and together they form one of the most important passageway complexes ● 82 in Prague.

EMMAUS MONASTERY (KLÁŠTER NA SLOVANECH) ★

SLAVONIAN LITURGY. This monastery was founded in 1348 by Charles IV who, with the support of Pope Clement VI, wanted to bring the Eastern and Western Churches closer together. Croatian Benedictines came to settle here as soon as the new monastery was completed in 1353; their job was to recopy the old Slav manuscripts and to perpetuate the memory of Slavonian, a language that they alone were authorized to use although they followed the Latin rite. In 1419, the Benedictines of Emmaus began to accept Hussitism and their monastery was saved; in 1445, they were allowed to renew the rules of their Order, and the monastery became the only one run by the Hussites. During the 16th century, the monastery was used by the sub-Utraquist Consistory, the Utraquists' highest council. After White Mountain ● 34, the monastery was passed over to Spanish Benedictines and then, in the 20th century, to another group from Beuron. The church was renovated in the Baroque manner in 1712, and in 1880 it was restored in an Early Gothic style. The roof was destroyed by bombing in 1945, but replaced in 1965-8 by modernistic spires. The building is now occupied by a number of Czech and European scientific institutes.
REGISTRUM SLAVORUM. The monastery rapidly became one of the most important cultural centers in Bohemia. In particular, it housed an outstanding scriptorium which produced a large number of works including the *Registrum Slavorum* in 1395. This register, which is also known as the "Slavonic Lectionary" and the "Coronation Service" of the Kings of France, consists of two separate books, the first in Cyrillic, the second in Glagolithic.

"REGISTRUM SLAVORUM"
This is the most valuable manuscript held in the Municipal Library of Rheims. The manuscript was brought here in the 16th century by the Cardinal of Lorraine, Archbishop and Duke of Rheims, and he offered it to the Treasury of Rheims Cathedral. From the time of Henry III onward, the kings of France took their vows on this lectionary.

FRESCOS. The cloister frescos are rare vestiges of Prague's Gothic mural paintings because, during the Hussite Wars, and between 1419 and 1421 in particular, many churches were badly damaged and works of art destroyed. The cloister in Emmaüs Monastery was built in 1360. It is now in a poor state of repair, but iconographical evidence coincides with representations on numerous stained-glass windows: on the upper level is a scene from the New Testament; on the lower level, one from the Old Testament. The message is clear: the Old Testament is a

prefiguration of the New Testament, and a number of stories from it anticipate various episodes from the life of Christ. The cycle is attributed to three artists, two of whom have been identified: Nikolaus Wurmser, a painter from Strasbourg, and Master Oswald, a painter at the Court of Charles IV. The third artist, who was responsible for the west and north wings, has still not been identified.

Above: external view of Emmaus Monastery; detail of a fresco; the interior of the Church of St-John-on-the-Rock.

CHURCH OF ST-JOHN-ON-THE-ROCK ★

This fine Baroque church (Kostel sv. Jana na Skalce) with its two steeples over the west façade was built in 1730 by Kilián Ignác Dientzenhofer. The beautiful, monumental, external staircase was executed by Schmidt in 1776–8 for a brotherhood of artisans in New Town. The statues on the façade are by Seeling and date from 1880, while Brokoff's statue of Saint John Nepomuk ▲ 233 on the high altar served as a model for the statue he made for Charles Bridge.

Manuscript in Cyrillic script.

NA SLUPI STREET

CHURCH OF OUR LADY OF THE ELIZABETHINES. Kilián Ignác Dientzenhofer built this church on the site of the summer palace of the Auxiliary Bishop J. Dlouhoveský z Dlouhé Vsi in 1724–5. The ST TEKLA CHAPEL next door boasts wonderful stucco decorations and a mural by Kracker depicting the life of Saint Tekla (1726).
CHURCH OF THE ANNUNCIATION. This church was built between 1360 and 1365, at the same time as the Servite

"St John Nepomuk keeps his right hand over us! May God grant us what he has given you, and may our language never rot in the grave!" These lines by the 19th-century writer Karel Havlíček-Borovský are known to every Czech.

BOTANICAL GARDEN
The Botanical Garden dates from 1845; it is really the university park, but is nonetheless open to the public. Although the Garden is quite small, there are delightful walks round the flowerbeds and greenhouses.

Monastery. It was founded by Charles IV, and is an interesting example of the restrained Gothic churches of the second half of the 14th century. It has a tower and a square nave with a vault supported by a single pillar. This former convent, which was rebuilt in the neo-Gothic style by Grueber in 1858, now houses a medical research institute.

VILLA AMERIKA ★

This house, best known as the "Villa Amerika", was originally a very beautiful summer pavilion which Kilián Ignác Dientzenhofer built for Count Michna of Vacinov on his return from Vienna in 1717. The interior design is particularly interesting for Johann Ferdinand Schor's frescos of 1720; the sculptures in the garden come from Braun's workshop. The villa is now the Dvořák Museum and recounts the composer's life through a range of personal belongings, including his viola and piano, as well as photographs of his public and private life and his works. Concerts are sometimes given here.

DVOŘÁK MUSEUM
Although Bedřich Smetana was the founder and standard bearer of the Czech School, Antonín Dvořák (1841–1904) is seen as the Czech composer par excellence. Better than any other, he expressed the relationship in the Czech Baroque tradition between the original characteristics of a form of music that was both national and universal. He was a brilliant composer of symphonies and chamber works, and in his oratorios he created a new tradition that has survived to this day.

Magnificent decoration in the Karlov Church.

OUR-LADY-OF-THE-ASSUMPTION-AND-THE-EMPEROR-CHARLEMAGNE (KARLOV)

This building has a most unusual appearance with its red roof and huge surbased cupola. After being founded by Charles IV in 1350, it was dedicated to Charlemagne and was intended to be an imitation of the Imperial Chapel in Aix-la-Chapelle. Only the masonry from this period survives. In 1575, Bonifác Wohlmut surmounted the church with a cupola 80 feet in diameter and in the form of an eight-pointed star. Like most churches in Prague, it was restored in the Baroque manner, and then renovated mainly by Kaňka in 1733–8.

SCALA SANTA. Only a few years earlier in 1798, Santini-Aichl constructed the *Scala Santa*, a series of steps which pilgrims had to climb on their knees. The interior decoration is a perfect example of Baroque theatricality, with the balconies adorned with lifelike pictures and polychrome statues depicting the life of Christ.

The outskirts

LETNÁ

From the vast Letná plateau, which is best approached along Paris Avenue ▲ *190* and Svatopluk Bridge, there are fine views out over Prague and the Vltava. The very edge of Letná overhangs the river, and from 1858 this part was laid out as a park. More remote sections were used for military maneuvers until the end of the 19th century. During the last century, sports facilities were also added, and after 1948 Letná was used for Spartakiads and other official celebrations. On May 1, 1955, a monumental statue of Stalin was erected on the slope overlooking the Vltava; Otakar Švec, the sculptor responsible for the statue, committed suicide the day after the unveiling. In 1991, the statue was pulled down but the plinth remains and on it now stands a gigantic metronome symbolizing time.

HANAVSKÝ PAVILION. This pavilion in the west of the park was built by Otto Hieser for the Jubilee Exhibition of 1891, and then transferred to Letná in 1898. Here, the neo-Baroque style is not so far removed from Art Nouveau. The pavilion was a gift from the Prince of Hanau to the city of Prague; it was designed to promote Hanau's steel products in Bohemia although, in the words of Petr Wittlich, a writer based in Prague, the Hanavský was more of an "amalgam of decorative moldings". The pavilion today contains a restaurant. In the east of the park, there is the fascinating NATIONAL TECHNICAL MUSEUM and, not far away, along Dr-Milady-Horakove Street, is a block of rented accommodation for teachers at 35 Kamenická ulice; it was designed by Otakar Novotný ▲ *185, 303* in 1923, and there are elements of Cubism ● *89* in both its structure and decoration.

HANAVSKÝ PAVILION
The first municipal swimming pool was opened next to this pavilion.

THE "BELVEDERE"
In the 18th century, Letná was called the "Belvedere" because of the magnificent views it afforded over Prague.

STROMOVKA PARK ● 20

This is one of the most beautiful parks in Prague, and was once a hunting ground for the Kings of Bohemia. John of Luxemburg made this lovely park a royal hunting reserve in 1319. In 1569 the lake was created, and in 1584 Rudolph II then linked the lake to the Vltava by a canal system that is still in operation. In 1804, the Governor of Prague, Jan Rudolph Chotek, opened the park to the public and the architect Georg Fischer designed the small neo-Gothic summer palace on the site of the building by Vladislav Jagiello.

EXHIBITION CENTER. In 1888, it was decided to commemorate the centenary of the first Prague Universal Exhibition of 1791. It was an opportunity to promote the new styles of architecture, emphasizing the use of glass and iron, as well as to herald recent industrial advances under the Dual Monarchy. The 1891 Exhibition consisted of 140 pavilions in the new "Exhibition Park" (now Výstaviště), east of Stromovka, and received almost two million visitors.

MUSEUM OF MODERN ART. The museum is installed in the former Palace of Exhibitions, on Veletržní Street. The building is an emblem of the functionalist style of architecture and was built between 1925 and 1929 to the designs of Oldrich Tyl and Josef Fuchs. It was partly destroyed by fire in 1974, and was then completely renovated in 1995 to become one of the exhibition halls of the National Gallery ▲ 227. The museum provides an exhaustive coverage of all the great European artistic movements of the 19th and 20th centuries. The collection of French painting is particularly splendid.

MUSEUM OF MODERN ART ✪
Over four floors the museum explores several artistic styles (including Symbolism, Expressionism, Cubism, Surrealism and Abstract Art) and disciplines (such as architecture, design and photography). The collection of French painting and art is exceptional, and includes works by such masters as Courbet, Delacroix, Rodin, Braque, Van Gogh, Cézanne, Gauguin, Matisse, Léger and Picasso.

PALACE OF INDUSTRY. The Palace of Industry, now the Czech Congress Building, is a masterpiece of the glass and iron architecture that anticipated Art Nouveau. It was the centerpiece of the 1891 Exhibition, being 680 feet long and covering 15,548 square yards. The architect Bedřich Münzberger was assisted by František Prášil, an engineer from the steel factory in Prague, who built the central part of the pavilion. The immense glass arcade which links the two towers consists of eight arches 70ft high, and weighs 500 tonnes. In Výstaviště it is still possible to visit the LAPIDARIUM from the National Museum's Department of Sculpture. A swimming-pool, an art movie theater and finally a lunapark complete the attractions.

TROJA CASTLE ★

It is thanks both to Count Václav Vojtěch Šternberk (c. 1640–1708) and to the origins of the palace of the same name at Hradčany ▲ 227 that this splendid castle on the banks of the Vltava was built at the end of the 17th century. Troja Castle was built between 1679 and 1691 as a summer pavilion for the Šternberk family, and was one of the first villas of any significance outside the city. What attracted the Count to the area was the proximity of the newly completed Royal Enclosure at Stromovka: this gave him the opportunity to offer hospitality to the King and his companions when they were out hunting and thus demonstrate his loyalty. In the late 17th century, the Domain of Zádní Ovenec – only the castle was called Troja – occupied the entire area, and incorporated all the Count's lands and vineyards. A boat departs daily for Troja from Rašin Quay, a short distance down river from Palacký Bridge. Alternatively, to take the one-mile walk from Stromovka Park, follow signs to the zoo and cross Cisářský Ostrov Island.

FRENCH INFLUENCES. Present-day Troja Castle, the work of the Dijon architect Jean-Baptiste Mathey, is a far cry from the original building designed by the Italian, Giovanni Domenico Orsi. Mathey seems to have worked here from 1685 onward. The first castle was flanked by two wings terminating in pavilions, a device that doubled the current width. However, the disappearance of these two blocks did little to affect the balance of the overall construction. J.-B.Mathey was greatly influenced by Roman classicism and the castles of the French Renaissance with their articulated pavilions, a design quite new to Prague. All the castle's architectural elements are painted red, while the walls are whitewashed. The garden, also in the French style, was laid out by Georg Seemann after 1698. It consists of various terraces in a star-shaped plan defined by

narrow paths. The supreme harmony of the garden is most fully appreciated by entering it, not through the side gate, but through the old, stately gateway whose Baroque ironwork has now been restored.
By taking this route, the visitor then approaches the magnificent monumental steps directly, and can simultaneously marvel at the castle's refined elegance.

MONUMENTAL STEPS. The double flight of steps, richly decorated with sculpture, is by Johann Georg Heermann (c. 1650–after 1700), a Dresden sculptor strongly influenced by the work of the Mannerist sculptor Bernini. Heermann was assisted by his nephew, Paul (1673–1732), and the decoration was completed in 1703. The scheme depicts a struggle between gods and giants; the defeated sons of Gaia support the head of the stairs. The subject matter is replete with political significance, and prepares the visitor for the story told in the paintings in the main hall – a metaphor for the Emperor's victory over the Turks at Kahlenberg (1683) and in Hungary (1686). The terrace is lined with a remarkable collection of decorated terracotta pots. The pots are adorned with festoons, little angels, heraldic motifs and busts of emperors. The artist responsible for them was a mysterious craftsman named Bombelli, of whom nothing is known except his work here and at Slávkov u Brna Castle.

PAINTED DECORATION. The monumental steps lead directly to the Imperial Banqueting Room, which is decorated with the same theme. The murals were painted by the brothers Abraham and Isaac Godyn, who came to the castle from Antwerp in 1690. Abraham began by painting the trompe l'oeil decorations in the corridors, and the Count then set him to work in the large reception room on the second floor. He worked here for six years on the paintings, which are devoted to a glorification of the Habsburgs. The guidebook to the castle explains the cycle of paintings to the visitor. The paintings in the other rooms are earlier, and of lesser quality; they are by Francesco Marchetti (before 1640– before 1707) and his son Giovanni, both from Trentino. The chapel, which they decorated in 1690, has a ceiling representing the apotheosis of the Count and his wife.

19TH–CENTURY CZECH PAINTING. Once in a poor state of repair, Troja Castle and its gardens have been restored on a number of occasions since they were purchased by the state in 1922. After 1976 it was decided to display here part of the collection from the National Gallery in the city of Prague. This led to further restoration work, and since 1989 the castle has housed Czech art from the 19th century – the second half in particular – and the early 20th century. Artists whose work has been exhibited here include Josef Čermák, Václav Brožík ▲ *319*, Julius Mařak, Antonín Chitussi ▲ *182*, Maxmilián Pirner, Jan Preisler ▲ *165* and Mikoláš Aleš ▲ *175*. A visit to this collection complements that in the Museum of Modern Art ▲ *317*.

THE IMPERIAL BANQUETING HALL
The decoration of this hall highlights the Habsburgs' principal virtues: moderation, clemency, and fear of God as manifested by piety. The Habsburgs' devotion to the Eucharist is the dominant theme of this décor, and it is illustrated on the wall by the legend of Rudolph I. The west wall celebrates Leopold I's triumph over the Turks.

The original Břevnov coat of arms included a branch (*břevno*) with three knots on a red background. The coat of arms opposite is a variant with a lion, the emblem of Bohemia, on a red background, and three branches with three knots on a blue background.

ST MARGARET'S CHURCH

"Its single nave, a version of the Germanic model of barn-like church, contains oval bays which weave in and out of one another, and whose arches rest on diagonal pilasters, The pilasters punctuate the white surface of the walls, which is itself embellished with secondary altars with painted trompe l'oeil decorations that are full of fantastic illusions."

Léon and Xavier de Coster

BŘEVNOV ABBEY

The foundation of this Benedictine abbey (Klášter sv. Markéty), the first religious houses for men in Bohemia, goes back to 993 and was jointly conceived by Duke Boleslav II and Saint Adalbert, Bishop of Prague. It was rebuilt on many occasions; the oldest parts date from the 10th century and only came to light during archeological excavations in 1964. The period between the 15th century, the era of Hussite reforms ● *32*, and the 18th century was a difficult time for the monastery, and it fell into serious decay; however, the monastery buildings, a garden, a church and a chapel were rebuilt in the Baroque style under the direction of Krištof Dientzenhofer between 1708 and 1745. The buildings that can still be seen today date from this period. The entrance to the monastery is through a door dating from 1740 ● *70* that was executed by Kilián Ignác Dientzenhofer. In 1990, Břevnov was returned to the Benedictines, and on February 13, 1991, it was declared a historic monument. The previous administration had only used it for storage.

ST MARGARET'S CHURCH. This church, which was built by Dientzenhofer between 1708 and 1714, is one of the most remarkable Baroque constructions in Bohemia. The powerful sweep of the walls, the generous undulations and the enormous skylights with carved pediments also make it one of the most typical. The ceiling frescos of the interior, dating from before 1721, are the work of Johann Jakob Steinfels and depict the legend of Saint Adalbert, to whom the church was originally dedicated. The church was only rededicated to Saint Margaret in the 14th century. The reredos on the high altar was made by Petr Brandl around 1720, and the whole church was restored between 1980 and 1983.

THERESA HALL. The Abbey's ceremonial hall is decorated with a fine fresco, *The Miracle of Saint Gunther* by Cosmas Asam (1686–1739), a Bavarian painter and architect, and one of the greatest German fresco artists and decorators of the 18th century.

CHURCH OF OUR-LADY-OF-THE-VICTORY AT WHITE MOUNTAIN

A chapel dedicated to Saint Wenceslas, patron saint of
Bohemia, was first built on the site of White Mountain
(Bilá Hora) ● *34* shortly after the battle in 1620.
However, Ferdinand II founded a Servite monastery
there in 1628 and ordered the construction of a
Chapel of Our-Lady-of-the-Victory to replace the
earlier church. In 1704–30, it was turned into a
place of pilgrimage. The architects may have
been Alliprandi or Santini-Aichl. The church
contains a copy of the painting of the Virgin
which a Carmelite, the Venerable Dominic of
Jesus-Maria, carried up to the front line. The
victory at White Mountain has often been
attributed to the miraculous intercession of
the Virgin Mary. Although the monastery
planned for this site was never completed, the
interior was decorated by the greatest artists of the
time: Reiner was responsible for the ceiling fresco
above the altar of Saint Rosalind, and Asam painted
the Assumption over the high altar. Other decoration
was carried out by Schöpf.

HVĚZDA SUMMER PALACE

This country residence dates from 1555–6, and its
name (Letohrádek Hvězda or Star Summer Palace) explains
its original conception. Archduke Ferdinand of Tyrol had it
built according to his own design, that of a six-pointed star,
inside the royal game reserve that had been selected by his
father, Emperor Ferdinand I. The pavilion was built by
Aostalli and Lucchese under the direction of the architects
Hans Tirol and Bonifác Wohlmut, and decorated by Italian
stucco artists, probably including Brocco. The ceilings on the
first floor have splendid stucco decoration depicting subjects
from mythology and ancient history. The basement
houses an exhibition that recounts the story of the
Battle of White Mountain in 1620; elsewhere the
castle has exhibitions of the work of the painter
Mikoláš Aleš (1852–1913) and the writer Jiří
Jirásek (1851–1930), both of them major figures
in the Czech National Movement.

In the 16th century
Hvězda Summer
Palace was topped by
a steeple, but this was
replaced by a cupola
in the 17th century.
The present roof
dates from the 18th
century.

A COUNTRY HOUSE
Villa Bertramka takes its name from its first owner, František Bertram. It was an affluent country residence built in an opulent, bourgeois style, and situated in the middle of one of the many vineyards that surrounded Prague at the time.

Detail of the score of Mozart's concert aria, *Bella mia fiamma* (right).

Interior of the villa: the drawing-room with the harpsichord used by Mozart.

VILLA BERTRAMKA ★

In the midst of the dilapidated Smíchov quarter, Villa Bertramka is an oasis of greenery and tranquility. At one time, the area was covered with vineyards, and access to the house was down a long avenue of chestnut trees. On April 23, 1784, the house was sold to Josefina Dušková, a celebrated singer married to the well-known pianist, teacher and composer, František Dušek (1731–99) ▲ *282*. Dušek was a key figure in the early days of Czech piano music, and he wrote many works for piano as well as a number of chamber pieces. He also taught several composers, including Leopold Koželuh, who succeeded Mozart as court composer to the Emperor. Indeed, the villa would have remained unknown if the

couple had not invited Mozart there on several occasions. The Dušeks had met him while Josefina was on tour in Vienna and Germany, mainly Dresden, and later in Salzburg in 1777. Then, in 1787, they collaborated with other admirers, including Count Thun, to invite Mozart to Prague where his *Seraglio* and *The Marriage of Figaro*, the previous year (1786) had been well received.

MOZART'S FIRST STAY. On his first visit to Prague in January 1787, Mozart did not stay at Villa Bertramka but with Count Thun ▲ *259*. On January 19, he conducted a concert of his music and, on the following day, a performance of *The Marriage of Figaro*. On that occasion, with the applause still ringing in his ears, he is said to have made his famous remark to Bondini, the theater manager, "My Praguers understand me!" Bondini promptly commissioned an opera specially for

Prague in return for the (usual) fee of 100 ducats and free accommodation for Mozart and his librettist, Lorenzo da Ponte. In early October 1787, while still working on *Don Giovanni*, the composer returned to Prague, accompanied by his wife, Constanze. He first lodged at the House "At the sign of the Three Small Golden Lions", which also belonged to the Dušeks, and then at Villa Bertramka. It was probably there, on the evening preceding the première on October 29, 1787, at the Estates Theater ▲ *281*, that he composed the overture to *Don Giovanni*.

K 528. Josefina Dušková is said to have locked the composer in the summer pavilion until he finished the concert aria, *Bella mia fiamma*. It was not commonly known at the time that Mozart had composed the aria, *Ah, lo previdi*, K 272, for her ten years earlier. Mozart was also a guest at Bertramka when he visited Prague in 1789; on that occasion, he went to see František Němeček, his first biographer, at Sadská.

"LA CLEMENZA DI TITO". Mozart's last official visit to Prague was during the summer of 1791 and on that occasion he was commissioned to write a new opera for the coronation of Leopold II as King of Bohemia in September 1791. *La Clemenza di Tito* was composed at Villa Bertramka in just eighteen days. It was an uncomfortable stay, and Mozart, who was ill, had to leave for Vienna as soon as he had completed the opera. It was a failure, although his bitterness was slightly assuaged by the success of *The Magic Flute* while he continued to work on his *Requiem*. He died on December 5, 1791, and the Czechs were the only people to honor his memory at the time ▲ *254*.

MEMORIAL TO MOZART. The Villa Bertramka was bought by the Popelka family in 1838 and in 1876, on the occasion of the centenary of Mozart's birth, they turned it into a memorial. The centenary of *Don Giovanni* was also celebrated there in 1887. In 1925, the last private owner, Matylda Slivenská, presented Villa Bertramka to the Salzburg Mozarteum and, in the late 1920's, part of the house was converted into a museum. After World War Two, the state took over responsibility for restoration and upkeep of the house, and founded a Museum that opened in time for the bicentenary of Mozart's birth in 1956. Further restoration took place in 1973 in anticipation of the bicentenary of *Don Giovanni* in 1987, and this phase of refurbishment gave the museum the appearance it has today.

Like the Smetana and Dvořák Museums, Villa Bertramka forms part of the

musical department of the National Museum. Concerts are given in the terrace garden and in the main sitting room.

Don Giovanni and Zerlina, characters in Mozart's *Don Giovanni*.

A LEGENDARY FOUNDATION. Kosmas, writing in the 11th century, and later Václav Hájek z Libočan in his *Kronika Česka* (*Czech Chronicle*) ▲ 233 of 1541, state that Libussa was the founder of Vyšehrad. According to Hájek, after the death of Čech, Krok was elected Duke (or Prince) of the Czechs. He had three daughters, of whom Libussa was the youngest, and they were all magicians and prophetesses; Libussa was the wisest and the most enlightened. After Krok's death, she was elected to succeed her father in 710, and founded Psáry Castle, as Vyšehrad was first known, where she lived and which she embellished and enlarged. She founded Prague Castle in 717. All this is legend, of course. In fact, Vyšehrad Castle was founded in the first half of the 10th century and was known as Chrasten and, from the end of the century, it belonged to the Přemyslids, who struck denarius coins there. It joined forces with the Castle to defend the town of Prague. After that, Vyšehrad was more or less abandoned until Charles IV gave it a new lease of life. It was felt that Nové Město had adequate defenses to the south by the rock, but it was not until the 17th century that Vyšehrad was properly restored, and a fortified and buttressed curtain wall was erected in 1654–80.

LIBUSSA. Krok's youngest daughter, the legendary founder of Prague, is also the legendary founder of the first royal dynasty of Bohemia. Realizing that the men did not like being governed by a woman, Libussa agreed to take a husband, and she nominated one in a prophecy. She indicated a field near the village of Stadice where a man would be working with two oxen. The man was called Přemysl (the Thinker), she said. Messengers were taken by Libussa's white horse to find him. Later, Přemysl Oráč (Přemysl the Ploughman) came to Vyšehrad, bringing with him his shoes made of the bark of the lime tree and his bag by which he wanted to record for posterity his peasant origins. At Vyšehrad, he married the princess and became the legendary founder of the Kingdom of Bohemia.

THE SITE AT VYŠEHRAD. The few ancient remains at Vyšehrad include the old Rotunda of St Martin (left), the fortifications and Ferdinand I's monumental gates. Between the first gate, the Tábor Gate (1655), and the Leopold I Gate (1678), there are vestiges

THE STORY OF PRAGUE: LIBUSSA'S PROPHECY
"I see a great fortress whose glory reaches up to the sky; I see a place in a forest thirty cubits from our castle [i.e. Vyšehrad] and on the edge of the Vltava . . . When you arrive there, you will find a man carving a threshold in the middle of the forest. As even great lords have to stoop before a low threshold, you shall name the castle that you shall construct on your journey 'Prague' (*Praha*), the Threshold (*Prah*)."

Vyšehrad coat of arms.

THE OUTSKIRTS ▲

of the fortifications that Charles IV had ordered to be built. To the right is one of the oldest Romanesque rotundas in Prague and Vyšehrad's oldest building, the ROTUNDA OF ST MARTIN; the entire structure dates from 1050–1100, except for the south gate, which was rebuilt as part of a restoration program in 1878–9. The other medieval religious buildings have disappeared, and only the scantiest vestiges of the Romanesque BASILICA OF ST LAWRENCE remain. Major archeological excavations are now taking place.

The tomb of the composer Antonín Dvořák by the

sculptor Ladislav Šaloun and, to the right, the arches of the cemetery. Vyšehrad Rock, overlooking the Vltava (below).

CHURCH OF ST PETER AND ST PAUL. Of the Romanesque Church of St Peter and St Paul (Kostel sv. Petra a Pavla), which was founded by Vratislav II, nothing remains except for the foundations, which are now covered by a neo-Gothic church of little architectural interest. The church dates back to the reign of Charles IV, who had it built from 1369. It has been much altered: during the 19th century, Josek Mocker ▲ 167, 190 attempted to give it a Gothic appearance and even the clocks (1902–3) are modern. It nonetheless has some interesting features, including a 14th-century Madonna of Humility showing the Virgin seated, and statues by Myslbek depicting characters from Czech mythology and including Přemysl the Ploughman. At one time, all of these groups decorated Palacký Bridge. There is also a rather unusual group of megaliths in the grounds.

CEMETERY. The small cemetery built in 1660 took on a new importance with the addition of a portico with neo-Renaissance arches and painted vaults in 1875. Most of the country's leading citizens are buried here, including the painters Václav Špála and Alfons Mucha and the writers Vítězslav Nevzal and Mácha, and many musicians, including Bedřich Smetana and Antonín Dvořák. The cemetery is dominated by a monument erected in honor of the country's founder guardian spirit and called *Slavín* (Place of Glory).

VYŠEHRAD, LEGENDARY CRADLE OF THE PRINCES OF BOHEMIA ✪ Vyšehrad is reached by walking up Vratislava Street as far as Prague Gate. A small museum set into the curtain wall, to the left, explains the history of the site. In the park stands the ancient Rotunda of St Martin, vestiges of the Gothic Spicka Gate, the Devil's Pillars and the Plague Column. The little candles that flicker after dark on the tombs of the illustrious dead give Vyšehrad's old cemetery, next to the the Church of St Peter and St Paul, a magical atmosphere.

CUBIST HOUSES IN VYŠEHRAD AND PODSKÁLI ● 89

At the foot of Vyšehrad rock are three examples of Cubist architecture by Josef Chochol (1880–1956), all of them built between 1911 and 1913. After studying in Prague, Chochol trained in Vienna in 1908 under Otto Wagner, like so many of his generation, including Engel, Roith, Janák, Kotěra and Plečnik. After a period as one of the better exponents of Rondo-Cubist architecture, Chochol opted for Russian Constructivism and then became attracted to Functionalism.
THREE-FAMILY HOUSE. The house at 6–10 Rašínovo nábřeži gets its name from the fact that it consists of three totally independent dwellings in one building.
ONE-FAMILY HOUSE. This house, which is considered to be Otakar Novotný's greatest achievement, is in Libušina Street next door to SEQUENS HOUSE (1912), also by Novotný. The two façades, which overlook the street and the garden, are finely distinguished.
APARTMENT BLOCK. This recently restored building at the end of Neklánova Street (no. 30) is an outstanding example of Cubist architecture. The decorative device over the first-floor windows is reflected in the cornice. Not a single detail has been neglected – neither the door and window handles, nor the form of the entrances, nor the ceramic tiles arranged diagonally on the staircase.

VINOHRADY

The royal vineyards planted by Charles IV in the 14th century – he also introduced seedlings and vine stock from Burgundy – extended throughout this quarter. Until the 19th century, it was called Královsky vinohrady, and it is

> "The moment war broke out, I could not
> stop thinking of Žižka's drum."
>
> Gustav Meyrink

now known simply as Vinohrady. The vineyards were abandoned in the late 18th century and partly replaced by rows of trees. Then, in 1875, the district began to be developed, with members of the Czech bourgeoisie, officials and civil servants settling here, as well as businessmen and people of independent means. In 1843, there were only 169 inhabitants; by 1869, the population had risen to 5318, then 14,831 by 1880 and to 52,483 by 1900. Vinohrady formally became a town in 1879 and was integrated into Greater Prague in 1922; it straddles three districts and contains a number of Secession and Art Nouveau buildings. A walk through Rieger Gardens (Riegrovy sady) toward Jiříz Poděbrad náměstí (George Poděbrady Square) takes in several streets well worth visiting, including Polská and Kroknošská.

MUNICIPAL THEATER (DIVADLO NA VINOHRADECH) ● *54.*
Between 1913 and 1920, the Municipal Theater's repertoire moved dynamically in the direction of Expressionism. From November 18, 1989, it became a meeting place of the Civic Forum ● *38,* the actors being among the leading lights.

CHURCH OF THE SACRED HEART. This brick-built church in Jiříz Poděbrad Square was built between 1927 and 1933 by the Slovenian Josip Plečnik (1927–57) ▲ *211, 213,* and is the most important building by this architect in Prague. After the war he was put in charge of restoring the Castle ▲ *211.*

Villa Gröbe in Havlíček Gardens was built between 1871 and 1888 in Italian Renaissance style for a businessman named Gröbe. Since 1953, it has been the House of Youth.

NATIONAL MEMORIAL
To the north of Vinohrady, on Žižkov Hill, is the National Memorial, erected between 1925 and 1932. The interior has mosaics depicting great moments in the nation's history; opposite the memorial is the equestrian statue of Jan Žižka (opposite) by Bohumil Kafka. Žižka, who died in 1424, was a brilliant horseman in Wenceslas I's retinue; he led the Taborite troops (Hussite radicals from the south of Bohemia) and defeated the Emperor Sigismond at the Battle of Vitkov (modern Žižkov) in 1420.

ZBRASLAV CONVENT ★

The convent buildings opening onto the main courtyard.

Zbraslav Convent occupies a marvelous rural setting 8 miles south of Prague, on the banks of the River Berounka a short distance before it flows into the Vltava.

A CISTERCIAN CONVENT. In 1292, on the site of a royal hunting pavilion, Wenceslas II founded a convent which he later gave to the Cistercians. The convent was finished in 1333, and the church, since destroyed, became a mausoleum for the last of Přemyslids. Wenceslas donated large tracts of land to the convent and it soon

prospered but, having suffered the ravages of the Hussite Wars and the Thirty Years' War ● 32, the buildings were restored in the early 18th century. The architect in charge of the restoration was Santini-Aichl (1677–1723), and the work was spread over the period 1709–27, with Kaňka taking responsibility for the last part. There are no traces of medieval design about this monastery; in fact, it is an excellent example of the Baroque-Gothic style for which Santini-Aichl ▲ 243, 254, 283 was famous. The convent was closed down in 1781.

U-SHAPED PLAN. The U-shaped buildings surround a main courtyard which acts as a cloister; a very low porch giving access to the courtyard was added later. The façade facing the river corresponds to the main hall, and is rounded. At the two ends of the "U" there are two pavilions and, on the south side, there is a small aedicule which breaks up the overall symmetrical design. Other pavilions punctuate the center of each of the wings, and they are topped with pointed roofs, including pagodas. The large windows on the first floor are underlined by a cornice supported by consoles.

MUSEUM OF ASIATIC ART
The ancient convent of Zbraslav today houses an exhibition of more than one thousand works of art from Japan, China, Tibet, India and South-East Asia. They are part of the collection of Asiatic Art in the National Gallery ▲ 227, founded in 1952, which today houses more that 12,000 works of art.

A CLOISTER DIVIDED IN TWO. The ambulatory within the cloister is, unusually, divided in two. The first corridor, each bay of which is covered by a vault with a pendentive, is broken up with huge windows. The second corridor, which is behind the first, is covered with barrel vaulting punctuated at regular intervals by windows in the separating wall. This second ambulatory is adorned with mezzanine windows, bays and gaps which allow plays of light and shade. In the corners of the cloister, there are two staircases, each of two flights, with the middle floor forming a balcony.

MURALS. Some of the rooms are decorated with paintings; the fresco in the refectory painted by Franz Xaver Palko in about 1770 is the most beautiful.

Statue in the grounds of the Zbraslav Convent.

Practical information

Key

X Children rates
♿ Disabled facilities
▯ Garden
P Parking
≋ Swimming pool
↑ Terrace
≋ View

◆ GETTING THERE

ADDRESSES

→ EMBASSY OF THE CZECH REPUBLIC

■ **United Kingdom**
28 Kensington
Palace Gardens
London W88 4QY
Tel. 020 7243 1115

■ **United States**
3900 Spring of
Freedom St. NW
Washington DC
20008
Tel. 202 274 9123
www.mzv.cz/
washington
– Consulate General
1109 Madison Ave
New York, NY 10028
Tel. 212 717 5643
www.mfa.cz/newyork

→ CZECH TOURIST AUTHORITY

■ **United Kingdom**
320 Regent Street,
Ste 29-31
London W1B 3BG
Tel. 020 7291 9925
www.czechtourism.
com

■ **United States**
1109 Madison Ave
New York, NY 10028
Tel. 212 288 0830
www.czechcenter.
com

BY AIR

→ FROM THE US
There are direct
flights from New
York to Prague with
ČSA Czech Airlines
and Delta Airlines,
with connecting
flights from other
US destinations. The
average travel time
New York to Prague
non-stop is 8 hours.
Delta Airlines
Tel. 800 241 41 41
www.delta.com
ČSA
Tel. 800 223 2365
www.csa.cz
Continental Airlines
Tel. 800 231 0856
www.continental.com
British Airways
Tel. 800 247 9297
(800 AIRWAYS)
www.britishairways.
com

→ FROM THE UK
There are daily
direct flights
London to Prague.

Average travel time
is two hours.
British Airways
Tel. 0870 850 9850
www.britishairways.
com
ČSA
Tel. 0870 444 3747
www.csa.cz
Low cost airlines
■ Easyjet
Tel. 0871 750 0100
www.easyjet.com
■ Sky Europe
Tel. 020 7365 0365
www.skyeurope.com
■ Bmibaby.com
Tel. 0870 264 2229
www.Bmibaby.com

BY ROAD

→ DOCUMENTS
A valid driving
license, car
registration papers
and insurance
documents.

→ ROAD TAX
Short-term permits
for motorway
driving can be
bought at the
border or at gas
stations.
Family car (under
3.5 ton): 800 Kč

BY TRAIN FROM THE UK

– Via Paris: Eurostar
to Paris Gare-du-
Nord, transfer to
Gare de l'Est for the
Paris-Prague Express
– Via Berlin: from
London-Victoria,
traveling via Ostend
and Cologne.
Rail Europe Direct
178 Piccadilly
London W1
Tel. 0870 837 1371
www.raileurope.co.uk
Information for
US residents:
www.raileurope.
com.us
EuropeOnRail
www.europeonrail.
com
Eurostar
Tel. 0870 518 6186
www.eurostar.com
French railways
www.sncf.fr

COST OF LIVING

■ A mug of beer:
35 Kč
■ 1 ticket to a

concert: 360 Kč
■ 1 dish in an
average restaurant:
175 Kč
■ 1 entrance
ticket to a museum:
70 Kč–100 Kč
■ 1 night in a
centrally located
hotel: 3,500 Kč
■ 1 entrance
ticket to a jazz club:
130 Kč
■ 1 CD: 450 Kč

CLIMATE

→ SPRING
min/max:
March: 32/45° F
April: 37/55°F
May: 48/64°F

→ SUMMER
June: 52/72°F
July: 55/75°F
August: 55/74°F

→ FALL
September: 50/66°F
October: 41/54°F
November: 36/43°F

→ WINTER
December: 28/34°F
January: 24/32°F
February: 28/34°F

DON'T FORGET

■ Travel insurance
valid throughout
the Czech Republic.
■ Student card,
giving discounts
(transport, concerts,
museums).
■ Credit card
numbers and
emergency
telephone numbers
in case of loss or
theft.

FORMALITIES

US and UK visitors:
no visa necessary
for stays of up to
90 days. Make sure
your passport is
valid for at least
six months from
date of entry.
No vaccinations
are needed. Other
nationalities: contact
the Czech embassy
for any visa
requirements.

→ CUSTOMS
One liter of spirits or
liqueur or 2 liters of

wine; 200 cigarettes
or 50 cigars.
Pets must have a
valid certificate of
vaccination against
rabies and proof of
a recent health
check, and either
an identifying
microchip or a
tattoo.

LANGUAGES

Czech is the national
language. English
and German are
widely spoken.

MONEY

The unit of currency
is the Koruna (Kč),
which is made up of
100 hellers (halér).
Notes come in 20,
50, 100, 200, 500,
1000, 2000 and 5000
Kč denominations.

→ EXCHANGE RATES
£1 = around 50 Kč
$1 = around 23 Kč
100 Kč = £2.30 or
$4.30
(at the time of going
to press)

TELEPHONE

To call Prague from
the UK or US, dial
the international
code (011 from US,
00 from UK), 420 for
the Czech Republic,
then the number
beginning with 2.

TIME DIFFERENCE

Prague is one hour
ahead of London,
and six hours ahead
of New York.

WEBSITES

■ *www.czechtourism.*
com
Site of the national
Czech Tourist Office.
■ *www.pis.cz*
Prague Information
service.
■ *www.travelguide.cz*
Hotels, restaurants,
camp sites. Online
reservations.
■ *www.heart*
ofeurope.cz
Guide to museums,
galleries and
exhibitions.
■ *www.prague*
experience.com

ACCOMMODATION

→ ACCOMMODATION IN PRIVATE HOMES

Many residents make available rooms in their homes to paying guests. It is best to book through an agency. However, there are many bed-and-breakfast signs in the streets of Prague, and you may decide to make your own arrangements. Prices vary according to the location and the season.

Ave Travel
– Main railway station (Hlavni Nadrazi), arrival hall
Daily 6am–11pm
– Wilsonova 8
Tel. 224 223 521 or 224 223 226
Daily 6am–11pm
– Na Příkopě 18
Tel. 224 226 087
Nov–March: Mon–Sat 9am–5pm; April–Oct: daily 9am–6pm
www.Ave-prague-hotels.com
– Ruzyne International Airport, arrival hall
Tel. 220 114 650
April–Oct: daily 7am–10pm.
Nov–March: daily 7am–9pm.

Rates
500–1,500 Kč per person per night, according to the season and location. Payment is made in Koruna or German Marks. Breakfast is usually included in the room rate, but it is advisable to check.

→ CAMPSITES
PIS and Čedok offices (see under Tourist information p.336) have a list of campsites in Prague and its surrounding area.
Categories
From 0 to 3 stars. Sites labeled 0 or * have cold water only. Those campsites in the ** and *** categories should provide electricity, hot water, eating facilities and a television room. Caravans and camping-cars are welcome, and individual bungalows or chalets are also available. All have communal bathrooms and cooking areas, as well as children's playgrounds. Located outside Prague, they can be reached by urban transportation.
Rates
From 100 to 240 Kč a night, according to the category.

→ HOTELS
Early bookings are recommended for the summer holidays.
Categories
Hotel ratings are based on a star system comparable to that used in Western Europe, determining prices and facilities. You may still encounter the older alphabet-based system: A* (deluxe) A, B*, B and C (in decreasing order).
Rates
Allow about £180/$338 for a five-star hotel, and about £20/$38 for a one-star hotel situated outside the city center. A room in a two-star hotel costs around £40/$75. A double room in a centrally located hotel costs at least £65/$122.

→ YOUTH HOSTELS
CKM Travel
Manesova 77
Tel. 22 721 595 and 222 241 137
Around 3,000 beds are provided by this organization, who will take the reservation and tell you where beds are available.
Prices
Prices vary according to the season.
Allow 200 Kč

(£4.50/$8.50) a night in a dormitory, 350 Kč (£8/$15) for a double room. A membership card entitles the holder to discounts.

AIRPORT

→ RUZYNĚ AIRPORT
Located 12½ miles northwest of the city center.
Tel. 220 113 314

→ AIRPORT TRANSFER
Shuttle
The best value option to get to the city center. Both Cedaz and Welcome Touristic Praha run shuttle vans between the airport and the city center (5.30am–9.30pm for Cedaz, 8.30am–7pm for Welcome). Departures every 30 minutes, journey time around 30 minutes. Tickets are available on board: 90 Kč. However you have to wait until the shuttle is full and it may go all over Prague before it gets to your hotel or its terminus, Náměsti-Republiky.
Buses 119 and 179
The cheapest way to get from the airport to Dejvická subway station (line A) or Nové Butovice Metro Station (Line B). Departs every

10 mins, journey time 30/40 mins. Cost: 12 Kč (lets you ride the bus and then transfer to the metro at Dejvická).

Taxis
One taxi firm has the monopoly on airport transfers. It charges a steep 600 Kč but check before you get in. A cheaper option is to phone one of the taxi firms listed in the Urban Transportation section once you have collected your luggage. To reach the taxi meeting point, take a right out of the arrivals terminal. And check that the price list, registration number and company name are displayed in the taxi before entering.

BEER HALLS, BARS AND CAFÉS
→ "PIVNICE", OR "HOSPODA"
A *pivnice* or *hospoda* is a Czech pub or beer hall. Bills are scribbled on the table. One slash means one beer (from about 25 Kč to 45 Kč, depending on the beer).

An extensive choice of beers
Each brewery produces its own beer from varieties of barley and hops grown in Bohemia. Among the hundreds of brands, the most famous are the golden and creamy-headed beers from České Budějovice and Plžen, such as *Pilsner, Pilsen Urquell* and *Budvar*. The quality of Plžen beer is the fruit of a long and respected tradition. Some beers, such as *Staropramen* are brewed in Prague.

Warning:
"Don't drink and drive" isn't just an empty slogan in the Czech Republic. *Fines are high for anyone breaking the "zero blood-alcohol" rule. Drivers may like to try one of the alcohol-free beers. The dark special beers (Ležák) have a very high alcoholic content.*

→ "VINÁRNA"
Vinárna are wine bars that also function as restaurants, and sometimes even as nightclubs. Wine is served by the bottle, the jug or the glass, with or without food. Some of the *vinárna* belong to wine-makers' cooperatives and sell only the wines made by these organizations. But most offer a varied list of local, national and foreign wines.

Vintage wine
The Czech Republic is a big producer of wine. The best are the dry and medium-dry white wines (*bilé víno*) from Bohemia, (*Bílá Ludmila* and *Mělník*), and the wines of southern Moravia (*Mikulov, Znojmo* and *Bzenec*). Slovakia also produces good wine. Don't forget to sample or even bring home some Czech specialties, *Slivovice* (plum spirit) *Becherovka* apéritif, and absinthe.

→ "KAVÁRNA"
These cafés, with their convivial and literary atmosphere, are the place to eat a plate of ham or cheese with a glass of beer, or nibble at pastries while sipping an expresso or Viennese or Turkish coffee (*káva*). Russian coffee comes with vodka. Tea is also served.

→ "CUKRÁRNA"
These are tearooms catering to the Czech sweet tooth. Waffles, cakes, fruit tarts (*koláče*), delicious donuts (*vdolky*), pancakes (*palačinky*), strudels, and poppy-seed cakes abound.

CELEBRATIONS AND FESTIVALS
January 14–21
International dance week
Mid May
Book Fair
Mid May–beginning of June
Prague International Spring Music Festival.
June
Concertino di Praga (Young Musicians' Master Classes); Contemporary Dance and Mime Festival.
July–August
Culture in the Prague summer (concerts, opera, theater, etc.).
August
Čedok Open (international tennis tournament).
September 28
St Wenceslas' Day.
September–October
Fall musical events.
October
International Jazz Festival.
November 17
Anniversary of the Velvet Revolution: demonstrations around Wenceslas Square.
December 26
Swimming competition in the Vltava, with water at 37º F!

DRIVING
Warning:
As said above, Czech law prohibits driving with any alcohol in the bloodstream, and seatbelts are compulsory. The speed limit is 70 mph/130km on freeways, 55mph/90kmh on main roads, and 35mph/50kmh in towns.

→ CAR RENTAL
Information
Rental agencies are located in the city center or at the airport. Addresses are available from tourist offices (see p. 336).

Rates
Czech agencies offer very good rates. Typical prices for A-category cars and gasoline: One–three days: 990 Kč per day. One week: 850 Kč per day.

→ PARKING
Parking spaces are scarce. If you park illegally, you may be fined or the car may be impounded. The city center is divided into three zones:
– Orange zone limited to 2 hours
10 Kč: 15 mins
40 Kč: 1 hour
Free between 6pm and 8am and on Sundays.
– Green zone limited to 6 hours. Zone for vehicles carrying tourists
30 Kč: 1 hour
120 Kč: 6 hours
– Blue zone reserved for Prague residents.

Main parking lots
The central train station, the National Theater and the Kotva store all have parking lots.

Park and Ride
There is also a "Park and Ride" system enabling visitors to park near one of the following subway stations and take trains into the city center (parking lots are guarded).
– Unlimited parking time: 10 Kč.
– Locations:
V Rybnickach (Line A, Skalka station)
Bucharova (Line B, Nové Butovice)
Radlická (Line B, Radlická station)

Zličín
(Line B, Zličín
station).
Hrnciska
(Line C, Opatov
station)
Holešovice Railway
Station (C-line,
Nádraží Holešovice
station)
Palmovka (B-line,
Palmovka station)

→ TRAFFIC
The roads that have
priority are signed
with a yellow square.
Warning:
*Beware of tramway
cars and buses
leaving their stops.*

→ EMERGENCY
NUMBER
ABA (Autoklub
Bohemia Assistance)
Tel. 1240

EATING OUT
→ STALLS
The cheapest and
fastest way of
eating. Food stalls
offer various types
of sausages and
regional hot dishes
for about 100 Kč
(£2.30/$4.30).
Salami and ham
sandwiches,
hamburgers (13 Kč),
potato cakes
(*bramboraky*), hot
dogs (25 Kč), grilled
sausages with
mustard, waffles,
beer and mulled
wine are also on
offer.

→ SELF-SERVICE
BUFFETS
These self-service
establishments
(called *Automat*, or
samoobsluha) offer
cheap lunches. They
are often full and
customers tend to
eat quickly, without
sitting down. Five
thick slices of bread
(with surimi, celery,
scrambled eggs, etc.)
and tea cost around
50 Kč. Roast chicken,
pork fritters and
potato cakes,
sandwiches, salads,
knedlíky (sliced balls
made of potato or

flour), and toasts are
also served with
beer, wine, tea or
coffee.

→ PUBS AND
WINE BARS
Good food is
cheaper than in
the traditional
restaurants (a good
meal rarely exceeds
150 Kč). The
surroundings are
attractive (albeit
often smokey) and
the service tends to
be faster. *Knedlíky*,
goulash, roast pork
with cabbage,
potato cakes,
chicken, soup, apple
strudel, cold meats
and cheese are
served with wine
and beer.

→ RESTAURANTS
A great number of
restaurants have
opened since the
Velvet Revolution.
Most are very good
value for money. The
most expensive
menu will cost you
around 1,500 Kč for
delicious dishes
served in exquisite
surroundings. For
350 Kč you can enjoy
a hearty lunch or
dinner with a glass
of wine or beer.

→ TIPPING
In pubs and cheaper
restaurants it is
normal to round up
the bill in front of
the waiter to the
nearest 10 Kč. In
smarter places it is
usual to leave 10%
of the bill. Some
places add a cover
charge or bill for
bread.

FINDING YOUR WAY
→ ADDRESSES
The name of the
street precedes the
number. In the
historic center the
buildings have a
double numbering
system:
Blue plaque
Indicates the
number.

Red plaque
This shows the
property registration
number, that is,
the building's
number in the
neighborhood
(never used in this
guide).

→ DISTRICTS
The city of Prague
(*Praha*) is divided
into ten districts.
The number of the
district (1–10)
appears as the
second figure in
the postal code.

→ HISTORIC CENTER
The historic heart of
the city is made up
of four different
areas:
■ Staré Město
(Old Town),
■ Nové Město
(New Town),
■ Hradčany
(the Castle),
■ Malá Strana
(Little City).

HEALTH
Health centers are
open from 7.30am to
5.30pm. Pharmacies
are open longer
(until around
6.30pm). Details of
night and weekend
services are posted
on the doors.
Emergency number
police, fire and
ambulance: 112
First aid
Palackého 5
Praha 1
Tel. 224 949 181
(emergencies)
Tel. 224 946 981
(dental emergency)
Open Mon–Fri
7pm–7am;
Sat–Sun 24 hours
Central pharmacy
Belgická 37
Praha 2
Tel. 222 519 731
or 222 513 396
Open 24 hours
**Emergency
medical service**
Nemocnice na
Homolce Hospital
(Foreign Pavilion)
Roentgenova 2
Praha 5
Tel. 257 271 111

or 257 272 146
After hours
tel. 257 272 191
**American Medical
Center**
Na Homolce Hospital
Janovskeho 48
Praha 7
Tel. 220 807 756
Open 24 hours

MAIL
**Central
post office**
Jindřišská 14
Praha 1
Tel. 221 131 111
Open 24 hours
24-hour post office
Hybernská 13
Praha 1
Tel. 224 225 845
Open 24 hours.
Mon–Fri 8am–5pm;
Sat 8am–noon

MONEY
→ ATM
There are many
ATMs throughout
the city center for
holders of Visa,
MasterCard or
American Express
cards.

→ BANKS
Banks are open
Mon–Fri 9am–5pm.
Exchange rates
are favorable (and
commission does
not exceed 2%).
American Express
Václavské náměstí 56
Tel. 224 800 111
Open Tue–Sat 9am–
7pm
Chequepoint outlets
on Staroměstské
náměstí 21 or 27
října 13 are to be
avoided as rates are
not good.
Komerčni Banka
Ná Příkopě 33
(Můstek subway
station)
Tel. 222 432 111
Open Mon–Fri
8am–5pm
**Zivnostenska
Banka**
Ná Příkopě 20
Tel. 224 121 111
Open Mon–Fri
8.30am–7pm

→ BUREAUX
DE CHANGE
Located in tourist

◆ STAYING IN PRAGUE FROM A TO Z

Newspapers, nightlife, parks and gardens

areas. Most are open daily 9am–11pm

→ EXCHANGE RATES
£1 = around 50 Kč
$1 = around 23 Kč
(at the time of going to press)
100 Kč = £2.30 or $4.35

→ LOSS OR THEFT
Notify your embassy or consulate (see p. 336) and the nearest police station as soon as possible. Report all stolen bank cards and checkbooks and have them stopped.
American Express
Tel. 222 800 111
Diners Club
Tel. 267 197 450
Mastercard/ Eurocard/Visa
Tel. 272 771 111

NEWSPAPERS
There are many newsstands, offering a good selection of international newspapers, especially daily, weekly and monthly English-language publications.

The Prague Post
Weekly newspaper published every Wednesday in English (usually doesn't appear on newsstands until Thursday). Its 'Night and Day' insert contains restaurant listings, and a calendar of local cultural events.
Cost: 50 Kč.
www.praguepost.com

Prehled Kulturnich Poradu V Praze
Monthly listing of cultural events in Prague. Available in the Information Offices in English or German.

NIGHTLIFE
→ CLASSICAL MUSIC
Orchestras and choirs hold performances in the streets of the Old Town, in churches, cloisters, former palaces and cultural centers. In summer they perform on bandstands, café terraces, in public parks and in the gardens of the Castle.

→ JAZZ
The International Jazz Festival takes place in October every year. Performances in jazz clubs start at 9pm. The best ones are:
Jazz Club zelezna
Zelezna 16
Tel. 224 239 697
www.jazzclub.cz
Open daily 3pm–1am; concerts at 9pm.
Reduta
Národní 20
Tel. 224 912 246
Open Mon–Sat 9pm–2am.
Tickets can be bought from 5pm on weekdays, and from 6pm on Saturdays.
Agharta Jazz Centrum
Krakovská 5
Tel. 222 211 275
Open daily 5pm–1am.

→ NIGHTCLUBS
Casual dress is tolerated in most places but is not always accepted. Many brasseries also operate as nightclubs and have their own dance floors.
Rock Café
Národní tř. 20
Praha 1
Tel. 224 914 414
Open until 3am
Radost
Bělehradská 120
Praha 2
Tel. 224 254 776
Roxy
Dlouhá 33
Tel. 224 826 293

→ ROCK
Rock is the favorite music of young people, of Václav Havel, and former opponents of the Communist regime, who took major figures of rock counter-culture such as Bob Dylan or the Velvet Underground, as models and ideological reference points. The most popular Czech groups are Krystof, Lucie, Cechomor, Monkey Business, J.A.R and Chinaskt.

→ THEATERS
Prices
A ticket costs from 45 to 800 Kč.
National Theater (Národní divadlo)
Národní tř. 2
Tel. 224 901 448
Wide-ranging program of plays, concerts and opera. Performances begin at 7pm on weekdays and 2pm on Sundays.
Estates Theater (Stavovské divadlo)
Ovocný trh 1
Tel. 224 901 448
This is one of the most important centers for theatrical activity.
Laterna Magika
Národní tř. 4
Tel. 224 914 129
Booking office open Mon–Fri 10am–8pm; Sat–Sun 3–8pm
Part of the National Theater, the Laterna Magika combines ballet, mime and theater performances with film showings.
National Marionette Theater
Žatecká 1
Tel. 224 819 322
Puppet shows.

→ TICKETS AND PROGRAMS
A monthly list of concerts, plays and films is available from the Prague Information Service, Prague Tourist Center (see under Tourist Information page 336 for both) and in hotels. Cultural events are also listed in the *Prague Post*. Tickets can also be bought at the door of the theaters, at some hotels, and at Čedok and BTI offices. Famous opera houses and theaters are often fully booked months in advance, but you may be able to get tickets from last-minute cancellations.
Ticketpro
Main outlet:
Prague Tourist Center, Rytírská 12
Praha 1
Open daily 9am–8pm
Reservations
– by telephone
Tel. 296 329 999
– by fax
Fax 234 704 204
– via Internet:
www.ticketpro.cz
– via email:
ticket@ticketpro.cz

BTI
(Bohemia Ticket International)
– Malé nám. 13
Tel. 224 227 832
Open Mon–Fri 9am–5pm; Sat 9am–1pm
– Na Příkopě 16
Tel. 224 215 03
Open Mon–Fri 10am–7pm;
Sat 10am–5pm;
Sun 10am–3pm
www.ticketsbti. cz

PARKS AND GARDENS
Petřín Park
East of Malá Strana (funicular or streetcars nos 12 and 22).
Letná Park
Situated between the Holesovice and Hradčany districts.
Vojan Park
In Malá Strana
Stromovka Park
The largest in Prague.
Vrtba Gardens
in Malá Strana, Karmelitská 25.
Open April-Oct: daily 8am–7pm
Hvězda Park
Final stop of streetcar no. 22.

PUBLIC HOLIDAYS

January 1
New Year's Day,
Day of Renovation
of the Independent
Czech State'.
Easter Monday.
May 1
Labor Day.
May 8
Liberation Day.
(1945)
July 5
St Cyril and
St Methodius Day.
July 6
Anniversary of the
death of John Huss.
September 28
Czech Statehood
Day'.
October 28
Independence Day
(1918).
November 17
Anniversary of the
Velvet Revolution.
December 24
Christmas Eve.
December 25–26
Christmas.

SHOPPING

→ OPENING TIMES
Most shops open at
10am and close at
6pm, Monday to
Saturday.
Department stores
close at 8pm. In
general, big city
center stores,
souvenir shops and
some bookshops are
open in the evening,
Sundays and even on
public holidays.

→ PAYMENT
Most shops accept
credit cards.
**Tax-free shopping for
foreign visitors**
If you purchase
goods costing more
than 1000 Kč in one
transaction, you can
get them free of
(sales tax), providing
you have a
certificate from
customs.

**→ BOHEMIAN
GLASSWARE**
There are several
varieties of Czech
glassware, the
most beautiful being
"Bohemia" (made
with lead to

strengthen the
glass), and the fine-
cut, fragile "Moser".
Moser
Na Příkopě 12,
Praha 1
Tel. 224 211 293
Open Mon–Fri
10am–8pm;
Sat–Sun 10am–7pm
Sklo Bohemia
Na Příkopě 17,
Praha 1
Tel. 224 210 574
Open daily 10am–
7pm
Celetná crystal
Celetná 15, Praha 1
Tel. 222 324 022
Open Mon–Thu
10am–8pm; Fri–Sun
10am–10pm
Magasin Kotva
Náměstí Republiky 8,
Praha 1
Open Mon–Fri 9am–
9pm; Sat 10am–7pm;
Sun 10am–6pm
Rott Crystal
Malé Náměstí 3,
Praha 1
Open Mon–Fri 9am–
8pm; Sat–Sun 10am–
6pm

→ BOOKS
Books are
inexpensive and
you will find in
Prague wonderful
antiquarian
bookstores.
Štěpánská and
Karlova streets are
good places to
browse, and you
never know what
treasured rarity you
might find there.

**→ COMPACT DISCS,
VINYL RECORDS
AND CASSETTES**
High in quality and
low in price, these
are widely available
in the streets and in
specialist stores:
Knihkupectuí Kafka
Staroměstské
náměstí 12
Tel. 222 321 454
Open daily
10am–6pm
**Bontonland
(Palais Koruna)**
Václavské náměstí 1
Tel. 224 225 277
Open Mon–Sat
9am–8pm; Sun
10am–7pm

→ CRAFTS

Česká Lidová řemesla
Melantrichova 17
(in the Old Town)
Mostecká 17
(in Malá Strana)
Both branches of this shop specialize in local crafts.
Thun
Pařížská 2, Praha 1
Sells china.
Botanicus
Ungelt, Praha 1
(Plus many other branches.)
Think Body Shop but cheaper.

→ SECOND-HAND SHOPS
For old bobbin-lace, embroidered tablecloths, books, engravings and so on.
U Prazskeho Jezulatka
Karmelitska 16
Tel. 257 532 441
Open daily 10am–noon, 1–6pm.
U Zlate Cise
Nerudova 16/212
Tel. 257 531 393
Open Mon–Fri 10am–6pm;
Sat–Sun 10am–5pm

→ MUSICAL INSTRUMENTS AND SHEET MUSIC
In order to export old instruments you will need to obtain a license from the Museum of Decorative Arts and pay a tax of 20%. In general, instruments more than a hundred years old are difficult to acquire, and they can only be bought through specialized channels.
Amati Kraslice
U Obecního domu (Naměsti republiky 5)
(behind the Town Hall)
Tel. 222 002 346
Open Mon–Fri 10am–8pm;
Sat 10am–2pm
Wind instruments specialists.

U Zlatého Kohouta
Michalská 3
Tel. 224 221 999
Open Mon–Fri 10am–6pm
Violin specialists.
Music Goca
Maiselova 1
Open Mon–Fri 10am–6pm
String instrument specialists.

→ OBJETS D'ART
A number of art galleries (which are listed in weekly and monthly programs) present paintings, drawings, prints and ceramics. Prints and

engravings are sold in the streets.
Warning:
Don't forget to check customs requirements with vendors.

→ TOYS
Puppets, wooden toys and traditional dolls hang in clusters in specialist stores.
Firma Ami
Nerudova 47, Praha 1
Tel. 257 532 735
Open daily 10am–6pm
Fantazie Kubenovci
Rytířská 19, Praha 1

→ ANTIQUES
Prague is not the best place to pick up antiques – small towns outside the city are – but you can still find some bargains here. Good places to search include:

Vetešnictvi
Vitězná 16, Praha 1
Art Deco Galerie
Michalská 21, Praha 1

→ GARNETS
The Bohemian home-grown gem.
Try: **Granat Turnov**
Dlouhá 30, Praha1
(also Panska 1)
www.granat-cz.com

TAXIS
Prague taxi drivers are notorious. In theory, fares are fixed at 22 Kč a kilometer, with a 30 Kč pick-up charge, and drivers are obliged to give a signed receipt from the meter. In practice taxi drivers often do not turn the meter on and simply demand whatever they feel they can get away with at the end of the journey. Or they have the meter rigged with so-called "turbo" devices which exaggerate the kilometers traveled. The worst offenders are the organized gangs which control the stands at the main railway stations and tourist zones. These drivers can demand 10 times the official fare or more and threaten violence if the tourist objects. We recommend you always telephone for a taxi. The following companies have the best reputation and most of their operators speak English:
■ Profitaxi
Tel. 261 314 151 or 14035
■ AAA Taxi
Tel. 233 113 311 or 14014

TELEPHONE
→ FROM THE POST OFFICE
Calling from the post office is a lengthy process. You must pay a deposit, then the operator will dial the number for you; at the end the operator gives you the change.

→ FROM TELEPHONE BOOTHS
Public telephones in the center of the city are usually in good order, but not those outside. Some take telephone cards (from 100 Kč to 280 Kč), available from post offices, Čedok offices, tobacconists and subway stations.

→ TELEPHONE NUMBERS
Following an update of the telephone system almost all Prague telephone numbers now have 9 digits, starting with 2. A local call is very cheap.
National enquiries
Tel. 1180
International enquiries
Tel. 1181
Emergencies Police
Tel. 158
Emergencies (medical help)
Tel. 155
Fire department
Tel. 150
Car breakdown services
Tel. 1230 or 1240

→ TO CALL THE UK
To call the UK from Prague dial 00 + 44 (UK) + the number

you require, omitting the initial zero.

→ TO CALL THE US
To call the US or Canada from Prague dial 00 + 1 (US/Canada) + area code and the number you require.

TOURIST INFORMATION
→ INFORMATION CENTERS
■ **Czech Tourist Authority**
Vonihradska 46, Praha 2
Tel. 221 580 111
www.czechtourism. com
■ **Prague Tourist Center**
Rytírská 12
Praha 1
Tel. 224 21 22 09 and 224 23 60 47
Open daily 9am–8pm
■ **Tourist Information Centers** (run by Prague Information Service, **PIS**)
– Staromětská radnice (Old Town Hall)
Tel. 12 444
Email: *tourinfo@pis.cz*
www.pis.cz
April-Oct: daily 9am–7pm (6pm Sat–Sun).
Nov-March: daily 9am–6pm (5pm Sat–Sun).
– Na Příkopě 20
Tel. 12 444
Email: *tourinfo@pis.cz*
www.pis.cz
April-Oct: daily 9am–7pm (6pm Sat–Sun).
Nov-March: daily 9am–6pm (3pm Sat–Sun).

→ TOURS
■ **Prague Sightseeing tours**
Tel. 222 314 661 and 222 314 655
Guided walks all over town and bus trips to outlying castles.
www.pstours.cz
■ **Pragotour**
Staroměstské náměstí (Old Town Hall), Praha 1
Tel. 236 002 562
Email: *guides@pis.cz*

Guided tours of the main sights with multi-lingual guides.
■ **Prague Walks**
Nezamyslova 7, Praha 2
Tel. 261 21 46 03
Walking tours with a theme: 'Old Prague pubs', 'The Velvet Revolution', 'Prague's ghosts' etc.
www.pha.comp.cz/pwalks/

→ EMBASSIES
■ **UK Embassy**
Thun Palace
Thunovská 14
11800 Praha 1
Tel. 257 402 111
www.britain.cz
■ **US Embassy**
Tržiště 15
11801 Praha 1
Tel. 257 530 663
www.usis.cz
■ **Canadian Embassy**
Muchova 6, 160 00 Praha 6
Tel. 272 101 800
www.canada.cz

→ LOST PROPERTY
Karoliny Světlé 5, Praha 1
Tel. 224 235 085
Open Mon–Fri 8am–noon, 12.30–5.30pm
For loss or theft of credit cards, see under "Money".

TRAINS
Hlavní nádraží
The Central Station is located at Wilsonova třída (Hlavní nádraží station, line C) and has several tourist information points. You can purchase tickets at the ticket offices or from automatic machines.
■ **Information**
Tel. 224 22 42 00

URBAN TRANSPORTATION
Prague's transportation system is very practical and inexpensive.
See map p. 384.

→ INFORMATION DESKS
There is an information desk in

five subway stations:
Muzeum (lines A, C)
Můstek (line B)
Andel (line B)
Nádraží Holešovice (line C)
Cerny Most (line B)
See also the website
www.dp-praha.cz

→ BUSES AND TRAMWAYS
Both tram and bus routes are shown at stops and on the city maps. While you are traveling, a recorded announcement indicates each stop as it arrives and the next one to come.
Day services
Between 4.30am and midnight
Night services
Between midnight and 4.30am
Buses
Lines nos 501 to 512
Tramways
Lines nos 51 to 58

→ FUNICULAR RAILWAY
Travels up Petřín Hill to the 'Eiffel tower' and gardens
It follows the direction Újezd-Nebozízek-Petřín.
Open daily 9.15am–8.45pm.
Every 10 or 15 minutes.

→ SUBWAY
The network consists of three lines indicated by different colors

and letters:
Line A: green
(Salka–Dejvická).
Line B: yellow
(Černy most–Zličín),
Line C: red
(Nádraží Holešovice–Háje).
Times
Daily between 5am and midnight.

→ TICKETS
Buy tickets at the subway station, newsstands, tobacconists, tourist offices and hotels.
Free
Children under 6 years of age and disabled people.
Concessions
50% reduction for children 6–15 years.

→ TARIFFS
No line change
Basic tickets cost 8 Kč (concessions 4 Kč). These are valid for 15 mins from the time you stamp your ticket on buses and trams, or for four subway stops.
Several changes
12 Kč ticket (concessions 6 Kč), valid 60 mins (90 mins at night and weekends)
Tourist period tickets
1 day: 70 Kč
3 days: 200 Kč
7 days: 250 Kč
15 days: 280 Kč

◆ GLOSSARY

COMMON EXPRESSIONS

Excuse me: *pardon*
Good morning: *dobré ráno*
Goodbye: *na shledanou*
Hello/Good day: *dobrý den*
Help!: *pomoc !*
How much?: *kolik ?*
I don't understand: *nerozumím*
No: *ne*
Please: *prosím*
Thank you: *děkuji*
What?: *jak ?*
What's your telephone number?: *jaké máte číslo telefonu?*
When? *kdy?*
Yes: *ano*

ACCOMMODATION

Bathroom: *koupelna*
Bill: *účet*
Camping: *kemping*
Do you have rooms?: *máte volné pokoje ?*
Full board: *plná penze*
Room in a private home: *pokoj v soukromí*
Single / double room: *jednolůžkový / dvoulůžkový pokoj*
Key: *klíč*
Night: *noc*
Reserve: *rezervovat*
Toilets: *záchod / toaleta*
Youth hostels: *mládežnická ubytovna*

CALENDAR

January: *leden*
February: *únor*
March: *březen*
April: *duben*
May: *květen*
June: *červen*
July: *červenec*
August: *srpen*
September: *září*
October: *říjen*
November: *listopad*
December: *prosinec*
Monday: *pondělí*
Tuesday: *úterý*
Wednesday: *středa*
Thursday: *čtvrtek*
Friday: *pátek*
Saturday: *sobota*
Sunday: *neděle*

COUNTING

One: *jeden / jedna / jedno*
Two: *dva /dvě*
Three: *tři*
Four: *čtyři*
Five: *pět*
Six: *šest*
Seven: *sedm*
Eight: *osm*
Nine: *devět*
Ten: *deset*
Fifty: *padesát*
One hundred: *sto*
Five hundred: *pět set*
One thousand: *tisíc*
Million: *milión*

CULTURE

Booking office: *předprodej vstupenek*
Change in a program: *změna programu*
Chamber music: *komorní hudba*
Concert: *koncert*
Dance: *tanec*
Fully booked: *vyprodáno*
Jazz: *džez*
Movies: *kino*
Musical (a): *hudební komedie*
Original version: *původní znění*
Theater: *divadlo*
Ticket: *vstupenka / lístek*

IN THE CAR

Beware of the train / tramway: *pozor vlak / tramvaj*
Breakdown: *porucha*
Car rental: *půjčovna automobilů*
Customs: *celnice*
Driving license: *řidičský průkaz*
Gasoil: *nafta*
Gasoline: *benzín*
Leadfree gas: *bezolovnatý benzín*
Oil: *olej*
To fill up: *natankovat plnou nádrž*

EATING

Beef: *hovězí*
Beer: *pivo*
Bon appétit!: *dobrou chuť!*
Bread: *chléb*
Cabbage: *zelí*
Cheese: *sýr*
Cold dishes: *studené jídlo*
Fish: *ryby*
Fork: *vidlička*
Game: *zvěřina*
Glass: *sklenice*
Ham: *šunka*
Hot dishes: *teplé jídlo*
Ice cream: *zmrzlina*
Knife: *nůž*
Lamb: *jehněčí*
Mutton: *skopové*
Pâtisserie: *zákusky-moučníky*
Pork roast: *vepřová pečeně*
Potato cakes: *bramborák*
Poultry: *drůbež*
Soup: *polévka*
Spoon: *lžíce*
Sugar: *sladký*
The bill, please: *u čet, prosím*
The menu, please: *jídelní lístek, prosím*
To your health!: *nazdraví!*
Waffles: *vafle*
Water: *voda*
White / rosé / red wine: *bílé / růžové / červené víno*

FINDING YOUR WAY

Avenue: *třída*
Bridge: *most*
Cemetary: *hřbitov*
Church: *kostel*
Crossroads: *křižovatka*
Garden: *sad*
House: *dům*
Island: *ostrov*
Left: *nalevo / vlevo / doleva*
Place: *náměstí*
Platform: *nábřeží*
Right: *napravo / vpravo / doprava*
Street: *ulice*

HEALTH

Aspirin: *acylpyrin / aspirin*
Blood group: *krevní skupina*
Cold (a): *rýma*
Dentist: *zubní lékař / zubař*
Clinic (dispensary): *zdravotní středisko*
Doctor: *lékař*
Hospital: *nemocnice*
I'm not feeling well: *je mi špatně*
Pharmacy: *lékárna*
Surgery hours: *ordinační hodiny*

MAIL

Address: *adresa*
Money order: *poštovní poukázka*
Parcel: *balíček / balík*
Post office: *poštovní úřad*
Postcard: *pohlednice*
Registered letter: *doporučený dopis*
Stamp: *známka*
Telegram: *telegram*
Telephone: *telefon*
Telephone card: *telefonní karta*
Telephone directory: *telefonní seznam*

MONEY

Auto-teller: *peněžní automat / bankomat*
Bank: *banka*
Bureau de change: *směnárna*
Cash: *hotovost*
Change: *směna peněz*
Commission: *poplatek*
Credit card: *úvěrová karta / kreditní karta*
Crown: *Koruna*
How long does it take to change...?: *jaký je kurs ?*
Money: *peníze*
Traveler's cheque: *cestovní šek*

STORES

Antique store: *stardžitnosti*
Baker's: *pekárna*
Bohemian glassware: *český křišťál*
Bookstore (second-hand books): *antikvariát*
Butcher's: *řeznictví*
CD: *kompaktní deska*
Closed: *zavřeno*
Cut / blown glass: *broušené / foukané sklo*
Department stores: *obchodní dům*
Doll: *panenka*
Embroidery: *výšivka*
Entrance: *vchod*
Exit: *východ*
How much is...?: *kolik to stojí?*
Lace: *krajka*
Open: *otevřeno*
Puppet: *loutka*
Sweets: *cukrovinky / cukrárna*
What is it?: *co je to?*

TRANSPORTATION

Avenue: *třída*
Book of tickets: *soubor jízdenek*
Discount: *sleva*
Transfer: *přestup*
Central railway station: *hlavní nádráží*
Exit: *výstup*
Funicular train: *lanová dráha / lanovka*
Next station: *příští stanice*
Stop: *zastávka*
Subway line: *trasa*
Terminal: *konečná stanice*
Traffic: *doprava*
Train: *vlak*
Validate: *označit*

- ⊡ < 3,000 Kč
- ⊡ 3,000 to 4,500 Kč
- ⊡ > 4,500 Kč

The ▲ symbol refers to the Itineraries section. The ◆ symbol refers to the map section. The key to the other symbols is given on page 329.

Abri

(off map C)
Jana Masaryka 36,
Praha 2
Tel. 222 515 124
Fax 224 254 240
www.abri.cz
Vinohrady (◆ C B6) sometimes called the Kensington of Prague, is a good hotel hunting ground for visitors who don't want or cannot afford to be right in the tourist vortex. This leafy 19th-century suburb is also full of restaurants and bars and it's only 15 minutes walk from Wenceslas Square. The Abri is a comfortable hotel with a restaurant and a charming terrace over the courtyard. Some of the rooms are small, but they are bright and have modern bathrooms. Twenty-six rooms.
⊡ P 🔼

Anna

◆ C C6
Budečská 17,
Praha 2
Tel. 222 51 31 11
Fax 222 51 51 58
www.hotelanna.cz
If you're prepared to be just outside the center this Vinohrady hotel is a bargain. It even has a smart pink neo-classical façade and the inside sports Art Nouveau flourishes. The rooms are not so extravagant but they are still comfortable and are equipped with modern bathrooms. Twelve of the thirty-

six rooms are in a cheaper annex. The National Museum is only a few minutes' walk down Vinohradská Street. Children's rates.*
⊡ 🔼 🏃

Betlem Club

◆ B B5
Betlémské náměstí 9,
Praha 1

CHARLES/OR

DŮM U KRÁLE JIŘÍHO/DR

Tel. 222 221 575
Fax 222 220 580
www.betlemclub.cz
Betlem Club has a great location in a quiet square in the heart of the Old Town, two hundred yards from Charles Bridge, and opposite the chapel where Czech hero John Huss used to preach, denouncing the wealth of the Church and the trade in indulgences. The two-story hotel is a bit kitsch but this is easily forgivable at this price. The rooms are comfortable, though a little retro in furnishing.

Breakfast is served in a rough stone cellar with medieval weapons hanging on the wall. Twenty-one rooms.
⊡

Casa Marcello

◆ B D2
Řásnovka 783,
Praha 1
Tel. 222 310 260
Fax 222 313 323

Situated in a quiet area near St Agnes Convent, Casa Marcello is full of character. It is a beautiful long building that follows the curve of a small alley, with an inner courtyard used in the summer. The bedrooms are all tastefully arranged, with well-equipped bathrooms. There is some beautiful furniture in the reception areas. Access available for disabled people. Twenty-seven double rooms and five apartments.
⊡ ♿ P

Dientzenhofer

◆ A E4
Nosticova 2,
Praha 1
Tel. and Fax
257 311 319
Set in an 18th-century villa behind Kampa Park, along the Vltava, this boarding house is a haven of peace. It is a hidden address in a quiet little street outside the usual tourist routes. In summer, breakfast is served on a terrace looking out onto the park. Access available for disabled people. Friendly atmosphere. Four double rooms and two suites.
⊡ P ♿ 🔼

Dum U Krále Jiřího

◆ B B5
Liliová 10,
Praha 1
Tel. 221 466 108
Fax 221 466 166
www.kinggeorge.cz
Close to Charles Bridge, Liliová Street is one of the most picturesque and tranquil streets in the Old Town. Fine old houses with red-tile roofs, interior gardens, and porches that open onto the grounds of a 17th-century convent or a seemingly abandoned garden. Fourteen comfortable rooms.
⊡

Dům U Velké Boty

◆ A C3
Vlašská 30,
Praha 1
Tel. and Fax
257 53 20 88
www.volweb.cz/rippl
A quiet family boarding house situated opposite the Embassy of the United States, in a very tranquil area. It offers a warm, friendly welcome

and spacious rooms with showers or baths, and looks out over a quiet little square. In summer, fireworks from the American Embassy light up Prague's night sky.
Eight rooms.
⊡

Elite
◆ **B** A6-B6
Ostrovní 32,
Praha 1
Tel. 224 93 22 50
Fax 224 93 0787
www.hotelelite.cz
The Elite is a stylish luxury hotel on the edge of the trendy bar district that extends from the National Theater toward Spálená. The rooms are a bit small and the elegant modern furnishings clash with the original Renaissance ceilings. Most look onto the hotel's pretty courtyard. Rather incongruously, breakfast is served in the Ultramarin bar which becomes a happening place at night with a nightclub in the cellar. Seventy-nine rooms.
⊡⊡⊡

Esplanade
◆ **B** E6
Washingtonova 19,
Praha 1
Tel. 224 501 111
Fax 224 229 306
www.esplanade.cz
Prague central railway station, an authentic Art-Nouveau building, is literally opposite the Esplanade, a stone's throw from Wenceslas Square. Owned by a foreign chain, this beautiful hotel enjoys a high reputation thanks to its luxurious décor and comfortable salons. The quality of the rooms varies, but you can view

them before making a decision. Rooms 711 and 712 have a magnificent view. Excellent restaurant. *Seventy-four rooms.*
⊡⊡⊡

Evropa
◆ **B** D6 ▲ *174*
Václavské náměstí 25, Praha 1

Tel. 224 215 387 (switchboard)
224 228 215 (reservations)
www.evropahotel.cz
Despite its slightly

run-down appearance, the Evropa still has great charm. A symbol of Art Nouveau, its façade has floral motifs and wrought-iron and ceramic balconies. Built in 1889 by the architect Bělský, it was rebuilt in the Art Nouveau style in 1903. Once you get past the heavy revolving door, you are transported into the enchanting

atmosphere of the early 20th century. Carry on past the reception area and enter the restaurant, which has a sumptuous décor of caryatids and stained glass. The old wooden elevator creaks a bit as it takes you to the upper floors, but the wrought-iron staircase is stunningly elegant. However, the bedrooms are of uneven quality so it is perhaps best to take a look at several of them before deciding whether to stay on. The bathrooms may not offer all modern amenities, but the Louis-XVI-style furniture and décor are unique and may compensate. You can enjoy breakfast in the gallery leading to the café of the hotel. This café is also open to non-residents (see p. 346). Ninety rooms and two apartments.
⊡⊡⊡

Four Seasons
◆ **B** A4
Veleslavínova 2a (street not marked on map; next to František u Křižovníků),
Praha 1
Tel. 221 427 000
Fax 221 426 666
www.fourseasons.com/prague
The new Four Seasons hotel has raised the standard that Prague's other luxury five-star hotels must try to reach. The hotel is right on the Vltava River, just on the edge of the Old Town, and has sweeping views of the Charles Bridge nearby and across to Prague Castle on the other bank. Because its site is so central

⊡ < 3,000 Kč
⊡ 3,000 to 4,500 Kč
⊡ > 4,500 Kč

the $60m-development provoked a huge controversy which dragged in even President Václav Havel, the Castle's occupant. But the sceptics have been proved wrong and the four interconnected old and new buildings blend in both with each other and the surroundings. From the river the new modern block is shielded from view by the neoclassical house and the fantastic 18th-century Baroque villa, all finished in yellow sandstone or plaster. On the Old Town side, the hotel is fronted by the richly detailed neo-Renaissance house with its domes and buttresses. Guests can specify which building they would prefer, but inside the maze of passages it is sometimes difficult to tell which century one is in. Even the rooms look similar – each of them is large, at around 430 square feet – though the ones in the neo-Renaissance House are easily distinguishable by their tall 12-foot ceilings. There are also twenty suites, including several on two levels with separate living and sleeping areas. For visitors to Mr Havel, the four-bedroom, 2,500-square-foot presidential suite – which takes up the whole first floor of the Baroque villa – should be the natural choice. Only around forty-five of the units have full river views but the superb Italian restaurant Allegro has a terrace facing

onto the embankment. One hundred and forty-two rooms. ⊡ ⼦ ♨ P &

Grand Hôtel Bohemia ◆ B D4
Královdvorská 4,
Praha 1
Tel. 234 608 111
Fax 222 329 545
www.grandhotel
bohemia.cz
Perfectly situated behind the Municipal House, this hotel belongs to the Austrian chain "Austria Hotels". The rooms are comfortable and the service of high quality. The halls are large and pleasant and the restaurant has a huge sitting capacity. With its balconies, stuccos and gorgeous ceilings, the neo-Baroque ballroom, called "Boccacio", is sometimes used for receptions and important dinner parties. Seventy-eight rooms. ⊡ ⌘ P &

Hoffmeister
◆ A F1
Pod Bruskou 7,
Praha 1
Tel. 251 017 111
Fax 251 017 120
www.hoffmeister.cz
The Hoffmeister, which belongs to the French "Relais & Châteaux" luxury chain of hotels, has an uncomfortable location, at the busy intersection outside Malostranská subway station, but it is a surprising oasis of calm away from the Malá Strana tourist tempest. In the 1920s it was one of the places to be seen and it is full of caricatures of the period, sketched by the current owner's father, Adolf Hoffmeister. Today it is more peaceful but

it still has a restaurant famed for its wine cellar. Thirty-eight rooms. ⊡ P &

Hotel Charles Bridge
◆ A E3
Josefská 1,
Praha 1
Tel. 257 53 29 13
Fax 257 53 29 10
www/hotels-of-prague.com/charles
The Charles is very popular with tourists, and for good reason. Set in a beautiful Renaissance gabled building, and freshly painted in green and white, this hotel is only 150 yards from Charles Bridge. Spacious rooms and beds. Twenty rooms. ⊡ ⼦

Josef
◆ B D3
Rybná 20,
Praha 1
Tel. 221 70 01 11
Fax 221 70 09 99
www.hoteljosef.com
The Josef is a new modern hotel in the Old Town for the style-conscious business traveler. The rooms are furnished with simple but luxurious modern furniture, and the superior ones have bathrooms with glass and metal walls. The hotel also has a top floor fitness center with its own terrace, a ground floor breakfast room looking out onto the hotel's own courtyard, and a trendy lobby bar. One hundred and ten rooms. ⊡ ⌘ P &

Hotel Palace Praha
◆ B D5
Panská 12,
Praha 1
Tel. 224 09 31 11
Fax 224 22 12 40
www.palacehotel.cz
The Palace opened

just before World War I and entered its heyday in the 1920s and 1930s when it entertained an international artistic cast including Josephine Baker and Enrico Caruso. It began its slow decline during the World War II, when it was frequented by the Gestapo, and was then left to molder quietly by forty years of Communist neglect. What you see today is the result of a massive reconstruction completed – with exquisite timing – just before the Velvet Revolution. The façade was left intact, with its beautiful Art Nouveau details around the windows, and the grand entrance, with its flanking statues holding glass lanterns, gives an idea of what it must once have been like. However, the inside, with its grand staircases and reading salons, was ripped out. In its place a modern hotel with 114 rooms and 10 suites was constructed. It could have been a disaster but care was taken to give a nod to the past by including Art Nouveau flourishes such as colored glass, mirrors and chandeliers, together with vaguely fin-de-siècle paintings and statues. There are places, such as the new American-style bar, where the influence of the 1920s is rather less obvious, but going into the dark paneled (and award winning) Gourmet Club Restaurant is

like entering a time capsule. A word of warning: the Palace is located outside the old town (opposite the new Mucha Museum), in the busy, main commercial district. One hundred and twenty-four rooms. Book well ahead for both hotel and restaurant.

Paříž

◆ **B** D4
U Obecního domů 1, Praha 1
Tel. 222 19 51 95 (swichtboard)
222 195 666 (reservations)
Fax 224 22 54 75
www.hotel-pariz.cz
The elegant canopy at the entrance, in authentic Secession style, is in itself a work of art ▲ 162. Art Nouveau enthusiasts (with the necessary means) usually elect to stay at the Paříž, which was fashionable at the start of the 20th century, when it was built. Other visitors may find the décor, immortalized by the Czech writer Bohumil Hrabal in "I Served the King of England", a little cold. In 1991 this stunning hotel, located next to the Town Hall, was returned to its former owners, the Brandejs, who restored it beautifully. It must be said that the rooms are a little small, but they are comfortable and well-equipped. The restaurant, with its Art Nouveau decorations, is truly magnificent. The service, however, lacks warmth. Ninety-four rooms.

Pod Věží

◆ **A** E3
Mostecká 2, Praha 1
Tel. 257 53 20 41
Fax 257 53 20 69
www.podvezi.com
This boutique hotel is, as its name suggests, just under the tower on the Malá Strana end of Charles Bridge. The view naturally is

superb, though it is really a bit too close to the constant stream of tourists crossing the bridge. The twelve rooms are classically elegant and there is also a restaurant facing the bridge.

Radisson SAS Alcron

◆ **B** D6, **D** D1-D2
Štěpánská 40, Praha 1
Tel. 222 82 00 00
Fax 222 82 01 00
www.radissonsas.com
The Alcron, like the Palace, was in its heyday in the 1930s when it hosted celebrated figures from around the world. During the World War II the hotel provided accommodation first for high ranking German officers and then at the end of the war for their Red Army conquerors. Under the Communist era it fell into steep decline, being famous more for prostitutes and secret policemen. The Radisson SAS group has now lovingly restored the hotel's stunning Art Deco interior and furnished the rooms up to luxury five star standard. The Alcron

restaurant is regarded as one of Prague's finest, The La Rotonde is almost as good. The Alcron is just off Wenceslas Square in the business district. Two hundred and eleven rooms.

Résidence Nosticova

◆ **A** E4
Nosticova 1, Praha 1
Tel. 257 312 513
Fax 257 312 517
www.nosticova.com
A fine establishment off the usual tourist routes. This fairly new hotel, housed in a 17th-century building, has been tastefully decorated by its Italian owners. A rough stone staircase leads to the bedrooms and apartments. Inside the rooms, fireplaces, canopied four-poster beds, mahogany furniture and tapestries make this hotel an ideal place for a romantic week end. Ten rooms (seven apartments and three bedrooms) – the bigger ones have a modern kitchenette.

Savoy

◆ **A** A2
Keplerova 6, Praha 1
Tel. 224 302 430
Fax 224 302 128
www.hotel-savoy.cz
This is Prague's luxury hotel par excellence. Top-class service and spacious rooms with terraces looking out over the Church of Loreto. Also available are a fitness center with sauna, a jacuzzi, a hairdressing salon, 24-hour room service and a beautiful library. Impeccable restaurant. Sixty-one

▣ < 3,000 Kč
▣ 3,000 to 4,500 Kč
▣ > 4,500 Kč

rooms and five
apartments.
▣ ♿ ✗ ⬆ ❄

Sax
◆ A C3
Jánský Vršek 328/3,
Praha 1
Tel. 257 531 268
Fax 257 534 101
www.sax.cz
*Superb environment
in a very quiet area
at the heart of
Malá Strana. Set
in an Empire-style
building, this
modern hotel is
built around a three-
story atrium. The
rooms are spacious
and well furnished.
The windows look
out over the
rooftops of Malá
Strana, Strahov and
the Castle. Very
romantic. Nineteen
rooms and three
suites.*
▣ ❄

U Krále Karla
◆ A C3
Úvoz 4,
Praha 1
Tel. 257 531 211
and 257 533 591
Fax 257 531 049
www.romantichotels.
cz
*The King Charles,
which lies just off
the steep tourist
climb up to the
Castle, must be
probably the most
beautiful hotel in
Prague. It's such a
riot of stained glass
and patterned
ceilings that it's
almost garish. It has
a fantastic baroque
façade and one's
first view of the
stained-glass skylight
over the narrow
central atrium is
breathtaking. The
rooms have antique
furniture, fireplaces,
and wooden-
beamed ceilings.
There is also a
restaurant.
Nineteen rooms.*
▣

U Kříže
◆ A E5-E6
Újezd 20, Praha 1
Tel. 257 313 272
Fax 257 312 542
www.ukrize.com
*Hotel-restaurant
in a renovated
16th-century
building, with a
view over Petřín
Hill, five minutes
from St Nicholas
Cathedral. Good*

U TŘÍ PŠTROSŮ/DR

*value for money.
Twenty-two rooms.*
▣ P ⬆

U Medvídků
◆ B B5
Na Perštýně 7,
Praha 1
Tel. 224 211 916
Fax 224 220 930
www.umedvidku.cz
*This boarding house,
run by young
people, is one of the
cheapest in the city
center, considering
its convenient
location between
Bethlehem Square
and the National
Theater. The house
may not look like
anything special, but
the rooms are
comfortable.
Excellent value for
money. Thirty-one
rooms.*
▣ ✗

Unitas
Bartolomějská 9,
Praha 1
Tel. 224 221 802
Fax 224 217 555
www.unitas.cz
*This Old Town
pension was until
the Velvet
Revolution a prison
and once
entertained future
President Václav
Havel. The cellar
rooms are bare cells
with metal doors,
while the upstairs
rooms boast carpets,
some furniture and
bright colored walls.
The shared showers
are a long walk
down the corridor in
your towel.
Smoking, drinking
and staying out late
are banned. Twenty-
seven rooms.*
▣ P

U Pava
◆ A F3
U Lužického
semináře 32,
Praha 1
Tel. 257 533 573 /
257 533 360
Fax 257 530 919
www.romantichotels.
cz
*The Peacock is
located in one of the
most beautiful*

squares of Malá
Strana, very close to
Charles Bridge. In
1991 the house was
saved from imminent
destruction,
renovated and
turned into a hotel
that managed to
keep an old charm
atmosphere. In 2000
the interior of the
hotel itself was
completely
refurbished in the
style of an English
stately home, with
slightly garish
results. There is also
a cellar restaurant,
and a sauna with a
whirlpool. Very
comfortable. Twenty-
seven rooms.*
▣ P ♿ ❄

U Staré Paní
◆ B B5
Michalská 9, Praha 1
Tel. 224 228 090
Fax 224 212 172
www.ustarepani.cz
*The Old Lady is a
good mid-range
choice in the heart
of the Old Town. The
rooms are nothing
special but the hotel
has charm, plus a
good restaurant, and
a well-known jazz
club. Eighteen
rooms.*
▣

U Tří Pštrosů
◆ A F3
Dražického
náměstí 12,
Praha 1
Tel. 257 532 410
Fax 257 533 217
www.upstrosu.cz
*This is one of the
oldest houses in
Prague, at the end
of Charles Bridge.
Legend has it that a
foreign delegation
came to meet
Emperor Charles IV
and had to spend
the night in the
company of three
ostriches that were
intended as a
present. The birds
became the symbol
of the house, as
illustrated in a fresco*

◆ PUBS AND BEER HALLS

Selected by Robert Anderson

on the façade. The rooms are spacious and comfortable, with beams on the ceilings decorated with rural motifs. Very good restaurant. Eighteen rooms.
⊡🅿🕏

U Zlaté Studně
◆ A E2
U Zlaté Studně 3 (not marked on map; the hotel is next to Starý Královský Palác), Praha 1
Tel. 257 011 213
Fax 257 533 320
www.zlatastudna.cz
Not to be mixed with U Zlaté studny below. This hotel is housed in a 16th-century Renaissance building, that once belonged to Rudolf II and later to the famous astronomer Tycho Brahe. Nestling just below the Castle walls it has some of the best views in Prague. All rooms have views and are stylishly furnished with replica antiques. The restaurant is also one of the best in Prague (see p. 349). Seventeen rooms and three suites.
⊡

U Zlaté studny
◆ B A4-B4
Karlova 3, Praha 1
Tel. and fax 222 221 113
This Old Town hotel has a marvelous façade, decorated with six statues, including one of St John Nepomuk, and looks out onto a small square at the entrance of the Clementinum. It is a prestigious address though, with only four spacious suites two double rooms. The suites have original vaulted

ceilings, parquet floors and antique furniture. A note of warning: the 16th-century house is on Karlova street which can be crowded day and night.
⊡🅿

U Zlatého Stromu
◆ B A4-B4
Karlova 6, Praha 1
Tel. and fax 222 220 441
www.zlatystrom.cz
A handsome three-story house with a gabled front locateed only 50 yards from Charles Bridge, this hotel-restaurant has recently been thoroughly restored. The beamed ceilings are quite low, as in most of the houses found in the Old Town. Public spaces and bedrooms contain some genuine Austrian antiques, such as trunks and painted wardrobes. The suites are tucked away under the eaves. There is a restaurant serving Czech cuisine, as well as a very discreet nightclub in the cellars. Twenty-three rooms.

U Žlute Boty
Jánský vršek 11, Praha 1
Tel. 257 532 269
Fax 257 534 134
www.zlutabota.cz
The Yellow Shoe is a pink Renaissance house in a quiet narrow street in one of the most beautiful parts of Malá Strana. Inside, the hotel is simple but cozy with wooden floors and ceilings. Many of the rooms have painted decorations but can be a little dark. There is also a small courtyard.

The hotel is great value for this part of the city. There are only eight rooms so reserve well ahead.
⊡▭

Hotel Waldstein
Valdštejnské náměstí 6, Praha 1
Tel. 257 533 939
Fax 257 531 143
www.avetravel.cz
The Waldstein is located in a quiet corner of Malá Strana next to the Senate, which was the palace of General Albrecht von Waldstein (Wallenstein) of Thirty Year's War notoriety. This Renaissance building has a small courtyard and a barrel-vaulted cellar breakfast room with its own well. The rooms have low timber-framed ceilings and are equipped with rather heavy antique furniture but modern bathrooms. There is no lift and half of the rooms are in nearby annexes. Twenty-four rooms.
⊡

The ▲ symbol refers to the Itineraries section. The ◆ symbol refers to the map section. The key to the other symbols is given on page 329.

The ▲ symbol refers to the Itineraries section. The ◆ symbol refers to the map section. The key to the other symbols is given on page 329.

PUBS, BEER HALLS

Báračnická Rychta
◆ A D3
Tržiště 23, Praha 1
Tel. 257 53 24 61
Open daily noon–1am
www.baracnickarychta.cz
A genuine old-style Czech pub with wood-paneled booths just off the tourist track among the alleys of Malá Strana. Solid food, good beer, outdoor tables in the summer, and a bewildering variety of live music in the evening.
◼🎵🏠

Kolkovna
◆ B C3
V. Kolkovně 8, Praha 1
Tel. 224 81 97 01
Open daily 11am–midnight
www.kolkovna.cz
Kolkovna is a fake – it's a new branch of the Pilsner Urquell chain – but it's great for all that. The Czech food is better than most, the pilsner is beautifully poured, and unlike many pubs it is bright and airy and not too smoky. Consequently it gets packed and service can be very slow.
◼

U Černého Vola
◆ A B3
Loretánské náměstí 1, Praha 1
Tel. 220 51 34 81
Open daily 10am–10pm
A real Czech pub in the Bohemian

◼ < 220 Kč
◼ 220 to 550 Kč
◼ > 550 Kč

Disneyland around the Castle! Although it's on the main tourist thoroughfare, the Black Bull thankfully keeps a low profile and requires determination to find. Once you've spotted the sign, stride confidently past the regulars blocking the doorway and try to find a spare part of a bench to squat on. You haven't come here to eat, but the bar snacks here are the real thing too. Smokey place.
◼

U Fleků
◆ D B1 ▲ 307
Křemencova 11,
Praha 1
Tel. 224 93 40 19
Open daily
10am–11pm
www.ufleku.cz
U fleků is probably the most famous pub in Prague but it's not quite clear why. Yes, it has a gorgeous Gothic room and it brews its own beer but it is also overpriced and full of tourist groups and oom-pah bands. No self-respecting Czech would ever step through the door. Watch the extras here as well – the nibbles on the table and the proffered Becherovka aperitif are neither complementary nor cheap.
◼ ◼ 🏠 ❄ 🎵

U Medvídků
◆ B B6
Na Perštýně 7
Praha 1
Tel. 224 21 19 16
Open daily
11.30am–11pm
The Bear Cubs is a big beer hall just off Národní, worth checking out for its Budvar beer and wide range of

traditional Czech dishes. It is slightly ersatz but mercifully low on tour groups or smoke.
◼

U Zlatého Tygra
◆ B B4-B5
Husova 17,
Praha 1
Tel. 222 22 11 11
Open daily
3pm–11pm
The Golden Tiger is a great Old Town pub that has been saved from the tour groups. Bohumil Hrabal used to be a regular here and a few tables are still reserved for local diehards to preserve the pub's character. It is reputed to serve the best Pilsner Urquell in Prague. If you have to eat with your beer, it provides some Czech favorites, as well as bar snacks. The pub is tiny so come early to have any chance of finding a bench.
◼

RESTAURANTS AND CAFÉS

Amici miei
◆ B C3
Vězeňska 5,
Praha 1
Tel. 224 81 66 88
Open daily
11am– 4pm,
6.30pm–11pm
Elegant Italian restaurant close to the Spanish synagogue in the Jewish quarter. In the summer you can eat outside on the pavement. Enjoy the great fish dishes, excellent wine list, and the smooth service.
◼ 🏠

Bakeshop Praha
◆ B C2-C3
Kozí 1,
Praha 1

Tel. 222 31 68 23
Open daily
7am–7pm
Bakeshop Praha is a great place to grab a sandwich or quiche as it is just a stone's throw from the Old Town Square. The bakery now offers coffee to go with its mouthwatering array of American cakes and muffins.
◼

Bellevue
◆ B A4
Smetanovo
nábřezí 18,
Praha 1
Tel. 222 221 443
Open Mon–Sat
noon–3pm, 5.30–
11pm; Sun 11am–
3.30pm, 7–11pm
In the past the Bellevue suffered from indifferent service, basic furnishings and an unimaginative cuisine, but its location on the banks of the Vltava made up for these negative attributes by offering a superb view of Malá Strana and of the Castle opposite. Today, however, both the high-quality décor and the cuisine make this restaurant one of the best in Prague. The Sunday brunch is a must. Piano music on weekday evenings and a jazz ensemble at the weekend.
◼ ❄ 🎵

Bistrot de Marlène
◆ D B4
Plavecká 4,
Praha 2
Tel. 224 921 853
Open Mon–Fri
noon–2.30pm,
7–10.30pm;
Sat 7–10.30pm
Owner and chef Marlène Salomon first opened her bistrot in 1995. The 15 years she spent in Provence

seem to have influenced the bright, sunny décor of her restaurant. The menu is often amended according to the produce available. Specialties include duck cutlet in bilberry sauce, pheasant terrine and foie gras.
◼ 🏠 🎵

Café at the Evropa Hotel
◆ B D6
Václavské
náměstí 25,
Praha 1
This grand café, on Wenceslas Square, is well worth a visit for its remarkable Art Nouveau décor. (See the hotel's description p. 340.)
◼

Le Café Colonial
◆ B B3
Siroká 6,
Praha 1
Tel. 224 81 83 22
Open daily
10am–midnight
www.lecafecolonial.
cz
Part café, part brasserie, the Jewish district's Le Café Colonial does everything from a coffee to a full dinner. Some dishes don't work and the tables are a little too close together but it's always a cool and relaxed standby.
◼

Grand Café Praha
◆ B C4
Staroměstské
náměstí 22,
Praha 1
Tel. 221 632 520
Open 8am–midnight
Located on the Old Town Square, it offers a good view of the astronomical clock, as well as some delicious sweets and coffees.
◼

Café Montmartre
◆ B B5
Řetězova 7,
Praha 1
Tel. 222 22 12 44
Open Mon-Fri
9am–11pm; Sat-Sun
noon–11pm
*Between the wars
this Old Town bar
used to be the place
to catch up with
Franz Kafka, Max
Brod, Gustav
Meyrink, or Jaroslav
Hašek. Now it's an
airy, quiet place to
get away from the
tourist throng and
recharge your
batteries before
making the final
assault on Charles
Bridge.*
◻

Café Slavia
◆ B A6 ▲ 298
Smetanovo
Nábřeži 1,
Praha 1
Tel. 224 21 84 93
Open 8am–midnight
*Built for Count
Lazansky, this was
the last palace to be
constructed for an
aristocrat. Opened
in 1863, it became
a favorite meeting
place for students
and intellectuals.
Smetana, the
composer, and the
writers Neruda and
Hašek were often
seen here. A symbol
of Czech dissidence,
the legendary café
was closed for a long
time, but was
completely
renovated and
reopened in 1997,
to the delight of the
people of Prague.
The décor has been
preserved, but there
is a new addition:
a very modern
restaurant with a
wonderful view over
the Vltava and the
Castle.*
◻ ◻ ▨

Circle Line
◆ A D3
Malostranské
náměstí 12, Praha 1

Tel. 257 53 00 21
Open Mon-Fri
noon–11pm; Sat-Sun
11am–11pm
*Extremely popular
with food lovers, this
new restaurant tops
the recommended
list in some gourmet
guides. The large,
vaulted room has
a sober décor and
the menu is quite
impressive: try the
fried veal liver or the
roasted chicken in
hot sauce.*
◻

BISTROT DE MARLENE/DR

Dahab
◆ B C3-D3
Dlouhá 33
(entrance in Rybna),
Praha 1
Tel. 224 82 73 75
Open daily
noon–1am
www.dahab.cz
*Bizarre thousand-
and-one-nights'
décor bar in the
Jewish quarter
serving passable
couscous and a
huge variety of
Arab-style coffees,
teas, and cakes.
For the full
experience, sit
on the carpets in
the back room
and order a hookah
pipe.*
◻

Dobrá Šajovna
◆ B C5-D6
Václavské
náměstí 14,
Praha 1
Tel. 224 23 14 80
Open Mon-Sat
10am–11pm;
Sun 2–11pm
*Cukrárna (tearoom)
with a great choice
of teas.*
◻

Flambée
◆ B B5
Husova 5,
Praha 1
Tel. 224 24 85 12

Open daily
noon–1am
www.flambee.cz
*You will find the
Flambée under a
porch in the narrow
Husova Street,
almost opposite
St Giles' Church.
It is set in rough-
stone, vaulted
cellars, reached
via a rather steep
staircase. The tables
are pleasantly
decked with flowers,
and the lighting is
rather subdued but
adequate. Paintings
and 17th-century
mirrors decorate the
walls. Specialties:
roasted partridge,
loin of stag.*
◻

Kampa Park
◆ A E3-F3
Na Kampě 8,
Praha 1
Tel. 257 53 26 85
Open daily
11.30am–1am
*Kampa Park is
famous for its
summer terrace
perched on the
Malá Strana
riverfront just
next to Charles
Bridge but it has
a cozy back parlor
and a bright airy
front room with a
view of the kitchen
too. The
international-style
food, especially the
fish, is pretty good
too.*
◻ ▨ ⌂

Kavárna
Obecní dům
◆ B B4
Náměstí Republiky 5,
Praha 1
Tel. 222 002 763
Open daily
7.30am–11pm
*One of the city's
most spectacular
cafés, worth visiting
just for its Art
Nouveau décor.
Located in the
former Town Hall,
it has been superbly
restored to its
19th-century glory:
period candelabras,
big mirrors, swathes
of marble and metal,
waiters in costume.
Elegant ladies,
passing tourists and
businessmen mingle
for a breather over a
coffee (káva or kafe)
or a pastry. The
service can be
indifferent and the
prices are steep but
it's still one of the
classiest places for
a coffee. You can
sit outdoors in the
summer but stay
inside for the best
view. Internet corner
also available.*
◻ ▨

Kogo
◆ B C4
Havelská 27,

■ < 220 Kč
■ 220 to 550 Kč
■ > 550 Kč

Praha 1
Tel. 224 21 45 43
Open daily
8am–11pm
www.kogo.cz
Kogo's remains the best mid-priced Italian restaurant in the city center. The pastas and desserts are superb and it can often be hard to get a seat. There is also a bigger flashier branch in the Slovanský Dům complex on Na Příkopě – this location just raised its menu prices 30 percent – which has a courtyard for summer dining but more variable cooking.
■

Mlýnec
◆ B 4B
Novotneho lávka 9 (not marked on map, but situated above the Smetana Museum), Praha 1
Tel. 221 08 22 08
Open daily noon–3pm, 5.30–11pm
Mlýnec's eclectic range of dishes suits every palate and will suit most wallet. For those lucky enough to grab one of the few tables on the terrace, it also provides a great view of the Old Town end of the Charles Bridge. Have an aperatif in one of the snugs while you wait for your table to be prepared.
■ ■

Nebozizek
◆ A D5
Petřínské sady 411, Praha 1
Tel. 257 31 53 29
Open daily
11am–11pm
www.nebozizek.cz
For one of the best views in Prague reserve a window table here and catch the furnicular

railway from Úzejd, getting off half way up Petřín Hill. The Czech cuisine is indifferent but for a romantic dinner it's hard to beat. And you've still got the walk down through Prague's most romantic park.
■ ■

Odkolek
◆ B C5
Rytířská 12, Praha 1
Mon-Fri 7am–8pm, Sat 8am–8pm, Sun 10am–8pm
Cukrárna (tearoom) where the bread and sweets can also be purchased to take away.
■

Palffy Palác
◆ A E2 ▲ 262
Valdštejnská 14, Praha 1
Tel. 257 530 522
Open daily
11am–11pm
Palffy Gardens have just been restored, providing an additional reason for reserving a table at the restaurant on the second floor of the 18th-century palace. As you go under the porch, you will more than likely hear musical scales being practised. Do not be surprised as Prague's Music Academy is just above. The restaurant has high ceilings, with stuccos and wooden floors, green plants and 15 tables. On the walls hang prints of famous musicians.Specialties: scallops and duck in orange sauce.
■ ■ ■

Parnas
◆ B A5-A6
Smetanovo nábřezí 2, Praha 1
Tel. 224 23 96 04
Open daily

noon–11pm
Parnas, like Bellevue, provides polished service, elegant surroundings, classic continental cuisine and a stunning view over the river. However, the consensus among the cognoscenti is that it has fallen behind its neighbor. See if they're right, go and do your own compare and contrast if you can afford it.
■ ■

Perle de Prague
◆ D B2-B3
Rašínovo nábřeží 80, Praha 2
Tel. 221 98 41 60
Open Tue-Sat noon–2pm, 7–10.30pm; Mon 7–10.30pm
www.laperle.cz
Situated on the river banks, above the National Theater, the "Dancing House" (Tančící dům) resembles a concrete building folded with grace and care. You will find the restaurant on the seventh floor of this unusual building; it has a bright dining room and large bay windows giving a exceptional view over the Castle. The ceilings are high and the tables are well spaced out. French cuisine: foie gras in puff pastry, roasted lobster and grilled turbot.
■ ■

Pravda
◆ B B2-B3
Pařížská 17, Praha 1
Tel. 222 32 62 03
Open daily
noon–1am
When it opened a few years ago Pravda swiftly became the place to see and be seen. It has remained hip and cool (and

expensive). The restaurant is full of the beautiful people, and has big windows onto Pařížská, the most expensive street in Prague where they all do their shopping. However, the jack of all cuisines approach to the menu does not always work.
■

La Provence
◆ B C4
Stupartská 9, Praha 1
Tel. 257 535 050
Open daily
noon–1am
La Provence was one of the first western-style restaurants to open in Prague's Old Town after 1989 and its relaxed style and competent provençal cuisine has kept it popular. Ignore the tacky go-go bar upstairs and head down to the cellar for good fish, a long wine list, and almost too comfortable seats. Early reservations essential.
■

Radost FX Club
◆ D F2
Bělehradská 120, Praha 2
Tel. 224 254 776
Restaurant and café open daily 9am–1am
www.radostfx.cz
Radost is a Prague institution – it's been around since the first expats hit these shores in the early 1990 – and is many things to many people: separate rooms house a music store, club, restaurant, bar, and café. But what it does best is food. The ambience is cool Bohemian chic, all velvet and brocade, with sofas and comfy chairs

clustered around low tables. Everything on the menu is delicous, whether you choose their giant burritos, spicy stirfries, sublime pastas, homeade soups, or myriad tofu-based creations. The servings are massive, the waitstaff is good-looking, the prices are reasonable, and they serve a wicked Bloody Mary at Sunday brunch. 🔌🎵

Restaurant Palác Kinských

◆ B C3
Týnská ulička 3, Praha 1
Tel. 224 81 07 50
Open Mon-Sat noon–3pm, 6–11pm
This cellar restaurant just round the corner from the Old Town Square offers excellent Continental and Czech cuisine in elegant surroundings. The service is particularly attentive. But it can be a bit quiet for those not particularly wishing to hear the sound of their own voice. 🔌

Siam-I-Siam

◆ B B4
Valentinská 11, Praha 1
Tel. 224 81 40 99
Open daily 10am–midnight
www.arzenal.cz
Prague's best Thai restaurant by a mile is hidden at the back of a fancy glass design store (Arzenal) near Staroměstská subway station. The few diners that find their way here use beautiful plates, cutlery and glasses from the store. Some of the

U MODRÉ KACHNIČKY/DR

U FLEKŮ/DR

U CISAŘU/DR

dishes are truly fiery, as Thai food should be. 🔌

U Cisaru

◆ A B3
Lorentánská 5, Praha 1
Tel. 220 51 84 84
Open daily 11am–midnight
www.ucisaru.cz

On your way up to Strahov Monastery, book a table at The Emperors. The windows look down onto the Malá Strana gardens, and in summer you can enjoy the coolness of the cellars, and admire the interesting medieval weapons

that decorate the rough stone walls. Lively Czech folk music is played at lunchtime, quieter piano music in the evening. The vast choice of wines is impressive. Czech cuisine features game specialties. 🔌🎵🎵

U Modré Kachničky

◆ A E4
Nebovidská 6, Praha 1
Tel. 257 320 308
Open daily noon–4pm, 6.30–midnight
www.umodrekachnicky.cz
One of the best restaurants in Prague. The emblem of this establishment is a "blue duck". Discreet colors, tinted windows, and prints and small pictures depicting hunting scenes displayed on the walls. Specialties are duck in orange sauce, rabbit old Bohemia style, and carp with cumin. Good wine list. Reservations are necessary. 🔌🎵

U Patrona

◆ A F3
Dražického náměstí 4
(street not marked on map, on the western edge of Charles' Bridge), Praha 1
Tel. 257 53 07 25
Open daily 11am–midnight
This tiny Malá Strana restaurant offers beautifully prepared continental dishes in an intimate and relaxed setting. The standard of the cuisine may not quite be up with the very best Prague can offer, but it makes up for it in atmosphere. In

◼ < 220 Kč
◼◼ 220 to 550 Kč
◼◼◼ > 550 Kč

summer ask for one of the balcony tables with a view. Garden open from April 1.
◼◼◼ ⌂ ⛰

U Zlaté Studně
◆ A E2
U Zlaté Studně 4 (not marked on map; next to Starý Královský Palác), Praha 1
Tel. 257 53 33 22
Open daily 11am–midnight
This hotel-restaurant perched under the Castle is another strong contender for the best view in Prague but it also serves superb continental cuisine, particularly fish, and mouthwatering desserts. Go in the summer for the terrace. See p. 343 for the hotel's description.
⊞ ⛰

Universal
◆ B B6
V Jirchářích 6, Praha 1
Tel. 224 934 416
Open daily 11.30am–1am
Universal has long been the leader among the pack of restaurants in the trendy area behind the National Theater (Národní Divadlo). The food is the Czech idea of French, with good salads thrown in, and the prices are very reasonable. A reliable choice before hitting the district's bars but very popular in the evenings.
◼◼

Na Verandach
(off map)
Nadrazni 84, Smíchov, Praha 5
Tel. 257 191 200
Bar and pub open daily 11am–midnight
The beer doesn't get any fresher than

that served at this restaurant, the house pub for at the Staropramen brewery. As many as five different types of beer are brewed on the premises and served, along with excellent Czech specialties like pork knuckle and duck breast. The menu is extensive, and offers tasty appetizers if you just want to snack and drink. A good place to go with a group.
◼

Vinarna v Zátíší
◆ B B4-B5
Liliová 1, Praha 1
Tel. 222 22 11 55
Open daily noon–3pm, 5.30–11pm
The flagship of the Zátíší group – which also includes Circle Line, Mlýnec and Bellevue – tends to be overlooked among its newer and flashier peers but it's still worth visiting for its old world elegance and classic continental cuisine.
⊞

Zahrada v Opeře
◆ D E1-E4
Legerova 75, Praha 1
Tel. 224 23 96 85
Open daily 11.30am–1am
This relatively new restaurant in the back of the old Czechoslovak Federal Parliament has quickly become a favorite, despite its unpromising location on the highway at the top of Wenceslas Square. The international cuisine is very good value and the restaurant space is airy and modern. Perfect for a bite after catching a performance at the State Opera.
◼

◆ PLACES TO VISIT

The ▲ symbol refers to the "Itineraries" section.
The ◆ refers to the map section.

PRAGUE

BERTRAMKA MUZEUM **W. A. MOZARTA** Villa Bertramka – Mozart Museum Mozartova 169, Praha 5, Subway B Tel. 257 31 74 65 / 257 31 84 61 Fax 257 31 67 53	*Open daily, April–Oct: 9.30am–6pm,* *Nov–March: 9.30am–5pm.* *Admission:* *museum: 110 Kč (50 Kč students); concerts 390 Kč* *(250 Kč students); Christmas concerts 450 Kč*	▲ 322
CAROLINUM Ovocný trh. 3 and 5 and Železná	*University building. Also used for exhibitions.* *Open daily 10am–5pm. Tel. 224 491 250*	▲ 278 ◆ B C4
FORMER TOWN HALL Staroměstská Radnice Staroměstské nám. 1 Praha 1 Tel. 224 482909	*Open April–Oct: Mon 11am–6pm, Tue–Sun 9am–6pm;* *Nov–March Mon 11am–5pm, Tue–Sun 9am–5pm.* *Admission: 30 Kč. Guided tour of the Town Hall* *Meeting Room every hour.* *One of the most efficient tourist offices is located on* *the first floor and organizes guided visits to UN-listed* *Czech towns and cities (see p. 336).* *The Town Hall also holds exhibitions on the history of* *the city of Prague and the Czech Republic.*	▲ 146 ◆ B C3
STRAHOV MONASTERY Kláster premonstrátů na Strahově Strahovské nádvoří 1 Praha 1/132 Library Tel. 220 51 66 71 x411 Gallery Tel. 220 51 72 78 *www.strahovmonastery.cz*	*The monastery is open to the public daily for the* *6pm service. The Library houses the Museum of* *Czech Literature, including the Theology and* *Philosophy Rooms: open daily 9am–noon and 1–5pm* *(admission: 50 Kč).* *For a guided tour of these rooms, contact the* *Museum four days before your intended date of visit* *to book the two-hour guided tour (400 Kč).* *The monastery also houses the Strahov Gallery:* *open daily except Mon. 9am–noon and 12.30–5pm.*	▲ 237 ◆ A A3

THE CASTLE   ◆ A C2-D1-D2-E1

CASTLE Hradčanské nám. Praha 1 Tel. 224 37 33 68 *www.hrad.cz*	*Castle area open daily, April–Oct 5am–midnight.* *Nov–March 5am–11pm.* *Castle information center (third courtyard) open daily,* *April–Oct 9am–5pm, Nov–March 9am–4pm.* *Admission: 120 Kč (three-day pass, giving admission* *to Old Royal Palace, St Vitus' Cathedral, Powder* *Tower and St George's Basilica). Guided tours* *Tue.–Sat. 400 Kč for groups of five people.*	▲ 200
FORMER PALACE OF THE **BURGRAVES (TOY MUSEUM)** (Museum Hraček) Jiřská ulice, Praha 1 *www.muzeumhracek.cz*	*Also called the 'House of Czechoslovak Children'* *Open daily 9.30am–5.30pm.* *Admission: 40 Kč.*	▲ 223
HOLY CROSS CHAPEL Second courtyard Praha 1	*Open daily 10am–6pm.* *Classical music concerts.*	▲ 213
LOBKOWICZ PALACE NATIONAL **MUSEUM OF CZECH HISTORY** Jiřská ulice 1/3, Praha 1 Tel. 257 535 121 *www.nm.cz*	*Open Tue–Sat 9am–5pm.* *Admission: 40 Kč.*	▲ 223
OLD ROYAL PALACE Starý královský palác Third courtyard *www.pribeh.hradu.cz*	*Open daily, April–Oct: 9am–5pm;* *Nov–March: 9am–4pm.* *Admission: 120 Kč (see Castle above).*	▲ 218
PRAGUE CASTLE **PICTURE GALLERY** Obrazárna pražského hradu Left under the porch leading to Powder Tower (Prašný most) Praha 1	*Open daily 10am–6pm.* *Admission: 100 Kč.*	▲ 212
ROYAL GARDENS Královská Zahrada Beyond Powder Bridge (Prašný most) Praha 1 Tel. 224 371 111	*Open daily, April–Oct 10am–6pm.*	▲ 224

RIDING HALL (U PRAŠNEHOMOSTU) Praha 1	*Open during exhibitions Tue–Sun 10am–6pm.* *(Note: this is not the Waldenstein Riding School,* *which is part of the National Gallery, at Valdštejnska 3)*	▲ 224
ROYAL SUMMER PALACE Castle gardens Praha 1	*Open during exhibitions Tue-Sun 10am–6pm.* *Used for National Gallery exhibitions.*	▲ 224
ST GEORGE'S BASILICA Fourth courtyard Praha 1	*Open daily, April–Oct: 9am–5pm; Nov–March 9am–* *4pm. Admission: 120 Kč (see Castle above).* *Admission free first Wednesday of the month.*	▲ 220
ST GEORGE'S CONVENT (NATIONAL GALLERY) To the left of St George's Basilica Klášter sv. Jiří, Praha 1	*Open Tue–Sun 10am–6pm.* *Admission: 50 Kč.* *Free first Wednesday of the month.*	▲ 220
ST VITUS' CATHEDRAL Third courtyard Praha 1	*Open daily, April–Oct: 9am–5pm;* *Nov–March: 9am–4pm.* *Adults 120 Kč, children and students 60 Kč.*	▲ 214
SPANISH HALL Second courtyard, above the Picture Gallery, Praha 1	*Visits by appointment.*	▲ 213
TENNIS COURT Mičovna Castle gardens, Praha 1	*Open daily during exhibitions 10am–6pm.* *Concerts, dance performances and plays.*	▲ 224
WHITE TOWER At the end of Golden Lane (Zlatá ulička), Praha 1	*Open daily 10am–5pm.* *Admission free.*	▲ 223

OTHER SITES IN PRAGUE

ARCHBISHOP'S PALACE Hradčanské nám. 16 Praha 1	*Not open to the public.*	▲ 226 ◆ A C2
BETHLEHEM CHAPEL Betlemské nám. Praha 1	*Open daily, April–Oct 9am–6pm;* *Nov–March 9am–5pm. Adults 30 Kč, children 20 Kč.* *Classical music concerts.*	▲ 286 ◆ B B5
BOTANICAL GARDEN Pražska Botanická Zahrada Nadvorni 134, Praha 7 Tel. 234 148 111 www.botgarden.cz	*Open daily, summer 9am–6pm; winter 9am–4pm.* *Free admission to gardens.* *Admission to greenhouses: 90 Kč.*	▲ 313 ◆ D C3-4
ČERNÍN PALACE Loretanské nám Praha 1	*Not open to the public.* *Houses the Ministry of Foreign Affairs.*	▲ 234 ◆ A A2
CHAPEL OF MIRRORS Zrcadlová Kaple (Klementinum) Křižovnické nám., Praha 1	*Open for concerts.*	▲ 151 ◆ B A-B4
CHURCH OF OUR LADY'S **ASSUMPTION AND CHARLES THE** **GREAT ON KARLOV** Kostel nanebevzeti Panny Marie v Nadeji a sv. Karla Velikeho na karlove Ke Karlovu 1, Praha 1 Tel. 224 92 21 78	*Open Sun 7am–5pm.*	314 ◆ D E4
CHURCH OF OUR LADY OF LORETO Loretánské nám. 7/100 Praha 1 Tel. 220 51 67 40	*Open Tue–Sun 9am–12.15pm, 1–4.30pm.* *Services Sat at 7.30am and Sun at 6pm.* *Admission 70Kč.*	▲ 235 ◆ A B2
CHURCH OF OUR LADY **OF PERPETUAL SUCCOR** **OF THE GAETANI** Kostel panny Marie Ústavíčné pomoci a sv. Kajetána Nerudova 22, Praha 1 Tel. 257 53 26 75	*Visits Tue and Fri 5.30pm, Sun 2pm and 3pm.*	▲ 255 ◆ A C2
CHURCH OF OUR LADY OF **THE ELIZABETHINES** Kostel panny Marie Na Slupi and Apolinářská Praha 2 Tel. 224 92 05 98	*Services Wed and Fri at 5pm and Sun at 9am.*	▲ 313 ◆ D C4

◆ PLACES TO VISIT

CHURCH OF OUR-LADY-OF-THE-SNOWS Kostel panny Marie sněžné Jungmannovo nám. 18, Praha 1 Tel. 222 24 62 43	*Open Mon-Fri 6.30am–7pm, Sat 7am–7pm, Sun 8am–7pm.*	▲ 290 ◆ B C5
CHURCH OF OUR LADY VICTORIOUS Panna Maria Vitežna Pražske Jezulatko Karmelitská 9, Praha 1 Tel. 257 53 36 46	*Open Mon-Sat 8.30am–6.30pm, Sun 9am–7pm. Small museum and souvenir shop inside the church open Mon-Sat.*	▲ 271 ◆ A D4
CHURCH OF OUR LADY OF TÝN Panna Marie pr ě d Tynem Staroměstské nám., Praha 1	*Services Sun 9.30am and 9pm, Wed-Fri 6pm, Sat 8am. Open to the public 9am–1pm.*	▲ 147 ◆ B C4
CHURCH OF OUR LADY UNDER THE CHAIN Kostel panny Marie pod retězem Lázeňská, Praha 1 Tel. 257 53 08 76	*Church built for the Order of the Knights of Malta. Open for services Mon-Sat at 5pm, Sun at 9.30am, 11am (Latin mass) and 5pm.*	▲ 273 ◆ A E3
CHURCH OF ST CLEMENT Karlova, Praha 1 Tel. 222 22 03 64 or 221 66 31 11	*Open for services Mon-Sat at 5pm, Sun at 7.30am, 8.30am, 10am and 11.30am.*	▲ 152 ◆ B A4
CHURCH OF ST CYRIL AND ST METHODIUS Kostel sv. Cyrila a Metoděje Resslova 9, Praha 2 Tel. 224 92 06 86	*Services Tue, Thu and Sat at 8am, and Sun at 9am. Memorial to the Czech resistance in the crypt: open Tue-Sun, summer 10am–5pm, winter 10am–4pm. Admission: 30 Kč.*	▲ 306 ◆ D B2
CHURCH OF ST FRANCIS SERAPHIM sv. Františka Serafiského Krisovnické nám. 3, Praha 1 Tel. 221 10 82 66	*Open Tue-Sat 4–8pm. Services daily at 7am. Concerts daily April–Oct at 9pm.*	▲ 153 ◆ B A4
CHURCH OF ST JOHN OF NEPOMUK Kostel sv. Jana-Nepomuckého U kasáren, Praha 1	*Open for services.*	▲ 233 ◆ A B2
CHURCH OF ST JOHN-ON-THE-ROCK Kostel sv. Jana Nepomuckého na skalce Vyšehradská 49, Praha 2 Tel. 224 91 53 71	*Service Sun at 6pm.*	▲ 313 ◆ D C3
CHURCH OF ST JOHN OF THE WASH HOUSE Kostel sv. Jan Křtitelle Říční and Všehrdova Praha 1	*Open for services.*	▲ 268 ◆ A E5
CHURCH OF ST LAWRENCE on Petřin Hill	*Open summer Mon-Fri 10am–4pm; open in winter by request. Services Sun at 11am and 5pm, and Tue at 5pm.*	▲ 270 ◆ A C5
CHURCH OF ST MARTIN-IN-THE WALL Kostel sv. Martina Martinská 8, Praha 1 Tel. 06 04 759 062	*Open for concerts. Look up www.martinvezdi.cz for concert information.*	▲ 283 ◆ B B5
CHURCH OF ST PETER AND ST PAUL Kostel sv. Petra a Pavla na Vyšehrade Vyšehradské sady, Praha 4 Tel. 224 91 86 37	*Open summer Mon, Wed-Thu and Sat 9am–noon, 1–5pm, Fri 9am–noon, Sun 11am–noon, 1–5pm; winter Wed-Sun 10am–noon, 1–4pm.*	▲ 325 ◆ D B6
CHURCH OF ST SIMON AND ST JUDE Kostel sv. Šimona a Judy Dušni / u milošrdnych Praha 1 Tel. 222 32 10 68	*Open for classical music concerts.*	▲ 184 ◆ B C2

CLAM-GALLAS PALACE Clam-Gallasův palác Husova 20 Praha 1 Tel. 224 22 24 96	Used for exhibitions. Open daily 10am–5.30pm. Admission: 60 Kč.	▲ 149 ◆ B B4
CLEMENTINUM (Klementinum) Karlova 1 Praha 1 Tel. 221 663 111	Tower open April–Oct: Mon-Fri 2–9pm, Sat-Sun 10am–9pm; Nov–Dec: Sat-Sun 10am–8pm. Library open Mon-Fri 9am–5pm, Sat-Sun 8am–7pm. Admission: 100 Kč. Houses the Chapel of Mirrors, also known as the Chapel of the Annunciation (open only for concerts).	▲ 150 ◆ D B6
DIAMOND HOUSE Spálená 4 Praha 1	Not open to the public.	▲ 310 ◆ D C1
FAUSTUS HOUSE Faustův dům Karlovo nám. 40 Praha 2	Not open to the public.	▲ 311 ◆ D C3
FOERSTER MUSEUM Pštrossova 17	Open for concerts.	▲ 306 ◆ D B1
GOETHE INSTITUTE Masarykovo nábř. 32 Praha 1 Tel. 221 962 111 Fax 221 962 250	Open Mon-Thu 9am–5pm, Fri 9am–2.30pm. Movies screened. Library: open Mon-Tue 2–6pm, Wed-Thu 10am–noon and 2–4pm, Fri 10am–noon.	◆ B A6 D B1
GOLTZ–KINSKÝ PALACE (NATIONAL GALLERY) Staromeštske nam. 12 Praha 1 Tel. 222 32 14 59	Open for exhibitions Tue-Sun 10am–6pm. Adults 110 Kč, children and students 50 Kč.	▲ 143 ◆ B C4
HIGH SYNAGOGUE Červená 2 Praha 1 Tel. 224 81 07 58	See Jewish Museum.	▲ 193 ◆ B B3
HVĚZDA PAVILION Pavillion Liboc (obora Hvězda) Praha 6 Tel. 235 35 79 38	Open April–Oct: Tue-Sun 10am–5pm (closes at 4pm in April and Oct). Admission: 30 Kč Subway A (Hradčanska), trams 8, 22 (to Vypich), 1, 18 (terminus).	▲ 321
JAROSLAV JEŽEK MEMORIAL – BLUE ROOM Památník Jaroslava Ježka Kaprova 10, Praha 1 Tel. 224 818 393	Open Tue 1–6pm. Admission 10Kč.	◆ C F4
JEWISH MUSEUM U Stary Skoly Praha 1 Tel. 224 81 94 56 or 224 81 00 99 www.jewishmuseum.cz Ticket sales U Stareho hrbitova 3a Tel. 222 317 191 rezervacni.centrum@ jewishmuseum.cz	The museum is made up of six different sites: – The Maisel Synagogue which houses the Museum of the History of Bohemian and Moravian Jews from the 10th to the 18th century (until the Emancipation). – The Spanish Synagogue which houses the Museum of the History of Bohemian and Moravian Jews from the Emancipation until today. – The Pinkas Synagogue which includes the Memorial to the Victims of Nazism. – The Jewish cemetery. – The Klaus Synagogue and the Burial Guild Ceremonial Hall house the Museum of Jewish Traditions All these sites are open Nov–March: Mon-Sat 9am– 4.30pm. April–Oct: Mon-Sat 9am–6pm; closed Sun and Jewish holidays. Admission to the Jewish Museum only: 300 Kč. Combined ticket for the Jewish Museum and the Old–New Synagogue: adults 490 Kč (children under 6 years free). Admission to the Old-New Synagogue only: 200 Kč.	▲ 184- 193 ◆ B BC3

◆ PLACES TO VISIT

JEWISH TOWN HALL Židovská radnice Maiselova 18, Praha 1	*Not open to the public.*	▲ 193 ◆ B B3
KLAUS SYNAGOGUE U Starého Hřbitova Praha 1	*See Jewish Museum.*	▲ 191 ◆ B B3
KORUNA PALACE Václavské nám. 1 Praha 1 Tel. 224 21 95 26	*Open Mon–Sat 9am–8pm, Sun 10am–6pm.* *Now a shopping center.*	▲ 174 ◆ B C5
LIECHTENSTEIN PALACE Lichten Štejnský palác Malostranské nám. 13 Praha 1 Tel. 257 53 42 05	*Houses the Music Academy.* *Open-air concerts held in the courtyard (April–Sep).*	▲ 250 ◆ A D3
MAISEL SYNAGOGUE Maislova 10 Praha 1	*See Jewish Museum.*	▲ 193 ◆ B B3
MÁNÉS GALLERY Masarykovo nábř. 250 Praha 1 Tel. 224 930 754 *www.galeriemanes.cz*	*Open Tue–Sun 10am–6pm.* *Admission: 50 Kč.*	▲ 303 ◆ B A6
MUCHA'S HOUSE Kaunický Palác, Panská 7 Tel. 224 216 415 *www.mucha.cz*	*Open daily, summer 10am–6pm, winter 11am–6pm.* *Admission: 120 Kč.*	▲ 232 ◆ B D5
MUSEUM OF CZECH LITERATURE Památník národního písemnictví	*Located in one of the Strahov Monastery's buildings* *(see Strahov Monastery).*	▲ 242 ◆ A A3
MUSEUM OF DECORATIVE ARTS Ul. 17. listopadu 2 Praha 1 Tel. 251 09 31 11 *www.upm.cz*	*Open Tue–Sun 10am–6pm.* *Admission: 60–120 Kč.* *Library hours: Mon noon–6pm, Tue 10am–8pm,* *Thu–Fri 10am-6pm.*	▲ 195 ◆ B B3
MUSEUM OF MODERN ART (NATIONAL GALLERY) Veletržní Palace Exhibition Hall Dukelských hrdinú 47 Praha 7–Holešovice Tel. 224 30 11 11	*Open Tue–Sun 10am–6pm. Admission free first* *Wednesday of the month.* *Visit of one floor: 100 Kč.* *Visit of two floors: 150 Kč.* *Visit of three floors: 200 Kč.* *Family admission 300 Kč.* *Note: there is an Internet café within the museum.*	▲ 317
MUSEUM OF THE CZECH RESISTANCE AND MILITARY MUSEUM Muzeum Odboje a dejin armády U Památníku 2 Praha 3 – Žižkov Tel. 973 204 900 *www.militarymuseum.cz*	*Open Tue–Sun 10am–6pm.* *Admission: 30 Kč (free on Tue)*	◆ C D1
NA SLOVANECH MONASTERY "EMMAUZY" Kiášter na slovanech Vyšehradská 49 Praha 1 Tel. 224 91 53 71 *www.emauzy.cz*	*Open Mon–Fri 7am–7pm.* *Admission 10 Kč.*	▲ 312 ◆ D B3
NÁPRSTEK ETHNOGRAPHICAL MUSEUM Náprstkovo muzeum Betlémské nám. 1 Tel. 224 49 75 00	*Open Tue–Sun 9am–5.30pm.* *Admission: 40 Kč.*	▲ 287 ◆ B B5
NATIONAL MUSEUM Národní muzeum Václavské nám. 68 Praha 1 Tel. 224 49 71 11 or 224 49 72 12 *www.nm.cz*	*Open May–Sep: daily 10am–6pm,* *Oct–April: daily 9am–5pm.* *Closed first Tue of the month.* *Admission 100 Kč. Free first Monday of the month.* *Library open Mon–Fri 9am–7pm.*	▲ 175 ◆ B E6

NATIONAL THEATER Narodni Divadlo Narodni třida 2, Praha 1 Tel. 224 90 14 4 8 *www.narodni-divadlo.cz*	*Open Mon–Fri 10am–6pm, Sat 10am–12.30pm,* *3–6pm. Guided tours available.*	▲ *294* ◆ B A6
NOSTITZ PALACE Nostický palác Maltézské nám. 1, Praha 1	*Classical music concerts.*	▲ *272* ◆ A E4
NOVÉ MĚSTO TOWN HALL Novoměstska radnice North of Karlovo nám. Praha 2 Tel. 224 947 131 / 224 947 190	*Open for exhibitions May 1–Sep 30: Tue–Sun* *10am–6pm.*	▲ *309* ◆ D C1
OLD-NEW SYNAGOGUE Červená ulice Praha 1	*Built in 1275, this is Europe's oldest synagogue still* *being used for regular worship (admission not* *included in ticket to Jewish Museum).* *Ticket to the Old-New Synagogue only: 200 Kč.*	▲ *190* ◆ B B3 ▲ *149* ◆ B B4
OLD TOWN'S NEW TOWN HALL Nová radnice Mariánské nám. 2, Praha 1 Tel. 224 48 11 11	*Open Mon–Fri 9am–6pm.*	
PETŘÍN HILL FUNICULAR RAILWAY Station na Újezde, Ujezd Praha 1	*Open daily 9.15am–8.45pm.* *Tickets: 12 Kč.*	▲ *270* ◆ A C5
PETŘÍN PARK Malá Strana Praha 1 and 5	*'Eiffel Tower' 60-meter-high observation tower. Open* *daily, April–Sep 10am–7pm; May–Aug 10am–10pm;* *Oct 10am–6pm. Open Nov–Dec: Sat-Sun 10am–5pm.*	▲ *269* ◆ A C5
PETŘÍN BELVEDERE Petřín Park Praha 1	*Open daily 10am–6pm.* *Adults 30 Kč, children 20 Kč.*	▲ *270* ◆ A C5
PETŘÍN VILLA AND GARDENS Holečkova parc Petřín Praha 1	*Open Tue–Sun 9am–5pm.* *Ethnographical Museum.*	◆ A D6
PLANETARIUM Kralovska obora 233, Praha 7 Tel. 233 37 64 52 *www.planetarium.cz/ENG/*	*Open Sat-Thu 8am–8pm.*	
POWDER TOWER Prašná Brána Na Příkopě 1, Praha 1 Tel. 224 063 723	*Open April–Oct: daily 10am–6pm.* *Admission: 30 Kč.*	▲ *167* ◆ B D4
PRAGUE CITY MUSEUM Muzeum hlm. Prahy Na Poříčí 52, Praha 1 Tel. 224 81 67 72 *www.muzeumprahy.cz*	*Open Tue–Sun 9am–6pm.* *Admission: 30 Kč.* *Admission free first Thursday of the month.*	▲ *169* ◆ B F3
ROTT HOUSE 3 Malé nám. Praha 1	*Open daily 10am–10pm.* *Houses a fine jewelry and Bohemian glassware store.*	▲ *148* ◆ B B4
ROTUNDA OF THE HOLY CROSS Konviktská and Karoliny Světlé Praha 1 Tel. 233 35 35 47	*Services Tue and Sun at 5pm.*	▲ *289* ◆ B A4
RUDOLFINUM **(HOUSE OF ARTISTS)** Alsovo nábrezi 79 Praha 1 Tel. 227 059 111	*Houses the House of Artists and the Czech* *Philharmonic Orchestra. Open for concerts.*	▲ *194* ◆ B A3
ST ADALBERT'S CHURCH Kostel sv. Vojtěcha Vojtešská 10, Praha 1 Tel. 224 93 05 77	*Services Mon-Sat at 9.15am, Sun at 9am and* *5.30pm.*	▲ *303* ◆ D B1
ST AGNES CONVENT **(NATIONAL GALLERY)** Kiášter sv. Anežky České U Milosrdných 17, Praha 1 Tel. 224 81 06 28	*Houses the National Gallery's collections of* *ancient Central European art.* *Open Tue-Sun 10am–6pm. Admission: 100 Kč.* *Admission free first Wednesday of the month.*	▲ *182* ◆ B C2
ST BARTHOLOMEW'S CHURCH Kostel sv. Bartoloméje Bartolonějská, Praha 1 Tel. 222 32 13 30	*Open for services at 11.30am.*	▲ *289* ◆ B B5

ST HAVEL'S (ST GALL'S) CHURCH Kostel sv. Havla Havelská, Praha 1	*Open for services Mon-Fri at 12.15pm and Sun at 7.30am.*	▲ 283 ◆ B C4
ST GILES' CHURCH Kostel sv. Jiljí Husova 8, Praha 1 Tel. 224 22 02 35	*Services Mon-Fri at 7am and 6.30pm, Sat at 6.30pm and Sun at 8.30am, 10.30am, noon and 6.30pm.*	▲ 285 ◆ B B5
ST IGNATIUS' CHURCH Kostel sv. Ignáce Ječná 2 and Karlovo nám. Praha 2 Tel. 224 92 12 54	*Services Mon-Fri at 6.15am, 7.30am and 5.30pm, Sat at 6.30am, 7.30am and 5.30pm, and Sun at 7am, 9am, 11am and 5.30pm.*	▲ 309 ◆ D C2
ST JAMES' CHURCH Malá Štupartská and Jakubská Praha 1	*Open Mon-Sat 9.30am-noon, 2–4pm, Sun 7.30am-noon, 2-4pm.*	▲ 160 ◆ B C3
ST JOSEPH'S CHURCH Kostel sv. Josefa Nám. Republiky 2 Praha 1 Tel. 222 31 45 72	*Open Mon-Fri 6.30am-5.50pm, Sat 6.30–8am, Sun 7.30am-7.50pm. Services Mon-Sat 7am and 6pm; Sun 7.30am and 9pm.*	▲ 163 ◆ B D3
ST JOSEPH'S CHURCH Kostel sv. Josefa Josefská 8 Praha 1 Tel. 257 31 52 42	*Open 12.30–2.30pm.*	▲ 258 ◆ A E3
ST NICHOLAS' CHURCH Staroměstské nám. 27 Praha 1 Tel. 223 225 89	*Open Mon 10.30am-4pm, Tue-Sat 10am-4pm. Open for classical music concerts.*	▲ 145 ◆ B B4
ST NICHOLAS' CHURCH Kostel sv. Mikuláš Malostranské nám. Praha 1 Tel. 257 534 215	*Open daily, summer 9am-5.30pm, winter 9am-4pm. Tower open March–Nov: Sat-Sun 10am-5pm. Admission: 45 Kč (church), 30 Kč (tower).*	▲ 251 ◆ A D3
ST SAVIOR'S CHURCH sv. Salvátora Křížovnické nám. 1, Praha 1 Tel. 223 313 884	*Open for classical music concerts and for service on Sun. at 8am.*	▲ 153 ◆ B A4
ST SAVIOR'S CHURCH Kostel sv. Salvátora Salvátorská, Praha 1	*Service Sun at 9am. Classical music concerts.*	▲ 184 ◆ B C3
ST THOMAS' CHURCH Kostel sv. Tomáše Letenská, Praha 1 Tel. 257 53 05 56	*Visits by request. Services in English and Portuguese.*	▲ 256 ◆ A E2
ST URSULA'S CHURCH Kostel sv. Voršily Národní třída 10 Praha 1	*Open for services Mon-Fri at 5pm in Czech, Sun at 10am in Slovenian and 11am in Spanish.*	▲ 292 ◆ B A6
ST WENCESLAS' CHURCH Resslova 6 and Dittrichova Praha 2 Tel. 224 91 10 69	*Open for services Sun at 10am (summer) and 9.30am (winter). Also used for exhibitions.*	▲ 307 ◆ D B2
SCHWARZENBERG-LOBKOWICZ PALACE AND MILITARY MUSEUM Jiřská 3 Praha 1 Tel. 257 535 121	*Open Tue-Sun. 9am-5pm Admission 40 Kč.*	▲ 230 ◆ A C2
SMETANA MUSEUM Muzeum Bedřicha Smetany Novotného lávka 1, Praha 1 Tel. 222 22 00 82	*Open Mon, Wed-Sun 10am-5pm. Admission: 50 Kč.*	▲ 156 ◆ B A4
SPANISH SYNAGOGUE Dušni 12 Praha 1	*See Jewish Museum.*	▲ 184 ◆ B C3
STERNBERG PALACE (NATIONAL GALLERY) Hradčanské nám. 15 Praha 1. Tel. 233 350 068	*National Gallery's collections of European Art. Open Tue-Sun 10am-6pm. Admission: 60 Kč. Admission free first Wednesday of the month. Café open Tue-Sun 10am-5.30pm.*	▲ 227 ◆ A C2

STROMOVKA PARK Bubeneč Praha 7	Open summer 9am–5pm, winter 9am–4pm.	▲ 317
SWEERTS-SPORCK PALACE Hybernská 3–5 Praha 1	Not open to the public. Houses the Philosophy Department of the University.	▲ 168 ◆ B E4
SYLVIA-TAROUCCA PALACE Na Příkopě 10 Praha 1	Not open to the public. Its three connecting courtyards house a casino, a theater and a Kosher restaurant.	▲ 171 ◆ B C5
TOWN HALL Obecní dům Nám. Republiky 5, Praha 1 Tel. 222 00 21 00	Cultural and information center open 10am–6pm. Offers guided tours of the city Sat noon, 2pm, 4pm, Sun 10am, noon, 2pm, 4pm, Mon 10am, noon, 2pm. Price 160 Kč. Tours last 40 mins.	▲ 164 ◆ B D3
TROJA CASTLE U Trojského zámku 1 Praha 7 Tel. 283 851 614 *www.citygalleryprague.cz*	Visits Nov-March: Sat-Sun 10am–5pm; April-Oct: Tue-Sun 10am–5pm. Admission: 120 Kč. Admission free first Tuesday of the month. Subway C (Nádrži Holešovice station), then Bus 112.	▲ 318
TÝN COURTYARD Týnský Dvůr, Malá Štupartská Access behind the Church of Our-Lady-of-Týn, Praha 1	Boutiques and restaurants.	▲ 160 ◆ B C4
U HYBERNŮ CHURCH Nám. Republiky and Hybernská, Praha 1	Not open to the public.	▲ 167 ◆ B D4
URBÁNEK HOUSE Mozarteum Jungmannova 30 Praha 1 Tel. 296 24 50 24	Open only for exhibitions and concerts Tue-Fri noon–6pm, Sat 11am–6pm. Bookstore: same opening hours.	▲ 290 ◆ B C6
VILLA AMERIKA Dvořák Museum Museum A. Dvořáka Ke Karlovu 20, Praha 1 Tel. 224 918 013	Open Tue-Sun daily 10am–5pm. Admission: 40 Kč. Guided tour in English 500 Kč. Classical music concerts April–Oct: Tue and Fri at 8pm.	▲ 314 ◆ D D2
VOJAN PARK Vojanovy sady U lužického semináře, Praha 1	Open April–Sep: daily 8am–7pm; Oct–March: daily 8am–4pm.	▲ 263 ◆ A E-F2
VRTBA GARDENS Vrtbovska zahrada Karmelitská 25, Praha 1	Open daily 10am–6pm.	◆ A D3
VYŠEHRAD CEMETARY Vyšehradské sady, Praha 4 Tel. 241 410 348 or 241 410 247 *www.praha-vysehrad.cz*	Open April–Oct: daily 9.30am–6pm; Nov–March: daily 9.30am–5pm.	▲ 325 ◆ D B-C6
VYŠEHRAD NATIONAL MEMORIAL on Vyšehrad Hill Tel. 241 410 348 *www.praha-vysehrad.cz*	Open April–Oct: daily 9.30am–6pm, Nov–March: daily 9.30am–5pm. Admission: 20 Kč.	▲ 327 ◆ D B6
WALLENSTEIN PALACE Valdsteinke nám. 4 Praha 1	Not open to the public. The entrance to the gardens of the Wallenstein Palace is in Letenska Street. Gardens open March 21– April and Oct: daily 10am–6pm; May 9am–6pm.	▲ 260 ◆ A E2
ZBRASLAV CONVENT **(NATIONAL GALLERY)** Bartonova 2 156 00 Praha 5 Tel. 257 921 638/639	Open Tue–Sun 10am–6pm. Admission: 80 Kč (family 120 Kč). Admission free first Tuesday of the month Bus 129, 241, 243 from Smichov Station (line B)	▲ 328
ZOO U Trojského zámku 120 Troja, Praha 7 Tel. 296 112 111 *www.zoopraha.cz*	Open daily March: 9am–5pm; April–Jul 9am–6pm; Aug–Oct 9am–7pm; Nov–Feb 9am–4pm. Admission: 60 Kč. Bus no. 112 from the Nadraži Holesovice subway station (line C), or from Trojska station (lines 5, 14, 17) then bus no. 12.	

◆ PLACES TO VISIT

THE OUTSKIRTS

KARLŠTEJN
www.hradkarlstejn.cz
Group reservations:
SPUSC, Sabinova 5, Praha 3
Tel. (+420) 274 00 81 54
rezervace@spusc.cz (no
bookings possible at the Castle)

By car: take the D5, come off
at Beroun east, then continue
for 9 miles on the 116

By train: from Smichov Station
in Prague or Hlavni nádraži

*Gothic castle built in 1348 by the emperor Charles IV to
accommodate the royal treasure. It contains a gallery of
portraits of Czech kings, a banqueting hall, royal chamber,
St Catherine's chapel and the Holy Rood chapel.
Guided tours of the castle (50 mins).
Open Jan–March: Tue-Sun 9am–3pm; April: Tue-Sun 9am–
4pm; May-June: Tue-Sun 9am–5pm; July–Aug: Tue-Sun
9am–6pm; Sep: Tue-Sun 9am–5pm; Oct: Tue-Sun 9am–4pm;
Nov: Tue-Sun 9am–3pm; Dec: Tue-Sun 9am–3pm.
(Closed for lunch noon–12.30pm in May-Sep and noon–1pm
in Oct–April)
Admission: 200 Kč. Guided tours of the castle and the Holy
Rood chapel (70 mins): 300 Kč (July to Nov. only).*

KOLÍN
Tourist office: Na Hradbach 157
Tel. 0321 712 021
www.mukolin.cz

By car: road n° E67 (D11) then
n° 38.

By train: from
Prague's Central Station

*A medieval town which has preserved its 13th-century town
plan and interesting sites: the Gothic cathedral of St
Bartholomew, the Baroque facades of Charles Square, and
the old Jewish ghetto with its synagogue (1642) and 15th-
century cemetery.
Tourist Office open Tue-Sun 9am–5pm.*

KONOPIŠTE
Tel. 0301 721 366
Reservations: Tel. 02 7400 8154
www.zamek-konopiste.cz

By car: freeway n° E 55 in the
direction of Brno then Benesov.

By train: from Prague's Central
Station

*A romantic manor house with rich Gothic, Renaissance and
Baroque interiors. It contains the Archduke Ferdinand's
arsenal, St George's museum, and luxurious rooms and
apartments. Beautiful park and garden.
Admission: 130 Kč.*

KŘIVOKLÁT
Tel. 0313 558 120
or 0313 558 440
www.krivoklat.cz

By car: road n° E50 (D5),
in the direction of Beroun,
then roads n° 116 and n° 236.

By train: from Smichov Station

*Late-Gothic royal castle, among the oldest in Bohemia,
housing Gothic art collections, a hunting museum, the
Fürstenberks museum (19th–20th-century art) and a library.
Walks on the ramparts provide panoramic views. Guided tours
of the castle:
Jan–Feb: Mon-Fri 9am–noon, 1–3pm (reservation required);
March: Tue-Fri 9am–3pm (reservation required), Sat-Sun
9am–3pm (open to the public); April: Tue-Sun 9am–noon,
1–3pm; May–Sep: Tue-Sun 9am–noon, 1–4pm;
Oct: Tue-Sun 9am–3pm; Nov–Dec: Tue-Fri (reservation
required), Sat-Sun 9am–3pm (open to the public); closed
noon–1pm every day.
Admission: 160 Kč. Children 120 Kč.
Groups of 10 or more must book.*

KUTNÁ HORA
Tourist office:
Palackého námesti 377
Tel. 0327 515 556/124
www.kutnohorsko.cz

By car: freeway D11 in the
direction of Hradez Kralové, exit
Nymburk-Kolin, then follow road
n° 38 to Kolin and Kutná Hora.

By train: from Masarykovo
Station to Kutná Hora-mesto
(central station) or Kutná
Hora-Hlavní nádreži (main
station, further out of town).

*A historic town which has been on UNESCO's world heritage
list since 1995.
Principal sites: the Gothic cathedral of St Barbara, the
cathedral of the Virgin Mary, the Gothic palace (the silver
museum), the Ursuline convent.
The tourist ofice offers guided tours of the town costing from
70 Kč to 210 Kč per person depending on the route.*

BIBLIOGRAPHY ◆

GENERAL BOOKS AND GUIDES

◆ ABEL SMITH (L.) and KOTALÍK (J.): *A Guide, Prague*, John Murray, 1991

◆ BATT (J.): *Czechoslovakia in transition, from federation to separation*, London, 1993

◆ BROOK (S.): *Philip's Prague, Architecture, History, Art*, London, 1992

◆ BURIAN (J.) and HARTMANN (A.): *Prague Castle*, London, 1975

◆ DENSTEIN (V.) and KOTALÍK (J.): *Prague*, London, 1979

◆ DUBČEK (A.): *Hope Dies Last, the Autobiography of Alexander Dubček*, London, 1993

◆ FLEGL (M.): *Prague*, Olympia Guides, Prague, 1989

◆ HUMPHREYS (R.): *Prague, the Rough Guide*, London, 1992

◆ KOVTUN (G.) (ed.): *The Spirit of Tomáš G. Masaryk*, an anthology, Basingstoke, 1990

◆ MICHEL (P.): *Politics and religion in Eastern Europe: Catholicism in Hungary, Poland and Czechoslovakia*, Oxford, 1991

◆ NEUBERT (K.): *The Treasures from the Past, the Czechoslovak Cultural Heritage*, Prague, 1992

◆ PLICKA (K.) and POCHE (E.): *Walks Through Prague, a photographic guide*, Prague, 1984

◆ RIPELLINO (A.): *Magic Prague*, Basingstoke, 1994

◆ RYBÁR (C.): *Jewish Prague: A Guide to the Monuments*, Akropolis Publishers, 1991

◆ SADEK (V.): *The Old Jewish Cemetery and the Klausen Synagogue*, Prague, 1989

◆ SKILLING (H.G.) and WILSON (p.) (eds.): *Civic Freedom in Central Europe: Voices from Czechoslovakia*, Basingstoke, 1991

ART AND ARCHITECTURE

◆ BIALOSTOCKI (J.): *The Art of the Renaissance in Eastern Europe, Hungary, Bohemia, Poland*, Oxford, 1976

◆ *The Czech Avant-Garde of the 1920s and 1930s*, ex. cat., London, 1990

◆ DODWELL (C.): *Jewish Art Treasures from Prague, the State Jewish Museum in Prague and its collection*, London, 1980

◆ DRAHOTOVA (O.): *Bohemian Glass*, Prague Museum of Decorative Arts, 1992

◆ FAROVA (A.): *Josef Sudek, Poet of Prague*, London, 1990

◆ *Gypsies, photographs by Josef Koudelka*, London, 1975

◆ HASALOVA (V.) and VAJDIS (J.): *Folk Art of Czechoslovakia*, London, 1975

◆ HOOLE (J.) and SATO (t.): *Alphonse Mucha*, London, 1993

◆ LAMAROVA (M.): *Czechoslovakian Cubism, architecture, furniture and decorative arts 1910-1925*, New York, 1992

◆ MARGOLIUS (I.): *Cubism in architecture and the applied arts, Bohemia France, 1910-1914*, Woolwich, 1979

◆ *Pavel Büchler, Untitled Portraits*, ex. cat., Glasgow, 1988

◆ *Rudolf Fila*, ex. cat., Glasgow and London, 1989

◆ SEIBT (F.): *Gothic Art in Bohemia: architecture, sculpture and painting*, Oxford, 1977

◆ ŠKVORESCKY (J.): *All the Bright Young Men and Women, a Personal History of the Czech Cinema*, Toronto, 1975

◆ VANN (P.): *Three Contemporary Czechoslovakian Artists*, Great Britain, 1990

◆ VLČEK (T.) and SEKALOVÁ (H.): *Bohemian Glass of the Art Nouveau Period*, Prague, 1985

HISTORY

◆ CHROPOVSKY (B.): *The Slavs, their Significance, political and cultural history*, Prague, 1989

◆ DAWISHA (K.): *The Kremlin and the Prague Spring*, London, 1984

◆ KEJŘ (J.): *The Hussite Revolution*, Prague, 1988

◆ KIRSCHBAUM (S.) and ROMAN (A.) (eds.): *Reflections on Slovak History*, Toronto, 1987

◆ MASARYK (T.): *The Meaning of Czech History, edited and with an introduction by René Wellek*, Chapel Hill, 1974

◆ SKALNIK-LEFF (C.): *National Conflict in Czechoslovakia and the Remaking of a State 1918–1987*, Guildford, 1980

◆ SVITÁK (I.): *The Unbearable Burden of History, the Sovietization of Czechoslovakia*, Academia, 1990

MUSIC

◆ HOLZKNECHT (V.): *Antonín Dvořák*, Prague, 1977

◆ LARGE (M.): *Martinů*, London, 1975

◆ MIHULE (J.): *Bohuslav Martinů*, Prague, 1972

◆ MORIKE (E.): *Mozart's Journey to Prague*, London, 1976

◆ TAUSKY (V and M.): *Janáček, Leaves from his life*, London, 1982

◆ TYRRELL (J.): *Czech Opera*, Cambridge, 1988; *Intimate Letters, Leoš Janáček to Kamila Stösslová*, London,1994

CZECH WRITERS

◆ ČAPEK (K.): *R.U.R. and The Insect Play*, London, 1961; *Three Novels*, London, 1948

◆ HAŠEK (J.): *The Good Soldier Svejk*, tr. Cecil Parrott, Alfred A Knopf / Everyman's Library, 1993

◆ HAVEL (V.): *Disturbing the Peace, a conversation with Karel Hvížďala*, London, 1990; *Open letter, Selected Prose, 1965–90*, London, 1990; *Summer Meditations, on politics and civility in a time of transition*, London, 1992

◆ HOLAN (V.): *A Night with Hamlet*, London, 1980

◆ HRABAL (B.): *I Served the King of England*, London, 1989

◆ KAFKA (F.): *Collected Stories*, tr. Willa and Edwin Muir, Alfred A Knopf / Everyman's Library, 1994. *The Trial*, tr. Willa and Edwin Muir, Alfred A Knopf / Everyman's Library, 1993. *The Castle*, tr. Willa and Edwin Muir, Alfred A Knopf / Everyman's Library, 1993. *The Diaries of Franz Kafka, 1910–1923*, edited by Max Brod, London, 1992

◆ KISCH (E.): *Tales from Seven Ghettos*, London, 1948

◆ KUNDERA (M.): *The Book of Laughter and Forgetting*, tr. A. Asher, Faber and Faber Ltd, 1992; *The Farewell Party*, Faber and Faber Ltd, 1993; *Immortality*, tr. P. Kussi Faber and Faber Ltd, 1991; *Jacques and his Master*, Faber and Faber Ltd, 1986; *The Joke*, tr. M. H. Heim, Faber and Faber, 1992; *Laughable Loves*, tr. S. Rappaport, Faber and Faber Ltd, 1988; *Life is Elsewhere*, Faber and Faber Ltd, 1986; *The Unbearable Lightness of Being*, London, 1984; *The Art of the Novel*, 2003; *Ignorance*, Faber and Faber Ltd, 2003

◆ NERUDA (J.): *Tales of the Little Quarter*, tr. E. Pargeter, Greenwood Press 1977; *Selected Poems*, Prague, 1984; *Prague Tales*, tr. M. H. Heim, Central European University Press 2000;

◆ *The Poets of Prague – Czech Poetry between the Wars*, London, 1969. *Malá Strana Tales*, London, 1957

◆ SEIFERT (J.): *An Umbrella from Piccadilly*, London, 1983

◆ *Three Czech Poets, Vítézslav Nezval, Antonín Bartušek, Josef Hanzlik*, with an Introduction by Graham Martin, Harmondsworth, 1971

LITERATURE ABOUT PRAGUE

◆ APOLLINAIRE (G.): *The Wandering Jew*, London, 1967

◆ CAMUS (A.): *Selected Essays and Notebooks*, Harmondsworth, 1970

◆ CHATEAUBRIAND (F.R.): *Memoirs of François René, Vicomte de Chateaubriand, Vol. 5*, London, 1902

◆ FERMOR (P.L.): *A Time of Gifts – On Foot to Constantinople*, London, 1983

◆ MAGRIS (C.): *Danube*, The Harvill Press, 1999

◆ *Prague, a Traveler's Literary Companion* (ed.) Paul Wilson, Whereabouts Press 1995

◆ ROTH (P.): *The Prague Orgy*, Jonathan Cape, 1985

◆ SYMONS (A.): *Cities*, London, 1903

◆ LIST OF ILLUSTRATIONS

Knopf Guide
Front cover:
Jewish Town Hall, litho
1898 © J.-L. Charmet /
Bridgeman Art Library.
Back cover:
Panorama of Prague,
Vincenc Morstadt,
watercolor, Prague
Museum © Dagli Orti.

Front endpaper:
Our Lady of Týn © S.
Grandadam, Créteil. Statues
on Charles Bridge, general
view of Prague, ph.
J. Sierpinski © Scope.
Interior of Veletžní Palace ©
V. Vasquez/Gallimard Guides
The Old Jewish Cemetery,
ph. J. Sierpinski © Scope.
The Castle, National
Museum, ph. S. Guilbert.
*Reliquary book and
polychrome sculpture*,
*Theology Room, Strahov
Monastery*, ph. G. Roli,
Milan. Malá Strana Square,
arcades, ph. S. Guilbert.
*From the nave toward the
apse*, St Nicholas, Malá
Strana © Scala, Florence.
Kampa, ph M. Frank. *Café
Slavia*, ph. Anne Garde,
Paris. Masaryk Quay
© V. Vasquez/Gallimard
Guides.
Vyžehrad Cemetery, ph.
J. Sierpinski © Scope.
10-11 *The Frozen Vltava*,
1820, photo, all rights
reserved.
12-13 *"Praha" bus in front
of the Castle*, postcard, all
rights reserved.
14 *Grocer's in the Old Town*,
photo, all rights reserved.
17 Charles Bridge and the
Vltava, ph. R.Holzbachová.
18 Petřín Hill, ph. Gallimard.
20 Stromovka Park, ph.
Gallimard.
22 Kestrels, ph. Štastný.
23 *Seal of Rudolph II of
Habsburg*, 1603, Archives
nationales, Paris © Lauros-
Giraudon.
24 *Přemysl the
Ploughman*, illustration
1891, ph. S. Guilbert.
Vyžehrad Code, stamp,
all rights reserved.
24-25 *Seal of Charles IV*,
1355, ph. J. Kašpar.
25 Fresco of *Charles IV*,
Chapel of Our Lady,
Karlštejn © Giraudon.
Vladislav II Jagiello,
illumination, ph. S. Guilbert.
Crown of Bohemia, stamp,
all rights reserved.
26 *Hussite charge*, M. Aleš,
drawing, 1902, Orbis pub.,
ph. S. Guilbert.
Jan Hus at the stake,
miniature, ph. S. Guilbert.
Louis Jagellon, Brožík, o/c
1909, ph. S. Guilbert.
27 *Rudolph II*, Flemish, late
16th c., Versailles © Lauros-
Giraudon.
Behem, detail, map of

Bohemia 1550, all rights
reserved.
Joseph II, Austrian, 18th c.,
Versailles © Lauros-
Giraudon.
28 *František Palacký*, J. V.
Hellich, o/c , Národní
Muzeum, ph. S. Guilbert.
*The Popular Guard and the
students exercising in 1848*,
detail, M. A. Witka, litho ©
Roger-Violet.
*President Masaryk arrives in
Prague, 1918*, from a
Hungarian newspaper of the
time © J.-L. Charmet.
29 *Beneš and Churchill*,
from "*La Vie
tchécoslovaque*" 1939,
Orbis, ph. S. Guilbert.
Demonstration in 1950 ©
Werner Bischof/Magnum.
*Demonstration in November
1989* © D. Lefevre/ VU.
*Press conference by Václav
Havel*, November 1989 ©
idem.
30 *Royal crown* © Národní
Muzeum.
Přemysl Otakar II,
illumination, 18th c., ph. S.
Guilbert.
Saint Wenceslas, o/c, Saint
Vitus' Cathedral, ph. S.
Guilbert.
George Poděbrady, ph. J.
Kašpar.
Vladislav II Jagellon,
postcard, all rights reserved.
31 *Ferdinand I*, Kupelwieser,
o/c © Art Museum, Vienna.
*Equestrian statue of
Rudolph II*, National Gallery,
ph. J. Kašpar.
Empress Maria-Theresa,
o/c 1890, Václav Brožík,
Town Hall, ph. S. Guilbert.
32 *Sigismund of
Luxemburg*, A. Pisanello, oil
on wood, Kunsthistorisches
Museum, Vienna, ph. E.
Lessing © Magnum.
Wenceslas IV, detail, votive
panel by Jean Očko de
Vlašim, distemper on wood,
14th c., National Gallery ©
Giraudon.
Portrait of Jan Hus,
engraving © Bibl. nat., Paris.
32-33 *Jan Hus at the stake*,
Ulrich Richenthal, wood-
block, 1483, Polonaise
library, Paris
© J.-L. Charmet.
33 *Hussite Fighter*, Krumlov
Codex, Prague Museum,
ph. S. Guilbert.
Jan Hus, Ulrich Richenthal,
watercolor © Giraudon.
34 *Ferdinand II of Habsburg*,
Justus Sustermans, Pitti
Palace, Florence ©
Giraudon.
*Frederick V leaves for the
hunt*, detail, Anthonie
Palamedes, priv. coll.,
Sussex © Giraudon.
Defenestration of Prague,
1618, A. Mucha, drawing
© Roger-Violet.
34-5 *Battle of the White
Mountain, 1620*, litho, Bibl.

nat., Paris © J.-L. Charmet.
35 *Execution in Prague,
1621*, engraving © Roger-
Violet.
Old Town Square, litho
1841, Prague Museum.
36 *President Masaryk*, V.
Dlouhý, drawing, 1926, ph.
S. Guilbert.
36-7 *President Masaryk
arrives in Prague, January
1919*, photo © L. de
Selva/Tapabor, Paris.
37 *Sudeten Germans
welcome the German Army*,
photo © AKG, Berlin.
Edouard Beneš, photo ©
Roger-Violet.
*E. Beneš' conference
credentials, Versailles 1919*,
ph. S. Guilbert.
38 *Swastikas*, all rights
reserved.
*March 1939, The Germans
enter Prague*, photo ©
Keystone, Paris.
39 *1944, Soviet troops and
units of the Czechoslovak
Corps enter Prague*, photo
© Édimédia, Paris.
Klement Gottwald, photo ©
Roger-Violet.
*R. Heydrich and A.
Eichmann*, photo © Roger-
Violet.
40 *Political poster against
the occupation of
Czechoslovakia*, Paris,
October 1968 © Roger-
Violet.
Prague 1968, poster, all
rights reserved.
*Demonstrators in Wenceslas
Square 1968*, photo
© J. Koudelka/Magnum.
Dubček, photo
© D. Lefevre/VU.
Prague 1989, Aleš Najrt,
poster, all rights reserved.
41 *Václav Havel on World
Human Rights Day,
December 10, 1988*,
photo © Lobo/VU.
The Velvet Revolution,
poster, all rights reserved.
42 *Kralice Bible*, Press of the
Czech Brethren, 1593, ph.
S. Guilbert.
Slavonic Gospel-book, detail
of Cyrillic writing, Reims
library.
Jan Hus, fresco, Bethlehem
Chapel, ph. R. Holzbachová.
43 *Vyšehrad Codex*,
Clementinum library
© Giraudon.
*Frontispiece of Complete
Works of J. A. Komenský*,
© Bibl. nat. Paris.
44 *Hračky*, Toy-shop design,
ph. S. Guilbert. *Na Baště*,
sign, 1757, ph. S. Guilbert.
Bilingual street name-plate,
ph. D. Rolland.
*Czech poster for the
newspaper "Zlatá Praha"*,
1895, Museum of
Decorative Arts, Paris,
Maciet Collection © J.
Vigne, Gennevilliers.
45 *Traditional costume of
Bohemia*, Pilsen region, c.

1890, Museum of
Decorative Arts, Paris,
Maciet Collection © J.
Vigne, Gennevilliers.
46 *The Singing-Lesson*,
wood-block, 1564,
all rights reserved.
Signature of Antonín Dvořák
all rights reserved.
*Antonín Dvořák conducting
an orchestra*, Antonín
Dvořák Museum
© Dagli Orti.
47 *Page of a gradual, telling
of the day when Jan Hus
was burnt at the stake*,
1569-1572, all rights
reserved.
Bedřich Smetana, photo
1866 © Interfoto, Munich.
Portrait of Bohuslav Martinů
ph. S. Guilbert.
Portrait of Leoš Janáček,
1970 © CTK Pressfoto.
48 *Concert by Kubelik in Old
Town Square* © Cedri, Paris
Concert in Strahov Church,
ph. G. Roli, Milan.
48-9 *Decorated violin*,
Gasparo de Salo, Brescia,
1584, ph. M. Krob.
49 *Concert by the
Philharmonia* © Cedri, Paris
*Massed choirs of the
"Šedifony"*, J. Šedivá, 1901-
1913, ph. M. Krob.
Giraffe piano, early
18th c., ph. M. Krob.
*Hurdy-gurdy, with a relief of
the Annunciation carved on
the lid, probably Bohemian*,
18th c., ph. M. Krob.
50 *The Drawing-Room
Polka*, Thierry Frères, detail,
litho 1844, Bibl. nat., Paris
© Roger-Violet.
*Bedřich Smetana at the
piano*, litho from a painting,
archives B. Smetana
© Dagli Orti.
Škoda Lásky, polka by
Jaromír Vejvoda and Vašek
Zeman, record sleeve, all
rights reserved.
51 *Musical score of the
"Esmeralda" opera*, František
Matěj Hilmar, 1838, all rights
reserved.
The Bartered Bride, Bedřich
Smetana, title page 1872, all
rights reserved.
The Drawing-Room polka,
Thierry Frères, detail, litho
1844, Bibl. nat., Paris ©
Roger-Violet.
52 *Stará pražská polka*,
record sleeve, all rights
reserved.
*Coronation Ball of Leopold
II*, František Heger, 1791,
Prague Museum, ph. S.
Guilbert.
Funfair in Hvězda park,
Viktor Barvitius, o/c 1861,
National Gallery, ph. S.
Guilbert.*Czech ball in
Pomněnka, 1848*, City
Archives, ph. S. Guilbert.
53 *Fan made for a student
ball, 1849* © Bibl. des
Langues Orientales, Paris.
Dancing school © B.

LIST OF ILLUSTRATIONS ◆

◆ LIST OF ILLUSTRATIONS

LIST OF ILLUSTRATIONS ◆

◆ LIST OF ILLUSTRATIONS

LIST OF ILLUSTRATIONS ◆

◆ LIST OF ILLUSTRATIONS

We would like to thank the following people for their help:

M. Petr Beránek
(Dir. Art Gallery, Ostrava)
Mme Vlasta Cibulová
(Villa Bertramka)
M. Guy Erismann
Mme Anna Fárová
(Sudek Collection)
M. Nicolas Galaud
(Municipal lib. Reims)
Mme Helena
Koenigsmarková
(Museum of Decorative
Arts)
Mme Méguernes
(Éditions Flammarion)
M. Zdeněk Mika
(Dir. Prague Museum)
Mme Danièle Monmarte
M. Arnauld Pontier
(Paris Museum)
Mme Hana Povolná
(Dir. Jewish Museum)
Mme Joëlle Ribas
(Bücher Publishers,
Munich)
Mme Jítka Sedlářová
(Moravská Galerie,
Brno)
Mme Dagmar Šefčíková
(Dir. National Gallery)
Mme Jana Vejdovská
(Tourist Office)
Mme Nina Všetečková
(Center for Musical
Information)
M. Klaus Wagenbach
(Archives Kafka)

Acknowledgements
Grateful acknowledgement
is made to the following
for permission to reprint
previously published
material.

◆ AYER COMPANY,
PUBLISHERS, INC.: Excerpt
from *Intimate Things* by
Karel Čapek, translated by
Dora Round. Reprinted by
permission of Ayer
Company, Publishers, Inc.,
N. Stratford, NH.
◆ ALFRED A. KNOPF INC.:
Excerpt from *The Book of
Laughter and Forgetting* by
Milan Kundera, translated by
Michael Henry Heim,
English
translation copyright © 1980
by Alfred A. Knopf, Inc.
Reprinted by permission of
Alfred A. Knopf, Inc.
◆ FARRAR, STRAUS & GIROUX,
INC.: Excerpt from *The
Prague Orgy*, by Philip Roth,
copyright © 1985 by Philip
Roth. Reprinted by
permission of Farrar, Straus
& Giroux, Inc.
◆ JONATHAN CAPE LIMITED
and DEBORAH OWEN LITERARY
AGENCY: Excerpt from *The
Thirty Years War*, by C.V.
Wedgwood (Jonathan Cape
Limited, 1938). Reprinted by
permission of Jonathan
Cape Limited, a division of
Random House UK Limited,
and Deborah Owen Literary
Agency, London.

◆ OXFORD UNIVERSITY PRESS:
Excerpt from *Dr Burney's
Musical Tours in Europe, Vol.
II* edited by Percy A. Scholes
(Oxford University Press,
Oxford, England, 1959).
Reprinted by permission of
Oxford University Press.
◆ RANDOM HOUSE, INC. and
GRANTA/PENGUIN BOOKS
LTD.: Excerpt from *The
Magic Lantern* by Timothy
Garton Ash, copyright ©
1990 by Timothy Garton
Ash. Rights outside the U.S.
from *We The People* (Granta
Books) administered by
Granta/ Penguin Books Ltd.,
London. Reprinted by
permission of Random
House, Inc., and Granta/
Penguin Books Ltd.
◆ CHARLES SCRIBNER'S SONS
and GRANTA BOOKS: Excerpt
from *My Golden Trades*, by
Ivan Klima, translated by
Paul Wilson, English
translation copyright © 1992
by Paul Wilson.
Rights outside the U.S.
administered by Granta
Books, London. Reprinted
by permission of Charles
Scribner's Sons, an imprint
of Simon & Schuster, and
Granta Books.
◆ SCHOCKEN BOOKS: Franz
Kafka diary entries for
November 18, 1911, and
March 14, 1913, from *The
Diaries of Franz Kafka,
1910–1913*, by Franz Kafka,
edited by Max Brod,
translated by Joseph Kresh,
copyright © 1948, copyright
renewed 1976 by Schocken
Books, Inc. Reprinted by
permission of Schocken
Books, published by
Pantheon Books, a division
of Random House, Inc.
◆ VIKING PENGUIN and JOHN
MURRAY (PUBLISHERS)
LIMITED: Excerpt from *A Time
of Gifts* by Patrick Leigh
Fermor. Copyright © 1977
by Patrick Leigh Fermor.
Rights outside the U.S.
administered by John
Murray (Publishers) Ltd.,
London. Reprinted by
permission of Viking
Penguin, a division of
Penguin Books USA Inc.,
and John Murray
(Publishers) Ltd.

◆ INDEX

368

◆ INDEX

◆ INDEX

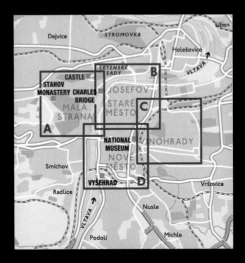

Map section

Key

- ▬ Freeway
- ▭ Expressway
- ▭ Main road
- ▭ Railroad
- ✠ Christian cemetery
- ✡ Jewish cemetery
- ✚ Hospital
- Ⓜ Metro station
- ✈ Airport
- ▲ Principal summits

◆ STREET INDEX

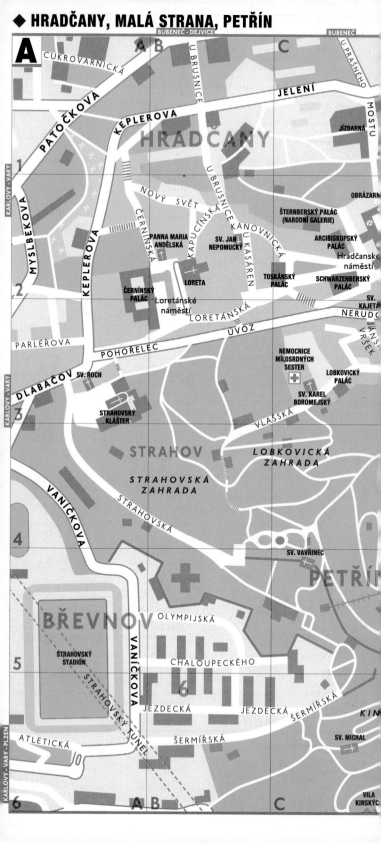

◆ HRADČANY, MALÁ STRANA, PETŘÍN

A

BUBENEČ - DEJVICE

BUBENEČ

U PRAŠNÉHO MOSTU

CUKROVARNICKÁ

PATOČKOVA

KEPLEROVA

JELENÍ

U BRUSNICE

JÍZDÁRNA

HRADČANY

NOVÝ SVĚT

U BRUSNICE

OBRÁZÁRN

KAPUCÍNSKÁ

ČERNÍNSKÁ

PANNA MARIA ANDĚLSKÁ

ŠTERNBERSKÝ PALÁC (NÁRODNÍ GALERIE)

KANOVNICKÁ

SV. JAN NEPOMUCKÝ

ARCIBISKUPSKÝ PALÁC

Hradčanské náměstí

U KASÁREN

LORETA

TOSKÁNSKÝ PALÁC

SCHWARZENBERSKÝ PALÁC

ČERNÍNSKÝ PALÁC

Loretánské náměstí

SV. KAJETÁ

LORETÁNSKÁ

NERUDO

MYSLBEKOVA

KEPLEROVA

UVOZ

VLAŠSKÝ VRŠEK

PARLÉŘOVA

POHOŘELEC

NEMOCNICE MILOSRDNÝCH SESTER

LOBKOVICKÝ PALÁC

DLABAČOV

SV. ROCH

SV. KAREL BOROMEJSKÝ

STRAHOVSKÝ KLÁŠTER

VLAŠSKÁ

STRAHOV

LOBKOVICKÁ ZAHRADA

STRAHOVSKÁ ZAHRADA

STRAHOVSKÁ

VANÍČKOVA

SV. VAVŘINEC

PETŘÍ

BŘEVNOV

OLYMPIJSKÁ

VANÍČKOVA

STRAHOVSKÝ STADIÓN

CHALOUPECKÉHO

STRAHOVSKÝ TUNEL

JEZDECKÁ

JEZDECKÁ

ŠERMÍŘSKÁ

KIN

ATLETICKÁ

ŠERMÍŘSKÁ

SV. MICHAL

VILA KINSKÝC

KARLOVY - VARY

KARLOVY - VARY

KARLOVY - VARY - PLZEŇ

A B C

1 2 3 4 5 6